# Sex Offenders and the Internet

# Sex Offenders and the Internet

**Kerry Sheldon**
*Psychology Department, University of Gloucestershire, UK*

and

**Dennis Howitt**
*Department of Social Sciences, Loughborough University, UK*

John Wiley & Sons, Ltd

*Other Wiley Editorial Offices*

John Wiley & Sons Inc., 111 River Street, Hoboken, NJ 07030, USA

Jossey-Bass, 989 Market Street, San Francisco, CA 94103-1741, USA

Wiley-VCH Verlag GmbH, Boschstr. 12, D-69469 Weinheim, Germany

John Wiley & Sons Australia Ltd, 42 McDougall Street, Milton, Queensland 4064, Australia

John Wiley & Sons (Asia) Pte Ltd, 2 Clementi Loop #02-01, Jin Xing Distripark, Singapore 129809

John Wiley & Sons Canada Ltd, 6045 Freemont Blvd, Mississauga, ONT, L5R 4J3, Canada

Wiley also publishes its books in a variety of electronic formats. Some content that appears in print may not be available in electronic books.

Anniversary Logo Design: Richard J. Pacifico

*Library of Congress Cataloging-in-Publication Data*

Howitt, Dennis.
    Sex offenders and the internet / Dennis Howitt, Kerry Sheldon
        p. cm.
    Includes bibliographical references and index.
    ISBN 978-0-470-02800-1 (cloth) – ISBN 978-0-470-02801-8 (pbk. : alk. paper)
    1. Internet pornography. 2. Child pornography. 3. Sex offenders. I. Sheldon, Kerry. II. Title.
    HQ471.H645 2007
    364.15′302854678–dc22
                                                                            2007019141

*British Library Cataloguing in Publication Data*

A catalogue record for this book is available from the British Library

ISBN 978-0-470-02800-1 (hbk) 978-0-470-02801-8 (pbk)

Typeset in 10/12pt Palatino by Thomson Digital, New Delhi, India
Printed and bound in Great Britain by Antony Rowe Ltd, Chippenham, Wiltshire
This book is printed on acid-free paper responsibly manufactured from sustainable forestry in which at least two trees are planted for each one used for paper production.

# Contents

# About the Authors

**Kerry Sheldon** is Lecturer in Psychology and Criminology at the University of Gloucestershire. She trained in investigative psychology at the University of Liverpool before obtaining her PhD in psychology at the Department of Social Sciences at Loughborough University. In between these, she worked for the probation service in sex offender treatment where she first encountered Internet sex offenders. She has substantial publications in the field of sex offending and the Internet.

**Dennis Howitt** is Reader in Applied Psychology in the Department of Social Sciences at Loughborough University. He is a Fellow of the British Psychological Society and a chartered psychologist. His books in the field of crime and sex abuse include *Paedophiles and Sexual Offences Against Children* (Wiley, 1995), *Crime, The Media and the Law* (Wiley, 1998) and *Child Abuse Errors* (Harvester Wheatsheaf, 1992). He is author of *Introduction to Forensic and Criminal Psychology* (2nd edition, Pearson Education, 2006). He has published books in the field of race with Kwame Owusu-Bempah including *Psychology Beyond Western Perspectives* (British Psychological Society, 2000) and *The Racism of Psychology* (Harvester Wheatsheaf, 1994). Amongst his well-known methods textbooks with Duncan Cramer are *Introduction to Statistics in Psychology* (4th edition, Pearson Education, 2008), *Introduction to SPSS in Psychology* (4th edition, Pearson Education 2008) and *Introduction to Research Methods in Psychology* (2nd edition, Pearson Education 2008).

# Acknowledgements

We are indebted to the following for crucial help in getting our research on Internet sex offenders under way: Samantha O'Hare, Sara Casado, Chris Edwards, Sandra Link and Jon Auty. And most of all, Mal Mellor, without whom the research would never have been finished and for the fun she provided as an antidote to the depressive effects of the interviews with offenders.

# CHAPTER 1

# Sex Offending on the Internet

We all know two basic things about the Internet: that it has changed our lives and that crime is rife. This book is concerned with how the Internet has changed the lives of sex offenders and created, in effect, a new category of sex offender – the Internet sex offender. The Internet has been characterised as a chaotic, lawless, and dangerous place – a digital Wildwest. Quite what this means in relation to sex offending against children is open to question. Despite what is often assumed, the Internet and the World Wide Web ('WWW' or 'the Web') are not the same thing. The Internet is a system or network of interconnected networks of computers that carries information such as email, files, online telephone services, and other forms of chat online. The WWW first began to be available to the public in 1991 and greatly facilitated the use of the Internet. It is just a subpart of the Internet and operates much like a stack of computer files (for example, text, images, and videos) accessed through the Internet. Along with email, the Web was responsible for the Internet's growth in popularity in the early 1990s (Renold *et al.*, 2003). Web browsers allow users to interact with WWW information.

The immediate dangers of the Internet are more than apparent after just a few moments surfing with the Internet service provider's content filters switched off. Searching using the keyword 'pornography' produces a seemingly infinite display of pornography. Our search resulted in images of group sex, male masturbation, 'fisting' (insertion of a fist into a vagina or anus) – plus a Web site on which the public are invited to post indecent pictures of themselves as an act of political protest! And this was only the start of our search. The material available can be extreme but, nevertheless, our search did not produce an avalanche of child pornography. Some sites refer to schoolgirls or teens but the images they present are of sexually mature women. References are made to 'barely legal' pornographic models but clearly illegal pornography simply did not appear. The so-called free-for-all of the Internet seems to be something of a misrepresentation. Of course, this may merely reflect the success of attempts to police the Internet and it should not be taken to mean that child pornography is unavailable via the Internet – merely that an unusual degree of determination and skill is needed in order to find it.

Not everyone using the Internet does so innocently. Perhaps the most dramatic evidence of this is the work of Demetriou and Silke (2003) who set up a 'bogus' Web site called *Cyber Magpie*. It was registered with Internet search engines, so enhancing its likelihood of being seen by people browsing. A number of hyperlinks were provided that allowed the user to:

- download legally available shareware and freeware;
- download well-known games such as *Tomb Raider*, which are commercially protected;
- view softcore pornography featuring men or women;
- view hardcore pornography;
- obtain XXX passwords that would give them access to illegal pornography sites (pay-to-view sites).

When the material was illegal, the links on the site were not functional. Of course, the purpose of this site was to examine what Internet users 'do' when faced with these temptations so, unknown to the users, the researchers were tracking the activity on the site. Very few users found the site while surfing the Internet for pornography. In fact 93 % of visitors to the site initially were seeking legal shareware or freeware. Nevertheless, 45 % of the users clicked the link to the softcore pornography on the site and rather more (60 %) chose the hardcore pornography link. Thirty-seven per cent went on the illegal pornography passwords page. Things were similar in terms of the games: 38 % of visitors to the site went to the illegal game download section, for example.

The conclusion is inescapable. Even when engaged in a perfectly legal activity such as searching the Internet for freeware to download, many users can be sidetracked into illicit activities. Demetriou and Silke (2003, p. 220) claim that 'On the Internet, the opportunity to commit crime is never more than three or four clicks away.' This offending is almost a byproduct of surfing the Internet. In comparison, it is not quite that easy for Internet child sex offenders – many mouse clicks and a great deal of knowledge is required before they find the child pornography they desire.

New technologies and pornography have gone together for decades, if not centuries. Photographs, movies and video are examples of new technologies that have enabled the production and consumption of pornography. The telephone's contribution perhaps is the indecent phone call and phone calls to sex lines; CB radio was used by prostitutes to contact possible clients (Luxenburg and Klein, 1984). Although the sex industry does not invent these technologies, it is responsive enough to be among the first to take advantage of the new media (Durkin and Bryant, 1995; Griffiths, 2000) and so took to the Internet quickly. It is said that in the 1980s the main users of the Internet were government, university academics and pornography seekers (Sprenger, 1999). The Internet provides a wide range of pornographic material (Fisher and Barak, 2000) ranging from conventional *Playboy*-type material through hardcore to the bizarre (for example, alt.sex.bondage.goldenshowers.sheep) (Griffiths, 2000).

Sex is claimed to be the most searched-for topic on the Internet (Freeman-Longo and Blanchard, 1998). Similarly, Sparrow and Griffiths (1997) analysed a million word searches on a search engine and found that the majority searched for pornography; the top eight word searches used terms related to pornography. However, these findings are not matched by other reports concerning the most popular Internet searches. For instance, Google, the US search engine reported its 10 most popular Internet searches in 2006. These included searching for video clips from Youtube.com which was the most popular search, the World Cup, the death of Steve Irwin, TV programmes *Prison Break* and *Big Brother*, Wiki (an online database), the lottery results, and the weather (Hickman, 2006). Other statistics suggest that the top ten searches do not include pornography but rather things like lottery results, horoscopes, tattoos, lyrics, ring tones, hairstyles, jokes and TV programmes (Burns, 2005).

## SEX AND THE INTERNET

Many of the activities and motivations of sex offenders on the Internet are redolent of those of many non-offending Internet users. There are numerous ways in which the Internet can or could be used for sexual purposes (Griffiths, 2000). The diversity is perhaps surprising and includes, according to Griffiths the following (Griffiths, 2000, pp. 537–8):

- Sex education: Web pages, discussion groups, and other aspects of the Internet may help the user to find materials for the purpose of sex education.
- Commerce involving sexually related goods: this would include the buying and selling of such items as sex books, sex videos, sexual aids, contraceptives and so forth for use offline.
- Online sexual entertainment and masturbation: the user seeks Web sites that permit the exploration and purchase of picture libraries, videos, online peep-show access, and textual materials perhaps in the form of access to chat rooms.
- Sex therapists: using the Internet to obtain details of sex therapists to consult for advice.
- The search for enduring intimate partners such as by using online dating agencies.
- The search for transitory sexual partners such as prostitutes or swingers.
- The identification of individuals via the Internet who will become the targets of sexually related crime. Examples of this would include cyberstalking and the grooming of children online.
- Online-only relationships. These would involve the initiation and maintenance of relationships through Internet resources such as email or chat-rooms.
- Gender and identity role creation. This may involve the creation of new personas online, which are used in online relationships.
- The seeking of digitally manipulated images for sexual entertainment or masturbation. This might include celebrity fake nude photographs where a

celebrity's face is superimposed on a picture of another person's naked body.

Virtually any of these could apply to the online behaviour of men with a sexual interests in children, of course.

Using the Internet for sexual purposes is often regarded in academic discussions as being either (a) 'pathological' or (b) 'adaptive' (Barak and King, 2000; Cooper et al., 1999). An adaptive perspective of Internet-related sexual behaviour is provided by Cooper and Sportolari (1997) who examined the notion of romance in cyberspace. They coined the term 'computer-mediated relating' (CMR) to describe the interactions taking place through the use of electronic mail (email). Rather than 'computer-mediated relating' promoting superficial relationships, online relating has a number of much more positive aspects. Predominantly, it reduces the importance that physical attributes can play in the development of attraction as well as promoting a focus on other factors such as propinquity, rapport, mutual self-disclosure, emotional intimacy and shared interests and values. It increases the chance of meeting like-minded others particularly for people who have difficulty meeting with people face-to-face (for example, someone who is overweight). Users can experiment by exploring more inhibited parts of their personalities and online communication allows individuals more control on how they present themselves including the freedom to deviate from typical gender roles (Turkle, 1995).

The Internet may also offer the opportunity for the formation of online or virtual communities in which previously isolated, disenfranchised individuals can communicate with each other around sexual issues (such as gay, lesbian, bisexual, transgender and abuse issues) with less fear of prejudice and discrimination (McKenna and Bargh, 1998). These individuals can become the 'majority' in their own community (Cooper, McLoughlin and Campbell, 2000). For instance, early work studied participants in Internet groups devoted to stigmatised aspects of identity – that is aspects of them that were potentially embarrassing and tended to be kept secret even from family and friends (such as homosexuality, bondage, sexual spanking or, fringe political groups) (McKenna and Bargh, 1998). The more that the Internet group members participated in the groups through, say by posting messages, the more they incorporated the previously taboo aspect of their identity into their self-concept. Feelings of self-acceptance of the stigmatised aspect were enhanced and they had a greater tendency to 'come out' to important friends and family.

Internet chat rooms have also become an acceptable way of meeting and dating other persons (King, 1999). Similar patterns have been found in the gay subculture. For instance, Tikkanen and Ross (2000) interviewed gay Swedish men who used the Internet and found that six out of 10 young men who used chat rooms had experiences of physically meeting at least one sexual partner. A quarter of the men had also met their current long-term partner in a chat room. So there was some connection between the offline world and the online world.

It could be argued that these positive features of the Internet become negative ones in the hands of paedophiles. The 'pathological' view of Internet sexuality dominates the literature. Durkin and Bryant (1995) argued that 'cybersex' allows a person to operationalise sexual fantasies that would otherwise have self-extinguished if it were not for the reinforcement of immediate feedback provided by online interactions. Early work suggested that sex offenders misuse the Internet in several ways; to traffic child pornography; to locate children to molest; to engage in inappropriate sexual communication with potential victims; to communicate with other persons with similar interests; and to form online communities and bonds (Durkin, 1997; Durkin and Bryant, 1995; Mahoney and Faulkner, 1997). Even the idea that the Internet may empower people who have otherwise felt marginalised (Granic and Lamey, 2000) has relevance for paedophiles who are traditionally an isolated group (Quayle and Taylor, 2002a). Quayle and Taylor (2002a) argue that the Internet may allow paedophiles to communicate freely with each other and that this may (a) reinforce the belief that their behaviour is valid and normal and is an expression of 'love' and not abuse and (b) that the Internet is a relatively safe environment to exchange images and text. Additionally the Internet may allow users to try out new roles and even to switch genders (Turkle, 1995) but this can include the paedophile who misrepresents himself in order to gain access to pornographic images and/ or to facilitate communication with children.

The pathological view is consistent with a medical model of social problems – one common way of conceptualising pathological Internet use is the notion of 'Internet Addiction' or compulsivity (Bingham and Piotrowski, 1996; Durkin and Bryant, 1995; Cooper et al., 1999; Griffiths, 2000; Putnam, 2000; Young, 1996, 1997a, 1997b; Young and Rogers, 1998). Problems associated with Internet use have also been reported in relation to other online behaviours such as gambling (King, 1999; King and Barak, 1999).

Internet addiction is generally characterised by behaviours such as investing more and more time in Internet behaviours to the detriment of other behaviours (such as spending time with family); negative feelings when offline; increasing tolerance to the effect of being online; and denial that there is a problem (Kandell, 1998, p. 1). It is argued that any Internet behaviour (such as downloading pornography, Web surfing, online gambling) can be defined as an addiction as long as it meets certain criteria such as salience, mood modification, tolerance, withdrawal symptoms, conflict and relapse (Griffiths, 2000). This perspective regards Internet addiction as behaviourally similar in character to other dependencies and compulsions and individuals who meet these criteria are thought to experience social, psychological and occupational harm (Caplan, 2002). Individual vulnerabilities related to the aetiology of compulsive online sexual behaviour are similar to those discussed in the literature (for example, Coleman, 1992) relating to sexually compulsive behaviour off-line (Putnam, 2000) including depression and difficulty coping with stress (Cooper et al., 1999) and interpersonal difficulties (Putnam, 1997). Factors unique to the Internet such as *anonymity, accessibility* and *affordability* help with Internet-use initiation (Barak and

Fisher, 2001; Cooper, 1998; Cooper, McLoughlin and Campbell, 2000; Cooper and Sportolari, 1997).

Research, some argue, has failed to show conclusively that Internet addiction or Internet sex addiction exists except, perhaps, in a small percentage of people (Griffiths, 2000). There is an overreliance on self-report measures, the criteria used for addiction lack the dimension of severity, there is no temporal dimension, there is a tendency to overestimate the prevalence of problems and no account is taken of the context of Internet use (Griffiths, 1999). Moreover, much of the research tends to focus on how theoretically and operationally to define 'pathological' or 'addictive' Internet use rather than on testing theories (Beard and Wolf, 2001). Terms vary from 'pathological' (Cooper et al., 1999) to 'excessive', 'maladaptive' (Caplan, 2002) and 'problematic' (Taylor and Quayle, 2003) and there are no standardised criteria for 'addictive' use of the Internet. Beard and Wolf (2001) were also critical of the term 'addiction' and raise the question of what it is that the individual is addicted to. The computer? The typing? The information gained? The anonymity? The types of activity in which the individual is engaged? Each of these may have a role to play in making the Internet reinforcing (Beard and Wolf, 2001). According to research by Meerker et al. (2006), use of erotica on the Internet is the factor that most predicts Internet addiction. Interestingly, the notion of 'addiction' is found to be a common description (or justification) employed by men who download and use Internet child pornography (Quayle and Taylor, 2002b).

Recent reviewers suggest that the addiction framework suffers from three flaws; a lack of conceptual or theoretical specificity (Caplan, 2002; Davis, 2001; Shaffer, Hall and Vander Bilt, 2000), a paucity of empirical evidence (Beard and Wolf, 2001; Caplan, 2002) and a failure to account for what people are actually doing online (Caplan, 2002). Chou, Condon and Belland (2005) review ideas like these and other findings concerning Internet addiction more positively.

In the context of child pornography, Quayle, Vaughan and Taylor (2005) suggest that escalating and problematic Internet use may not only be a function of the specific contents of the material but also a function of the role that the Internet plays in meeting emotional needs. They found that some of the psychological functions of child pornography that emerged from their interviews with Internet sex offenders (Quayle and Taylor, 2002b) corresponded with seven subcategories derived from a questionnaire exploring general problematic Internet use in non-offenders (Caplan, 2002):

- mood alteration;
- perceived social benefits available online;
- negative outcomes associated with Internet use;
- compulsive Internet use;
- excessive amounts of time spent online;
- withdrawal symptoms when away from the Internet;
- perceived social control available online.

# CHILD PORNOGRAPHY AND THE INTERNET

Much of the concern about the Internet and sex offending centres on the issue of child pornography. As far as can be ascertained, child pornography is the major activity that constitutes Internet-related sex crime at the present, certainly in terms of convictions. There are other crimes, as we will see, but concern about the Internet and child sex offences has quintessentially involved indecent child abusive images of children. Child pornography existed before the Internet. However, public concern and interest in the topic was not intense and academic interest in the topic minimal. This is surprising given the intense political activity involving social scientific research applied to adult pornography since the 1960s. Few social scientific research topics have been as at the centre of attention from government. There are numerous examples of 'government' committees and commissions to investigate the effects of pornography (for example, Commission on Obscenity and Pornography, 1970; Committee on Pornography and Prostitution, 1985; Everywoman, 1988; US Attorney General's Commission on Pornography, 1986; Williams, 1979). The number and cost of such investigations suggest that they served a major political purpose. Interest in child pornography, in contrast, has never resulted in the equivalent levels of research activity. There is a sense in which the issue of child pornography is so ideologically constrained that research may be regarded as superfluous. Before the Internet, child pornography was considered to be a small and specialist issue – an adjunct to the broader problem of pornography of all sorts.

Since the early 1990s there has been considerable change in how child pornography is represented – this is not simply that the issue has had an increased salience but that child pornography has been redefined to de-emphasise its erotic aspects and to promote the idea that child pornography is imagery of the sexual abuse of children. The intensity of media coverage reporting convictions for Internet-based pornography offences, police operations netting seemingly thousands of child pornographers and high profile cases of major and minor celebrities found in the possession of child pornography, have helped focus public attention on child pornography and the Internet. Paradoxically, despite the attention, there is a great deal yet to be known about how the Internet actually opens up new avenues for old forms of abuse. Why are some men, seemingly with no history of sex offences against children, nevertheless drawn to collect vast amounts of Internet child pornography? Such men enter a criminal justice system lacking resources other than to treat them as 'hands-on' contact offenders against children. It is not surprising, then, that practitioners faced with men who dispute that they are child molesters have had difficulty in assessing precisely what do to help them avoid future reoffending. The basic question of whether or not Internet offenders differ from contact offenders has received insufficient attention, yet is at the core of social policy in dealing with Internet pornography.

## THE PROBLEM WITH CHILD PORNOGRAPHY

Conceptually, child pornography can be approached in two distinct ways (Taylor and Quayle, 2003). The first is to regard it as the end point of a process of production that imbues the material with various implicit and explicit characteristics. These characteristics ensure that the material meets the requirements of consumers of child pornography. For example, it is argued that consumers tend to dislike child pornography that portrays child sex as distressing or painful for the child victim (Taylor and Quayle, 2003). Imagery that suggests that the child is actually enjoying his or her victimisation may be their preference (Taylor and Quayle, 2003). Thus child pornography commonly portrays the victim as 'smiling'. In other words, a key production value in child pornography involves indications that the children are willing and also taking pleasure in the sexual activity that is, in fact, their abuse. This sort of imagery may facilitate the generation of sexual fantasy in which children are, in imagination, sexually compliant and, perhaps, complicit. Some users of child pornography may reject child sex imagery in which children appear obviously distressed or unhappy. Cognitively, users of child pornography deny the harm caused by the sexual abuse of children and unhappy, distressed victims would challenge this belief. According to Taylor and Quayle (2003), sometimes child pornography videos have soundtracks on which the 'producer' can be heard instructing the children to look to the camera and smile.

The second viewpoint does not concentrate on the content of the child pornography production but considers the process of viewing child pornography. There is a sense in which the term 'viewing' fails to adequately describe the activities of users. Although some users of child pornography talk of 'viewing' it, this implies a passivity that is belied by fuller consideration of what users do with the material, which goes beyond mere viewing. Users actively engage with the material since they are known to frequently collect, catalogue and index the child pornography that they accrue (Tate, 1990, p. 112). Psychologically, they sexually fantasise to the material and masturbate to climax (Taylor and Quayle, 2003). An instance of this active involvement is that they may fantasise that the child is performing the depicted sexual acts upon them and not the individuals they see in the pornographic image.

If users of child pornography confine themselves to masturbation and fantasy alone, some might ask (as do Internet offenders themselves) why society needs to control their activities. It might be argued that they are not harming the children themselves. In many cases, there is no 'direct' link between the user of child pornography and the abuse of the child featured in the photos or videos. Viewing photographs of other sorts of crime is not construed as a crime and fictional creations of other crimes, although they may receive some censure as in the case of media depictions of violence, is not punished in general. Furthermore, large numbers of people are known to have sexual fantasies of inappropriate and illegal acts such as rape (Crepault and Couture, 1980; Greendlinger and Byrne, 1987; Leitenberg and Henning, 1995) though their fantasies have not been legislated against.

Part of the answer to this is in the following list of reasons why Society should be concerned about the use of child pornography images (Taylor and Quayle, 2003):

- Users of child pornography fuel the market by creating a demand. It is argued that supplying material to meet this demand results in the further abuse of children. In this way, users of child pornography collude in a process that does further harm to children. Pictures, films and videos function as a permanent record of the original sexual abuse. Consequently, the memories and traumas of the abuse are maintained as long as the record exists. Victims filmed and photographed many years ago will nevertheless be aware throughout their lifetimes that their childhood sexual victimisation continues to be exploited perversely. More traditional forms of child pornography such as videos or photographs had limited circulation and were easily destroyed or otherwise removed from circulation, but once on the Internet the infinite reproduction of the material is possible and total destruction of an image unlikely. Take the example of pictures of children on a public nudist beach, which can be made without the knowledge of the children or their parents. Not only does the circulation of such photographs breach a child's and family's privacy and safety but it transforms an innocent situation into a sinister and disturbing one in which the child is used for the sexual satisfaction of paedophiles. Despite this, a trauma may not be caused to the child or family as they are unaware of the offender's actions and the pictures were not of a child being abused.
- Deviant sexual fantasies based on Internet images may fuel a need to sexually abuse other children directly by users of such material. Generally the literature (for example, Healy, 1997; Quayle and Taylor, 2002a) assumes that pornography plays a critical role in generating inappropriate sexual fantasies in the viewer and stimulating sexual arousal. Further, when the viewer masturbates to the material this reinforces their sexual response to it and encourages repetition (Laws and Marshall, 1990). Moreover, there is a process by which inappropriate sexual fantasies begin to escalate and guide the offender to sexual criminal behaviour that temporarily satisfies the fantasy. This idea is quite common and, on the face of things at least, plausible. Nevertheless, some argue that the evidence of a link between adult pornography and sexual aggression is unconvincing (Howitt and Cumberbatch, 1990; Seto, Maric and Barbaree, 2001) so why should child pornography be different? According to Seto, Maric and Barbaree (2001), it may be individuals with a predisposition to respond to pornography who 'are the most likely to show an effect of pornography exposure and are the most likely to show the strongest effects' (Seto, Maric and Barbaree, 2001, p. 46). This idea of vulnerable predispositions is far from new in discussions of the effects of the media and mass communications although any evidence in its support is suspect or missing (Howitt and Cumberbatch, 1990). It is, nevertheless, an argument of the adverse effects of pornography albeit one limited by the

predispositions of the user. Of course, the research on adult pornography has been interpreted differently by various researchers and reviewers – for example, some suggest that the evidence is more consistent with a no-effects model (Howitt, 1998a) or even a beneficial effects model (for example, Baron and Straus, 1987). Taylor and Quayle's (2003) position is a little different. They argue that a graver risk comes from child pornography encouraging its users to take indecent photographs of children. They provide anecdotal evidence from interviews in support of this association. For example, 'when I made this video tape I was copying these er movie clips...that I had downloaded er...I wanted to be... doing what they were doing' (Taylor and Quayle, 2003, p. 25). However, 'encouraging' may be the wrong word and it may be simply that availability allows those with such a predisposition to offend against children to use child pornography in this way.

- Using child pornography to groom children into sexual abuse. This is partly through a process of 'desensitisation' in which the child is familiarised with adult-child sexual activity (Burgess and Hartman, 1987). For instance, the material might be used to initiate a child into how to perform the sexual acts 'correctly'. What is sexual abusive behaviour could be presented as 'fun' or educational. Furthermore, such sexual acts may in this way be presented as 'normal' in the minds of children in order to encourage them into sexual poses or sexual behaviour. Of course, this is not about the viewing of child pornography as such because it involves the use of the pornographic material in the grooming process. Only once the offender has the intention to abuse a child can the material contribute to the offence.

## WHAT IS CHILD PORNOGRAPHY

One standard English dictionary defines pornography as the 'writings, pictures, films, etc., designed to stimulate sexual excitement, the production of such material' (from the Greek *pornographos* meaning 'writing of harlots' – *Collins Concise Dictionary*, 4th edition, p. 1152). Another defines pornography as 'the explicit description or exhibition of sexual activity in literature, films, etc., intended to stimulate erotic rather than aesthetic or emotional feelings' (*Concise Oxford English Dictionary*, 8th edition, p. 927). These two definitions overlap greatly, certainly enough to imply some consensus. Both suggest that pornography is material intended to produce sexual excitement in those that use the material. However, both definitions fail to identify just what it is about the material that makes it pornographic rather than, say, erotic. For example, are photographs of anything that may be intended to stimulate others sexually pornographic? Is a picture of a slinky model on the catwalk pornographic by these definitions? Of course, another criticism of these definitions is that in most jurisdictions, especially the Anglo-American judicial systems, pornography in itself has never been illegal nor attracted sanctions. The test of acceptability is often the effect of the material on those likely to use it. While pornography is not illegal in these systems, obscene material is. Obscene material will tend to deprave and corrupt the user, although such a criterion has inevitably been open to interpretation and dispute. The history of censorship is replete with examples of the shifting standards that have applied in determining whether material is obscene and the contents of material which is regarded as obscene.

In the light of this brief discussion, it should be apparent that the definition of child pornography has more ramifications. The definitions of 'a child' (it is not always a real child) and 'an indecent image of a child' are multifaceted issues. The criteria may depend upon social, cultural, temporal, psychological and legal factors together with moral, sexual and religious norms dominant in society (Healy, 1997). Especially in relation to child pornography, there has not been a simple march through time from repression to liberalisation, as there seems to have been with adult pornography. Instead, in many cases, liberal ideas have been reversed or attempts have been made to reverse them. So, for example, when a television newsreader is prosecuted for bath-time pictures of her children, this is a move away from liberal positions.

In this context, the Council of Europe (1993) has drawn attention to the Lolita clothing fashions for children and expressed concern about the eroticisation of children in commercial advertising. Highly sexualised images of children commonly appear in the mass media. Such images encourage the idea that children are sexual as well as prematurely escalating children into a world of adult sexuality (Adler, 2001; Elliot, 1992; O'Connell 2000). Furthermore, some mainstream images as well as softcore pornography often intentionally attempt to make women look, and behave, in a more childlike manner (Adler, 2001). This eroticisation of childhood extends well beyond the issue of child pornography. The interrelation between the two is unknown and can only be a matter of conjecture. Nevertheless, it is undeniable that child pornography and eroticised images of children strike at basic concerns about childhood sexuality and the sexual exploitation of children.

The three following definitions of child pornography give the flavour of some of the issues that make this such a complex matter:

- The Council of Europe (1993) defined child pornography simply as 'any audio-visual material which uses children in a sexual context'.
- ECPAT defines child pornography as '... any representation, by whatever means, of a child engaged in real or simulated explicit sexual activities or any representation of the sexual parts of a child for primarily sexual purpose' (Optional Protocol to the Convention on the Rights of the Child cited on http://www.ecpat.net/eng/CSEC/faq/faq.asp, 9 April 2003). The global network, ECPAT International, seeks to eliminate the commercial sexual exploitation of children and has representation in over 60 countries. The name stands for End Child Prostitution in Asian Tourism, but it changed its name in 1996 to mean End Child Prostitution, Child Pornography and Trafficking in children for sexual purposes. The organisation distinguishes a 'softcore' form of child pornography from 'hardcore' pornography – softcore

child pornography may involve naked and seductive imagery of children but does not feature children engaging in sexual activity, which is the characteristic that distinguishes hardcore child pornography:

- The current definition of The International Criminal Police Organization's (Interpol's) Specialist Group on Crimes Against Children is not dissimilar: '. . . Child pornography is created as a consequence of the sexual exploitation or abuse of a child. It can be defined as any means of depicting or promoting the sexual exploitation of a child, including written or audio material, which focuses on the child's sexual behaviour or genitals' (see http://www.interpol.int/).

There is some common ground between these definitions in their emphasis on the sexual nature of the representation. This appears to be in part an attempt to distinguish innocent childhood images such as those on a beach or in a pool with their family. Furthermore, classical iconography and other artistic representations of children (such as representations of naked angels or saints in the form of children) would seem to be excluded. Images of the innocence or purity of children would also seem acceptable though, paradoxically, these are features of childhood which paedophiles claim to appreciate. Explicit pictures of children's genitals or photographs/film of their sexual abuse are probably readily classified as child pornography; innocent photographs involving child nudity may, in the wrong hands, be used for perverse sexual gratification. Convictions have been quashed because the content of the imagery and not the sexual purpose to which it is put is the criterion of illegality. How it was used or its effects on the child involved are not the issue (Edwards, 1995). So among the sorts of images that may be problematic are those involving apparently innocent situations such as children undressing, bathing, on the beach, swimming, nudity and semi-nudity. The case of *R. v Graham-Kerr* in 1988 illustrates the problem. A swimming pool instructor had taken a photograph of a seven-year-old boy naked at a swimming pool. The instructor admitted that he became sexually aroused when he took the picture and also when he viewed the picture. Nevertheless, the conviction was overturned on the grounds that a photograph of a naked boy is not in itself indecent (Edwards, 1995).

Historically, child pornography was linked with photographs and magazines with limited circulation. This remained the case with the introduction of video recordings around about the 1980s. Nevertheless, drawings, text and other media may also be relevant – something that seems to have been anticipated in some of the definitions. In fact, ECPAT (1996) anticipated that child pornography can be found on, or in, several different types of media. The Internet, of course, is not confined to any particular type of representation and this is true for pornography that may exist in textual, photographic, graphic, and video formats.

## LEGAL APPROACHES TO CHILD PORNOGRAPHY

Potter Stewart, Associate Justice of the US Supreme Court, famously said of hardcore pornography 'I know it when I see it' (Simpson, 1988). This might apply equally to child pornography. Whether a definition of child pornography is possible that would prove satisfactory on an international basis is a moot point. The General Assembly of the United Nations, when signing the Convention of the Rights of the Child in 1989, undertook to protect children from all forms of sexual exploitation and sexual abuse and this included the exploitative use of children in pornographic performance and materials (Renold *et al.*, 2003). Nevertheless, according to the National Society of the Prevention of Cruelty to Children, the lack of a universally accepted definition of what constitutes child pornography has hampered progress in tackling the problem (Renold *et al.*, 2003).

A range of factors make an internationally acceptable definition of child pornography difficult. These are the definition of 'a child' and 'indecency' and the problem of pseudo-images. We turn to these now.

## What is a Child

The legal definition of a child differs between jurisdictions, as does the legal minimum age of consent to sexual intercourse and, indeed, the age at which an individual can legally participate in pornography or even erotic photography. In the UK, to take one example, the age of being legally able consent to sexual intercourse is 16 years whereas, with certain limitations, an individual has to be 18 years or over in order to legally participate in sexual photography (Gillespie, 2005c).

The United Nations Convention on the Rights of the Child (UNCRC) in 1989 defined a child as a person under the age of 18 years (Renold *et al.*, 2003). In the economically advanced countries of West, childhood is generally regarded as ending at 18 years of age (Taylor and Quayle, 2003). This, however, means that in many places children are legally able to give consent to sexual intercourse and marry.

Historically there has been wide variation in the lowest age for legal consent to sexual activity (Howitt, 1995a). Nevertheless, this minimum age has tended to increase over the centuries for heterosexual intercourse while tending to decline for homosexual intercourse. Taken on a long timescale, the minimum ages of consent to sexual intercourse and marriage have generally been identical in most cultures with respect to heterosexual relationships. Homosexual relationships, by contrast, present a much more complex situation. Currently, gay marriage is only possible in a small number of legal jurisdictions, of course, and the homosexual age of consent is historically unrelated to that for heterosexual couples. However, the UK Sexual Offences (Amendment) Act 2000 changed the age of consent for male homosexual activities (including anal sex) from 18 years to equal that of heterosexual and lesbian sexual activities of 16 years (it is 17 in Northern Ireland and 18 in Jersey). The following time sequence gives some indication of the broad trends which provide a wider perspective:

- 1275: men were prohibited from having sexual intercourse with a girl of under 12 in English law;

- 1533 until 1861: anal sex involving men was punishable by death;
- 1576: carnal knowledge of a girl of 10 years or under with or without her consent was defined as rape;
- 1875: The Offences Against the Person Act raised the age of consent for females to 13 years, which was increased to 16 years in 1885 – however, carnal knowledge of a girl between 13 and 16 years was only illegal if the man was 24 years of age or above;
- 1956: sexual intercourse with a girl under 16 years of age – with or without her consent – became punishable by two years imprisonment or life if the girl was under 13 years;
- 1967: homosexuality was legalised (1980 in Scotland) for males of 21 years of age and above;
- 1993: non-consensual anal intercourse becomes classified as rape;
- 2000: homosexual consent was set at 16 years for most of the UK but 17 years in Northern Ireland.

So what is legal at one time and place may be illegal at another. Seemingly, as the age of heterosexual consent has increased over the years, the age of biological sexual maturity has declined (Gluckman and Hanson, 2006; Howitt, 2006b). It has been argued that increases in the age of consent are a response to the demands of developing industrial societies for an increasingly educated workforce (Killias, 1991).

For heterosexual intercourse even in fairly recent times, minors of 15 years of age could legally consent to sexual activities in some US jurisdictions (Ruxton, 2001); in Portugal the age of consent is 14 years (Petit, 2004); in Sweden the age of consent is 15; in Switzerland it is 16 (Petit, 2004). In most of the UK, all sexual activity with under 16s, whether heterosexual or homosexual, is now covered by the same laws (Sexual Offences Act 2003). Some nations have no age stipulation, leaving it to be determined on an individual basis, for example by stating that children becomes adults once they reach puberty. Internationally, the age of consent can vary from as low as 12 through to 18 years, although in many European countries it is more likely to be 16 (Renold et al., 2003). It is seemingly becoming more common to replace a simple age criterion of legality with a more complex formulation which it is partially dependent on the age and power differential between the individuals engaging in sexual intercourse.

In many cases, however, the legal age of consent to sexual activities is younger than the age at which one can consent to participating in pornography, which is typically 18 years (Europol, 2005; Petit, 2004). For instance, in Spain the age for consensual sexual activity is 13 whereas the age within child pornography legislation is 18 years (Europol, 2005). This means that the production and possession of child pornography are crimes, even if the child involved can legally consent to sexual intercourse. Such arrangements may protect young people who have passed the age of consent but whose judgement is not sufficiently mature for them to consent to be photographed or filmed in the same sort of sexual activity. Similarly, in some jurisdictions young people under the age of 18 years can marry and therefore it is possible for a married young person of 16 years to engage in the visual or audiovisual recording of consensual sexual activity with their adult (18+) partner. Yet under the United Nations Convention on the Rights of the Child such a practice could be defined as producing or possessing child pornography (Renold *et al.*, 2003). In Britain, the Sexual Offences Act of 2003 protects 16 and 17 year olds from involvement in indecent photography although, if married or in a stable relationship, the consensual taking of such photographs is permitted so long as nobody other than the couple is involved in the sexual act or is shown the photographs. In other countries the legal age for participating in pornography may be set at 18 but there may be exceptions for those aged 17. In Switzerland children are allowed to participate in the production of pornographic material provided that they give informed and free consent and are above 16.

Many countries within the European Union have laws against possessing, producing and distributing child pornography – for example, Belgium or Cyprus – but definitions of child pornography vary between jurisdictions (Europol, 2005). Similarly, in some countries outside the European Union, possession of child pornography material is a crime, for example New Zealand (National Center for Missing and Exploited Children, Press Release, April 2006). However, in countries like Russia and Thailand the law does not distinguish between child and adult pornography and, as long as there is no intent to distribute it, its possession is not a criminal offence (Shytov, 2005). The International Centre for Missing and Exploited Children in collaboration with Interpol reported that, of the 184 Interpol members they studied, 95 countries had no laws concerning child pornography, in 138 countries possession of child pornography was not a crime and in 122 countries there was no law that specifically addressed the distribution of child pornography via computers and the Internet (National Center for Missing and Exploited Children, Press Release, April 2006). The Council of Europe Cybercrime Convention is, to date, the only multilateral treaty to address the problem of computer-related crime and it bans child pornography (Shytov, 2005).

There is another perhaps more practical problem. Child pornographic images circulate and the police, for example, may never actually find out who the child is for very obvious reasons (Taylor and Quayle, 2003). As a consequence, the age of the person in the pornography has to be estimated from the evidence in the picture or film. Taylor and Quayle (2003) indicate that determining a child's age from the viewing a picture and in the absence of other knowledge about that victim is very complicated. When the child is very young the judgement is far easier than for an adolescent. There can be considerable variation in the development of secondary sexual characteristics such as breasts or pubic hair. Thus, some adults may appear as immature children if, say, they are flat-chested or have little or no pubic hair.

## What is Indecency?

The question of what constitutes an *indecent* image of a child is likely to receive different answers in different legal jurisdictions. Standards have certainly varied historically. The legislation that allows for the prosecution of child pornography in the UK is extensive but of great significance is the fact that the Protection of Children Act 1978 created new offences in terms of the taking, distribution, exhibition, advertising and possession of indecent photographic images of children and pseudo-images (which appear to be real images of a child). However, the judgement as to what constitutes indecency is a matter for courts of law and is not dependent on simple definition to be found in statute (Gillespie, 2005b).

Possession and distribution of child pornography is a criminal offence in the US, of course. Crucially, however, in the case of *Ashcroft* v. *Free Speech Coalition* in April 2002, the Supreme Court ruled that a real child must be involved in the pornographic material otherwise its possession and distribution did not constitute an offence (Akdeniz, 2006; Shytov, 2005). This meant that the burden was on law enforcement to prove that the child(ren) in the child abuse images were real children in order to prove that abuse had occurred. This made US legislation different in this respect from developments internationally, including the UK, where pseudoimages are also prohibited (Taylor and Quayle, 2003). One consequence of this US law, unanticipated at the time, was that the police were obliged to identify who the children were in the images in order to make charges of possession of 'child pornography'. Holland (2005) argues that the result was that this kick-started victim identification in the US, which was not previously a priority. It also influenced victim identification practices worldwide because US enforcement agencies had to make queries worldwide regarding the images they had seized.

It is clear that what is defined as child pornography differs somewhat from jurisdiction to jurisdiction. As a consequence, international cooperation of law enforcement agencies may be constrained. Thus photographs that are not universally illegal have to be ignored in international initiatives. Inevitably, international variation in definitions of what is illegal or obscene results in pressure for a common international standard for both legislation and policing.

How pornographic images are regarded is influenced by the broader context of legislation beyond that specifically dealing with obscenity. In the US, for instance, the case of *Miller v. California* (1973) resulted in an important decision relevant to the question of how obscenity is to be defined. The Supreme Court decision in this case suggested that if the material was pornographic then the protection of the First Amendment may apply but this would not be the case with obscene material (Mehta, 2002). Difficulties arise because different types of communities in the US vary in how they regard the acceptability of pornographic material. Mehta suggests that in the fundamentalist Bible Belt areas of the US, many sexual acts would be regarded as obscene or offensive by a large proportion of the population. Elsewhere, in cosmopolitan cities such as Los Angeles or New York, where attitudes to sexual matters may be more liberal, different standards would apply. The legal decision by the Supreme Court allowed for local areas to define their own standards concerning pornography and what is obscene. The Miller decision also outlined a three part test of obscenity (the *Miller Standard*). These three conditions need to be met in order for an image or written work to be obscene (Mehta, 2002):

- the typical person applying current standards would judge the work assessed in its entirety to be oriented to appeal to prurient interests;
- the work depicts or describes in a patently offensive way sexual conduct specifically defined as obscene by the applicable state law;
- when considered as entirety, the material lacks any 'serious' value in terms of its literary, artistic, political or scientific content.

A 'yes' answer to each of these three components of the Miller test constitutes obscenity, but the test is inevitably socially constituted without absolute standards. Thus the Miller Standard applied in different communities may well yield different decisions. Furthermore, failure to meet any of these criteria for obscenity renders the free speech protection of the First Amendment applicable. Perhaps the Miller Test illustrates the problems on setting a single national standard for obscenity – and the likelihood that the Miller Test would not work successfully as an international standard.

There are jurisdictions in which the definition of child pornography is demonstrably more precise than, say, in UK legislation. Section 263 (1) of the Canadian Criminal Code states, according to Mehta (2002, p. 323), that child pornography includes photographic, film, video, and electronic media portrayals of:

1. A person under the age of 18 years engaging in sexual or explicit sexual activity or depictions of them being so engaged.
2. Depictions of predominantly sexual organs or anal areas of a person under the age of 18 years for sexual purposes.
3. Written or visual representations that 'advocate or counsel' sexual activity involving a person under the age of 18 years are also an offence under the Code.

The production of pornography using 'child-like' models or the use of props (such as scouting and guiding uniforms) suggesting that the model is younger than their real adult age is prohibited. According to Mehta (2002, p. 323), Canadian legislation seeks to 'suffocate the market for such material'. It prohibits both the possession and distribution of child pornography.

Similar, legislation in the Irish Republic refers to the sexual qualities of the prohibited material. According to the Irish Child Pornography and Trafficking Act (1998), child pornography includes visual representations of:

1. A child engaged in or depicted to be engaged in explicit sexual activity.
2. A child witnessing these activities.

3. The genital or anal regions of children for sexual purposes as a dominant characteristic.

## Pseudo-images

As we have mentioned, the pseudo-photograph is particularly problematic. Whereas the doctoring of old analogue-process silver-based photographic images was very difficult to achieve convincingly, digital technologies have changed that. There are now 'pseudo' photographs involving 'virtual' children and events that did not happen, which have been constructed by software packages (Taylor and Quayle, 2003). There are highly indecent fake nudes of many movie stars circulating on the Internet and, indeed, many mass-market movies use digital technologies to an entirely different creative effect. The ability to alter images digitally means that non-sexualised pictures of real children can be sexualised to appear as pornography. For instance, a child in a swimming costume may have the costume removed or a baby who is holding a toy in one picture can now appear to be holding a man's penis (Healy, 1997; Lanning, 2001; Taylor and Quayle, 2003). Of course, the human mind is able to change and create sexual fantasies from otherwise innocuous material. For example, Howitt (1995b) found that perfectly licit images of children were converted into sexual fantasies by some offenders. What is different, of course, is that pseudo-photographs do the fantasy work of the offender. This makes it more likely that pseudo-photographs are incorporated into an offender's sexual fantasies.

Pseudo images also raise practical issues. How old is a virtual child? How is it possible to have a crime without a real victim? The question of where the criminal act takes place could also be an issue though perhaps equally so for 'real' child pornography. Is the crime where the image is produced, where the image is hosted, or where the image is viewed? Indeed, pseudo-pornography might be thought by some to be victimless in the sense that there is no specific victim. However, harm to the victim is not a criterion that has been applied in court. It is mainly a problem where the underlying belief is that the user of child pornography colludes with the actual victimisation of a child.

Some jurisdictions include pseudo-images in the definition of child pornography, although implementation of this has sometimes proven problematic. Initially, in the US, the Child Pornography Prevention Act (1996) defined child pornography as: 'any visual depiction including any photography, film, video, picture or computer generated image or picture ... where such visual depiction is, or appears to be, of a minor' and any sexually explicit image that is 'advertised, promoted, presented, described, or distributed in such a manner that conveys the impression' it depicts 'a minor engaging in sexually explicit conduct' (OYEZ Project, 2002). The words 'appears' and 'conveys the impression' would seem to ensure that virtual child pornography is included in the definition. Opponents of this, including the American Civil Liberties Union, favoured the criminalisation of the production of child pornography because this would help prevent the sexual abuse of children. Nevertheless, they argued that because there is no 'actual' child in pseudo-pornography and the events are not 'real' (in that there is no real child) then such images should not be criminalised because there is no harm or victimisation involved. Others such as The Free Speech Coalition, an adult-entertainment trade association, alleged that 'appears to be' and 'conveys the impression' were vague and penalised material otherwise protected by the First Amendment (The OYEZ Project, 2002). They asserted that people's private thoughts cannot be regulated and that to criminalise pseudo-pornography violates the principle of 'freedom of speech' (Akdeniz, 1997). Indeed, what followed was the *Ashcroft v. Free Speech Coalition* judgement that rendered the 1996 Act inoperable (Akdeniz, 2006). The legislation failed against the precedents of legal judgements based on the First Amendment, which enshrines the freedom to engage in lawful speech. The 1996 Act prohibited material that was not obscene by the Miller standard and did not involve the abuse of a real child (OYEZ Project, 2002).

The situation is different in the UK where pseudo-images are covered by legislation unaffected by effective legal challenges. Indeed, a Home Office Task Force has considered whether sexually explicit drawings or cartoons ought to be treated in the same way as pseudo-images (Home Office Press Release, 14 December 2006). Arguments supporting the criminalisation of pseudo-pornography echo those points referred to earlier as to why viewing pornography can be problematic – that abusers use child pornography to entice other children into the same behaviour and whether the child in the pornography is real, or artificial, is irrelevant (McCabe, 2000; McCabe and Gregory, 1998).

There are numerous ambiguities and uncertainties in legal definitions of illicit child pornography. This is normal in the sense that all legislation undergoes a process of clarification and redefinition in the courts, for example. Unfortunately, cooperation between different countries on child pornography is likely to be hampered by differences in legislation. Child pornography may be created in one country, distributed from half way round the world, and consumed in a different hemisphere. Extraterritorial legislation, such as that in the UK, Canada and Ireland, enables the prosecution of those who sell or possess child pornography abroad. One limitation is that these extraterritorial laws apply only to those countries were possession and distribution is itself criminal (Renold *et al.*, 2003).

## PSYCHOLOGICAL PERSPECTIVES OF CHILD PORNOGRAPHY

Care is needed about why legal definitions of child pornography are important. The law and psychology are two very different conceptual systems that rarely clearly overlap (Howitt, 2006). Even if legal standards were identical internationally, this consensus would not necessarily lead to a psychological definition of child pornography that would be helpful to researchers. Inevitably, precisely how child pornography is defined contributes to determining those who are convicted and those who may come to the attention of researchers as a consequence. As a result, research in different countries and at different times may not refer to exactly the same range of offending behaviours.

Possibly the most prevalent view of child pornography among the research community is that it represents a record of child sexual abuse – although there may be no requirement that an adult is present in the picture. There was a gradual progression from early to later definitions whereby references to child sexual abuse become more apparent. One very early definition by Tyler and Stone (1985, p. 314) mentions exploitation rather than abuse:

> Child pornography refers to pictorial depictions of children in sexually explicit poses or acts. Unlike sketches, drawings and statues which may or may not have employed live child models, pictorial depictions require that a child must be exploited in order to product the published product.

Similarly tentative is Tate's (1990, p. 2) commentary that:

> The word pornography conjures up a 'nudge-nudge-wink-wink' reaction. Child pornography is not pornography as it is understood by the man and woman in the street. It is not the glossy centerfolds of Playboy nor even . . . of hard-core pornography.

> Child pornography is 'not pornography in any real sense; simply the evidence recorded on film or video tape – of serious sexual assaults on young children' (Tate, 1992, p. 203).

However, shortly after this, Kelly and Scott (1993, p. 116) described child pornography in the following terms:

> Each piece of child porn involving adults (or in some cases animals) is a document of the sexual abuse of a child who was required for its production. Not all child porn involves adults in the picture, but photographs and films which include children in the frame involve adults outside who control the situation and children's behaviour within it: demanding of and/or instructing the children in what the photographer requires from them. This too is a form of sexual abuse. Every piece of child pornography, therefore, is a record of the sexual use/abuse of the children involved.

Not all authors were moving in similar directions. So, in contrast, Svedin and Back (1996, p. 9) defined child pornography much as any other pornography would be defined as a 'text, image (photo, slide, film, video or computer programme), that is intended to evoked a sexual feeling, fantasy or response in adults' but this is exceptional. A few years later Edwards (2000, p. 1) was defining child pornography as ' . . . the record of the systematic rape, abuse and torture of children on film and photograph, and other electronic means'. And Lanning added the final important element of permanence when he stated that child pornography 'represents the permanent record of the sexual abuse or exploitation of an actual child' (Lanning, 2001, p. 72).

Of course, the more recent definitions suggest that child pornography is evidence of child abuse and not simply illegal content. Thus child pornography is a picture of a crime scene but also criminal in itself. DI Terry Jones, then of the Greater Manchester Police Abusive Images Unit, commented that 'pornography' is the wrong word, choosing instead 'child abuse images' which he believes correctly presents the nature of the material (personal communication, 28 May 2003). Of course, pseudo-pornography cannot be regarded as evidence of a crime scene.

Apart from pseudo-images, which are generally problematic, definitions of child pornography as images of child sexual abuse actually fail to specify what is meant by child sexual abuse. The definition of this is crucial but has a taken-for-granted character in the definitions of child pornography.

## CONCLUDING COMMENTS

Pornography, as such, is not illegal in many jurisdictions since the test of its legitimacy is whether it meets the criteria of obscenity – the tendency to deprave or corrupt. This test requires that the pornography would adversely affect the user. Even expressing child pornography in terms of a capacity to generate fantasy that might be regarded as corruption or depraved is problematic. Then, what for many of us would be acceptable images, might be defined as child pornography. The range of materials that can evoke fantasies in men who express a sexual interest in children varies widely – from photographs displayed in family albums, which show no overt erotic sexual content, to a picture of the rape of a child (Howitt, 1995b; Taylor and Quayle, 2003). Taylor and Quayle (2003, p. 30) view this as a 'continuum of increased deliberate sexual victimization'. The concept of a 'continuum' has led to a grading system developed by the researchers and will be described in Chapter 2.

Internet Sex Offending, to date, seems to be dominated by the issue of child pornography. There are new offences being defined that deal with other aspects of online paedophile behaviour. Nevertheless, although there are some media reports of cases such as grooming children over the Internet, the number of convictions for these is not clear and, even more evidently, they have hardly begun to be tackled by researchers apart from the occasional case study.

The definition of child pornography is partly determined by cultural factors and the seriousness with which child pornography is regarded in legislation is far from universal even in Western nations. In particular, one could point to the issue of pseudo-images as being illustrative of the range of responses found in legislation. In some jurisdictions, pseudo images are treated no differently from real images of child sexual abuse; in others such images are disregarded in terms of illegality.

# CHAPTER 2

# The Issue of Child Pornography

It is generally difficult to know the prevalence of child pornographic images including those circulating on the Internet and, in some cases, it is not clear how available statistics are obtained or even what they mean. According to the Home Office Task Force on Child Protection on the Internet (2003) there are approximately one million images of child abuse in circulation on the Internet and this number grows by 200 each day. UNICEF estimates that 90 % of paedophile-related investigations involve the Internet in some way (cited in Robbins and Darlington, 2003). On the other hand, a two-year police investigation in Leeds in the North of England identified 31 paedophile sex rings involving nearly 50 perpetrators and over 300 children. But only three of the 31 paedophile rings investigated were involved in the production of child pornography (Wild, 1987; Wild and Wynne, 1987). On the other hand, a study of 36 self-defined survivors of ritual sexual abuse found that 13 of them reported being used in child pornography (Scott, 2001). Whereas another British study questioned 3,000 adults between 18 and 24 years of age and found that less than 1 % claimed to have had pornographic photographs or videos taken of them when they were children under 16 years of age (Cawson *et al.*, 2000).

There is no internationally agreed basis for recording crimes where the Internet played a significant part. Indeed, many countries do not record whether a computer was involved in the commissioning of a crime. So the available evidence comes from limited sources. In the US, between 1995 and 2003 there were 4,439 prosecutions relating to child pornography offences, of which 3,294 led to convictions and 2,849 resulted in imprisonment. The average prison term given between 1995 and 2002 was 45 months though in 2003 this rose markedly to 53 months (Akdeniz, 2006). Further, during 2002, 60 % of the child exploitation cases investigated involved distributing child abuse images online or using the US mail service (US Postal Inspection Service, 2002).

Reliable assessments of the amount of child pornography on the Internet are difficult. The Internet is too large and changes too quickly (Calder, 2004) to sample meaningfully or reliably and it is difficult to know what an appropriate sampling frame from which to draw samples would be. The lack of legal protection for researchers downloading child pornography for research purposes in countries like the UK does nothing to reduce the difficulties of obtaining worthwhile data. Thompson and Williams (2004) reviewed the case law and other issues related to this. Thompson's academic career has involved important research on of anti-pornography campaigns as well as critical accounts of notorious sexual abuse cases, *inter alia*. As such, he was a highly influential, independent voice on topics of crucial important to families throughout the United Kingdom. Yet he describes his victimisation by Internet child pornography legislation despite no child pornography pictures being found by the police on his computer. Although legislation related to child pornography offered protection or a legal defence to people other than the police with a legitimate interest in the problem of child pornography, gradually things changed such that such defences were excluded through simple legal procedures. The legal protections applied to 'possessing' child pornography; there was no legal defence allowed for the 'making' of child pornography. So by prosecuting for making child pornography there was no defence even for academics working in the field. Downloading and making are regarded as synonymous in law.

So objective evidence concerning child pornography on the Internet is scant. The difficulties are compounded by the lack of a uniform system amongst agencies for recording child pornography offences. This can make assessing the number of victims and the number of offenders arrested a somewhat hit-and-miss process. Despite the problems, it is regarded as important to establish the extent to which individuals and networks of abusers produce, circulate and use child pornography (Kelly and Scott, 1993). Only with such knowledge can proactive solutions for resource management, Internet regulation and abuse detection be developed.

Aside from guesstimates from many different parts of the world, North America has been the main provider of evidence about how much child pornography is available, the content of this material, its usage and how many children are involved. Data from the UK are mainly restricted to prevalence surveys, case studies of organised child abuse, Home Office figures, 'hotlines', media reports and police seizures. Caution is required when interpreting any of this evidence and a variety of sources probably need to be consulted given the pervasive methodological problems in the available research.

## CONVICTIONS FOR CHILD PORNOGRAPHY-RELATED OFFENCES

Convictions for child pornography-related offences give some idea of the growth over the last few years. Table 2.1 gives a summary of some British Home Office statistics. These fail to differentiate the type of medium involved, such as whether the postal service is involved or the Internet. Nevertheless, there is a clear increase in convictions for these crimes, which has escalated in recent years. In fact, a more detailed analysis of these data suggest a very substantial increase in convictions in the years 2002–3. There are various reasons for this. Obvious ones include the rapid increase in the use of the

**Table 2.1**  Number of defendants on average per year found guilty at all courts for offences relating to indecent photographs of children in England and Wales 1990 to 2003

| Type of offence | 1990–4 | 1995–9 | 2000–3 |
|---|---|---|---|
| Taking or making indecent photographs of children | 36.4 | 87.4 | 497.3 |
| Possession of indecent photographs of children | 35.2 | 80.2 | 140.8 |

Internet for all purposes since the mid 1990s, which has been accompanied by increasing police interest in the exchange of indecent child images and in chat rooms (Jones, 2003). Furthermore, the impact of massive police operations such as Operation Ore which began in May 2002 in the UK (Bright, 2003; Howlett, 2003; O'Carroll and Morris, 2003; Renold *et al.*, 2003) may have been influential. As of April 2005, this police operation in the UK involved 4,283 searches being made and leading to the arrest of 3,744 men, 1,848 have been charged, 1,451 convicted, plus an additional 500 having received cautions (Akdeniz, 2006). These are significant numbers given that the numbers convicted each year are not large.

## INTERNET SURVEILLANCE

The UK Internet Watch Foundation (IWF) uses a hotline system to actively monitor the Internet for illegal material. The IWF is the only agency, other than law enforcement agencies, which can legally view child-abuse images (Sexual Offences Act 2003). The Foundation was established in 1996 as a joint initiative involving government (the Home Office and the Department of Trade and Industry), Internet Service Providers (ISPs) and the police. Funding comes from the Internet industry as well as telecommunications companies and the European Commission (Carr, 2003; Renold *et al.*, 2003; Robbins and Darlington, 2003). Data are collected from the public that inform the organisation via email of any suspected illegal material seen on the Internet (Akdeniz, 2001; Robbins and Darlington, 2003). Staff of the Internet Watch Foundation then investigate complaints. If well founded, the Internet Watch Foundation informs the police and National Criminal Intelligence Service but also, crucially, asks all British Internet Service Providers to remove the offending site. If the ISPs do not comply then the police may take further action (Akdeniz, 2001a; Robbins and Darlington, 2003). The main focus is on child pornography, obscene adult pornography and criminally racist material. Other activities include supporting the labelling work of the Internet Content Rating Association, recommending that ISPs should not carry certain newsgroups and education and promoting awareness about content and general usage of the Internet with parents and children (Robbins and Darlington, 2003).

In 2003, hotline reports to the Internet Watch Foundation had reached over 19,000 from 11,000 in 2001, although this fell to 17,000 in 2004 (Internet Watch Foundation, 2004). However, the underlying trend was up because the annual number increased to almost 24,000 in 2005 (Internet Watch Foundation, 2005). Of course, reporting may be affected by a number of factors. Apart from the obvious possibility that illegal material on the Internet fluctuates, it is also possible than anti-spam security measures on computers have resulted in fewer offensive hits on computers being registered. Furthermore highly publicised police activity may make the public more aware of the penalties that may follow visiting pornography Web sites and distributing abusive images of children. Of course, figures on the number of reports do not in themselves reflect illegal content. It is interesting to note that in 2005 over 6,000 reports were regarded as 'valid' – in other words that illegal content was found. However, this leaves almost 18,000 reports that were not substantiated as having illegal content. Most reports from the public (89 %) concerned child pornography, which, inevitably suggests, that substantial numbers of reports of child pornography on the Internet were, for some reason, not valid. Of the confirmed illegal child pornography content, almost half was to be found on commercial or pay-per-view sites (IWF, 2005), although this is not the main source for offenders.

Changes have also occurred in terms of where the material originates in the World. Child pornography hosted from the US has declined whereas Russian sites have increased (IWF, 2005). It is argued that the main geographical areas providing child victims used for child pornography are Russia, the Ukraine and other former Soviet Union countries, South East Asia and Central and South America (Europol, 2005) where it is thought that a lack of legislation is facilitating this illegal activity (Sommer, 2003). The Internet Watch Foundation also reported in 2005 that Asian countries contributed a moderate amount of the potentially illegal content. Most striking is the fact that UK located sites have declined to less than 1 % of reports (IWF, 2005).

At best, these figures can only reflect the reporting figures through the hotline. The figures cannot tell us directly how much child pornography is actually available on the Internet. Furthermore, what might be available to Internet users lacking the motivation to seek out child pornography may be very different from that available to motivated individuals with the skills to find the material in otherwise little used corners of the Internet. Despite the claims of the Foundation and the government, it is uncertain that the hotline reflects the extent of child pornography on the Internet (Akdeniz, 2001a). It is also questionable whether closing down UK Internet sites significantly affects the amount of child pornography circulating. To be sure, material may be removed by UK ISPs but how often does it reappear in another guise? Material may be removed from UK ISPs but nevertheless remain on ISPs in other countries (Akdeniz, 2001b).

## MEDIA REPORTS

Media reports, while in a sense not directly assessing the extent of child pornography, set the agenda for what people think the situation is. It is relatively easy to use the Internet as a source of newspaper articles and news programmes – the difficulty is the sheer volume of coverage. Searching for media articles on the Web sites of newspapers and news programmes (for example, the *Telegraph*, the *Guardian*, *BBC News*) for references to sex offending produces a wide variety of articles. A regular feature is newspaper articles reporting individual cases and police seizures consequent to police operations. British broadsheets and tabloids alike have substantially increased their coverage of paedophile/paedophilia since 1996 (Soothill, Francis, Ackerley, 1998). This cannot be accounted for by increases in the number of offenders passing through the courts because the proportions of sex offenders in the prison population remained stable despite the increase in media coverage. It is well known that media coverage of crime news shows little relationship with objective indicators of the extent of crimes (Howitt, 1998a). Of course, there are signs that the public is willing to voice concerns about the threat posed by sex offenders against children which would include Internet offenders (NSPCC, 21 January 2003, press release).

Media coverage provides accounts of individuals arrested for the possession of many thousands of indecent images of children. What is the overall effect of this emphasis in media coverage? Do the many thousands of indecent images of children obtained via the Internet create the impression that the problem of Internet child pornography is huge? Or perhaps such arrests encourage some of the public to believe that the problem is under control. Therefore is current public thinking about sex offending and the Internet out of proportion to the scale of the problem (Renold *et al.*, 2003)? Are we witnessing a moral panic about the extent of paedophilia in which the media pay a crucial role in fuelling the panic (Silverman and Wilson, 2002)? Phrases such as 'paedophile ring' are culturally laden with meanings and implications, which may be difficult to sustain as a description of such paedophile activity. One effect of the media coverage may be to create the impression that there are many paedophile rings or networks operating when, in reality, it is often the case that one offender is sending banned material to another over the Internet. Furthermore, the implication is often that the quantity of images that an offender downloads is an indicator of their deviancy (Sullivan and Beech, 2003). Indeed, many of the downloaded images that are totalled for Internet offenders may not feature children at all but involve legal material or adult pornography. The public generally does not access research articles or books that may modify the impressions created by the media. As a consequence, their perception of the debate on pornography will be disproportionately influenced by news coverage (Howitt and Cumberbatch, 1990).

Furthermore, Internet child pornography images are mainly derived from videos so a single video may be the source of perhaps thousands of still images (Taylor, Quayle and Holland, 2001). Of course, the fact that one picture is capable of being disseminated many times makes estimates of how many children are involved in child pornography images even more difficult. Despite its inherent dramatic value, just what bearing does the conviction of an individual who had one million images on his computer have on the impression of the degree, extent and control of child pornography distribution on the Internet?

## POLICE SEIZURES AND OPERATIONS

High-profile police operations against Internet child pornography began in
the mid-1990s and the first arrests following these occurred in the latter part
of that decade (Jones, 2003; Renold *et al.*, 2003). Some police forces have
dedicated units to tackle the availability and distribution of indecent images
of children (Jones, 2003). For instance, in the UK, the Greater Manchester
Police (GMP) initially seized very few such images but this increased with
the establishment of a specialised unit. To illustrate, during 1995 the
Manchester unit seized a total of 12 images – all in video or stills format
rather than on a computer hard drive for example. There was a remarkable
increase to 41,000 images by 1999. However, all but three of the images were
in some form of computer format. Of course, such a massive increase in the
number of detected images probably reflects the hoarding of thousands of
images rather than a commensurate increase in the number of offenders. For
example, in 2001 one offender in this police area was found to have
accumulated 50,000 child images and over three gigabytes of movie files.
The force, of course, was inclined to the view that their figures confirm the
wide-scale availability of such material and the relative ease by which it can
be accessed (Jones, 2003).

There have been a number of high-profile police operations at both the
national and international levels and some of these are listed in Table 2.2.
Police operations do not necessarily reflect the scale of offending at a
particular time. It is worthwhile discussing two particularly important police
operations in some detail – these are not mentioned in Table 2.2.

### Operation Cathedral

Ronald Riva, a child molester, was arrested in California. This led to a trail that
finally exposed the W0nderland Club. The police found links between Riva
and Ian Baldock in Hastings in the UK. After his computer had been
confiscated in England, over 40,000 child images of a sexually explicit nature
were found. The W0nderland Club (0 is a zero not 'o') was a global Internet
channel set up in the 1990s to expedite the exchange of child pornography.
Possibly it was named after Lewis Carroll's *Alice in Wonderland* book. It had
been operating for about four years before homes and premises were raided
by the police in 12 countries on 3 September 1998. Coordinated raids took
place simultaneously in Australia, Austria, Belgium, Finland, France, Germany, Italy, Norway, Portugal, Sweden and the US.

The organisational structure could be described as a 'pyramid system' in
that men would need to have obtained at least 10,000 pornographic child
images as a condition of being able to join and trade images with other men.
The club had a chair, a treasurer, board of members and a set of rules
enshrined in the *Traders Security Handbook*. Security was provided by powerful
gatekeeping and encryption software – one was a computer program known
as Alice. Higher status was accorded to those who had the most material to
distribute (Akdeniz, 2001c; Calder, 2004; Dowd, 2003; Fields, 1998; Silverman

**Table 2.2**   Major police operations

| Operation name | Date, place and details |
| --- | --- |
| First Out (Akdeniz, 2001b) | 1994 – Fellows and Arnold had stored thousands of indecent child Internet photographs on a work computer (at the Department of Metallurgy of Birmingham University). It was ruled that computerised images could be regarded as photographs and this set a legal precedent. |
| Starburst (Renold et al., 2003) | 1995 – Started in the UK and identified 37 suspects worldwide. |
| Innocent Images (Renold et al., 2003) | 1995 – FBI operation that generated 186 convictions by March 1998. |
| Modem (Akdeniz, 1997) | 1996 – Local operation by Durham police after information received from their German counterparts. It led to the raid on St Joseph's presbytery and subsequent arrest of Father McLeish. The police found 8,998 image files, including child and adult pornography and drawings; two hard disks referred to as 'nice' and 'naughty'; thousands of explicit email messages exchanged with other paedophiles; encryption software and a private code 'overhead the moon is beaming'. He also admitted to 12 charges of indecent assaults against two boys of 10 and 12, distributing and possession with intent to distribute and being involved in the importation of child pornographic videos. |
| Kimble (Jones, 2003) | 1999 – 16 targets were identified. This operation commenced partly as in-house police training. For two months staff monitored paedophile activity within Internet newsgroups. During a search in the Greater Manchester area a video was found that showed an individual abusing his stepdaughter. He had no prior convictions. |
| Queensland (Renold et al., 2003) | 1999 – 24 UK police forces arrested 14 men and one woman and seized 19 computer systems. |
| Appal (Jones, 2003; Silverman and Wilson, 2002) | 2001 – 48 targets were identified as suspected of distributing child pornography; 26 police forces were involved. This led to the discovery of previously undisclosed child abuse but also six of the targets were under 17 and one was 13 years old – he had 321 child abuse images downloaded from the Internet. He became the youngest person in Britain to be placed on the Sex Offender Register. |
| Snowflake (Jones, 2003) | 2001 – The first UK investigation that analysed objects contained within the images. The offender received six life sentences for serious crimes against children. |
| Magenta (Renold et al., 2003; Silverman and Wilson, 2002) | 2002 – 34 UK police forces raided 75 addresses after 74 hours of online monitoring. Twenty-seven people were arrested ranging from 15 to 59 years of age. One of the notable features of this inquiry was the close involvement of an Internet filter company from Cheshire called SurfControl. The kit developed dramatically reduced the amount of time needed to filter out innocent chatroom traffic taking place all over the world and hone in on illicit transactions, providing names and addresses. |

*(Continued)*

**Table 2.2**  (*Continued*)

| Operation name | Date, place and details |
| --- | --- |
| Atlas (BBC News, 2005c) | 2003 – Norfolk Police carried out weekly raids on homes resulting in 48 convictions. Police seized 129 personal computers, 48 laptops, 55 hard discs and thousands of DVDs, CDs and floppy diskettes. |
| Callidus (BBC News, 6 May 2005) | 2005 – Italian, Danish, Polish, Norwegian, Maltese and Dutch police were involved in investigating 100 people involved in chid pornography on the Internet. Pictures and videos were seized and 20 people in France were arrested. Investigators used French software especially developed for the purpose of tracking internet users and identifying victims. |
| No name (BBC News, 2006) | 2006 – Michael Studdert (a former vicar) and Thomas O'Carroll (a paedophile rights campaigner) were jailed after a child porn 'library' was uncovered at the former vicar's home. Additional charges included possession, making and distributing child abuse images. The collection, which took 50 years to put together, was discovered after undercover police infiltrated a group known as the International Paedophile Child Emancipation Group and its subsidiary, Gentlemen with an Interesting Name. |

and Wilson, 2002). About 100 men were arrested worldwide. The operation netted a total of three-quarters of a million images together with 1,800 digital video clips. Some of the children in the images were only a few months old. One of the eight British men charged (this included three computer consultants) later committed suicide (Akdeniz, 2001c). It is noteworthy, however, that despite this being the largest ever international police operation at the time, the men only received between 12 months and 18 months in prison – substantially less than the maximum of three years that could have been given at that time (Akdeniz, 2001c; Renold *et al.*, 2003). The club possessed the facility for offenders to film sexual abuse as it took place and to transmit to other members although it was not established that the convicted British men participated in this (Dowd, 2003). Some of the men contributed to early research on their motivation and behaviour (see, for example, Quayle and Taylor, 2002b).

## Operation Ore

This British police operation was the result of the US Postal Inspection Service mounting Operation Avalanche. A Texan Web site belonging to Landslide Inc. was the target of this investigation. The site sold 'adult keys', which provided a gateway to many Web sites containing adult pornography but also some sites that contained child pornography. It is claimed that the Web site had a special button for child pornography. Some suggest that the company obtained a £1 million-a-month profit from the site. Details of 75,000 repeat users of the site were found on a computer. These were people who had paid for access using their credit cards. The FBI passed on to the British police possibly in excess of 7,200 names of individuals suspected of purchasing child pornography via this company (Bright, 28th September 2003; Howlett, 2003; O'Carroll and Morris, 2003; Renold et al., 2003).

Of most interest in this context were the events in the US. A list of Landslide subscribers in the US was contacted in a sting operation. The subscribers were offered the opportunity to purchase child pornography through the postal service. Many did not respond to the invitation – presumably, part of the reason for this is that some were not interested in child pornography. However, some did purchase the child pornography. One-hundred-and-forty-four purchasers of the child pornography were investigated further (ABC News, 2001) and 30 % of them were found to have known contact offences against children. It would be fallacious to assume that 30 % of all of the Web site's clients were contact abusers against children (Irish Examiner, 2004). The remaining 70 %, presumably, consisted of men with no contact offences but an interest in indecent portrayals of children. Just how typical the 'purchasers' of the bogus child pornography were of Internet pornography offenders in general we do not know. Furthermore, we do not know what proportion of contact offenders are also consumers of child pornography.

Claims have been made that Operation Avalanche demonstrated that Internet pornography offences and contact offences against children are closely linked. However, one could not claim on the basis of Operation Avalanche that there is a certain or even a strong link; a better description is that the link is somewhat weak as few took up the offer of the bogus child pornography. The Operation Ore investigation attracted political and media attention for a number of years, partly because of the number of high profile figures arrested.

## RESEARCH STUDIES OF THE EXTENT OF INTERNET CHILD PORNOGRAPHY

There is no doubt that child pornography offences lead to excellent headlines, but this is unsystematic information that should not be regarded as particularly important in terms of research. There are more systematic studies of Internet child pornography available. It should be remembered that research is essentially prevented in some jurisdictions because research is not accepted as a defence to child pornography charges. Not surprisingly, then, much of the systematic research on child pornography is not very recent.

Utilising a 'research team' from the Carnegie Mellon University in Pittsberg, Rimm (1995) downloaded over a four-month period, pornographic mages from five Usenet newsgroups and also obtained listings from 69 commercial adult bulletin board systems or BBSs. This yielded 917,410 descriptions or images. However, the analysis concentrated on the adult bulletin board system files, which amounted to 450,620 files, of which only 292,114 were categorised. The rest of the BBS files were either ambiguously described or had no description at all and so could not be included in the analysis. The descriptions of the images were coded in terms of the presence of a number of dominant themes. However, as some files contained more than one theme then the dominance of some themes may be inflated. Rimm coded the files in terms of the categories of *paedophilic/hebephilic* (nude portraits of prepubescent children and hardcore sex acts including young-looking boys and girls), *paraphilic* (including transvestism, transsexualism, sadomasochism, fisting, urophilia, coprophilia, voyeurism, bestiality and incest), *hardcore imagery without paraphilic allusions*, and *softcore pornography*. The basis of his coding was The *Diagnostic and Statistical Manual for Mental Disorders*, fourth edition (DSM-IV)

This was a highly publicised and controversial study. One needs to be careful about the overinterpretion of the research. Academics have debated the study in terms of its 'accuracy and originality' and 'the ethics of the researcher' (Mehta, 2001 p. 696). For instance Rimm's qualifications to lead a research study were rather thin. He was, in fact, an undergraduate student.

Consumers all over North American and 40 other countries were accessing paedophilic and paraphilic pornography using their computers, Rimm concluded. There were 2,685,777 downloads of material in this category which would amount to 48.4 % of all downloads from the selected 68 commercial adult bulletin boards systems sites. It is argued that misleading information was supplied by Rimm concerning the percentage of pornography to be found on Usenet which itself constituted 11.5 % of Internet traffic at the time of the research. Rimm (1995, p. 1914) claimed that '84.5 % of Usenet images are pornographic'. This has been seriously questioned because the study only used newsgroups with an 'alt.binaries' prefix, which is not representative of all Usenet sites. Of the 32 newsgroups he surveyed, 17 contained pornographic images (p. 1867). During one week, out of 5,033 image postings, 4,206 were made to pornography newsgroups. That is 83.5 % of images were posted to pornographic newsgroups. However, this figure of 83.5 % was extrapolated to all Usenet postings. Furthermore, the 83.5 % includes all types of images including an uncertain number of pornographic ones. Basically his figures suggest that a lot more postings are made to pornographic newsgroup sites (alt.binaries prefix ones) than to other newsgroups – a very different picture from the one that Rimm paints.

Rimm had stated that approximately 70 % of pornography on the Usenet originated from the Bulletin Board System and that half (48.4 %) of the BBS contained paedophilic and paraphilic images. This, of course, would constitute an alarmingly high figure for child pornography and paraphilic images available through the Bulletin Board System. By recalculating the figures reported in Rimm's article, Hoffman and Novak (1995, p. 8) argued that:

> Less than half of 1 % (3 % of the 11 %) of the messages on the Internet are associated with newsgroups that contain pornographic imagery. Further, of the half of 1 %, an unknown but even smaller percentage of

messages in newsgroups that are associated with pornographic imagery actually contain pornographic material.

Taken, then, to its logical conclusion, the percentage of newsgroups that would contain child pornography would be even smaller.

Rimm's interpretation of his data was sensational rather than measured, so it provided some policymakers with all the evidence they needed to argue their case for legislation, although Rimm's evidence is unsound (Hoffman and Novak, 1995). His data cannot be used to estimate the amount of child pornography in circulation though Hoffman and Novak's recalculation may provide us with a picture that is somewhat more accurate.

A more trustworthy study was work in Canada by Mehta (2001). This involved 9,800 randomly selected images from 32 Usenet newsgroups (for example, alt.sex.bondage, alt.sex.paedophilia) between July 1995 and July 1996. The intention was to document the kinds of images online including real and/or pseudo images of children and adolescents. Twenty per cent of images involved children/adolescents, compared to a figure of 15 % obtained in an earlier study (Mehta and plaza, 1994). This 20 % was made up of the following:

- nude images of children/adolescents not involved in sexual activity – 5.1 %;
- 'hebephilic', clearly showing an adolescent with secondary characteristics involved in sexual activity – 10.6 %;
- 'paedophilic' images emphasising the genital region of a child, or sexual activity involving children lacking secondary sexual characteristics – 4.4 %.

The view is commonly promoted that child images on the Internet are the result of commercial greed. In fact images depicting nude children, nude adolescents and paedophilic themes were more likely to be posted by non-commercial sources than commercial ones. The pornography posted on commercial sites was more likely to involve images of adult multiple participants, vaginal and anal penetration, fellatio and cunnilingus, ejaculation, bondage, homosexual sex and bestiality. Care is needed with these statistics because whether the company had posted the image or someone else had placed them there could not always be determined. It was not possible to tell whether the commercial source intended or wanted to have particular images circulated in Usenet.

## THE WORK OF COPINE

COPINE at the University of Cork in the Republic of Ireland has made an important contribution to our knowledge of the contents of Internet child pornography. COPINE is the acronym for Combating Paedophile Information Networks in Europe. This project was legally permitted to develop a database of child pornography, which provides information concerning (a) the extent and (b) the nature of child pornography. The material used was obtained from 60 newsgroups known to host child pornography. Internet child pornography in other areas of the Internet has received scant attention although discussion of this is to be found in Jenkins (2001).

The material was classified, in part, according to its age – old material (over 15 years old), new (less than 10 years old), and recent material (between 10 and 15 years old) (Taylor, Quayle and Holland, 2001a). The database is said to include 'most of the material publicly available' and 'represents a very large sample of the total amount of material in public circulation and is wholly based on Internet sources' (Taylor and Quayle, 2003, p. 31). To the extent that this is the case, these researchers have provided us with an invaluable overview of Internet child pornography. The COPINE researchers provided a widely accepted grading system or typology consisting of various types of imagery. Ten different 'levels' of image content are described, which approximate a scale from the least extreme to the most extreme types of content. Each 'level' is given a name and the sorts of imagery it refers to has a description. According to Taylor, Holland, and Quayle (2001), the scheme is:

- *COPINE level 1: indicative.* This includes pictures of children that might be regarded in some contexts as innocuous. So pictures of children in underwear or wearing bathing costumes at play typify this level but are typical of family snapshots. Other aspects of the content or the context in which the pictures were found determine whether the material is inappropriate. Quayle and Taylor did not elaborate on this but, obviously, such pictures are likely to have been used inappropriately if they are found on an offender's computer alongside more explicit material.
- *COPINE level 2: nudist.* This includes pictures of nude or semi-nude children taken in legitimate nudist settings and obtained from legitimate sources.
- *COPINE level 3: erotica.* This comprises surreptitiously taken pictures of children in their underwear or exhibiting a greater degree of nudity.
- *COPINE level 4: posing.* This consists of deliberately posed pictures in which the children are fully or partially nude.
- *COPINE level 5: erotic posing.* As level 4 but with the added characteristic that the children are in provocative or sexualised postures.
- *COPINE level 6: explicit erotic posing.* As level 5 but with a greater degree of emphasis on the children's genital areas.
- *COPINE level 7: explicit sexual activity.* These images involve sexual touching, mutual or self-masturbation, oral sex and sexual intercourse by children but adults are NOT to be seen.
- *COPINE level 8: assault.* This is sexual assault in which the adult assaults the child through the use of touching with the fingers.
- *COPINE level 9: gross assault.* This category involves grossly obscene pictures involving an adult and depicting penetrative sex, masturbation or oral sex.
- *COPINE level 10: sadistic bestiality.* The most extreme level of content in which a child is tied up, bound, beaten, whipped or otherwise experiencing an ordeal which is painful. Alternatively, the pictures will involve an animal in the sexual behaviour.

The grading system includes pictures that would not be defined as child pornography by legislation anywhere. For instance, level 1 – non-erotic/non-sexualised pictures of children – includes the sorts of pictures that might be found in a typical family photo album. It could be argued that by having a grading system of seriousness implies a 'slippery slope', which may result in interest in extreme child pornography. In defining their position, the authors argue that collections of child pictures *per se* are not necessarily inappropriate. However, the context of the collection or its organisation may reflect inappropriate interest in the pictures (Taylor, Holland, and Quayle, 2001). Indeed, level 1 images could be the subjects of fantasy. Howitt (1995b) in his case studies of 11 men drew attention to how entirely innocent imagery can be used by offenders to promote and sustain fantasy.

Many similar comments could be made about level 2 images, which can feature children nude in artistic or nudist settings. Again the context in terms of the motivations of the producer or the viewer will be significant. A photograph in a gallery would make its artistic intent clear but the same picture among a collection of pornography might appear to suggest that such pictures may be turned into sexual material by some adults (Taylor and Quayle, 2003). In some jurisdictions level 2 pictures may or may not be illegal (Taylor, Holland and Quayle, 2001). Level 3 images may be a particularly problematic area because in some ways they may be no different from family-album photographs except that they involve some exploitation (Taylor, Holland and Quayle, 2001). For example, images taken with telephoto lenses in order to hide the photographer's intentions may be involved – that is, surreptitiously taken pictures at swimming pools and on beaches. It could be argued that this behaviour is wrong because it turns places in which children should be able to play in safety and security into sexual events (Taylor and Quayle, 2003).

In the UK (and probably elsewhere), the likelihood is that the police would generally not investigate pictures below COPINE's level 5. Furthermore, it is actually unlikely that pictures at levels 4 and 5 would be illegal (Jones, personal communication, 28 May 2003). It is difficult to imagine any pictures with a COPINE classification level of 8, 9 or 10 being legal since they involve adults or animals involved sexually with children – typically they are pictures of sexual assaults or rapes (Taylor, Holland and Quayle, 2001; Taylor and Quayle, 2003). Much the same would apply to COPINE's level 7 category though the perpetrator may not be seen in these pictures (Taylor and Quayle, 2003).

Monitoring the content of child pornography on the Internet using the COPINE scheme revealed that approximately two new children per month appear in photographs on the newsgroups studied. Over 1,000 illegal photographs per week are posted onto Usenet newsgroups (Taylor, Quayle and Holland, 2001). An increase in 'domestic' production (the pictures are taken in dwellings) is evident (Taylor and Quayle, 2003) as well as an increase in material from South America and Eastern Europe (graded at levels 5 and 6) (Taylor, Quayle and Holland, 2001). The COPINE project also conducted a six-week monitoring exercise in 2002, which found 140,000 child images posted, of which 35,000 were completely new. Twenty new children had been abused to produce them (Renold *et al.*, 2003). It would seem that the numbers of pictures and the numbers of children abused to obtain them are very different because multiple images can be used of any one child. Often the identification of a victim in child pornography eludes the investigator. So it is problematic just how many children are involved and who exactly they are. A 30-year-old photograph of a victim is unlikely to lead to identification – and the victim for many reasons may not be willing to come forward.

The COPINE database holds more than 150,000 separate still pictures and 400 video sequences (Taylor and Quayle, 2003). Of the pictures categorised as level 7 (explicit sexual activity) and above, 7 % were new pictures of females and 26 % new pictures of males. Children between nine and 12 years of age contribute 41 % of the new girl pictures and 56 % of the new boy pictures. White children (both boys and girls) are more likely to be depicted in level 7 activity and above. Asian children are more likely to appear in levels 5 and 6. There is a marked absence of black children altogether in the archive. Taylor and Quayle (2003, p. 41) argue that collectors of child pornography prefer 'thin, fair children, where genitalia are clearly visible and where there are no secondary characteristics'.

The Sentencing Advisory Panel (2002) published guidance on what factors should be taken into account in deciding the correct level of sentence in relation to those who collect, view and distribute child pornography. The two primary factors that increase the likelihood of, and length of, a custodial sentence are the extent of the offender's involvement with the material and the *nature* of the indecent material (rather than the quantity). The former ranges in severity from possession of material for personal use to wide-scale commercial distribution. In relation to the nature of the material, the Court of Appeal prompted by the Sentencing Advisory Panel (2002) decided that it would be useful to classify images in terms of indecency and adapted COPINE's index scale (Gillespie, 2005d). The Sentencing Advisory Panel (2002) is an independent body that provides advice to the Sentencing Guidelines Council. One of the purposes of the COPINE scale was to help law enforcement agencies to categorize images (Taylor, Holland, and Quayle, 2001) but Gillespie (2005d) points out that the Court of Appeal misrepresented the use of the scale in that it was never intended to be a scale of severity of the offence but was a description of the sort of content involved. Nevertheless, the 10-stage COPINE was reduced to a five-level sentencing structure (Gillespie, 2003, 2005d). COPINE levels 5 and 6 became the new SAP level 1 and COPINE levels 7 to 10 all equated to one SAP level each (Gillespie, 2005d). This results in the following scheme:

- *SAP level 1:* images depicting erotic or explicit erotic posing. This category ranges from erotic posing (deliberate sexual or provocative poses) to explicit erotic posing (emphasis on genital area).
- *SAP level 2:* sexual activity between children, or solo masturbation by a child. This category is explicit sexual activity but confined to children only.
- *SAP level 3:* non-penetrative sexual activity between adult(s) and child(ren). This includes images of sexual assaults on children by adults.

- *SAP level 4:* penetrative sexual activity between child(ren) and adult(s).
- *SAP level 5:* sadism or bestiality.

The higher the SAP level of the material, the higher the sentence.

Other aggravating factors that would increase sentencing include showing or distributing material to a child, posting images in public areas where they could be found accidentally, being responsible for the actual production of the images, and the age of the child (Gillespie, 2005d). In some cases, where a large amount of SAP level 2 material has been distributed (sexual activity between children or solo masturbation by a child), three years or more is recommended. It is not clear why the three year term is chosen but the sentence is now in line with the average sentence for a serious indecent assault, which is three years (Gillespie, 2003). Conditional discharges and fines are reserved for those offenders in possession of small amounts of pseudo-images or SAP level 1 (images depicting erotic or explicit erotic posing) pornography for personal use only. Given the arguments noted earlier for criminalising pseudo-pornography, pseudo images are treated as less serious (in terms of sentencing) than photographic images of real children.

If one is found in possession of SAP level 1 material, at a commonsense level, this is less reprehensible than being found in possession of SAP level 5 material – or distributing the pornography. Offenders may feel the same too. Yet, there is no research evidence, to date, which has explored the idea that the sort of child pornography downloaded is an indication of a person's greater or lesser risk to children (Carr, 2003). The inverse may well be true. The lower SAP level material might, to the offender, depict more realistic and attainable abusive situations. This might suggest that children could be at greater risk from a low SAP level offender.

The COPINE extremity grading allows for a degree of discrimination in terms of the contents of Internet child pornography. Nevertheless, the system says little or nothing about how the viewer of the images interacts psychologically with the material. It also cannot account for the processes involved between the Internet, images, and the user of the images. According to Taylor and Quayle (2003), the child pornography collections of offenders are not simply an aggregate of individual images. Internet child pornography often consists of 'series' of pictures having distinct names and serial numbers within the series. One common feature, though not precisely documented, is the extent to which Internet child pornography tends to be still photographs captured from a video (Taylor, Holland and Quayle, 2001). The series have narrative qualities in the sense that they may show a child engaging in a particular behavioural sequence – for example, the child may be shown at different stages in the process of undressing. Sometimes, the producer of the pornography does not post the set of pictures in their exact temporal sequence – this results in some users spending time looking for the missing photographs in the series (Taylor and Quayle, 2003). More recent child pornography sometimes includes linking textual narrative to provide an enhanced narrative structure to the sequence of images such that the user is in some respects included in the narrative. Taylor and Quayle (2003) point out that the narrative generally leads to the most extreme picture or pictures. The narratives may help the user engage with the victim in the pornography and assist in the maintenance and generation of sexual fantasy (Taylor, Holland and Quayle, 2001). The search for and finding of the missing pictures from a user's collection is behaviourally highly reinforcing and may add to the psychological importance of the sequence of images. This is illustrated in the following interview from Taylor and Quayle (2003, p. 39):

> You know I suppose I was deliberately going for groups...em...so you get like an idea of the full event that was going on so I suppose like I come back here it's probably more like action which is probably later on I went to em...movie format...I you know so you get an idea of...the full continuation rather than just one photo...or like a snapshot.

Applying the COPINE grading system, it is possible to summarise the characteristics of massive sets of pictures (Taylor and Quayle, 2003). For example, they studied a particular set of images that is believed to involve a total of 36 girls aged between 1.5 and seven years old. In this series, the total number of pictures exceeds 3,000 and these are distributed in 100 different individual picture series of between 30 and 60 'stills' – believed to be from video. The same children are presented at different ages. Judging from their data, there seems to be over 50 picture sequences that show sexual victimisation at COPINE level 7 or above (explicit sexual activity but not directly involving an adult). Individual children could be identified and five of the 36 girls are portrayed in two or more series. Only these five girls are featured in pornography at about the COPINE level 7 or above. For instance, one girl is displayed on pictures ranging from level 5 to level 9, from about the ages of three to seven. Thus we get a clear indication of the extent in terms of time of involvement and seriousness of the sexual acts of some of the children in the pornography. In other words, some of the pornography documents the extent of the long-term abuse of children. Taylor (1999) and Taylor, Quayle and Holland (2001) note that the age of children involved in Internet pornography (particularly females) is reducing. Children under the age of five years of age may be particularly vulnerable because of their limited ability to refuse participation and their greater difficulty in disclosing to adults because of their lack of language skills.

More recently, Taylor and Quayle (2003) refer to the increase in home production facilitated by changes in the advancement of photography, from instant cameras to scanners and more recently mobile phones. Another characteristic of Internet pornography is the speed by which even free images can accumulate from a few to many thousands. Fast acquisition can be facilitated by the use Internet Relay Chat, which can allow others to access the contents of an individual's hard drive (Taylor, Quayle and Holland, 2001). Taylor and Quayle (2003) describe one offender whose collection grew in about six months from 3,000 to about 40,000 using the Internet. Before the Internet, men might have had to trade pornography via word of mouth or through the post, both of which increase the risk of detection. The storage of the images is also relatively easy and only a few DVDs or other storage discs are needed to store what is far in excess of what a few hundred magazines could contain – and perhaps with a much lower risk of detection as a consequence (Tate, 1990).

## CONCLUDING COMMENTS

The extent of child pornography on the Internet may not be the key issue. Any child pornography is too much child pornography. It could be argued that the extent of child pornography should have no necessary bearing on public attitudes. But, of course, this is mistaken because an Internet rife with child pornography both indicates that the material is not effectively controlled and that there is a substantial audience for this material. Public alarm, from this point of view, is both appropriate and justified. That we cannot say with certainty just how much child pornography there is on the Internet probably reflects the inadequacy of the question. Perhaps more important questions to address include the issue of how easy it is to obtain child pornography on the Internet if one really is intent on finding it – and, conversely, just how easy is it to inadvertently stumble across child pornography when one is not looking for it.

Caution is needed as to just what the statistics promoted about pornography on the Internet actually mean. The most careful studies seem to suggest that there is a problem but one that is largely exaggerated. In particular, the idea that child pornography is imagery of child abuse would demand that we need to know just how much new child pornography there is and just how many victims are shown on the Internet. It would seem that a lot of child pornography has been repeatedly recycled from the 1970s although there is a steady stream of new child pornography. This may be no more than one new child each week although that child may have numerous images posted. And we must remember that this is worldwide, which puts the issue into sharper perspective. Of course, compared to what we know about child abuse and its frequency, these are not large figures. They also fit in with what we know from the victims of child abuse about their involvement in child pornography – relatively small numbers of them report any involvement in sexual abuse that was photographed or videoed.

A different perspective is that the amount and accessibility of child pornography on the Internet raises questions about the extent of sexual interest there is in children and the potential impact of the Internet in increasing this interest. These are complex issues to be addressed in later chapters.

# CHAPTER 3

# What we Know about Paedophilia

We know about paedophiles and paedophilia and develop this understanding of their sex offending in a political context. This political environment includes, of course, the government but also the general public, professionals working in the field of child protection, psychologists, psychiatrists and others. Each of these is integral to the direction that ideas about paedophiles develop. Paedophiles and paedophilia are not ivory-tower research topics but matters about which most people have strong opinions. The intensity of the anti-paedophile feelings throughout the community is almost tangible. Paedophiles are regarded as among the most (if not the most) heinous criminals of all. They are thought to be at great risk of reoffending because they are addicted to sex with children. They lie, distort, and manipulate. Consequently, anything they have to say is of little worth. Many, including the media, use words like 'evil' to describe them and their activities. What makes them even more frightening is that they are organised and form 'paedophile rings'. This social construction of paedophiles is not wrong but is considerably overstated. There is no such thing as 'the paedophile' – they vary.

The social and cultural image of paedophiles affects our thinking in a number of ways. It is not the job of a researcher to merely re-confirm what the public believes it knows but inevitably researchers are influenced by and may share aspects of public opinion. Equally, in such a politicised area of research, there is a risk that any departure, no matter how small, from the consensus about paedophiles will be misconstrued as making excuses for their behaviour or, in some other way, condoning it. For example, to suggest that paedophiles have themselves been victims of sexual and other abuse in childhood may arouse a critical reception. It is easy to see why. Many children have been sexually abused but few of them grow up to be abusers. Hostility to certain sorts of explanations is understandable yet has to be regarded as a problem when it straightjackets the way paedophilia and paedophiles are understood.

## THE NATURE OF CONTACT PAEDOPHILE OFFENCES

The public generally learns about sex offending through the media (Howitt, 2002) and consequently, given the nature of media reporting, the image is of violent, predatory and sensational crimes (Brown, 2005). But these seem to be the exceptions rather than the rule and few sexual offences against children involve homicide, brutality, sexual mutilation or significant injury (West, 1996). Perhaps more important is that the victims probably both know or trust the perpetrators (Elliot, Browne and Kilcoyne, 1995). 'Stranger-danger' may fuel the media and public fears but it misrepresents sexual crimes against children (Brown, 2005). Children are most in danger in private locations rather than public places (Elliot *et al.*, 1995). Our understanding of what is involved in sex offences against children comes from two main sources: victims and offenders (Howitt, 1995a). However, there are numerous difficulties in summarising the characteristics of offences against children other than in the broadest terms. Among the problems are variations in the legal definitions of sexual crimes against children, the differences between different data-collecting settings, differences in sampling techniques employed and the lack of a standard definition of abuse. Consequently, there can be substantial differences in terms of the trends found in different studies (Howitt, 1995a). Relying on victim studies alone would suggest that offences perpetrated on girls largely do not involve contact and that any contact abuse that does happen is more likely to be genital fondling (Finney, 2006; May-Chahal and Cawson, 2005; Wyatt, 1985). Studies using offenders paint a somewhat different picture. For instance, Craissati and McClurg (1996) based on data from a group of sexual perpetrators from a community project in South East London reported that overall 29 % of men were convicted of non-penetrative acts whilst the remainder 71 % were convicted of penetrative offences.

## HOW MANY PAEDOPHILES AND PAEDOPHILE OFFENCES ARE THERE?

Jenkins (2001) estimates that the 'core population' of Internet users of child pornography worldwide is between 50,000 and 100,000, although this would exclude casual browsers. This is very much a guesstimate but needs to be considered alongside the issue of the numbers of men in general with a sexual interest in children. It would be of great significance if there were a definitive answer to the question of how many paedophiles there are. A figure of 1 in 10 people would be disturbing and might perhaps change our thinking mark-edly. A figure of 1 in 1000 people would perhaps be disturbingly low. A figure of 1 in 5 people – what would that tell us? Of course, the number of paedophiles there is depends partly on how the term is defined. Quite clearly, rather fewer paedophiles exist if the stringent DSM criteria are employed than if a more general definition of paedophiles is used – such as 'people with a sexual interest in children'. The question becomes more complicated when the issue of whether paedophilia has to be expressed physically against a child is considered. There are heterosexual people, after all, who never have sexual relationships with another person. Why should that not be the case with paedophiles?

We probably cannot answer the question of how many paedophiles there are precisely. The National Criminal Intelligence Service (2003) argues that the precise number of paedophile sex offenders in the UK is unknown. But an approximate answer – or rather a variety of answers – is available from a variety of types of information. For example, we might use prevalence studies (how many individuals have ever been sexually abused as a child) or incidence studies (how often children are sexually abused on average in a particular period of time). The Foreign and Commonwealth Office (2004) claimed that there are 230,000 people in the United Kingdom involved in paedophile activity. However, the basis of this claim is not stipulated but it would mean approximately one paedophile for every 260 people (men, women and children) in the country. The number of victims might give us some clues. Between the years of 1980 and 2001, there were a total of about 70,000 crimes of gross indecency with a child and unlawful sexual intercourse were reported to the police (National Criminal Intelligence Service, 2003). This amounts to 3,500 offenders approximately each year if each offender were to commit one crime (Howitt, 2006b). This estimate may be very inaccurate given that there were only 3,400 paedophiles serving sentences in 2004 in total and that these would have entered prison over a period of several years. There is also the 'tip-of-the-iceberg' problem whereby only a proportion of crimes are reported. In this context, it should be noted that Finkelhor and Lewis (1988) found that in a telephone survey, 10 % of males admitted that they had sexually abused a child.

Other samples of 'normal' individuals have been asked hypothetical questions about whether or not they would be willing to commit illegal sexual acts – especially if they believed that they would not be arrested or punished. A familiar study of this sort asked students whether they would rape if there were no sanctions on them. Over a third said that they would (Malamuth, 1981a). Briere and Runtz (1989) reported that 21 % of US college male students admitted to having some sexual attraction to children. Seven per cent of them said that there was some likelihood that they would have sex with a child if they could get away without adverse outcomes for themselves. This is a surprising outcome because we might expect that such feelings would be underreported such that the base rates are actually higher (Fisher, 1994). While indicating on a questionnaire that one might in certain circumstances commit a sexual offence is quite different from actually offending, nevertheless one in five of college students had indicated some sort of sexual interest in children.

The results of phallometric (plethysmographic) studies also have a bearing here. Phallometric studies involve recording any change in a man's erection when shown 'erotic' images. Hall, Hirschman and Oliver (1995) recruited a sample of males through newspapers. While these are volunteers and may be a biased sample, the findings of the study provide food for thought. The men were shown various picture slides depicting such images as clothed and nude girls below puberty and nude women. They were also played explicit sound tapes, which featured consensual intercourse involving an adult woman, the rape of a child and also violence against a child. The men sexually aroused by child stimuli also tended to be aroused by adult stimuli, for example. About a quarter of the men showed a larger erection to child pictures than they did to pictures of adult women. Twenty per cent of the men in this study reported a sexual interest in children although far fewer, just 4 %, said that they had acted on their sexual interest in children. Of course, the fact that the men who showed sexual arousal to images of children were also aroused by other stimuli may suggest that they were not paedophilic. That is, the men most easily aroused by explicit material of all sorts were the most likely to be aroused by paedophilic stimuli. We should also be cautious because responses in such studies can be faked in a number of ways (Howitt, 2002). While we would not claim this as an established fact, it is notable that in these studies there are indications that one in five men may have a paedophilic interest in children. One man in 10 may have been involved in sexual activity with children.

Given the high news profile of paedophilia, the temptation is to assume that paedophile crime resulting in conviction is quite frequent. This does not seem to be an accurate reflection of the trends in crime statistics. Taking the number of victims as an indication of how common paedophile activity is, we find relatively low numbers in England and Wales. By far the most common sexual offence against children recorded in the UK is indecent assault of a female under 16 years of age. Between 2000 and 2003, this offence led to an average of 1,719 convictions or cautions (Smith, 2005). A caution is an admonition at a police station given by a senior police officer. For some purposes it is counted as a conviction. All of the figures refer to frequencies and *not* rates per 100,000 of the population for example. The average frequencies for other crimes against children include:

- indecent assault against a boy of less than 16 years – 364 per year;
- unlawful sexual intercourse with a girl under 13 years – 65 per year;
- unlawful sexual intercourse with a girl under 16 years – 442 per year;
- rape of a girl under 16 years – 239 per year;
- rape of a boy under 16 years – 31 per year;
- buggery by a male of a male under 16 years – 67;
- buggery by a male of a female under 16 years – 15 per year;
- attempted rape of a female aged under 16 years – 37 per year;
- attempted rape of a male aged under 16 years – five per year;
- incest with girl under 13 years – 10 per year;
- inciting girl under 16 to have incestuous sexual intercourse – three per year;
- abuse of trust (including sex offender notification offences) – 420;
- gross indecency with boys – 101 per year;
- gross indecency with girls – 196 per year.

It is also worthwhile noting that certain sex offences may show substantial decline over the years. For example, figures for indecent assault on a female under 16 years of age declined by 23 % between 1985 and 2003. Similarly, indecent assault on a male under 16 dropped 27 % in the same period. There was a decrease of 68 % in unlawful sexual intercourse with a girl aged 13 to 15 years. There was a similar decrease of 50 % for unlawful sexual intercourse with a girl of less than 13 years. The early figures are taken from the Home Office (1997).

Of course, these changes are difficult to interpret or – more bluntly – could mean just about anything. One possibility is that they reflect the increasingly better management of sex offenders and indicate an important reduction in offending behaviour. However, the tip-of-the-iceberg issue of reporting rates could again be relevant (Russell, 1984). Typically, it is suggested that less than 10 % of sexual offences are reported to the authorities and 1 % of offences end in arrest (Russell, 1984). The evidence is clearest in terms of adult victims. MyHill and Allen (2002) reported that only 18 % of the rapes that were reported to the British Crime Survey had been reported to the police. The British Crime Survey examines the public's experiences with crime. It is claimed to represent a fuller picture of crime than official statistics because it avoids the problems of 'crime reporting' behaviour by the public (Maguire, 2002) and 'attrition' (Soothill, Peelo and Taylor, 2002). Attrition in the criminal justice system is the filtering process that occurs between a crime being committed and the person who committed it being sanctioned by the police or courts. Therefore, even if a sex offence has been reported it does not necessarily lead to the arrest, conviction and imprisonment of the offender. Cowling (1998), for instance, argued that only 8 % of reported rapes led to a conviction. There may be several reasons for this: the perpetrator not being found, evidential considerations, convictions being made for lesser offences, or agreed plea bargaining (Soothill, Peelo and Taylor, 2002).

The following is significant in that it appears to indicate much higher rates of sexual offences than are revealed by conventional crime statistics. The British Crime Survey (Finney, 2006) found that among a sample of 13,038 women and 10,546 men aged between 16 to 59 years old in 2004/05, 23 % of women and 3.1 % of men had experienced, at least once since the age of 16, a 'less serious sexual assault'. This included indecent exposure, sexual threats and unwanted touching. Much lower figures were reported with regard to rape and attempted rape; 5 % of women and 0.4 % of men experienced at least one such incident since the age of 16 years. Assault by penetration or attempted assault by penetration (penetration of the vagina or anus by an object or body part) similarly accounted for fewer reports; 2 % for women and 0.2 % for men. Overall, 23.5 % of women and 3.4 % of men experienced at least one sexual assault (including attempts) of any kind. The more serious assaults were more likely committed by perpetrators known to the victim than strangers. The victim-offender relationship was the reverse for less serious sex offences.

The US Department of Justice Criminal Victimization study for 2004 in contrast indicates that 47 % of rapes and sexual assaults are reported to the police. These changes in reporting rates may reflect public attitudes, more stringent criteria for prosecutions, and so forth. They may also reflect old offences finally being reported to the police following changes in the law since offences involving abuse of trust did not follow the decline. Such offenders doubled in two years following the introduction of the relevant legislation. This may well be the consequence of knowledge of the offence gradually leading to more reporting.

Due to such inherent problems in crime statistics, some argue that the best estimates of the prevalence of child sexual abuse lie in community surveys (Grubin, 1998). Nevertheless, even these estimates vary depending on the method of collecting data. Postal surveys, for example, are likely to produce different rates from in-depth interviews (Howitt, 1995a). The definition of sex abuse used also makes a difference. For example, it is crucial to know whether non-contact forms of abuse are included (Wyatt and Peters, 1986). A good illustration of the issue comes from a South African study. In this high rates of abuse for men were found but two-thirds of these did not include any physical contact (Finkelhor, 1994a). Despite these problems, there do seem to be patterns in sexual abuse. For example, the rates of sexual abuse for female children are more or less consistently higher than those for male children. Furthermore, intrafamilial abuse is more common for girls than for boys (Grubin, 1998). Another fairly consistent trend is the low level of disclosure of abuse found when participants are asked about their experiences of abuse (Finkelhor, 1994a).

An important early study of the national prevalence of child sexual abuse in the UK was conducted by Baker and Duncan (1985). Female interviewers surveyed over 2,000 people both male and female. The lower cut-off point for inclusion was 15 years of age. Participants were told that:

> A child (anyone under 16 years) is sexually abused when another person, who is sexually mature, involves the child in any activity which the other person expects to lead to their sexual arousal. This might involve intercourse, touching, exposure of the sexual organs, showing porno-graphic material or talking about sexual things in an erotic way (Baker and Duncan, p. 458).

Based on this, 12 % of females and 8 % of male children had been sexually abused below 16 years of age. About half knew their abusers before the abuse and 14 % of cases were incestuous abuse. Boys on average were abused at 12.0 years of age whereas girls were abused at the younger age of 10.7 years on average. There are, of course, problems with the study such as just what is meant by a sexually mature person, because anyone post puberty could be regarded as sexually mature. Furthermore, quite how some of the other terms would be interpreted is not clear. For example, just what is meant by 'pornography' and talking about things 'in an erotic way'? Baker and Duncan (1985) estimated that in excess of 4.5 million adults had been sexually abused as children. For the cohort of children of under 16 years of age, this would mean that approximately 1.1 million would be sexually abused at some stage. It is important to note that over half of the cases involved no physical sexual contact between the child and the sexually mature person and largely these involved indecent exposure.

For the most part the abuse was a single experience (63 %) or repeated abuse by the same person (23 %). Fourteen per cent were abused by two or more individuals. Sexual intercourse occurred in 5 % of cases. Scaling these figures back to the original sample rather than those who had been abused, 7 % of the full sample had been abused without physical contact, 6 % had been abused with contact, and 0.7 % had been subject to sexual abuse involving penetrative sex.

In a more recent study May-Chahal and Cawson (2005) examined the prevalence of all forms of child maltreatment in the UK involving 2,869 men and women aged 18 to 24 years old. Trained interviewers interviewed the participants. The study explored the prevalence rates of physical abuse, emotional abuse, absence of care, as well as sexual abuse. In relation to sexual behaviour a wide range of possibilities were covered from being shown pornography, to being encouraged to watch people performing sex acts (not pictures), to exposure of sexual organs and sexual intercourse, all while under the age of 16 years. Respondents were also asked whether these events happened against their wishes and if the other person was five years older or more. If they answer 'yes' to any of these questions then a series of follow-up questions were asked including the age at which this first happened and the relationship of the person to them. Sexual behaviour was categorised as abuse if the other person was a parent or carer; the behaviour occurred against the respondents wishes; or the consensual sexual acts involved a person other than a parent who was five or more years older when the child was aged 12 or under. The responses were also analysed according to whether the abuse was contact (for instance, kissing, fondling, sexual intercourse) or non-contact (for example, exposure, showing pornography). The most frequently recorded experiences of sexual abuse were:

- indecent exposure; 10 % of females and 3 % of males reported this type of sexual abuse;
- being touched or fondled on one's sex organs or other private parts of the body'; 8 % of women and 2 % of men; and
- being hugged or kissed in a sexual way' was reported by 7 % of women and 2 % of men.

However, what of the more serious forms of abuse which might be more damaging? Here are some of the findings:

- contact abuse by parents or carer: 1 % of children;
- non-contact abuse by parents or carer: less than 1 % of children;
- contact abuse by other relative: 2 % of children;
- contact abuse by someone unrelated but known to the child: 8 %;
- non-contact abuse by someone unrelated but known to the child: 3 % of children;
- contact abuse by an adult stranger: 2 % of children;
- non-contact abuse by an adult stranger: 2 % of children.

In total, 16 % of respondents had been abused sexually in some way – either through contact or non-contact. In addition, 6 % of respondents reported being involved in consensual sexual behaviour when aged 13 to 15 with someone 5 years or more older (other than a parent).

Asking offenders themselves is an obvious approach to estimating the extent of paedophilic offences but one that inevitably raises the spectre of paedophiles being untruthful manipulators. Hence any data supplied by them are likely to be regarded as suspect. Among the most famous work in this field is that by Abel and various co-workers (Abel *et al.*, 1987). It is much cited by researchers because a large number of offences were disclosed by the sex offenders studied (Howitt, 2002). The researchers took considerable steps to ensure the confidentiality of their participants who included, among others, child molesters. One classic 'fact' emerging from this study was that 5,611 sex offenders claimed to have committed a quarter of a million sex offences. The data are probably most dramatic for rapists who, on average, admitted to seven rapes. However, this figure is actually a skewed estimate of the offending since the median figure for offences was just one rape. That is to say, at least half of the rapists admitted to just one rape. More important here is the data for offenders against children. By way of illustration, the paedophile offenders against males (non-incestuous cases) admitted 43,100 offences. However, the numbers of victims was large at 22,981. This yielded a mean of 1.9 offences per victim. Incest offenders against female targets, not surprisingly, had very few victims in total but they repeatedly victimised them. Thus the average was 1.8 victims per offender but 45.1 offences per victim.

This study is routinely cited as showing that sex offenders habitually offend. However, this is a very misleading interpretation. It would be more accurate to conclude that the majority of sex offenders offend against a small number of victims on just a few occasions (Grubin, 1998). The study had various methodological problems, which may have encouraged overreporting by the offenders. The offenders were offered therapy if they confessed their crimes, which may have been the preferred outcome for the men (Abel *et al.*, 1987). Thus they had some motivation for admitting high frequencies. They were also likely to have been the among the most troubled and deviant sex offenders since they themselves had sought help with their problems (Mair, 1995).

## APPROACHES TO CLASSIFICATION

One of the basic tasks of research is the process of classification. Not only is there a need to define what is meant by 'paedophile', but the simple question needs to be addressed of what the different types of paedophilia are. There is no prior reason to assume that all paedophiles can be understood in the same way. But, if this is the case, then what typologies of paedophilia help us in understanding paedophiles better?

## The Clinical Approach to Classification

Different disciplines have different ways of conceptualising what, in many ways, are identical situations. Concepts need to be assessed in terms of fitness for purpose – whatever that purpose is. A person who sexually molests a child might be considered a paedophile from a psychiatric or psychological perspective. Nevertheless, from the point of view of the law and the criminal justice system, this term may not be appropriate or helpful – *perpetrator, sex offender* or even *predatory sex offender* may be more useful terms to lawyers and others working in the criminal justice system. This is because the offence lies in the criminal behaviour and not in having a sexual orientation towards children. Different authorities use different terms that, while overlapping to a degree, are also distinct (Cohen and Galynker, 2002; O'Dononhue, Regev and Hagstrom, 2000). Whatever terminology is used, the choice often carries its own message or meaning. *Child molester* is a common term for people who have directly involved themselves sexually with a child. There is no assumption that the child molester has been arrested or convicted. Furthermore, child molester does not imply necessarily an underlying psychological state such as paedophilia, which may seem to explain the offending.

The term paedophilia (actually *paedophilia erotica*) has its modern origins in the work of the founder of the discipline of sexology, Kraft-Ebbing, in his book *Psychopathia Sexualis* first published in 1886. Its origins are more ancient, of course, as it is basically a Greek word, which compounds the word for child (*pais*) with the word for love or friendship (*philia*) together. Thus, it is literally the love or friendship of a child. It is said to have been used instead of the word *pederasty*, which refers to homosexual relationships between adolescent boys and adult males. Therefore, our modern usage of the term paedophilia is more general than its original meaning (as it includes girls) and does not solely refer to sexual activity with adolescents.

Krafft-Ebbing considered paedophilia to involve the following major elements:

- It is a sexual interest in children that is persistent over time.
- The sexual interest in children is a central feature and, in the clearest cases, the only apparent sexual orientation of the paedophile. In less clear-cut instances, a sexual interest in children will be the paedophile's major or dominant sexual orientation.
- The term is confined to children or those at the beginning puberty.

When Krafft-Ebbing published his book, in the United Kingdom the Criminal Law Amendment Act of 1885 had allowed girls to marry at the age of 13 years though they could not consent to sexual intercourse outside of marriage until the age of 16 years. According to D'Cruze (2004) the harm done to adolescent girls by sexual intercourse was seen to be 'moral' harm. Otherwise, if they were married, the act of marriage constituted an ongoing consent to sexual intercourse with her husband. Not only is this of interest in terms of how we construe the harm done by adult-child sex but, further, it suggests why puberty was essentially Krafft-Ebbing's upper defining point for paedophilia. Similarly, for much of the century in which Krafft-Ebbing was writing, the age of consent to sexual intercourse was 10 years in the USA, for example. Thus, it is perhaps not surprising that Krafft-Ebbing chose to define paedophilia by reference to puberty given that generally the age of consent was very young in his time in comparison to modern developed nations.

*Hebephilia* is a term sometimes given to a sexual interest in postpubertal young people. However, the common usage of the term paedophilia in everyday talk nowadays generally includes those interested in postpubertal children as well as those interested in prepubertal children.

Whether or not we should view *paedophilia* as a clinical term that may reflect a sexual disorder is, perhaps, a matter of choice. The word existed before it was adopted by psychiatry, as we have seen, and there is nothing precise about the way in which the word 'paedophile' is used in everyday language. Nevertheless, the term paedophilia is to be found in the American Psychological Association's *Diagnostic and Statistical Manual of Mental Disorders-Version IV* (DSM-IV-TR; American Psychiatric Association, 2000). It is one of the paraphilias – which includes other conditions such as fetishism, transvestitism, masochism and voyeurism. In lay terms these might be called by the pejorative term *sexual perversions*. Paedophilia, along with other paraphilias is described as a 'sexuality and gender identity disorder'. A number of conditions have to be met in order to meet the requirements of a diagnosis of paedophilia according to the DSM-IV-TR:

- intense, recurrent and intense sexually arousing fantasies have been experienced over a minimum period of six months, or urges or behaviours that involve sexual activities with a prepubescent child or children (generally aged 13 or younger);
- clinically significant distress or impairment in social, occupational, or other important areas of functioning to the offender are caused by these fantasies, sexual urges, or behaviours; and
- the offender must be a minimum of 16 years of age and at least 5 years older than his/her victim(s)' (American Psychiatric Association, 2000, p. 528).

Not surprisingly given its roots in psychiatry and medicine, the APA classification system characterises the familiar disease model of social problems. The medical profession was highly involved in early social interventions to deal with societal problems such as drunkenness, inebriation and poverty (Howitt, 1992b). A disease model suggests strongly that paedophilia can be treated with medical methods such as drugs and even surgery (cf. Ward, Polaschek and Beech, 2006). Reports of surgical castration for sex offenders appeared in the literature dating back to the nineteenth and twentieth centuries (Rosler and Witzum, 2000) and laws legislating against the procedure were passed in several European countries in the 1920s (Ortmann, 1980). Some studies have shown that sexual offending recidivism rates to have dropped following surgery (Bremer, 1959; Ortmann, 1980; Sturup, 1968). In the 1960s and 1970s a number of research reports described how sexual offenders could be treated with anti-psychotic or *neuroleptic* drugs (tranquillisers where a calming effect is required). Such drugs are medications typically used in the management of schizophrenia (Bartholomew, 1964). However, it was found that such drugs also lower sexual drive (Maletzky and Field, 2003). Also redolent of the disease model is the idea that paedophilia is an addiction (McGregor and Howells, 1997) that escalates unless treated or otherwise prevented. Although paedophilia may conceivably be regarded a mental disorder (for example, in the sense that paedophiles show some distinct thought patterns), this does not justify the assumption that paedophilia is a psychotic disorder which prevents the sufferer from functioning in society. When we also consider that many sex offenders against children are adolescents (Anderson *et al.*, 1993; Davis and Leitenberg, 1987; Finkelhor, 1980; Flanagan and Hayman-White, 2000; James and Neil, 1996; O'Shaughnessy, 2006; Veneziano, Veneziano and LeGrand, 2000), the idea that paedophilia is psychotic behaviour becomes of even more limited usefulness.

Polaschek (2003) argues that diagnostic classification achieves little in terms of understanding the aetiology of a condition, making decisions about the risk posed by an individual or indicating what treatment is appropriate. Indeed, DSM-IV-TR fails to achieve these objectives in terms of paedophilia. There are other criticisms of the diagnostic category approach:

- DSM-IV-TR does not mention factors believed by many to be related to child sexual abuse such as cognitive distortions and self-regulation problems.
- Just how does one establish the basic requirement of paedophilia which is that the individual has recurrent intense sexual fantasies, urges or behaviours? There may be good reason for the individual to deny or minimise such feelings or actions, for example (Haywood and Grossman, 1994).

Especially pertinent here is the question of what does the psychiatric classification of paedophilia mean in terms of the men who are arrested for downloading Internet child pornography? The diagnostic category of 'paedophilia' involves terms such as 'recurrent', 'intense' and 'clinically significant distress'. What precisely do these mean and is it not likely that the imprecision of the terms encourage subjective interpretation by psychiatrists, psychologists, and other professionals working with such offenders (Bickley and Beech, 2001; O'Dononhue, Regev and Hagstrom, 2000; Ward *et al.*, 2006;)? In the six months period, how often do the feelings or behaviours have to occur to make them 'recurrent'? If an offender 'binges' his offences over just one week in the six months is he showing recurrent feelings or behaviours? What should we make of the offender who repeatedly molests children but either does not have (or denies having) 'intense fantasies' about children? What is intense about an intense sexual fantasy? Is it the potential of the fantasy to be sexually arousing, or is it one that is vivid in the sense that it is clear, colourful, and involves several senses such as vision, sound, touch and smell?

No more than 25–40 % of sex offenders against children show a sexual interest in them with a frequency of recurrence and intensity commensurate with the DSM criteria (Marshall, 1997). Thus, the DSM category of paedophilia does not include the majority of those who sexually offend against children (Bickley and Beech, 2001) and also contributes nothing to provide a basis for understanding these putative non-paedophile offenders.

The six-month period stipulated appears to be arbitrary and does not connect with other, possibly illegal, acts that the offender may commit. Thus we should not classify as paedophile a man who experiences a three or four-month period of the most intense sexual fantasies of sex with prepubescent children but then offends against a 13-year-old boy. According to the DSM, the man should not be classified as paedophile though it is difficult to see why not. Probably most practitioners would not take the six-month period literally but then this makes the definition subjective and open to a range of interpretations.

The idea that a paedophile's fantasies, urges and behaviours cause him distress or impairs his social functioning excludes some offenders who otherwise meet the DSM's criteria. Of course, some offenders express distress and regret in interviews about their offending although the numbers who do so as a result of their offending rather than as a result of getting caught for their offending is not known. Significant social impairment may also be a feature of some paedophiles but not all. Many seem to function perfectly adequately socially, occupationally and in most other respects much of the time. A good example of the problems that this aspect of the APA definition causes is illustrated by the child-love advocacy groups, such as the notorious North American Man/Boy Love Association (NAMBLA). This has members who openly advocate the mutual value of friendship and sex between adults and children. In this sense, paedophilia is not simply a sexual orientation but is also a way of life that has the support of an entire paedophile subculture (De Young, 1988, 1989; Taylor and Quayle, 2003). One of the aims of such pro-paedophilia groups is to redefine paedophilia as something natural and positive rather than in terms of the dominant abhorrence it receives. Members of such groups claim to see nothing wrong with consensual adult-child sex and actually advocate the benefits. As a consequence, we could exclude such members from the definition of paedophilia simply because they do not appear impaired socially or psychologically though they seem to be amongst the ones most committed to sex between adults and children. According to Ward *et al.* (2006) the DSM classification is restricted in its empirical scope since it excludes those who many would most readily identify as paedophiles.

In summary, the DSM classification does little to advance our theoretical understanding of the aetiology or maintenance of paedophilia, or of the offence process (Bickley and Beech, 2001). Indeed, the restrictive nature of the medical definition may actually hinder the understanding of this type of behaviour. Moreover, given the criticisms noted above, it would seem that a more flexible and dynamic definition is needed – one that does not rely on rigid classifiers such as age difference or the number of months that thoughts persist. A more appropriate definition for defining a paedophile would be 'someone who has a sexual interest in children'. The danger is, of course, that the lack of a consensual and universal definition of paedophilia makes it difficult to compare studies using different definitions.

## Theory-led Classifications

Sometimes, early theories of sexual offending against children included simple typologies of perpetrators. One frequently used distinction is between those who molest children within, and those who molest children outside of, the family. This dichotomy is linked to another influential idea – that of fixated and regressed sex offenders (Groth and Birnbaum, 1978). Regressed offenders offend within their family (making them more-or-less incestuous offenders) whereas fixated offenders offend outside of their family unit. The distinction appears frequently though its value is not altogether clear:

- *Regressed offenders*. These are defined as more-or-less 'normal' men whose usual sexual orientation is to other adults. Furthermore, socially they are primarily oriented towards other adults. It is argued that stress or pressures of normal life (for example, conflicts with wives or partners, problems at work) pushes them to regress to sexual involvement with children. Not surprising, regressed offenders are seen as being more likely to be married or in a satisfactory adult sexual relationship. They are also more likely to offend against children within their family.
- *Fixated offenders*. These are people who from adolescence are primarily sexual orientated to young people. Rarely are they married and their sexual targets are young people who are strangers or acquaintances. They tend not to target youngsters in their family. They may have had some sexual experiences with adults but this involvement may often be described as coincidental because there seems to be no intent or motive towards adults.

Despite its common currency among practitioners and researchers, there are reasons to be cautious about the classification because some offenders may target women with the purpose of offending against their children and sexual activities with a woman can be accompanied by paedophilic fantasies. Furthermore, using family factors as an explanation for the offending can be viewed as an excuse (Howitt, 1995a, 2002, 2006a). Other researchers (for example, Cowburn and Dominelli, 2001) have pointed out that when clinicians refer to fixated offenders they essentially suggest that the men are incapable of being treated – whereas when referring to regressed offenders the implication is that that they are responsive to treatment. This is almost to suggest that one type of offender is 'better' and the other is 'worse'. This has implications for the judicial and treatment system and perhaps public perceptions. Howitt (1995a) drew attention to the similarity between the concepts of fixated and extrafamilial offenders as well as the similarity between the concepts of regressed and incestuous or intrafamilial offenders. It is, therefore, worth noting that incestuous offenders are less likely to re-offend than extrafamilial offenders (Howitt, 2006b) although whether this constitutes a case in favour of the fixated/regressed dichotomy is another matter. The typology would classify all but a few incestuous offenders as regressed offenders. One consequence of this is that they are not usually regarded as paraphilic (Groth, 1982; Julian, Mohr and Lapp, 1980; Quinsey, 1986).

If we assume, for the moment, the following: (a) incestuous offenders engage in sexual activity with children because 'circumstances' push them towards it and (b) they are not really sexually attracted to children, then several things should follow. Most importantly, they should have few offences against children outside their family (and also adult women). But this seems not to be the case. Researchers have reported difficulty in effectively differentiating incestuous from non-incestuous child molesters using phallometry (Studer *et al.*, 2002). Phallometry (also known as plethysmography) basically records the enlargement of a man's penis in response to various sexual stimuli such as pictures of nude children. Studer *et al.*, found that just over 40 % showed their strongest erection to erotic child pictures irrespective of whether they were incestuous or non-incestuous offenders. There was evidence that 37 % of incestuous offenders had their greatest sexual response to imagery of adults whereas only 19 % of non-incestuous offenders did. It is also understandable based on the self-evident fact that regressed (incestuous) offenders have sexual relationships with adults. Furthermore, 30 % of the non-incestuous offenders had their primary sexual attraction to prepubescent children compared to 13 % of the incestuous offenders. However, these are only moderate trends compared to the substantial overlap between the incestuous and non-incestuous groups.

What is the validity of the next assumption of the fixated/regressed dichotomy – that regressed offenders confine themselves to children within the family? Again Studer *et al.* (2002) reported that over 40 % of the incestuous group had also offended sexually against children outside of the family. A different study by the same research team found that 53 % of incestuous biological fathers had child victims from beyond their family (Studer *et al.*, 2000). The difficulties are compounded by the finding that some incestuous offenders had also raped adult women. This makes the idea that they regressed 'under stress' to sex with children less tenable – why did they not respond under stress by resorting to sex with an adult women, even rape? Thus there are problems in differentiating clearly the two types of offender in terms of their sexual functioning and it not possible to claim that the signs of paedophilia are rare in one group but common in the other.

The concept of the fixated/regressed dichotomy appears in the Massachusetts Treatment Centre, Child Molester Typology (Version 3) (Knight and Prentky, 1990). This consists of two main axes: 'fixation/regression' (Axis 1) and 'amount of contact with the victim' (Axis 2). Axis 1 separates those individuals with an enduring interest in children from those without such an interest or for whom the interest is transitory. Axis I can be further separated into high or low levels of social competence, for example, success in employment. Axis 2 refers to the meaning for the offender of the contact with the victim. Six types of offenders can be derived based on a number of hierarchical decisions. The first decision is how much time an offender spends with or near children (though this excludes contact that parents normally spend with their children). For those with high contact the meaning or implications of this contact also needs to be evaluated. This decision generates two types of offenders: (a) those who perceive themselves in a loving relationship with a victim (*interpersonal* offender) and (b) those whose primary motivation is to use the victim to achieve self-gratification (*narcissistic* offender). If the amount of contact is low, the amount of physical injury caused to the victim and the presence (or absence) of sadistic fantasies are considered this produces four more types of sex offender – *exploitative, sadistic, aggressive,* and *overt sadistic* offender.

There are problems with this typology, some of which are the consequence of its origins in archival information such as that obtained from prison and other records. It also employs the offender's most recent offence and this may not typify his offending behaviour. Some have questioned whether the distinctions highlighted by this typology might actually be the consequence of the offender's experience in abusing children rather than reflecting qualitatively different types of offender (Taylor and Quayle, 2003). Knight and Prentky (1990) identified 24 different types of offender theoretically. Caution is needed, however, because a substantial minority of types (11 out of the 24 possible ones) are fairly rare. Furthermore, in developing the typology, incest-only offenders were excluded so the classification has little to contribute to clinically understanding this group (Bickley and Beech, 2001).

## Pragmatic Approach to Classification

Potentially, amongst the most important information needed regarding sex offenders is their likelihood of recidivism as well as decisions about just what sort of help could be provided in terms of treatment (Blackburn, 1993). There is a range of different methods of predicting an offender's future behaviour. Among the commonest is the use of past behaviour to predict their future risk of offending. This may be referred to as 'actuarial' prediction (Hall, 1996) as it is based on simple numerical relationships found empirically and categorises individuals in terms of levels of risk – low, medium and high. The classification approach works by having a sample of offenders about whom a certain amount of, say, background information is known as well as the extent to which they subsequently re-offend. The background factors that are found to correlate with reoffending can be used to estimate whether a new offender (who was not a member of the original sample) is highly likely to reoffend or not (Bickley and Beech, 2001).

Static risk factors are the most common to be used in assessments of future risk of reoffending. These are factors that do not change over a lengthy period of time (Bonta, 1996). Examples include prior sex offences, male victims, age of first offence, and stranger victims (Friendship and Beech, 2005; Hanson and Bussiere, 1998; Prentky, Knight and Lee, 1997; Quinsey, Rice and Harris, 1995). Hanson and Bussiere's (1998) review of 61 studies found that long-term recidivism was best predicted by static factors such as prior sex offences. Static risk factors are included on many of the standard risk assessment instruments such as Static-99 (Hanson and Thornton, 2000) which assess the risk of sexual and/or violent recidivism over a specified period of time. The Static-99 instrument was developed by combining two other scales – the Rapid Risk Assessment of Sex Offence Recidivism (RRASOR, Hanson, 1997) and Thornton's Static Anchored Clinical Judgement Scale (SACJ and SACJ-MIN, Grubin, 1998) (Friendship and Beech, 2005). It is widely used in clinical practice with sexual offenders and in research (Friendship, Mann and Beech, 2003a, b; Maguire *et al.*, 2001). The Static-99 (Hanson and Thornton, 2000) has recently been simplified into the Risk Matrix 2000 and includes assessing the risk of sexual offending, non-sexual violence and a composite risk of sexual or non-sexual assault (Thornton *et al.*, 2003).

Such assessment instruments are typically regarded as being superior to the unaided judgement of clinicians about the likelihood of re-offending. Nevertheless there are difficulties with the more objective approaches (Ward *et al.*, 2006). Risk assessments are only as accurate as the data they are developed on. Subsequently they are sometimes criticised because they are often based on official recidivism rates which are argued to be an underestimation of the real extent of the problem (Beech, Fisher and Thornton, 2003). Furthermore, predictors which are very common actually produce the best predictions of recidivism. In contrast, predictors which are rare lead proportionately to more mistaken predictions (Howitt, 2006a). And what of individuals who show unusual characteristics? Will this result in poor predictions? Assuming that past criminal behaviour is a good predictor of future criminal behaviour, it may nevertheless be more important to predict who is likely to be rehabilitated back into the community than who will reoffend. Moreover, by their very nature, such predictions are 'atheoretical' and based solely on statistical relationships. As such, they cannot address the reasons for the behaviours they attempt to predict (Krauss *et al.*, 2000). Furthermore, predicting recidivism tells us little about the overall deterrent effect that the criminal justice system may have in preventing others from offending (Taylor and Quayle, 2003).

An alternative to static factors in such assessments is the use of 'dynamic' risk factors, which may help predict reoffending (Hanson and Harris, 2000). Dynamic risk factors are characteristics that can change or could change with treatment (Bonta, 1996; Ward *et al.*, 2006) and when changed could result in a corresponding increase or decrease in recidivism risk (Hanson and Harris, 2000). Dynamic risk factors can be further subdivided into 'stable dynamic' factors and 'acute dynamic' factors (Hanson and Harris, 1998, 2000). Stable dynamic risk factors include cognitive distortions justifying offending behaviour or sexual deviant preferences (Hanson and Harris, 1998). Stable dynamic risk factors are expected to remain unchanged for months or years and consequently interventions aimed at creating enduring improvements need to target stable dynamic risk factors (Hanson and Harris, 2000). Deviant sexual interests has been identified as a strong predictor of sexual recidivism (Hanson and Bussiere, 1998).

In contrast, 'acute dynamic' risk factors can rapidly change (over days, hours and even minutes) and include such factors as victim access, stress or drunkenness (Hanson and Harris, 1998). Dynamic risk factors may be harder to assess and open to greater interpretation than static risk factors but they may have more value in establishing whether treatment has worked – whether someone needs treatment – and are more pertinent to theory. Beech *et al.*, (2003) acknowledge that actuarial risk assessment is cost effective in managing offenders but should be included as part of a broader assessment strategy that includes stable and acute dynamic risk factors. Thornton (2002) developed the Structured Risk Assessment (SRA), which has developed into the Structured Assessment of Risk and Need (SARN) that has been piloted by HM Prison Service (Webster *et al.*, in press). The SARN makes a combined risk assessment of an individual using static risk factors such as criminal history as well as dynamic risk factors including sexual interests, distorted attitudes, socio-affective functioning and self-management (Friendship and Beech, 2005).

Actuarial prediction deals with statistical probabilities rather than certainties (Ward *et al.*, 2006). Each offender is compared with the research findings based on a group of (similar) offenders and their behaviour. As such, the prediction cannot handle individual patterns well although these may have a strong bearing on future offending behaviour (Bickley and Beech, 2001). Such approaches are based on information concerning offending history, so there are difficulties in predicting the behaviour of individuals who lack any previous offending history, of which many Internet sex offenders are good examples (Burke *et al.*, 2001; Carr, 2003; Quayle *et al.*, 2000; Seto and Eke, 2005; Taylor and Quayle, 2003; Wolak, Finkelhor and Mitchell, 2005). Is it appropriate to take a history of Internet offending and apply what we know about the effects of a history of contact offending? We do not know enough about contact and Internet offenders to make such an assumption. Furthermore, there is a large difference between frequency of reoffending and the severity of offending (Grubin, 1998). The familiar question of whether Internet sex offenders are likely to progress to contact offending is pertinent in this context.

## THEORIES OF PAEDOPHILIA

Theories of paedophilia are numerous. Some theories, however, have achieved a primacy in the professional and research writings in this field whereas others are largely ignored. Currently the most popular theories of paedophilia generally involve a multifactorial approach (Ward *et al.*, 2006; Ward and Siegert, 2002). Unfortunately, the popularity of a theory does not necessarily reflect its empirical support or even its logical consistency.

### Finkelhor's (1984, 1986) Four Preconditions Model of Paedophilia

No comprehensive discussion of paedophilia can avoid the inclusion of Finkelhor's preconditions model of paedophilia. This is not a matter of its integrity as a theory but merely a reflection of its influence on professional groups such as probation officers, social workers, psychologists, and therapists (Fisher, 1994). The model is at the root of virtually every cognitive-behavioural approach to therapy with sex offenders. The key assumptions of Finkelhor's model that offending against children is complexly and multiply determined are embedded in the day-to-day work activities of most practitioners dealing with paedophiles.

The Finkelhor model suggests that there are four preconditions that need to be considered in relation to paedophile offending. Each precondition includes many factors that Finkelhor argued may contribute to the offending behaviour. The belief is that all preconditions must be present if a sex offence is to occur:

- *Motivation.* In order to offend there needs to be motivating factors that push the offender towards some form of interaction with children beyond what is normative. There are three important sources of motivation considered in this model: (a) an emotional congruence with children, (b) the child can provide sexual gratification and (c) because alternative sources of sexual gratification lack the power to satisfy or because they are unavailable.
- *Overcoming internal inhibitor.* An assumption of the model is that paedophiles like other people are socialised during their development in ways that tend to inhibit sexual approaches to young people. In order for offending to occur, therefore, the offender needs to overcome his internal inhibitors through a process of disinhibition. Such disinhibitors may include alcohol and drugs but also cognitive disinhibitors where the offender-to-be uses excuses or justifications for the sexual approach.
- *Overcoming external inhibitors.* Many social factors in the lives of children help to protect them from abuse. An offender needs to alter the situation or create a situation in which abuse is possible. In other words, the offender may need to find a situation that he can exploit. So, for example, the offender may befriend a lone parent, take advantage of the mother's absence from close supervision of the child, or possibly create sleeping conditions that make the child vulnerable to the offender (Budin and Johnson, 1989; Christiansen and Blake, 1990; Elliot *et al.*, 1995).
- *Overcoming the victim's resistance.* The final obstacle to offending is the resistance of the victim to the sexual approach. So part of the offender's behaviour is designed to reduce victim resistance. This can be achieved in various ways including offering gifts or treats as a form of bribery or gradually introducing, step-by-step, behaviours directed towards sexual activity with the child (Christiansen and Blake, 1990; Elliot *et al.*, 1995; Okami and Goldberg, 1992; Smallbone and Wortley, 2000).

The final two preconditions do not refer to the psychological characteristics of the offender, as such, but rather describe the process of offending. Thus they are not causal factors in offending (Ward and Siegert, 2002). The last two preconditions, especially the final one, encompass many of the behaviours by which the 'grooming' process takes place. Grooming is a general description of the sequence of behaviours employed by the offender in order to make the victim less resistant to the eventual sexual abuse. The offender may 'groom' the child into sexual activity over a considerable period of time. However, such systematic and planned preparation does not always occur (Sullivan and Beech, 2003).

The preconditions model, despite its great influence, is now somewhat dated. Rather more powerful models are beginning to supersede it. A number of weaknesses in the model have been identified. Its lack of adequate empirical grounding is a crucial one (Howitt, 2006a suggests it has little or none). Some consider it to be inadequate as an explanatory theory but may fare a little better as a way of describing the offending process (for example, Ward *et al.*, 2006). As such, it may be of value in helping offenders to understand the different aspects of their offending. Ward *et al.* suggest that the Finkelhor model might be described in their terms as a Level III theory. This means that it is a micromodel of 'how' offending occurs – it is not a model of why offending occurs. It is also suggested that Finkelhor's approach lacks 'internal coherence' because theories using quite different explanatory processes are mixed together despite the fact that they are contradictory. For example, the psychoanalytic notion of fear of females is included together with descriptions of early conditioning experiences (Ward and Hudson, 2001). This makes the theoretical adequacy of the model difficult, or it might be better to say impossible, to test. Furthermore, the model stresses triggering events (some-times described as proximal causes) of sexual offending (for example, stress) and tends to neglect predispositional (distal) factors, such as experiencing sexual abuse in childhood, that emerge from developmental experiences. Such distal factors might be considered to be better developed in the 'pathways model' (Ward and Siegert, 2002) which we discuss later in this chapter.

Generally, Finkelhor's model has been very positively regarded and extre-mely influential. By stipulating that a variety of factors may contribute to paedophile offending yet insisting that no factors are crucial in themselves, the Finkelhor model becomes largely untestable empirically. A factor that does not withstand empirical testing does not undermine the theory because it is only one of a number of influential factors. So, in this sense, the model has adversely influenced the development of theory. Moreover, the Finkelhor model has dominated the thinking of therapists. This means that therapy has tackled the wide variety of factors assumed to be involved in offending behaviour. Cognitive-behavioural therapy has largely been evaluated as an entirety and the effectiveness of specific components of therapy have rarely, if ever, been researched. Therefore, at most, what we know is that in general cognitive behaviour therapy is moderately effective - but what aspects of therapy do good are not clear.

## Hall and Hirschman's Quadripartite Model

This approach points out that offenders demonstrate a wide range of difficul-ties that are causally related to their offending behaviour. It was originally developed as an explanation of rape (Hall and Hirschman, 1991) but was extended shortly afterwards, to deal with child molestation (Hall and Hirschman, 1992). The model once again identifies four primary factors to account for child molestation:

- Physiological sexual arousal: individuals exhibit strong sexual preferences for children and typically have a history of sexual offending.
- Cognitive distortions: individuals think of children as competent sexual partners who are able to make informed decisions about when to have sex and who with.
- Affective dyscontrol: this refers to problems identifying and managing one's emotions. An individual may not be able to accurately identify certain feelings or may confuse them in some way, for example sexual desire and loneliness.
- Personality problems: this refers to more trait-like features. It is proposed that offenders display a wide range of interpersonal and personality deficits, for example, attachment difficulties. These are argued to stem from early adverse developmental experiences such as physical or sexual abuse or parental divorce.

These four factors make the individual vulnerable and when they exceed a certain threshold level and the offender has the opportunity to offend then sexual offending is likely. For any given offender, one of these factors may dominate the process, which culminates in offending behaviour. The model, as a consequence of this assumption, suggests that there are different types of offender differentiated by which factor dominates. The different types of offender may be associated with different treatment needs (Ward, 2001). Different factors push individuals beyond the threshold for offending, so appropriate treatment for any individual must address primarily the dominant factor for him. Ward (2001) argues, however, that there are a number of weaknesses inherent in this model. For example, do the factors act independently or is there a synergy between them? What are the links between feeling sad, becoming sexually aroused and having sex with a child (Ward *et al.*, 2006)? Equally, there is a lack of clarity as to the nature of the personality problems that may be responsible for tipping the individual over his threshold for offending. Finally, it is not possible to identify where the critical threshold is, whether it is the same for all offenders, or how this idea can be used to prevent sexual offending.

## Marshall and Barbaree's (1990) Integrated Theory

Marshall and Barbaree's integrated theory assumes adverse developmental histories in childhood result in certain vulnerabilities in those affected, which result in adolescents who are unable to deal with the surge of sexual urges characteristic of puberty. Offenders are both unable to cope properly with, or adequately understand, their emotions. Consequently, offenders satisfy their sexual and emotional needs in a deviant way through inappropriate contact with children. The offenders' sex and aggression drives (which are claimed to share the same brain structures) become 'fused' together it is suggested.

Some of the cultural, social, psychological, situational and biological factors that are associated with sex offending become more understandable as a consequence of the theory. The model encourages the examination of pre-viously neglected areas such as the style of attachment to significant others in the offender's life. The theory's emphasis is on the emotional self-regulation difficulties which offenders should exhibit according to the theory. That is, they handle their emotions poorly and inappropriately. One difficulty is that only a small proportion of paedophiles appear to have such problems in emotional self-regulation (Hudson, Ward and McCormack, 1999; Ward, 2002).

Ward (2002) makes a number of criticisms. Notably, the theory seems unable to explain why individuals sometimes wait until adulthood to com-mence their offending career. Certainly the key stage in the theory is adolescence, which, consequently should be the start of the offending pro-blem. However, whether this means that the offender who begins sexually abusing children well into adulthood is a difficulty for the theory is a moot point. Another of Ward's criticisms is probably more apposite. He suggests that the centrality of aggression in the model, although appropriate for rape, is not pertinent to much child sexual abuse, which generally does not involve physical force or violence.

## Ward and Siegert's (2002) 'Pathways Model'

In an attempt to bring together some of the positive features of the previous models of paedophilia, Ward and Siegert (2002) developed the 'pathways model'. Many of the factors that are central to the earlier models, such as the idea of multicausality, are included in it (Ward *et al.*, 2006). There are assumed to be four basic psychological mechanisms, which, if any are dysfunctional, may result in sex offences against children. These factors are described as mechan-isms to indicate that they are psychological processes that cause specific out-comes (or effects). The four mechanisms are intimacy or attachments deficits, sexual scripts, emotional regulation and cognitive distortions. Four subtypes of sexual offenders are said to result from the dominance of one of these (dysfunc-tional) mechanisms. A fifth subtype has a more-or-less even balance of the four dysfunctional mechanisms. Offenders of this subtype are identifiable as the pure paedophile. Offending occurs when an offender's particular pattern of vulner-ability to offending interacts with situational factors conducive to offending.

The five pathways (and types of offender) are as follows:

- *Intimacy deficits*. The offender possesses normal sexual scripts but has intimacy and social skills deficits. The primary causal factor within this pathway is insecure attachment styles and subsequently the offender has problems establishing satisfying adult relationships. He may be particularly vulnerable to offending during periods of loneliness, or where a preferred partner is unavailable. The child becomes a surrogate partner.

- *Deviant sexual scripts.* A sexual script is a cognitive representation that guides people in their sexual relationships and behaviour. Quite clearly, men and women, for example, have different sexual scripts. Sexual scripts are built up in the mind socially and depend to a degree on a person's particular developmental experiences. These cognitive representations guide a person in their sexual relationships and behaviour. Individuals in this pathway have distortions in their sexual scripts but also a dysfunctional relationship schema. It is thought that these individuals have been sexually abused and have become prematurely sexualised or were brought up in a deviant socialisation environment. The distortion in the sexual script, however, relates to the context of sex. They will seek impersonal sex when they feel aroused and will see sex and intimacy as representing the same thing. Consequently, relationships will be unsatisfying and non-lasting and the offender may seek sex with children after rejection by an adult.
- *Dysfunctional emotional regulation.* This pathway identifies individuals with normal sexual scripts, but dysfunctional mechanisms for emotional regulation. Two kinds of emotional dysfunction are thought to be particularly related to sexual offending. Firstly, individuals might have problems controlling their emotions (such as anger) and sexually abuse children as a way of punishing their partners or simply because they have lost control of their behaviour. Secondly, individuals have difficulty calming their feelings and may use sex as an emotional coping strategy, i.e. to improve their mood. It is argued that compulsive masturbation during adolescence to improve self-esteem and mood could create an early link between sex and emotional wellbeing (Cortoni and Marshall, 2001).
- *Cognitive Distortions*: This pathway contains individuals with normal sexual scripts but who hold pro-criminal attitudes and beliefs. In a sense such men are 'generalist' rather than 'specialist' offenders (Greenberg *et al.*, 2000). That is, they are likely to commit a whole variety of criminal acts, such as driving, violent and property offences. These individuals are thought to have patriarchal attitudes and a sense of their own superiority as well as a disregard of social norms regarding children and sex. The types of cognitive distortions that paedophiles hold (Ward and Siegert, 2002) include the belief that they are 'entitled to sex', 'that the world is a dangerous place whereas children are not a threat', 'the uncontrollability of one's behaviour' and that 'sex with a child is not harmful and is in fact beneficial to the child'.
- *Multiple dysfunctions.* This group of offenders has dysfunctions in all of the above areas. They are also likely to have a history of sexual abuse and/or sexual activity at a young age. They are described as 'pure' paedophiles whose preferred sexual partner is a child.

The different pathways to child sexual abuse imply different types of treatment for the abuser. The four pathways are very similar to the four stable dynamic risk domains discussed by Hanson and Thornton (2000). These are deviant sexual interests, distorted attitudes, socioaffective functioning and poor self-management. In this way there is a clear intervention strategy appropriate for each since each of these could be made central to therapy (Drake and Ward, 2003a; b). If the offender has a dominant dysfunction, say, in that their cognitions are distorted, then this needs the most attention in therapy.

The authors of the theory have identified some of its problems (Ward and Siegert, 2002; Ward *et al.*, 2006). In particular, and like some other theories, the model needs to be subjected to rigorous empirical validation. The causal mechanisms it proposes have not been subject to direct empirical testing with appropriate vigour (Ward *et al.*, 2006). Instead, the theory tends to lean heavily on ideas from other areas of psychology, such as script theory. Just how the different causal mechanisms interact with each other is not clearly explained. Ward and Siegert, themselves, argue that a satisfactory theory needs to cope with sexually abusive behaviour's development, onset, and maintenance. The model, however, neglects the issue of the maintenance of the offending behaviour (Brown, 2005; Rich, 2006). Their limited discussion of it suggests that abusing a child itself can change the offender's sexual script and also that vulnerability factors may lead to the continuation of the offending behaviour. This assumption, however, may not be well founded, Furthermore, the maintenance of offending is likely to be related to the positive and negative reinforcers associated with offending, which may be a consequence of an offender's personal pattern of vulnerability factors.

Brown (2005) indicates that the model is much easier to apply retrospectively – that is, after the offender has been identified and assessed. Whether or not the model could be used to identify offenders-to-be is not known. That is, could it be used to identify potential paedophiles early and before they have offended sexually against children? Consequently, the model may not be useful in preventing abuse. For example, Brown argues that paedophiles characteristically demonstrate insecure attachments to others in their lives, but as a causal factor it acts in combination with many other factors. Consequently, she believes that even if it were possible to identify men with insecure attachments, it would be difficult to identify who would then go on to offend.

This model seems to be aimed at the needs of practitioners and so it lacks the ability of some descriptive models to explain offending behaviour to the offender. The pathways model is too complex and lacks a major focus on the social processes involving in sexual offending against children (Brown, 2005). The model, regarded as a model for therapy, is not in line with current treatment regimes in which all sex offenders are subject to much the same treatment programme using group work and fairly strict manuals for their implementation. However, Brown argues that as the pathways model has four key factors which apply to all offenders, to some degree, it may be possible to produce treatment programmes in which individual offenders complete as much or as little of the treatment in these key areas as he requires. In this way, treatment would deal with individual needs whilst still catering for a wide range of offenders.

## Sexualisation Explanations

None of the above theories or models of paedophilia provide us with much of an explanation of why paedophiles are sexually interested in children. Indeed, the pathway model talks of sexual scripts, for example, and indicates that these may be dysfunctional in sex offenders. But, in general, sexual offending is presented much as if it were a byproduct of other dysfunctional aspects of the offender's cognitions or personality. Yet, the crucial thing for any theory of paedophilia to account for is that offenders are sexually aroused by children. Why is this? While this is a patently obvious question to ask, it has been sidestepped. The most obvious explanation has had a mixed history – that is, that childhood sexual experiences in some way, in some circumstances and in some people lead to sexual offending. Put this way, this probably does not seem a particularly radical suggestion yet it is one that has sometimes suffered a harsh response. The reasons why are partly based on research but they are also concerned with the politics of sexual abuse research – what it is acceptable to offer as explanations and what is not.

There are many reasons why children are sexually abused and why there may a link between that abuse and growing up to abuse children sexually as an adult. For example, childhood attachment has been theoretically linked to childhood sexual abuse (Smallbone and McCabe, 2003). In particular, Alexander (1992) writes that insecure relationships are often found in families characterised by sexual abuse. There are a number of possible additional factors: (a) absence of parent(s), (b) maternal unavailability, (c) marital conflict, (d) the presence of a step-father and (e) poor relationships with parents are all predictors of increased risk of child sexual abuse. Insecure children are more susceptible to sexual abuse because of their need for emotional support, which initially their abuser may exploit. The insecurely attached child may have fewer psychological resources to deal with and resist the abuse. Of course, the long-term effects of sexual abuse will vary with the quality of family and other support available to the victimised child (Alexander, 1992). Some children appear resilient to the potential long-term negative effects of sexual abuse and lack serious or clinical levels of symptoms or problems (Rosenthal, Feiring and Taska, 2003). Parental support has been associated with less psychological distress, less abuse stress and fewer negative appraisals of the abuse experience, themselves and others (Elliot and Carnes, 2001; Spaccarelli and Kim, 1995). Family support and good quality relationships with a non-offending parent can be an important factor in maintaining school performance, activities and peer relations after abuse (Spaccarelli and Kim, 1995). Similarly, boys and girls who report more satisfaction with their caregiver's support following abuse disclosure also report less depression and better self-esteem one year later and support from friends is associated with less sexual anxiety (Rosenthal et al., 2003).

There are several proposed explanations for why sexual abuse in childhood contributes to adult sexual offending against children. The most straightforward is the social learning theory (see, for example, Bandura, 1977), which basically assumes that behaviours are learnt from others in the social environment. However, a number of other explanations have been offered including:

- Sexually abused men overcome the trauma they suffered by taking the anger out on other children (Howitt, 1995a).
- There is a 'career progression' from being an abused child to being an abuser (Howitt, 1995a).
- Premature sexual experiences interfere with the future development of intimate relationships, causing the individual to view children as partners who can be controlled without the need to negotiate all the difficulties inherent in adult relationships (Grubin, 1998).
- Abusing other children can protect a person from the worst aspects of his own abuse. He rationalises what happened to him as positive and, therefore, there is no reason why he should not do it to others (Grubin, 1998).

However, whether childhood abuse causes someone to become an abuser has been a controversial issue. If there is a link between being abused and becoming an abuser one would expect to find the prevalence of childhood sexual abuse to be greater in sex offender populations compared to controls. Generally there is evidence supporting this (see, for example, Cohen *et al.*, 2002; Craissati and McClurg, 1996; Glasser *et al.*, 2001). However, there is a degree of inconsistency in the findings and the proportions of sex offenders suffering sexual abuse as children compared to controls varies across studies (Craissati, McClurg and Browne, 2002).

Unfortunately, methodological problems plague the findings. Much of the evidence for cycles of sexual abuse is provided by retrospective reports. This, of course, leads to doubts about the reliability of the information provided. Some see this as rendering a cycle of sexual abuse theory untenable. For instance, perpetrators may *over-endorse* their own personal abuse history as a way of justifying their offending, for purposes of good clinical presentation or as a way of attempting to lessen the legal consequences of their behaviour (Hanson and Slater, 1988). Hindman's (1988) study is commonly quoted as evidence that sex offenders tend to fake a history of childhood sexual abuse. They were told that they would undergo a lie-detector test to ascertain the veracity of their childhood abuse claim and, if the claim was proven false, they would be returned to prison. Only 29 % of the men claimed to have been sexually abused when they were threatened in this way compared to 67 % when there was no such threat. However, denying a history of childhood abuse may have been the safest way to avoid reimprisonment: 'Given that the lie-detector is a controversial instrument, it might well be the safest course of action since no-one would take action against them if they had denied the abuse, despite it having occurred' (Howitt, 1995a, p. 58).

Equally, the rates of childhood abuse in the lives of sex offenders may actually be *underestimated*. There are several possible reasons for this including: (a) a reluctance to report abuse due to the stigma attached to it; (b) fear that they will appear guilty because they admit to being victimised (Hanson and Slater, 1988); (c) an inability to cognitively process the memories due to their traumatic nature and as such their memories are denied or distorted (Cohen *et al.*, 2002), and (d) simply because they do not see their abuse as 'abusive' rather than, say, consensual (Howitt, 2002).

There are other methodological issues such as the unsuitability of comparison groups used in some studies (Hanson and Slater, 1988). For instance, the use of police officers (for example, Groth, 1979) which might result in the rates of abuse for offenders being overestimated because police officers would partly be selected for their jobs because they demonstrate emotional stability. The definition of sexual abuse will also affect the research outcomes. Studies using definitions of sexual abuse that include non-contact abuse will tend to produce higher reporting rates than studies using a narrower definition requiring sexual contact (Kelly, Regan and Burton, 1991). Further, studies commonly use questionnaires, or simply ask the direct question 'have you been abused?' which may increase the tendency to deny having experienced abuse. The recognition of childhood abuse may take an adult a long time to achieve and may even require therapy. Not surprisingly, focused interviews can produce greater reporting of childhood abuse than self-completion questionnaires (Wyatt and Peters, 1986).

The notion that abused individuals become abusers themselves may be enduring because it has intuitive validity (Federoff and Moran, 1997). But one crucial weakness of the 'cycle of abuse' theory is its failure to explain why most sexual abusers are male and most victims are female (Hilton and Mezey, 1996). Furthermore, if something like 10 % of the population were victims of childhood sexual then why are 10 % of the population not sex offenders (Finkelhor *et al.*, 1990; Murphy and Smith, 1996)? The problems are compounded if, say, on average 20 % of sex offenders claim to have been sexually victimised as children (see, for example, Williams and Finkelhor, 1990) as the 'abused becoming an abuser' theory can only explain a small proportion of paedophile careers (Groth, 1979; Finkelhor, 1984; Hansen and Slater, 1988; Howitt, 1995a). Similarly, many men who have been abused do not go on to abuse children. The tenability of the cycles of abuse thesis can only be enhanced if a larger proportion is abused than some studies report and if there is something different about the victimised men who become abusers. Factors which may protect the child from the worst effects of sexual abuse include good self-esteem and sexual knowledge; availability of support; success in activities that reflect parent's pride; having long-term goals; and monitoring by parents from further abuse (Prendergast, 1993). These may be lacking in the childhoods of many abusers.

## Sexualisation Model

It is not hard to understand the lack of enthusiasm for the 'cycles of abuse' idea despite its simplicity. Moreover, the mechanism by which sexual abuse in childhood leads to paedophilia in adulthood is left for conjecture (Howitt, 1995a). Howitt (1995a; 2006a) asserts that research should not concentrate *exclusively* on the effects of childhood sexual abuse but should explore the influence of all aspects of early sexualisation on the offender such as peer sex. One possible consequence of early sexual experiences is that the paedophile will start to see sexual contact for children as normal because it was a normal event in his experience. In this context, childhood sexual abuse is only the start of a process that may end in paedophilic activity.

Adult-child sexual contacts are, in part, regarded as problematic because of the power differentials between adult and child. Yet child-child sex is regarded as a healthy, or normal, part of growing up so long as there are no discernible age (or power) differences between the children (Howitt, 1995a). Research creates a picture of adult-child sex as extremely harmful and indeed this may well be the case for some children. Traumatic childhood abuse is responsible for the early sexualisation of at least a proportion of sex offenders-to-be. There is also some reason to believe that the nature of the abuse may have a bearing on its effects. For example, penetrative sex, female perpetrators, repetition of abuse and other atypical abusive acts may have more of an adverse effect on the victim and possibly lead to paedophilia in adulthood (Howitt, 2006a). Conversely, there is an occasional study that suggests that some adult-child sexual experiences can be of positive value to a child (Sandfort, 1992). Much the same argument is commonly put forward by pro-paedophilia organisations (such as the North American Man/Boy Love Association – NAMBLA). However, there is no good reason to assume that child-child sexual contacts cannot be harmful and contribute to the development of paedophilia (Howitt, 1995a). Of course, potentially child-child sex is a politically much more fraught issue than adult-child sex for which the political solution is simple – it is illegal. Yet at the same time just what is different about sexual activity between two children, which renders it harmless, compared with adult-child sexual activity? Suggestions of power differentials have superficial validity but just what is the nature of these differentials – how can they be precisely defined?

But what of the suggestion that (theoretically at least) child-child sexual activity may be conducive to paedophilia (Howitt, 1995a)? It is not improbable that pleasurable experiences may be repeated on later occasions. Furthermore, early experiences with underage partners might create a preference for young sex. Moreover, sexual attractiveness is commonly equated with 'youthfulness' in our society. Offenders will describe being attracted to the physical attributes of a 14 year old (like soft skin) rather than the age as such. These attributes may be identical characteristics to those of a 16 year old. The main difference between the two situations is legality (Howitt, 1995a).

Howitt (1995a, p. 66) proposed two reasons why studying sexualisation in offenders is important;

- That sexualisation should be common and universal in the lives of offenders and should account for more offenders than the cycle of abuse theory on its own.
- Early sexualisation might have a strong influence on sexual fantasy and behaviour, and there should be similar themes between the two.

The sexualisation model does partly explain the tendency of offenders to abuse the victim in a way that replicates their own experience of abuse (Hilton and Mezey, 1996). For instance, Howitt (1995b) presents several case studies illustrating connections between aspects of early sexual experiences of some offenders and features of their abusive behaviour in adulthood. Further, Haaspasalo, Puupponen and Crittenden (1999, p. 98) refer to the concept of isomorphic behaviour: 'That physically abused children tend to commit physically violent crimes whereas sexually abused children are prone, in adulthood, to sexual violence including paedophilia, child molestation and rape.'

They reported a case of a 38-year old recidivist. The sexual acts perpetrated by him, the ages of the victims and his patterns of grooming were almost identical to those in the perpetrator's own childhood experiences. The reason for isomorphism of sexual offending may be that it involves repeating strategies for achieving basic feelings of safety and security (Howitt, 2002). Cohen *et al.* (2002) found that the concordance between childhood experiences of a given sexual act and paedophilic performance of the act averaged 58 %. For seven of the eight acts (fondling, kissing, tongue kissing, masturbating an adult, adult touching child's genitals, fellatio on adult and sexual intercourse) the average was 66 % ranging from 50 % to 100 %. The one exception was anal intercourse, which was not reported as being repeated. Naturally, offenders may be replicating the abusive acts performed upon them as a child during adulthood not because of some form of symbolic reference but because of influential situational factors: expediency; acts that reduce the risk of discovery; or acts that are sexual preferences developed in adulthood.

Finally, the concept of sex offenders experiencing early sexualisation is in line with the current recognition that sex offending in childhood cannot and should not be neglected (James and Neil, 1996). Indeed, significant amounts of sexual abuse against children are actually committed by juveniles (Anderson *et al.*, 1993; Davis and Leitenberg, 1987; Finkelhor, 1980; Flanagan and Hayman-White, 2000; James and Neil, 1996; O'Shaughnessy, 2006; Veneziano, Veneziano and LeGrand, 2000). For instance, US studies have shown that 39 % of all victims aged between six and 11 years of age and 40 % of those victims aged below six years are sexually assaulted by juveniles (Snyder, 2000).

## CONCLUDING COMMENTS

Of course, that is not all that we know about paedophiles. There are plenty of other ideas that are worth considering. But it should be clear that if we know anything about paedophilia then that knowledge is very tentative and even tenuous. There are increasing numbers of research studies of some pertinence but, as ever in research, the problem is not the number of studies but the number of ideas that are of any assistance to understanding. Perhaps the task of understanding may be too large. There are strong indications that childhood may be importance in its development yet it seems clear that, at least in a proportion of cases, men do not engage children sexually until adulthood and perhaps later. This is a huge span of time to study. So where do we get our knowledge from? We do not know which children will become paedophiles so we cannot track their progression from an early age. Yet if we start at the other end of the process then it is difficult to be sure what adult offenders tell us about their early lives has any validity at all.

So, in a sense, our knowledge of paedophilia is as if through a mist. The mist is partly the mist of time, which affects our understanding of what it was about the early lives of offenders that led them into offending. But there is an equally important mist – that which is the consequence of the ideologically based nature of our understanding of sex offenders. As a modern folk-devil, our discussions of the paedophile tend to be within clearly proscribed limits. To go beyond these limits is to risk censure that one's academic work is dangerous or pro-paedophile. This even applies to ideas such as the notion that paedophiles have a history of being sexually abused themselves or even the idea that it is possible to gain some insight into paedophilia by listening to what paedophiles have to say. Perhaps things are more conducive to such ideas nowadays. Weak descriptive theory has tended to dominate the field thus drawing attention away to what for some of us would be a key question – why paedophiles?

As we have indicated, there is some consensus and some ideas are quite recurrent. But we would argue that there are no theories available at the moment that synthesise what we need to know about paedophilia. We probably know more about where not to look for explanations of paedophilia than where to look. Thus, there is little or no enthusiasm for genetic, biological, biochemical and similar explanations of paedophilia. There is a sort of agreement that childhood development is in some way important in understanding how paedophiles are made. There is an idea that paedophile's cognitions are different in ways which may be conducive to offending. There is the view that offenders may be changed away from offending by changing their cognitions. These may be important statements but they lack clarity so that we cannot be confident that researchers will soon begin to be able to address some of the more profound issues to do with offending against children.

The relevance of all of this to Internet offenders is dependent on the extent that they can be seen as truly paedophiles.

# CHAPTER 4

# Creating and Controlling the Internet Sex Offender

> The discourses of paedophilia and sexuality have undergone profound transformations, and it is the axis of age, and the distinction between child and adult sexuality, that is of utmost social, community and parental interest and concern. Within the last two decades, in most Western societies there has been nothing short of an explosion of social panic surrounding paedophilia and purported paedophile networks. Just as the 'homosexual' was catapulted to centre stage at the turn of the nineteenth century, now it is the 'paedophile' that has emerged as a highly salient and potent figure almost a century late. (Angelides, The emergence of the paedophile in the late twentieth century)

Concerns about sex offending and the Internet mainly grew alongside modern proactive child protection initiatives and anti-pornography legislation. In many ways, child protection was the major social concern of the 1970s and has continued to grow in scope and importance since then. What is particularly modern in child protection is the idea of 'pro-action' rather than 'reaction'. While concerns about the physical, psychological, emotional, and sexual safety of children became heightened from the 1970s onwards, there has been a sea change based on the belief that the abuse of children is not merely preventable but that this is a realistic and practical aim.

Thus the so-called 'discovery' of child abuse in the second half of the twentieth century is somewhat misleading. At its core, it implies a sudden new awareness of child abuse, which previously did not exist. This is belied by the considerable historical evidence (for example, Calder, 2005) which suggests that violent abuse was well known among the general public and extreme instances of it, in particular, were likely to be condemned. Similarly, awareness of child sexual abuse goes back much earlier than the second part of the twentieth century and there is evidence of awareness of child sexual abuse going back to Victorian times if not earlier (Howitt, 1992a, 1995a).

Of course, child protection was organised differently in the past and attitudes towards abusers seemingly very different. The precise history varies from country to country in detail. In the UK, the watershed moment marking the change from the old way to the new way was the outcry following the killing of seven-year-old Maria Colwell at the hands of her stepfather. The resulting public inquiry in 1974 investigated why her death had been allowed to happen. The public inquiry made numerous recommendations including ones aimed at the better integration of the different agencies involved in the protection of children. The mechanism for this was to be area child protection committees (originally known as area review committees). Increasingly, formal policies and procedures geared towards guiding the practices of child protection professionals were developed. In addition, a system of case conferences was introduced, which brought together the relevant professions and agencies to discuss the situation of particular children and families (DHSS, 1974, 1976). Typifying the emerging proactive approach was the introduction of 'at risk' registers (now known as child protection registers) containing the names of all children in an area about whom child protection issues had been raised (Thomas, 2005).

Another way of putting this is that the death of Maria Colwell instilled the idea of the predictability and preventability of child abuse into professional work with children and the expectations of the public. Social workers, especially, increasingly began to be seen as having an abuse-prevention role, not merely a palliative one. Consequently, they were pilloried for failing to recognise danger signs so putting children at risk. The criminal justice system, itself, has been characterised in recent decades by this drive towards crime prevention – a topic that had been much neglected throughout the earlier history of the criminal justice system (Moss and Stephens, 2006).

## CHILD SEXUAL ABUSE

Child sexual abuse became a matter of profound social concern in the early 1980s and, consequently, a major issue on the agendas of social workers, teachers, police and others. The lessons learned from the physical abuse of children had not transferred to sexual abuse. So, at the beginning of the 1980s in Britain, area child protection committees could not effectively deal with child sexual abuse and procedures to help guide practitioners were not in place (Mrazek, Lynch and Bentovim, 1983). The factors that gave rise to the increased focus on sexual abuse are numerous and complex. One should not underestimate the impact of the women's movement and feminism in both promoting the core ideas of sexual politics and providing practical means of helping women and children. Women were developing an increasingly central and powerful voice in Society. Academia, apart from the contributions of feminists, was influential because of seemingly groundbreaking research. In the US, the sociologist, David Finkelhor, had a major impact on ideas about sexual abuse (Finkelhor, 1986). He, and others, provided a significant and important research base documenting the widespread sexual abuse of children. This does not mean that such research was entirely novel. A half century or so earlier, a succession of surveys had been carried all pointing to the same conclusion – that large numbers of men and women had been victims of the unwanted sexual attention of adults when they were children (see, for example, Gagnon, 1965; Hamilton, 1929; Kinsey *et al.*, 1953; Landis, 1940, 1956; Salter, 1988; Terman, 1938, 1951). However, for all intents and purposes, these early surveys just gathered dust on academic library shelves, seeds which did not germinate.

Of course, historically the sexual abuse of children was punished. This is easily seen in the historical trends in published statistics on sexual crimes (Howitt, 1995a). The emergence of sexual abuse as an issue of social importance may have increased the expectation that offenders should be prosecuted. However, in previous decades action would be taken against offenders when the sexual abuse was clear-cut and evident. The urgency of the belief that sexual abuse can and must be prevented is crucial to understanding what had changed (Thomas, 2005). The move was from mere reaction to proaction – from the punishment of crime to its prevention.

This change created its own problems. There was a notorious period during which misguided proaction itself was responsible for major problems. The most significant instance of this came in 1987 with the 'Cleveland Affair'. A number of children in the north of England had been (mis)diagnosed by doctors as having been sexually abused on the basis on of a faulty medical diagnostic test (Howitt, 1992a). The *anal dilation test* involved the medical touching of a child's anus in the belief that an anus damaged by abuse would not react the same way as that of a child who had not been sexually abused. However, claims of the test's efficacy were unfounded and it was likely to give false positives for sexual abuse. The report of the consequent public inquiry (Cleveland Report, 1988) further sensitised childcare practitioners to the issue of sexual abuse but also called for agencies to rethink their policies and working practices. Once again the call was for agencies to work together with greater levels of integration – as well as to work closely with parents. The Children's Act 1989 enacted many of the recommendations from the Cleveland Inquiry. At root, the problem was that professionals were imbued with the belief that it was possible to be proactive in preventing abuse rather than simply wait for crimes to be reported to the authorities (Howitt, 1992a). There emerged a flurry of instances where social workers and others appeared to have lost their grip on reality according to the media and the general public. 'Paedophile rings', satanic abuse and ritual abuse were the basis of (unfounded) allegations of sexual abuse (for example, in the Orkney Islands – see the Clyde Report, 1992). Despite the intensity of attention given to them, objective evidence for many of these allegations never did emerge (La Fontaine, 1998) and the suspicion was that the authorities were the problem. Curiously, however, these more bizarre allegations seem to have had little impact on public policy compared with the monumental changes following the Cleveland Report. For example, the report *Working Together to Safeguard Children* (Department of Health, 1999) largely ignored these cases that, with hindsight, are best regarded as evidence of the growing imperative to prevent child sexual abuse.

Through all of these changes and developments, the media played a crucial role in publicising the failings of the child protection system. Most directly, in

1986 the BBC broadcast the programme *Childwatch* to launch the organisation Childline (Thomas, 2005). This provided a free telephone helpline for children who felt themselves in difficulties to call. Not only did the programme raise public awareness but it disturbed 'previously untouched sensitivities' (Parton, 1991, p. 93). Taking the media as a barometer of public opinion, there was an 'explosion of interest' even among serious newspapers about sex offending against children (Soothill, Francis and Ackerley, 1998, p. 882). Indeed, paedophiles had become headline news.

## THE GATHERING ACTION AGAINST CHILD PORNOGRAPHY

Government concerns about pornography became increasingly evident from the 1960s onwards. In various countries, different governments organised committees and commissions to investigate the effects of pornography on society and on the individual users of pornography. The conclusions of these deliberations ranged from damning condemnations of pornography to virtual exonerations so far as adult pornography was concerned. Little in all of the research commissioned in the course of these investigations involved child pornography in any way.

Increasingly, it is believed that countries such as Thailand, India, and South America are among the major sources of child pornography together with Eastern European countries where Westerners are the amateur producers of child pornography (Taylor and Quayle, 2003). Traditionally, however, Western nations (Western Europe and North America) were the major source of child pornography. During the late 1960s and 1970s a number of Western countries, especially Western European countries, relaxed the censorship of pornography (Tate, 1990). Particularly important was that on the 1 July 1969, Denmark legalised all forms of pornography, including child pornography. The only restriction was that anyone caught selling obscene pictures or objects to children under 16 years of age were liable to a fine (Tate, 1990). Even where legislation did not change, some governments permitted the production and distribution of child pornography simply by failing to enforce existing laws (Tate, 1990).

The majority of child pornography circulating commercially had private origins (Schuijer and Rossen, 1992). Private material is sometimes 'swapped' and thus becomes vulnerable to appropriation but sometimes it is sold to commercial interests. Typical of the material circulating around the 1970s would be black-and-white photographs of poor quality. Experts insist that a substantial part, if not most, of the currently available material had its origins 30 or so years ago (Taylor and Quayle, 2003). The Color Climax Corporation of Denmark made 36 or more 10-minute films for the 'Lolita' series (Tate, 1990). The films involved young girls mainly aged between seven and eleven being sexually abused, mainly by men. Their titles say much about their contents – *Incest Family*, *Pre-Teen Sex*, *Sucking Daddy* and *Child Love*. Another Danish producer of child pornography, Willy Strauss, is alleged to have published 1,500 pornography magazines. Again their titles said much about their contents – *Anna and Her Father* and *Bambina Sex*. Another Danish company, COQ International, catered for the boy market by producing magazines such as *Piccolo* and *Uncle Joe* (Tate, 1990). Care should be taken not to assume the worst of the contents of some of these publications. For example, one of COQs publications *Boy* consisted, for the most part, of nudist-type photographs (Schuijer and Rossen, 1992).

Holland had its own producers of child pornography. *Lolita* was a child pornography magazine produced by Joop Wilhelmus. The magazine title became synonymous with child pornography (Tate, 1990). Its contents included pictures of children being abused. In addition, readers were invited to provide new child pornography images to be published in the magazine. It would appear that no great financial incentive was involved and that a magazine copy was given in exchange for each new child photograph – though the sum of $350 was offered in the magazine if Wilhelmus could take the photographs himself. The magazine also had a contact service for its readers: 'English gentleman, 37, paedophile, wishes to meet a mother with Lolita daughter or lady with paedophile feelings with view to marriage' (Tate, 1990, p. 59).

The magazine was not closed down until 1987.

The US similarly began production of child pornography in the 1970s although this was quite a complicated situation. In particular, Tate (1990) refers to the British-born Eric Cross living in Florida in the early 1970s. Cross was responsible for the *Lolitots* series of photomagazines. In 1974 he had invited a 10 and an 11 year old girl on a holiday trip with the knowledge of the girls' parents. At a hotel, Cross took several hundred nude photographs of the girls before they went back to their parents. However, the Protection of Children Against Sexual Exploitation Act 1977 for the first time prohibited the use of children in pornography anywhere in the US. Because of this Act, he took his pictures to Europe to be published and then imported them back into the US in the form of the three magazines *Sweet Linda*, *Sweet Patti* and *Sweet Linda and Patti*. This circuitous route became the pattern for US producers of child pornography. This same material is still available and is a substantial part of the child pornography currently available. Police seizures of child pornography collections regularly include this early material (Taylor and Quayle, 2003). Of course, child pornography videos or magazines are easily turned into digital images on the Internet. According to Taylor and Quayle, this early child pornography material can often be identified on the Internet from the file name it is given. *Lolita* material is referred to as LL. So a code such as LL21-17 would be the seventeenth picture taken from the 21st *Lolita* video.

But the circumstances of its production have no necessary relationship to the process by which child pornography comes to be recognised as a social problem. According to Schuijer and Rossen (1992), the earliest media coverage indicating a huge child pornography trade occurred at the end of the 1970s in the US, England and Scandinavia. The publication of Robin Lloyd's *For Money or Love: Prostitution in America* (1976) is held to be the start of interest. In this he claimed that there was a boy-prostitute network involving 300,000 boys. Although this was a totally hypothetical figure others cited it as a firm fact.

Judianne Densen-Gerber, who was director of Odyssey House treatment clinics for drug addicts, set about mobilising public opinion using this very statistic. Suddenly articles about child pornography began to appear in newspapers, including respectable ones, much more frequently. Furthermore, in 1977 a subcommittee of the Committee on the Judiciary of the House of Representatives met in a series of meetings which ensured that child pornography was a substantial news item for half of that year. In Schuijer and Rossen's (1992, p. 1) words 'A platform was established by crusaders against child pornography, and in the prevailing climate of moral panic their cries for stronger measures received wide political support.'

Proposals for the first US federal law dealing with child pornography were reviewed at a series of hearings. The very first of these features the 300,000 hypothetical-guess as to the number of boys engaged in boy prostitution. Densen-Gerber merely doubled this to deal with girl child prostitution. Furthermore, the chair of the hearing doubled this figure on the specious grounds that not only were one million runaways at risk of child prostitution but a further million school dropouts. According to Schuijer and Rossen, estimates made at this time of such things as the numbers of children involved in child pornography, the money to be made, and the damage done to children had no precise foundation in available evidence. There is an element of truth in each case but the actual figures are much lower.

In Holland in the 1980s, one police raid was said to have netted eight cubic meters of child pornography. The police described how the pictures and videos depicted children being used against their will and with looks of horror on their faces. In the US it was being claimed that there were regular auctions in Amsterdam in which children were for sale for prostitution and child pornography. Child pornography was held to be half of the trade in pornography. Yet a senior police officer explained later how easy it was to stop the sale of child pornography in shops since the shops claimed that only 1 per cent of their sales were child pornography. Financially it was not in the interest of the shops to have difficult relations with the police. It was suggested that $5 to 10 billion was being made annually from child sex and pornography according to Child Defence International (Schuijer and Rossen, 1992).

The personal computer was gradually to outstrip anything that the video recorder could do. A user of child pornography from the Internet is not constrained by geographical boundaries in terms of obtaining material. Computers have flexibility in terms of things like cataloguing the material yet feel misleadingly secure. Access to a computer could be restricted by the use of a password to ensure some privacy even from other members of the household (Tate, 1990). But evidence of the use of the Internet by men sexually interested in children was to appear in the work of the Attorney General's Commission (The Meese Commission) (1986). President Ronald Reagan commissioned an investigation into pornography and the pornography industry from his Attorney General, Edwin Meese. Meese found that child pornography users mainly used bulletin boards on the Internet. Bulletin boards are functionally the precursors of the WWW in terms of their ability to bring people together. They are based on software that allows users to connect to a computer system and to download items of software, as well as other forms of data. The user is able to exchange messages with other users of the system. At this time, users would be paying for the analogue telephone line and the users of the bulletin board would generally live close together because of the cost. Some bulletin boards were themed around the issue of sex so paedophilic messages, not surprisingly, began to appear on some of them. It was proposed in 1983 by a member that the North American Man/Boy Love Association should start its own electronic bulletin board (Tate, 1990). In Britain in 1985, a Mike Parker started a bulletin board used by paedophiles and had 500 regular users – some seeking child pornography. This was closed down after a police intervention though no charges were made against Parker (Tate, 1990).

The development of the Internet and the WWW necessitated changes in the laws controlling pornography and, especially, obscenity. Had the law that applied in the 1970s not changed with the arrival of the Internet, then it is doubtful whether any Internet child pornography would ever have been prosecuted. The law on obscenity in the UK was historically quite straightforward in that it was contained within the Obscene Publications Acts of 1959 and 1964 (Akdeniz, 2001a; b; c). There was no legislation against pornography but there was legislation against obscenity. The test of obscenity within the legislation was that items are obscene if, taken as a whole, they would: '...tend to deprave and corrupt persons who are likely, having regard to all relevant circumstances, to read, see or hear the matter contained or embodied in it' (Akdeniz, 2001b, p. 5).

Under the Obscene Publications Act the offence was that of publishing such material for gain – possession did not constitute an offence. The Act covered tangible items such as computer discs. However, computer users can, of course, 'publish' obscene images to other computers using modems and telephone lines, which constituted another legal loophole in need of rectification (Akdeniz, 1997).

Significantly, the Criminal Justice Act 1988 penalised the possession of indecent photographs of children. So the crime was no longer limited to the activities of the producer of child pornography. The Protection of Children Act 1978 had made it an offence to take or permit to be taken and to make, to distribute or show indecent photographs of persons under the age of 16 years (or have the material in one's possession with the intent of distributing or showing it). The same Act also made it illegal to publish or cause to be published advertisements indicating that the advertiser distributes or shows indecent photographs of young people or has the intent of doing so. However, neither of the Acts defined 'indecency' and it is left to the courts to interpret its meaning (Gillespie, 2005b). A former head of the Metropolitan Police's Paedophile Unit argued that a test of indecency linked to the *intentions* of the photographer would be beneficial because some offenders obtain sexual gratification from images that may not be considered objectively indecent (McLachlan, 2002). Consequently, some photographs are available that are blatantly indecent, and some that are indecent simply because of the photographer's intent. Proving intention, though, is difficult. The context of the photograph in the life of the individual provides clues as to the intention (for example, was the photograph stored with images of child rape). The difficulty occurs when there is no such evidence to prove intention, leaving any such determination due to purely subjective means.

The Criminal Justice and Public Order Act of 1994 covered technological changes such as those produced by the Internet and was stimulated by a growing fear of child pornography (Akdeniz, 2001b). The meaning of the word 'publication' was clarified so that it covered the electronic transmission of material. The Act criminalised making pornographic material available to download by another person using a password (Akdeniz, 2001b). The Act extended the word 'photograph' to include photographs that had been manipulated in ways that make the results look like a picture of child abuse (Gillespie, 2005c). Pseudo-photographs can be the result of digital manipulation. Morphing, as it is sometimes called, is made easy thanks to computer technology and sometimes it is difficult to distinguish pseudo material from the 'real' thing. Gillespie (2005c) points out that not all pseudo-images are necessarily sophisticated and some images are obviously manipulated. Gillespie gives the example of an individual in possession of a picture of a naked adult woman with the head of a child being 'pasted' onto it. Gillespie explains that in this circumstance the court ruled that it was not a pseudo-photograph because it was two separate images but if it were photocopied, or scanned then, it might breach the law about pseudo-images. One reason for the legislation against pseudo-images is as an anti-evasion measure (Akdeniz, 2006). In other words, people accused of possessing images may claim that the pictures are pseudo rather than real and it may be impossible to prove that it is a real child (Akdeniz, 2006; Gillespie, 2005c).

Computer technology has made image manipulation extremely easy and distinguishing between fake and real photographs can be difficult (Akdeniz, 1997; 2001b). One might, of course, argue that no actual harm is done to the children in pseudo-photographs (Lanning, 2001). Pornography featuring real victims involves the permanency, longevity and circulation of images of the sexual abuse of children. This argument cannot apply to pseudo-photographs. However, common arguments favouring the illegality of pseudo-photographs suggest that they are instrumental in nature. For instance, pseudo images might be traded for images involving 'real' children (Lanning, 2001). Moreover, photographs of children engaged in sexual activity might act as learning instruments in the 'grooming' process or be employed to entice other children into the same behaviour (Attorney General's Commission, The Meese Commission Report, 1986; Tate, 1990; Taylor and Quayle, 2003; Wyre, 1987). Both real and pseudo-photographs could be used equally for this purpose (Akdeniz, 2001b). Of course, the law now provides tough penalties for 'grooming' offences or for 'causing or inciting' a child to be involved in pornography (Sexual Offences Act 2003). Others argue that criminalisation of pseudo-photographs is based on morals (Ost, 2002).

Similarly, child pornography can be blamed for the incitement of offences such as when an offender uses it as a stimulus in preparation of his offending (Marshall, 1988). A pseudo-image may be just as potent as a real image in fuelling the sexual fantasies of paedophiles. Therefore, in this light, whether an image is real or artificial is irrelevant. However, this sort of pornography use is limited (Condron and Nutter, 1988; Howitt, 1995b: Langevin *et al.*, 1988; Nutter and Kearns, 1993). Indeed, if an individual generates fantasy from pornography then one might be concerned about the risk of fantasy becoming reality. The empirical evidence (so far as adult pornography is concerned) for such a link is very limited (Seto, Maric and Barbaree, 2001).

Legislation has also increased sentencing for those involved in child pornography. Possession of indecent photographs has been augmented to an 'indictable offence' in other words requiring trial by jury in a Crown Court (Criminal Justice and Court Services Act 2000) with maximum penalties increasing from six months to five years imprisonment. Similarly, maximum penalties for taking, making, showing and distributing indecent material have increased substantially from 3 to 10 years imprisonment (Protection of Children Act, 1978).

## CONTROLLING INTERNET AND OTHER SEX OFFENDERS

For all intents and purposes, Internet sex offenders are subject to much the same punishments and control as any other type of sex offender in the UK. We have seen that different standards apply internationally and, to date, there is no complete comparative study of the way in which Internet sex offenders are punished, controlled and monitored in comparison to regular child molesters. Since, in the UK, Internet offences qualify for the offender to be included into the Sex Offender Register, then that register and the ensuing controls may dominate the lives of Internet offenders once their sentences have been served. Indeed, even if the offender escapes a conviction in court for some reason, the system can require their registration through other means, as we shall see. Partly, modern legislation can be viewed as indicative of the general seriousness with which sex offences are regarded but it also exemplifies a potentially complex system of controls on the lives of Internet offenders once in the system. This is despite the lack of clear evidence at the time that Internet offenders are indeed similar to other sex offenders in terms of their likelihood of reoffending or the risk that they will reoffend with a contact offence. Many of the controls only make sense if it is assumed that what is appropriate for contact offenders is equally applicable to those whose offending has been confined to child pornography.

## THE MODERN CLIMATE OF CONTROL

Instances of modern legal changes designed to control the activities of sex offenders and prevent their further re-offending are legion. According to Hudson (2005), legislation in the UK has incorporated the following changes in recent years:

• greater sentencing tariffs given to 'dangerous' sexual and violent offenders (The Criminal Justice Act 1991);

- UK citizens can be tried in UK for offences committed abroad (The Sexual Offences (Conspiracy and Incitement) Act 1996);
- DNA tests can be given to sex offenders while serving a sentence (The Criminal Evidence (Amendment) Act 1997);
- mandatory life sentences for offenders committing a second serious sexual or violent offence (The Crime (Sentences) Act 1997);
- most serious sex offenders obliged to 'register' their personal details such as their address with the police (The Sex Offenders Act 1997);
- Sexual Offenders Orders restricting the behaviours of sex offenders within the community (The Crime and Disorder Act 1998);
- sexual activity in the context of 'an abuse of trust' made illegal for the first time (The Sexual Offences (Amendment) Act 2000);
- restraining orders limiting offenders' movements and disqualifying most sex offenders from working with children (The Criminal Justice and Court Services Act 2000); and,
- serious offenders even on first conviction could be imprisoned indefinitely for public protection (Criminal Justice Act 2003).

All of this amounts to unprecedented controls on sex offenders.

## CURRENT LEGISLATION: SEXUAL OFFENCES ACT 2003

The Sexual Offences Act 2003 consolidated many earlier laws and widened and strengthened some earlier provisions. Notably, it pushed the age limit for the legal protection of children upwards to include 17 year olds (Renold *et al.*, 2003). It also included measures to deal with Internet child pornography and grooming. The precise provisions of the Act vary according to the age of the child involved. For the first time, inciting a child younger than 13 years to sexual activity became an offence. This was due to the law's previous inability to deal with the case of the man who persuaded two 11-year-old girls to strip naked in front of him but used no violence or threats and did not touch the girls but was not prosecuted because his behaviour did not fit any offence under English Law (Thomas, 2005).

Abuse of a position of trust legislation (Sexual Offences (Amendment) Act 2000) was tightened to make it an offence for a person aged 18 or over to involve a person under 18 years of age in sexual activity (for example, sexual touching, causing or inciting sexual activity, sexual activity in the presence of a child and causing a child to watch sexual activity) where he or she is in a specified position of trust in relation to that child. Such positions of trust include where a child is detained in an institution (for example, a detention centre), cared for and accommodated in a home (for example, a care home), and where an adult is looking after a child in an educational establishment and the child is receiving education (for example, college).

The Sexual Offences Act 2003 also protects children until they reach 18 years in family relationships. Family relationships include situations where someone is living within the same household as a child and assumes a position of trust or authority over that child as well as relationships defined by blood ties, adoption, fostering, or common law relationships. The Act introduced a new set of offences specifically dealing with the exploitation of children up to the age of 18 through prostitution and pornography (for instance paying for sex with a child; causing or inciting child prostitution or pornography; controlling a child prostitute or a child involved in pornography; and arranging or facilitating child prostitution or pornography). Trafficking offences also included those involving child victims.

The Act recognised that typical behaviours of paedophiles do not always involve physical contact yet cause some children psychological distress. Consequently, indecent exposure, sexual activity in a public toilet and voyeurism were all established as offences. Grooming behaviour was also criminalised – whether or not it was computer based. Grooming is the process of gaining a child's trust and possibly setting up a situation whereby the adult is alone with the child with the intention of committing some sort of sexual activity. The UK Act established as a crime circumstances in which an adult contacts a child under 16 years of age on the Internet, face-to-face meetings, or via the telephone on at least two occasions and then attempts to meet that child with the intention of sexual abuse either on that or a subsequent occasion.

## GROWING CONTROLS ON OFFENDERS: SEX OFFENDER REGISTRATION AND NOTIFICATION

A key move towards the effective management of known sex offenders was the Sex Offender Register, with or without, community notification. The State of Washington in the US introduced both in 1990. They are among the most familiar of a spate of activities and initiatives designed to exercise greater control on offenders and to protect children. Howitt (2006b) describes how anyone with the minimum of effort can check the names of registered sex offenders in many of the states of the US, such as Virginia (Malesky and Keim, 2001). The Jacob Wetterling Act of 1994 was an American federal law that required states to create sex offender registers. Initially, there was no requirement for US states to develop a system of notifying the public about who was on that list. Megan's Law of 1996 changed that by introducing community notification of 'dangerous' sex offenders though the precise method of implementation was for each State to decide (Thomas, 2005). Megan was Megan Kanka who, in 1994, at the age of seven years, was abducted from her New Jersey neighbourhood, raped and murdered. She had been enticed into the home of a convicted sex offender living just over the road from her with the promise that he would show her his puppy. That he was a twice-convicted sex offender was unknown to Megan's parents and the rest of the community (Tewksbury, 2002; Thomas, 2005).

Community notification is the US phrase to describe the process of public dissemination of information from the Sex Offender Register (Thomas, 2005). The assumption of the law is that by officially notifying communities of a sexual offender living locally, parents and others can in some way protect children against future victimisation (Fitch, 2006; Hudson, 2005). The community would be better protected because those sex offenders undergoing extensive notification will know that they are under surveillance and thus will be deterred from reoffending (Malesky and Keim, 2001; Zevitz, 2006).

Precisely how the public is informed about sex offenders in their community varies. The US notification provisions operate on a three-tier system of risk assessment (Brooks, 1996). Tier 1 refers to those low in risk of reoffending. Tier 2 incorporates those with a moderate risk of reoffending (information regarding such offenders is passed onto schools and other organisations caring for children). Tier 3 refers to those who are a high risk of reoffending (information is also distributed to families living with a stipulated distance of the home of the offender). Therefore, only those offenders classified as high risk (Tier 3) are subject to full community notification (Hudson, 2005).

The manner of notifying communities varies between states; sex offenders may be required to wear identifiable clothing (Hudson, 2005), posters or flyers may be displayed that list their crimes and the cost of these are met by the offender (Fitch, 2006), sex offender registry 'Web sites' may be set up (Malesky and Keim, 2001) and offenders may be required to put a sticker on the bumper of their cars (Winick, 1998). Some States have databases of sex offenders, which can be accessed locally through the police (Fitch, 2006). Lovell (2001) describes the inter-state variation as involving (a) different risk assessment procedures, (b) different procedures by which the public are informed and (c) the penalties involved when the public engages in vigilante actions against sex offenders. The onus is on those who receive information about dangerous sex offenders to use that information responsibly. Further legislation quickly followed Megan's Law in the US including The Pam Lychner Sexual Offender Tracking and Identification Act of 1996. This required that the worst sex offenders remain on the Sex Offender Register for life and later legislation has introduced further stringencies on, for example, recidivists (Bureau of Justice Assistance, 2006).

At one level, the argument in favour of sex offender community notification seems self-evident - parents knowing that there are sex offenders living nearby can protect their children. Fifty-eight per cent UK adults believe that convicted paedophiles should be 'named and shamed' (MORI/News of the World, 2000). But there is some evidence that suggests that things are not that simple. For example, it is known that registration compliance by sex offenders is greater in the UK (which does *not* have community notification) than in the US (which does) (Howitt, 2006b). One obvious interpretation of this is that community notification deters offenders from registration. This means that their whereabouts is unknown so, consequently, the police, for example, do not have access to this important information. In Washington State reoffending by sex offenders was 22 % but it declined to 19 % following Megan's law (Silverman and Wilson, 2002). This, though, was not a statistically reliable decline.

The question still remains of whether community notification laws are beneficial. In a rare study exploring sex offenders' responses to US community notification, Elbogen, Patry and Scalora (2003) found that two-thirds of sex offenders believed that it was an incentive to not reoffend. In contrast, the same study argued that notification has several negative effects. Specifically, being labelled as a sex offender may result in men feeling that they have less self-control and consequently they may be less motivated to participate in treatment, for example. Sex offenders may show a degree of unfamiliarity with the relevant law which suggests potential accidental breaches as a result of misunderstandings. The feelings of unfairness might potentially translate into increased or decreased recidivism though there is not direct evidence on this.

Freeman-Longo (1996) identified 24 concerns related to public notification, including, *inter alia*, the impact on the victim and the offender's family. Some studies suggest that incest sex crimes are less likely to be reported by a family for fear that their details will become common knowledge (Edwards and Hensley, 2001). Fitch (2006) conducted a review of the evidence for community notification in the US in States including Louisiana, California, Washington State, Minnesota and Vermont and argued that there was very little to suggest that community notification had an impact on offending. There was no evidence that community notification had a positive impact on offender recidivism rates or that it resulted in fewer assaults on children. There was also little to suggest that paedophiles used the publicly available information to contact other offenders. In terms of the success of community notification, Fitch found that some practitioners spoke of the increased use of risk assessments, better information sharing and additional funding for treatment and surveillance. Fitch points out, however, that these good practices were distinct from the community notification element for which there was no evidence of benefits. Furthermore, there was very little monitoring of vigilantism, which is believed to be underreported and under-recorded. She also suggested that there may be exaggerated fears among the general public as the laws exaggerate the true level of offender recidivism.

The UK does not have a 'Megan's Law' although MAPPA arrangements have the discretion of notifying the public on a 'need-to-know' basis (Fitch, 2006). This can involve telling immediate neighbours, previous victims, schools, community centres and so on. However, in December 2006, the Child Exploitation and Online Protection Centre, which describes itself as a 'virtual police station', posted a 'most wanted' list on its Web site. This consisted of 'missing' child sex offenders who had breached various notification requirements. The Centre was anxious to locate them and their names, aliases, photos, physical descriptions, age, height, build, location, distinguishing marks and any other potentially helpful information was posted. In other words, information about known sex offenders was being made public.

Public calls for access to the Sex Offender Register also emerge from time to time especially in response to significant and highly publicised cases. In particular, public demands heightened in 2000 following the unprecedented media coverage of the abduction and murder of Sarah Payne by Roy Whiting – a predatory paedophile – who was living nearby in the community. Whiting had been previously imprisoned for the abduction and indecent assault of a 9-year-old girl. He was a registered sex offender known to the local Multi-Agency Public Protection Panel. The *News of the World* started published photographs and names of known sex offenders in its controversial 'naming and shaming' campaign which led to a week of demonstrations, acts of public disorder and vigilantism in several areas (Thomas, 2005), sometimes against entirely innocent individuals. One incident involved vigilantes who vandalised the home of a doctor – a paediatrician (Allison, *Guardian*, 2000) leading to the then Home Secretary, David Blunkett, stating that 'we cannot open the register to vigilantes who do not understand the difference between paediatricians and paedophiles' (Thomas, 2005, p. 167).

The UK sex offender registration legislation grew out of a Home Office consultation paper *Sentencing and Supervision of Sex Offenders* (Home Office 1996a). This proposed that convicted sex offenders should notify the police of any change to their address. Of course, this idea had been mooted for a while and the Police Superintendents Association was most supportive of calls for such a register (Thomas, 2005). The UK Sex Offender Register began 1 September 1997 following the requirements of the Sex Offender Act 1997. The Register was assumed to serve as a crime prevention measure, a means of identifying suspects, and conceivably as a deterrent (Plotnikoff and Woolfson, 2000).

Professionals such as the police and probation officers felt, generally, that disclosure of the whereabouts of sex offenders to the general public would not be beneficial (Maguire *et al.*, 2001). Plotnikoff and Woolfson (2000) found that the police are supportive of the Register for improving working relationships with other agencies and, subsequently, improving the quality of offender information. The police, however, also reported negative aspects of the Register including the creation of unrealistic expectations of the public, resources being diverted from other higher risk offenders and inadequate resources for the monitoring of offenders (Plotnikoff and Woolfson, 2000).

The journal *Community Care* conducted a survey of 200 social workers on their views of the register's usefulness. Most felt it diverted attention to the idea that sexual abuse of children is carried out by strangers ('stranger danger') and away from the crucial fact that children are more at danger of being sexually abused by their own or extended families (Valios, 1998). Mental health workers suggested, similarly, that parents may be led to feel that an adult in the community is 'safe', say, to babysit their child simply because their name is not on the Sex Offender Register (Malesky and Keim, 2001). Furthermore, Sex Offender Registers, by and large, involve convicted offenders but other 'dangerous' individuals who have not been convicted may go by ignored (Fitch, 2006).

Plotnikoff and Woolfson (2000) found compliance with the registration process to be good at 94.7% in the UK but it can be argued that there is a difference between whether or not the Register works procedurally and whether children are protected by it (Thomas, 2005). It is particularly difficult to evaluate the impact of the Sex Offender Register by using the UK Criminal Statistics figures because some offences that require registration (such as possession of indecent photographs of children) are not sexual offences as defined in the criminal statistics (Plotnikoff and Woolfson, 2000). There were also no published figures on reconviction rates among offenders with a registration requirement. (Although more recent newspaper reports of research suggest that very few registered sex and violent offenders reoffend with a serious offence while on the Register (*Daily Telegraph*, 2004)). Sex offender disclosure to the general public risks the possibility that offenders become socially ostracised, reinforcing some of the emotional responses that triggered their offending behaviour (Edwards and Hensley, 2001).

However, the Home Office is currently undertaking an in-depth review of sex offender management and Megan's Law in the UK. In 2006 the Under Secretary of State for Criminal Justice and Offender Management visited New Jersey to learn more about the implementation of community notification laws in the US (Carvel, 2006).

## ONCE CONVICTED: SENTENCING AND CONTROL

Generally, sentences for contact offences against children have increased over the years as well as new offences being introduced. Mandatory life sentences have been introduced for serious sexual and/or violent offenders on a *second* conviction (Crime (Sentences) Act 1997, section 2), unless there are reasons for not doing so stated publicly in open court by the judge. Detention may also be extended until death by the Home Secretary (Hudson, 2005). Moreover, there are the somewhat controversial 'imprisonment for public protection' sentences (Hudson, 2005). These 'absolute prevention' measures (as opposed to 'harm-reduction' measures) (Laws, 1996) allow the justice system to detain those assessed as posing a 'significant risk to the public' and being 'dangerous' after they have committed a relevant sexual (or violent) offence such as rape of a child (Criminal Justice Act 2003, section, 225; Gillespie, 2005a). In other words, a sex offender's length of prison sentence could be indefinite, with release dependent on judgements of 'risk' by a parole board. Not surprisingly, the civil liberties group Liberty questioned whether such sentences are acceptable under the European Convention on Human Rights (Liberty, 2002).

Clearly, there are issues concerning the vague and subjective nature of 'dangerousness' in this context, hence making the identification of 'dangerous' people problematic. There were similar penalties during the 1970s 'dangerousness debate' – for example the 'reviewable sentence' (Butler Committee, 1975; Floud and Young, 1981). But these were successfully rejected due to the problem of false negatives – that is, the extended incarceration of a person based on the incorrect prediction that they *will* commit another offence (Bottoms, 1977).

Sex offenders may be seen as getting out 'too early' and that a five-year sentence should mean five years in prison (Thomas, 2005). The Crime and Disorder Act 1998 introduced the concept of 'extended supervision' which is an extended period of supervision tagged onto the custodial sentence

(Thomas, 2005). Freedom is limited during this period of extended supervision. The length of the extended licence for a sex offender is 10 years. Thus
this considerably extends supervision of 'high risk' offenders. Similar supervision may apply when a sex offender is sentenced to a 'community sentence'.
The sentence is in the form of a community rehabilitation order (previously
probation order) which can include additional conditions in terms of behaviour that should, or should not, be done. A sex offender might, for example,
be ordered to (a) attend a sex-offender treatment programme, (b) not to take
employment or leisure pursuits bringing them into contact with children, and
(c) not to visit the home of a child or receive visits from a child without the
permission from the service (HMIP, 1998). Similar contingencies may be
applied to ex-prisoners released on licence. The public's perception of community rehabilitation orders is that they are not a punishment (Gillespie,
2003). In contrast, the Community Punishment and Rehabilitation Order adds
to the element of punishment such as requiring greater numbers of hours
working in the community.

Compliance with supervisory orders, additional conditions and ensuring
their enforcement have become increasingly important (Thomas, 2005). Technological solutions have been put forward for helping the supervision of sex
offenders. This includes the use of polygraph testing (Travis, 2004). In parts of
the world the polygraph evidence is not acceptable in court; in other countries
it is (Howitt, 2006b). It is also fairly commonplace in the US and there are at
least 70 other countries in the world where the polygraph is used extensively
(Grubin and Madsen, 2005). The use of the polygraph is also increasing in
countries that previously shunned its use as evidence of guilt. For instance, in
the UK the government has initiated trials of the use of the polygraph in the
supervision and management of sex offenders when they are released back
into the community (Grubin *et al.*, 2004; Madsen, Parsons and Grubin, 2004).
Thus denials by paedophiles that they are targeting school playgrounds or
parks where children are playing can be assessed using polygraph techniques.
It is argued that this has prevented the sexual abuse of further victims and led
to the re-imprisonment of some offenders (BBC News, 27 November 2005).
Tagging in conjunction with mobile telephones may provide systems for the
tracking of offenders on some form of community licence across a wide
geographical area (Doward, 2003). 'Reverse monitoring' systems, similar to
those used in the US, have been piloted. For this, the monitoring equipment is
in the possession of the potential victim and it is the approach of the offender
that triggers the alarm (Whitfield, 1997). Other proposals of a technological
nature include identifying the eye's unique characteristics using a scanner
(Home Office, 2002).

The toughening process has also applied to the Sex Offender Register. For
instance, initial reporting requirements were altered from 14 days to three
days and are required to be in person at a police station (email and post are not
permitted). The police now have powers to photograph and fingerprint
offenders on initial reporting for registration (Criminal Justice and Court
Services Act 2000). Sanctions for failing to comply with the requirements of
registration can be as high as five years in prison. Some have suggested that

strengthening the Register in this way is an attempt to circumvent the demands by the public for full access to the names of offenders within the community (Thomas, 2005).

Other recent changes to the Sex Offender Register procedures include registrants reporting changes to their situation (for example, accommodation) within three days at a police station and in person; being required to report to a police station annually; reporting stays at other addresses of more than seven days (previously 14 days); and National Insurance numbers being used as a form of identification (Sexual Offences Act 2003; Thomas, 2005). Furthermore, offenders who receive a conditional discharge for an offence are now subject to registration as if they had been convicted and sentenced (Sexual Offences Act 2003) – which is a situation very removed from dealing with convicted paedophiles who were the initial driving force of public worries (Hebenton and Thomas, 1996).

The length of time of registration depends on the age of offender, the age of the victim and the length of sentence. For instance, registration for an adult offender who receives a custodial sentence of thirty months or more is for life. If the custodial sentence is between six and thirty months then registration is for 10 years but this declines to seven years for sentences of less than six months. Registration is for five years if the offender is cautioned (formal reprimand at a police station by a senior police officer) or if the sentence is not custodial. These periods of registration are halved for offenders aged less than 18 years at the time of the offence (Hudson, 2005; Plotnikoff and Woolfson, 2000; Sentence Advisory Panel, 2002; Thomas, 2005).

An offender on the Sex Offender Register will also be subject to monitoring arrangements while in the community. These are Multi-Agency Public Protection Panels (MAPPP) which involve statutory involvement of the police, probation and prison services to work jointly to establish arrangements for the assessment and management of sexual offenders in the community (Criminal Justice and Court Services Act, 2000 sections 67 to 68). Offenders dealt with by MAPPPs include registered sex offenders, violent offenders sentenced to 12 months or more in custody, other sexual offenders who are not required to register on the Sex Offender Register and offenders who, having served their sentence, still pose a risk to the public. This group of offenders must have a previous conviction (committed anywhere) which indicates that they are capable of causing serious harm (Criminal Justice and Court Services Act 2000 sections 67–8).

There are a number of further provisions available to help manage sex-offending behaviour to achieve greater community safety (Home Office, 15 April 2004; Thomas, 2005). For instance, a range of more innovative measures has been introduced:

• *The Sexual Offences Prevention Order* (SOPO): this is a new civil order that has been introduced by the Sexual Offences Act (2003). It is actually a combination of two pre-existing orders – the sex offender order and the restraining order (Gillespie, 2005d) and are both described as an 'injunction-type order' (Gillespie, 2005d, p. 14) in that they prevent the offender from doing anything named within the order. For instance, the police can apply for an order if anyone with a known history of previous sexual offences against children is seen as demonstrating 'trigger' activities (such as acting 'suspiciously' near a children's playground). The order then prohibits the person's activities. For example, the order could prevent an individual from hanging around a school or going to children's playgrounds. It also requires individuals to register if they have not already done so. Breaching the order is a criminal offence and individuals can receive a sentence of up to five years in prison (Sexual Offences Act 2003). Therefore, the offender's conduct may be perfectly 'lawful', but it may result in criminal sanctions.

- *The Foreign Travel Order.* This is designed to deal with sex offenders against children attempting to travel abroad thus putting children there at risk. The police apply for the order against an individual who is then unable to travel to specified countries or even to travel abroad at all (Sexual Offences Act 2003, sections 114–22). Failure to comply is a criminal offence.

- *The Notification Order.* This enables the police to apply for notification for anyone with a relevant sexual offence abroad who is regarded as a public risk on arrival in the UK (Sexual Offences Act 2003). Having received a notification order, the individual has to be registered on the Sex Offender Register and is thus subject to all of the requirements of the Register.

- *The mandatory block.* Generally speaking, this involves the use of a disqualification order that places a legal ban on certain people being allowed to work with children. A person, on sentencing for a sexual offence against a child, may be issued such a disqualification order (The Criminal Justice Act 2003). If the disqualified person applies for, or obtains, work with children then they are committing an offence. After 10 years, adult offenders may appeal the disqualification to the Care Standards Tribunal. A juvenile offender can appeal after 5 years.

- *The 'police check'.* This is a system by which applicants for public employment involving access to children are subjected to a process of pre-employment screening. This would include teachers, social workers, youth workers and the like. Failures of the system have produced public outcries and media headlines. For instance it was found that the police held intelligence on Ian Huntley (convicted of two child murders in 2003) regarding nine earlier suspected sexual offences. None had been disclosed to employers when he was given a caretaker's job at the college where he had access to children. In 1993 a Home Office review showed that over the seven years when the 'police check' was operating, the number of checks rose dramatically (Home Office, 1993). Because of the pressures on the police consequently a new Criminal Records Agency was proposed (Home Office, 1996b).

- *Enhanced disclosure.* The Criminal Records Bureau started in 2002. It has direct access to the Police National Computer. Enhanced disclosure is for those working in child care and standard disclosure is for those with some contact with children. Enhanced disclosure is very similar to the old 'police check' but, instead of going to the police, employers simply go to the Criminal Records Bureau who search their databases for conviction records and approach local police forces for any further information they need (Thomas, 2005). Enhanced disclosure also requires the Criminal Records Bureau to access two lists – the 'Consultancy Service' and 'List 99'. Essentially being included on these lists bars an individual from working with children. These have since been renamed as the 'Protection of Children Act List' and the Department of Education and Employment List' (Thomas, 2005). Employers can use these two sources of data in order to screen would-be employees.

## INTERNATIONAL CONSIDERATIONS

The international situation concerning legislation on child sexual abuse is inevitably extremely complex and it is impossible to offer a definitive statement on this matter. There is the problematic nature of child abuse, no standard way of categorising child sexual abuse and huge variations in legal definitions between countries and regions. As an example, in Poland sexual intercourse with a family member (including adopted daughters, for example) is punishable by a prison sentence of between three months and five years (International Criminal Police Organization (Interpol), 2005). This contrasts with a sentence of two years in Sweden for sexual intercourse with one's offspring and just one year for sexual intercourse with one's sibling.

Sex offending is an international problem. The United Nations describe the sexual exploitation of children as a global phenomenon which is to be found in both developing and developed countries and which is becoming increasingly complex due to its transnational scope (UN, 1996). And international agencies and countries are responding to the problem or at least acknowledging that child sexual abuse does occur. The Council of Europe asked its member states to review their legislation and practice to better protect children (Council of Europe, 1991) and the European Union has made the same demand of its members following public demonstrations in the streets of Brussels against a child murderer in Belgium (Thomas, 2005). International concerns also centre on child prostitution (General Secretariat, 2003) and Internet sex offending (Renold et al., 2003).

Legislation is far from the only response to sexual abuse. 'Circles of Support and Accountability' projects in Canada and the USA bring the community into helping manage the offender (Silverman and Wilson, 2002). They have been piloted in the UK by Thames Valley and Hampshire Probation Services and the Lucy Faithful Foundation (Birmingham) (Hudson, 2005). Aimed at high-risk offenders who have little or no support in the community, the 'circle' comprises of four to six community volunteers who provide support through weekly meetings, telephone conversations and help with resettlement (Quaker Peace and Social Witness, 2003).

## CONCLUDING COMMENTS

One message dominates legislation about sex offenders and has increasingly done so over the last two or three decades. That is, that sex offenders have to be punished and that these punishments are frequently inadequate and need extending. The multitude of changes in legislation for sentencing of sex offenders may be bewildering in detail but boil down to this simple trend of escalating punishment. In addition to this increase in punishment, there are other measures that restrict the activities of sex offenders in the community. All of these amount to attempts to minimise the threat of sex offenders (Hudson, 2002). Inherent in the legislation is the presumption that sex offenders are persistent reoffenders and are extremely dangerous either now or, if not now, at some time in the future. Researchers have contributed to this view that sex offending is habitual and almost like an addiction which will escalate if not checked (for example, Abel *et al.*, 1987). On the other hand, crime statistics and research evidence consistently paint a different picture – one in which sex offenders have relatively low recorded crime rates and tend to be the least likely group to reoffend (see, for example, Hanson and Bussiere, 1998). This is known to be the case in England and Wales, Europe and North America (Grubin, 1998). Of course, sex offending is very much an unreported crime (Grubin, 1998) so some may wish to argue that low recidivism rates simply reflect low reporting and detection rates. Probably the best statement of the situation is that there are many sex offenders who offend but then desist from reoffending but there is also a much smaller number who constantly reoffend and who are difficult to deter (Fisher and Thornton, 1993; Grubin, 1998; Hanson and Bussiere, 1998). For the former group of offenders, current legislation may seem draconian; for the latter group of offenders, legislation may appear barely to suffice.

Sex offenders receive disproportionate attention compared with their numbers. Society, in general, finds their offences repulsive and heinous and child victims are a major source of concern and sympathy (Mair, 1995). Some criminologists see measures such as the Sex Offender Register as mechanisms primarily designed to allay public fears about the threat posed by sex offenders (Hudson, 2005). Much the same has been said of community notification. These may appear to provide a rapid and firm government response to outcries about sex offending (Garland, 2001). Megan's Law in the US took no more than two months to enact (Hudson, 2005) leading to the claim that it was a quick-fix appeasement of public outrage (Brooks, 1996). While the UK does not have a Megan's law, the Multi-Agency Public Protection Panel was quickly given the task of providing an annual report of how many registered sex offenders there were in a specified area following the Sarah Payne murder (Hudson, 2005). Perhaps for similar public relations reasons, the Home Office began recruiting lay advisors to Multi-Agency Public Protection Panels in 2004 as part of the Panel's strategic decision-making process (Home Office, 15 April 2004; Hudson, 2005). Some have suggested that this may have been in order to deal with calls for community notification (Hudson, 2005; Thomas, 2005; Kemshall and Maguire, 2003).

Such is the legislative environment surrounded by the pressures of public opinion into which the issue of Internet sex offending emerged. While some Internet sex offenders may receive lighter sentences compared to child molesters, this is hardly true of their treatment once their sentence is served. Internet sex offenders will receive the same treatment when back in the community as any other released sex offender. They will remain on the Sex Offender Register for a number of years and, consequently, their behaviours will be reviewed and monitored.

All of this, however, does little about those offenders who are not caught.

# CHAPTER 5

# What Internet Sex Offenders Do

It would be a simple matter to become an Internet child pornographer. A paedophile could easily scan a child pornography magazine for storage on their hard drive or perhaps onto compact discs in order to make them portable (Quayle and Taylor, 2002a). An image, once in digital form can be endlessly reproduced without putting image quality at jeopardy. Equally, the paedophile could search the Internet for pornographic images and these images printed out or displayed on the computer screen. It would be easy to send the child pornography images to another e-mail address. Of course, all of this would make the user vulnerable to detection and prosecution, so somewhat less obvious methods are often employed.

Files on the World Wide Web are, technically, hypertext pages (http://) which are linked together so that the user can quickly move from one link to another. Web Browsers are computer applications which facilitate access to the World Wide Web. Some files are to be found on password protected websites which generate revenue by selling products and services (Sommer, 2003). Having located such a website and having paid the entry subscription fee, images, for example, can be viewed on screen or downloaded to the user's computer. In many countries, Internet Service Providers would close down any website which use their services for illicit purposes since effective ways exist for identifying the owners of illicit websites (Internet Watch Foundation, 2004; Sommer, 2003). As a consequence, paedophile websites are more likely to be set up in countries where legal controls, in general, or controls on the Internet, in particular, are weak (Sommer, 2003). The Internet Watch Foundation Annual Report (2004) drew attention to the increasing number of websites hosted in countries like Russia and Asia (IWF, 2004). Western men interested in children sexually visit such websites to increase their collections (Durkin, 1997; Taylor and Quayle, 2003; Sommer, 2003).

Jenkins (2001) discusses the complexity of the Internet methods by which child pornography can be obtained while minimizing the legal risks to the user. Some of the more important components are as follows:

## Usenet

It is believed that the major source of pornographic material on the Internet is the USENET (Carr, 2003; Renold *et al.*, 2003; Taylor, Quayle and Holland, 2001; IWF, 1998, 2000). The USENET is a well-established global Internet service (Sommer, 2003) dating from 1980. It consists of tens of thousands of themed 'newsgroups' where a catalogue of messages, called 'articles', on the same general topic can be found. This is not modern technology for the most part and hence does not allow participants to interact on a real-time basis. Instead users can drop into the service from time-to-time to update themselves on the discussions (Sommer, 2003). Each article has a brief description of what it contains to help the user decide whether to download it or not. The articles may simply be read or a reply can be sent either privately by email or publicly on the newsgroup. The result is a chain of comments, some with attachments, which form a 'message thread' (Brookes, 2003). Newsgroups tend to be organised into categories according to their major focus. These categories include alt (alternative lifestyles), misc (miscellaneous), rec (recreational) and so forth which give users some indication as to the contents of the newsgroup. So alt.sex.fetish.feet would contain discussion of the sexual nature of feet, alt.sex.stories would contain stories range from 'tame' bondage to snuff ones, and on alt.sex.zoophile sex with animals would be the topic (Kim and Bailey, 1997). The use of USENET has grown significantly. Figures indicated that in 1996, there were something like 13,000 to 14,000 newsgroups (Blatchford, 1996) which had increased to 30,000 to 40,000 by 2001 (Taylor, Quayle and Holland, 2001) and reached 80,000 by 2003 (Robbins and       Darlington, 2003; Renold, *et al.*, 2003). A wide variety of topics from education and science to alternative lifestyles are covered. Many of the sex related newsgroups deal with serious, legitimate issues such as homosexuality (Blatchford, 1996) and only a very small number are thought to carry child pornography (Sommer, 2003; IWF, 1998; 2000; 2003).

Newsgroups offer anonymity to paedophiles (Sommer, 2003). They are 'places' where men may discuss the type of victims they would like to meet, exchange sexual fantasies, and to obtain suggestions about potential victims (Quayle and Taylor, 2001; McGrath and Casey, 2002). Sex offenders may use such discussion forums to ask for practical advice such as regarding computer problems or the availability of new software (Quayle and Taylor, 2002a). They also request, swap and post pictures from and to others who share similar sexual interests in children (Durkin, 1997; Quayle and Taylor, 2002a, b; Quayle, and Taylor, 2001). Pornographic images are believed to be employed as a kind of currency; they legitimatize paedophile activity and create a sense of community (Sommer, 2003; Quayle and Taylor, 2002b; Taylor, Quayle and Holland, 2001). Pornographic images can remain on a server for some time allowing communication with like-minded people to increase dramatically. Even if the authorities locate an image, this does not mean that the distribution of it is impaired or stopped. Once an image becomes available on the Internet, it can be downloaded by any number of users and can be reproduced repeatedly (Healy, 1997). Most Internet service providers offer Usenet access as part of their normal Internet package but some restrict access to newsgroups with an obvious illegal content. However, they can still be accessed by opening an account with a commercial uncensored newsgroup service provider, for example.

Users of child pornography can exchange with each other by 'going direct client-to-client' (DCC). This means that they leave the Internet Relay Chat server system and set up a direct computer-to-computer link (Sommer, 2003; Quayle and Taylor, 2002a). *Panzer* is a popular facility for individuals wishing to swap substantial amounts of files. This automates file trading such that the user does not have to be continually present. This is also referred to as Fserver (short for file server). One of its advantages is that users can access parts of another person's hard drive in order to exchange files (Taylor, Quayle and Holland, 2001a). People trading in child pornography want new material in exchange for sending theirs (Sommer, 2003). Programs such as *Panzer* enable the individual to set a ratio system in place whereby a proportion of files have to be returned in exchange for the files that are sent.

## Peer-to-peer

*Peer-to-peer* is another method for sharing large numbers of files. It was originally developed for sharing music files (MP3) as in the case of *Napster* (Sommer, 2003). *Kazaa* also exploits this system to enable users to share files and upload or download material. Participants connect to a central computer that extracts from their computer a list of files that can be shared. A master database is generated which users can search for files that they wish to download. Once an individual identifies a file they want, the service puts them in touch with the original computer that holds it. The central computer never holds the images or files (Brookes, 2003; Sommer, 2003). Some anonymity is possible through the use of pseudonyms though techniques are available to reveal actual identities (Brookes, 2003). Since this is a good file transfer system, it became an important means of exchanging child pornography images and other illicit material (Brookes, 2003; Renold *et al.*, 2003; Carr, 2003).

## Bulletin Board Systems

*Bulletin Board Systems* are 'high tech party lines by which users can send and receive messages, run conversations, and upload and download files' (Durkin and Bryant, 1995, p.183). Bulletin boards are as they imply – a place where messages can be left and read. Sometimes they also offer chat rooms. They have been part of the activities of child pornographers since the 1980s (Tate, 1990) since they facilitate contact between individuals with similar interests. Just about any sexual interest can be dealt with. The service is accessed by contacting the service's inbound telephone number which can be obtained from porn or computer magazines – and, of course, directly from other paedophiles. Users of the service may be asked to complete a registration process and to pay a fee (Durkin and Bryant, 1995). Bulletin boards required neither licenses nor registration in most countries (Healy, 1997).

## CU-C-ME

*CU-C-ME (See You, See Me)* is a video-conferencing protocol allowing the user to use a camcorder to transmit live video images to other computers in the same network anywhere worldwide (Kim and Bailey, 1997; Taylor and Quayle, 2003). This type of teleconferencing allows the users to send text as well as to see and hear other users. Anonymity is lost, of course, and users cannot easily pretend that they are someone that they are not. Such a system allows the real-time transfer of images of sexual acts and on command (Kim and Bailey, 1997). Thus the system in conjunction with readily available digital equipment provides the capacity of virtually anyone to become a pornography 'producer' at home (Thomas and Wyatt, 1999; Healy, 1997). Computers come with built in microphones and speakers and digital cameras which can convert photographs, slides, negatives, and text into computer characters. There are also video capture devices which can record images from a video camera or VCR directly into the computer. It is thought that paedophiles in the *Orchid Club* videotaped themselves sexually abusing five to ten year old girls and then streamed some of the images live on the Internet. One particular example was the sexual abuse of a five-year old girl with at least 11 men watching. The abuse was 'interactive' in that the 'viewers' posted requests to the abusers as to the kind of sexual activities they would like to see happen next (Kim and Bailey, 1997).

## Chatrooms

A chat room typically appears as a small window on the computer screen. Chat rooms are cyber-places where numbers of people 'chat' (type) simultaneously to each other. Everyone's 'chat' shows on the screen in real-time. It is possible to chat in private to another person and, of course, the topics can be anything including cybersex and arranging to meet. Users can make material available to others via file transfer or live web cam images. A degree of anonymity is achieved by the use of pseudonyms. A considerable array of different styles of chat rooms are available through major Internet service providers (Home Office, 2003; Taylor and Quayle, 2003; Brookes, 2003). Chat rooms are thought popular with adolescents (Home Office, 2003). Many of them have an instant messaging service to let users know when their friends are on-line. Concerns have been raised about chat rooms since they allow paedophiles direct and immediate contact in real time with potential victims. Other concerns include the possibility for chat with a child to occur in private such that the conversation is unmonitored by other users (Home Office, 2003). Furthermore, companies which provide instant messaging services require users to register and provide personal information (e.g. age, gender and location etc). However, this information can be visible to other users and is sometimes shared (Home Office, 2003).

## HOW INTERNET OFFENDERS OPERATE

While there are clearly different Internet facilities which may allow sex offenders against children access to children and child pornography, it is important to consider precisely how offenders use the Internet in their offending behaviour. The development of strategies for preventing Internet crime may be partly dependent on just how well we understand the on-line behaviour of paedophiles. Among the important questions that need to be asked from this perspective are:

- How do offenders locate child abuse images?
- Which Internet areas and resources do Internet sex offenders exploit to commit their crimes?
- What behaviours do the offenders manifest both on- and off-line?

During our intensive interviews with Internet-Only, Contact-Only and Mixed-Internet Contact sex offenders, we gathered considerable amounts of information about their activities (see Box 5.1 for details of our research methodology). Internet offending occurred mostly in domestic settings as the majority of offenders used their home computers. Home is both a convenient and relatively secure setting but other locations were used, For instance, about one in five offenders used a computer at work or at a university when committing their crimes - riskier settings for illicit activities since large organizations such as universities actively monitor for illegal use of the Internet. Locations such as Internet cafés were rarely used presumably because of their public nature.

---

**BOX 5.1: THE OFFENDER STUDY**

The major methodological features of our study of 51 sex offenders against children are described here. Since the study started with the premise that we knew little about Internet offenders compared to the traditional contact offenders, the study was designed to be a comparative study of these two groups of offender. The participants (90 %) were largely recruited from prisoners in vulnerable prisoners units. The remainder were recruited via the probation services. As such, the sample is clearly more representative of offenders receiving custodial sentences for their offending. However, they do represent a greater variety of offenders than previous in-depth studies in which involve members of a particular Internet paedophile 'club', for

---

example. All the 51 offenders that we studied were white males and all but were two were British. Participants were volunteers and were classified both in terms of their index offence(s) and any previous child sexual convictions identifiable from their criminal records. There were three distinct groups that we identified:

- Internet-only paedophiles: Adult men (over 21 years) whose index sexual offence(s) and any previous sexual conviction(s) involve Internet child pornography. Internet pornography offences include the downloading (the legal definition is 'making'), distribution or possession of indecent images/videos of children from the Internet. This group had no *known* history of direct contact offences against children, 19 % ($n = 3$) had a history of previous Internet pornography offences There were 16 cases.
- Contact-only paedophiles: These are adult men who had no known convictions for Internet offences involving children or child pornography. Mostly these offenders had employed direct physical sexual contact with their victims (e.g. indecent assault, rape, gross indecency, and so forth). Thirty six per cent of them had previous convictions for contact sexual offences against children. These offenders constituted the largest group that we studied ($n = 25$).
- Mixed Internet-contact offenders: Adult men whose index sexual offence(s) and any previous sexual convictions involved both Internet pornography and direct physical sexual contact with children. Two men were the exception to this. One participant had Internet pornography offences and a gross indecency offence, which involving masturbating in front of a group of children and propositioning them into acts of gross indecency and another participant's offences included Internet pornography offences and an offence against the telecommunications act, which involved grooming a child over the Internet (prior to the new offence of grooming). These two participants were included into the study in the mixed-offence group. All but one participant in this category had no previous contact offences against children. This was the smallest group that we studied ($n = 10$).

All of the men participated in psychometric testing and also an in-depth qualitative interview. We also systematically assessed 33 background characteristics including date of birth, nationality, sentences received, numbers of indecent images involved in the conviction, and psychiatric history from the data sources available to us. The psychometric assessment was conducted on an individual testing basis. For the most part, standard assessment measures were employed as the basic resource though these had to be adapted or consolidated in some cases to be suitable for use with Internet offenders as well as contact offenders. The choice of measures used was intended to include the major psychological variables which our knowledge of the research and professional literature suggested were in some way involved in offending. We placed particular emphasis on integrative theories of child sexual abuse. The in-depth qualitative interviews were predicated on the need to find out some very basic information about Internet offending as well as contact offending. These interviews provided us with rich data, which, in part, could be used in conjunction with the psychometric data to supplement our understanding. Furthermore, we were interested in the processes involved in offending, which cannot adequately be assessed using quantitative data only. Wherever possible, we tried to quantify the qualitative material. The interview schedule consisted of over 40 questions covering four distinct aspects of paedophile offending (Ward and Siegert, 2002) such as insecure childhood attachment and adult attachment deficits, deviant sexual fantasy and experiences of sexual victimisation, inadequate coping strategies, and cognitive distortions. Further questions were included in order to find explanations of the index offending and to help elucidate the meaning of the quantitative data.

The three groups of offenders were very similar in age, with the means being in the range 46 to 47 years in each case. The age that we used was their age at the time of the index offence conviction. In this light, it is important to note that the average sentence in months for the three groups did differ. Internet-only offenders had an average sentence of 28 months compared to 51 months for contact-only offenders and 52 months for mixed Internet-contact offenders. The groups differed in terms of their numbers of previous convictions. The contact-only group had on average 14 previous convictions whereas the Internet only and mixed groups averaged one previous conviction in each case.

The three groups did differ in terms of the number of years they spent in education. Internet-only offenders averaged 14 years in education, mixed Internet-and-contact offenders 13 years and contact offenders only 11 years. Similar education differences favouring Internet sex offenders has previously been found by Burke, Sowerbutts, Blundell and Sherry (2001). This is keeping with the offender groups' occupations before conviction. Sixty three per cent of Internet offenders had been employed in a professional rather than a manual worker capacity. Contact offenders had overwhelmingly been employed is manual occupations (84%). Mixed offenders had been employed equally in manual and professional occupations. Sullivan and Beech (2004) found that a third of the professionals who abused the children in their care admitted accessing Internet pornography and one in ten of them had used the Internet in order to contact children.

But, in other respects, the three groups were very similar. There was no difference in terms of having had psychological treatment for their offending, or having dependants, or their marital status at the time of the index offences. Despite this, it is notable that Internet offenders were more likely to be with a partner when we interviewed them than were contact offenders. This may reflect the negative impact of the conviction on the relationships of contact offenders.

The use of disinhibitors such as alcohol and drugs was not common as only one in eight of the Internet-only offenders used such substances at the time of offending compared to over a third of Contact-only offenders. These low figures for the Internet offenders suggest that they are less inhibited about Internet crime than contact offenders are about their offending.

Adult-pornography sites are often the initial starting point in the offenders search for child pornography (Taylor, Quayle and Holland, 2001). Once on the adult pornography site, the user can usually search through a variety of hyperlinks. He may be tempted to sample links whose titles are suggestive of child pornography content. For other users, abusive Internet use started with a direct search for child images. The search for child pornography is initially a trial-and-error process through involving an active searching strategy. The user needs to acquire new computer and Internet skills and improve existing ones. Initially, offenders use obvious but telling key words such as 'child', 'pornography' or 'pre-teen' keyed into well-known web-based search engines such as *Yahoo*! and *Google*. This is a primitive and unsophisticated approach since any form of 'keyword' searching usually generates many 'hits' that lack the desired content. Extensive lists of 'hits' are time consuming if not unwieldy. More sophisticated users may employ more specialised search terms such as 'boy-love'. This term is frequently used by paedophiles to justify, normalise and rationalise their behaviours with children (De Young, 1988). 'Lolita' would be another more-sophisticated keyword (Brookes, 2003). This refers to the film directed by Stanley Kubrick, released in 1963, based on Nabokov's book. The name is synonymous with child pornography and adult-child sex. Advanced searches such as these would reduce the number of hits to explore before the desired material is reached. This is exemplified by the experiences of the following offender whose searches progressed from 'Lolita' to 'Ukrainian nymphets':

> First I typed in looking for "Lolita" . . . browsing I got "Lolita buffet" . . . and one of the links was "Ukrainian nymphets" . . . so I typed that in instead and what there was a whole host of sites! . . . well I just had to see what was on that . . . keep going down pages and pages of sites to see what I could access, some . . . were blocked, some . . . weren't, some you had to pay to get into . . . I'd put "Ukrainian nymphets" into Google almost all the time because that opened the door to all these sites [20: Internet Offender]

The use of such terms as part of search strategies presupposes that the offender has an existing interest in paedophilic images – words like inadvertent, accidental, or unexpected simply do not describe the process adequately despite their use by some offenders. Quayle (2004) argues that downloading is invariably a purposeful activity. Whilst it may be relatively easy to accidentally access adult pornography, this seems rarely, if ever, the case in relation to abusive images of children. The process of obtaining child material was an active one in all of the cases we studied. Offenders employ online 'nicknames' or pseudonyms partially to avoid detection but also to signal their sexual preferences to others online:

My user name...was at the time...daddy4uk...I can see it can look suggestive...my email address was different...but anything with the word dad in it like mine...use to attract people...anything like underage lover, cheerleader lover...school teacher...you can tell...its about children, it indicates their preferences [10: Internet Offender]

A minority of offenders (between 10% to 25%) accessed sites by 'back-door' methods which avoid payment. One Internet offender explained how he discovered websites from which he could obtain passwords to adult and child pornography sites. Using these passwords, he could enter 'pay-per-view' websites but not through the home page which usually requires the security information. 'Backdoor' methods mean that credit card details do not have to be supplied:

It was called...a backdoor site where there are lists of either user names or passwords...basically on the website...there would be the http code so you'd click on it and then you would either get the series [of images]...rather than have to go through the username and password to get into a pay-per-view site...you'd go through the back door so you would have access to the images and you wouldn't have to have paid for them...having discovered that possibly two-ish years into my offending that was my sum reference point really [12: Internet Offender]

Some employed technical software to accumulate child abuse images with lessened effort on their part. Perfectly legitimate programs such as *Newsbin Pro* allow the user to trawl through Newsgroup sites effortlessly once the system has been set up. The programs search specified Newsgroups or categories of Newsgroups for pertinent files which are then downloaded onto the user's own computer. The programs have user-adjustable settings. For example, by selecting only picture or video files (by the file name extensions such as jpeg or mpeg) and by concentrating on bigger files which are more likely to be photographs or video, the likelihood of finding the desired material is increased. The use of such a program distances the user from his offending behaviour as it is done more-or-less automatically. For the following offender, child pornography images were part of a wider collection of material ranging from non-sexual (e.g. pictures of trains) to sexually legal (adult pornography) and illegal images (paedophilic and bestiality):

I ended up with a programme called Newsbin Pro...you can set it up to run automatically...I set criteria that you can download any file bigger than 10 kilobytes so it would miss out news files and only pick out jpegs, movie files...digital images because the file size was too big for anything else...I set this thing going 24 hours a day...[then] I could off load [49: Internet Offender]

*Newsbin Pro* has mainly legitimate uses, of course. However, its ability to automatically download files while the user sleeps, its ability to explore individual newsgroups and groups of newsgroups and, for example, to organize MP3 files attracts illegitimate users. For the Internet sex offender, it speeds up the process of obtaining material and probably makes for a more thorough search.

## FAVOURITE INTERNET LOCATIONS USED BY OFFENDERS

There are certain prime locations on the Internet used by paedophiles -. newsgroups; chat rooms, communities; peer-to-peer; and web cams which allow abuse to be transmitted in real time (Brookes, 2003). The offenders we studied provided some support for this though certain locations were more commonly used than others (see Table 5.1).

Three quarters or more of the Internet offenders we studied had used Websites and these constituted the commonest resource from which images would be viewed and downloaded. Usually, though not always, the user had to pay a subscription fee to 'enter' the site. The following offender used the notorious pay-per-view site known as 'Landslide'. Many users of this site were eventually arrested as part *Operation Ore* in the UK and *Operation Avalanche* in the USA. For a fee, the user was supplied with an 'adult key' or 'adult pass'. This was a 'code' to gain access to sites containing all sorts of indecent images including, on some sites, child pornography:

> The actual site that was involved, was...Landslide...the files came through as zip files...you had to download the zip file to your computer, put your code in and then you could see what was on it...young girls without any clothes on...generally they are between...10 and 15 [years old] [15: Internet Offender]

Some users tended to restrict themselves to free to view material or tasters which encourage the user to graduate to paid-for material. Offenders who did not to use their credit cards online had three principal reasons:

- *'I was able to obtain them for free'*, and hinted that there was a moral difference between paying for images and not paying.
- *'I don't believe in providing succor to the industry'* which, in a sense, counters the view that Internet pornography users encourage the further abuse of children by resourcing the industry.

**Table 5.1**  Reported Internet resources used by Internet-only and mixed Internet/contact offenders

| Internet resources | Type of sex offender | |
| --- | --- | --- |
|  | Internet | Mixed |
| Web sites | 75 % | 80 % |
| Newsgroups | 56 % | 60 % |
| Chat Rooms | 31 % | 20 % |
| Emails | 25 % | 20 % |
| File-sharing(e.g. P2P) | 19 % | 10 % |

• Forensic awareness, in that avoiding the use of credit cards reduces the chances of detection and possibly conviction.

Newsgroups were the second most commonly used Internet location where illegal material was obtained; over half of the Internet users reported use of this resource. The following offender concentrated on two newsgroups which he found to contain sexualised images of pre- and post-pubescent girls including sexual contact with adults. Black cat scans he described as 'David Hamilton type' photographs. Hamilton is a highly commercially successful photographer known for very soft-focus, grainy images of nude or near nude adolescent girls. He has been the focus of criticism especially in the USA and UK, similar to that which the work of Jock Struges and Sally Mann has attracted (Anderson, 1997; Scott, 2005; Stanley, 1991; Warmoll, 2005). Their work includes nude photographs of children, although not in sexual situations.

In the headings there were quite a few that related to either Lolita's or young girls ... of those newsgroups there were only really two that I looked in one was called "black cat scans" ... predominantly pictures of ... pre-pubescent girls ... in various states of undress, partial or full nudity ... posed ... The other one that I looked at was ... "alt.binaries.mclt" ... "MCLT" actually stood for "my collection of Lolita's and teens" ... there were a lot of images again of a similar vein ... young, pubescent ... there were a few images that I did have that were more abusive ... some of them yes I can't deny I did find arousing ... the girls were smiling, looking happy, there wasn't any evidence of coercion or force I liked those [31: Mixed Offender]

There is concern that chatrooms intended for adolescents are used by paedophiles to groom their victims on-line (Brookes, 2003). Around a quarter of the Internet offenders we studied used chatrooms. But their preference was for ones of an adult nature which, in some cases, offered instant messaging services. This meant that indecent images could be sent embedded in e-mails or as e-mail attachments:

You go into an adult chat room ... called "chat teen pictures" ... if you hang about long enough somebody will message you ... depending on what sort of nickname you're using ... they ask "well you got any pictures?" ... you type back pictures of what? Oh girls or boys, whatever' .... And they ... send it to you [9: Internet Offender]

Other offenders, about a quarter of our sample, obtained indecent images from SPAM e-mail (which, in a sense, they did not solicit) or as a consequence of being on a 'private' mailing list. Peer-to-peer (P2P) programme sharing (e.g. *Kazaa*) is another major concern in relation to child exploitation (Sommer, 2003). However, less than 20 % of our offenders used such services.

The situation with the Internet changes rapidly and what may be true at one point in time may not be the case even a year later. So, for example, the *Internet*

*Watch Foundation* or equivalent organisations may close down sites providing pornography directly. It is important to note the resourcefulness of the offenders in relation to the Internet. Given the nature of their search and distribution activities, any claims by Internet sex offenders that they came across the material 'by mistake' seem unwarranted. The process is much more of a determined, active process to which the terms accident, unintentional, and unexpected have little or no relevance. The majority of offenders mentioned using at least two different Internet sources of child abuse imagery. There is clearly intentionality to the men's on-line behaviours which they frequently deny despite the evidence.

Visual material was not the only thing downloaded. Some, but not many, offenders would download paedophilic, including incest, stories. Some also wrote such stories. A small number of Internet offenders explained to us that they wished that they *had* collected stories but their reasons were largely pragmatic and showed a level of forensic awareness. They knew that the written word was not illegal and that they could not be prosecuted for having a collection of stories about adult-child sex.

## ONLINE AND OFFLINE SEXUAL ACTIVITIES

When the sexual activities of paedophiles are tabulated (see Table 5.2), it is notable that solitary child-oriented activities such as masturbation and cataloguing dominated what they did both online and off. They were much more common than other forms of behaviour such as role-playing and grooming which seem to require more social skills. Viewed in this way, masturbation, not surprisingly, was the most frequent sexual activity related to children that offenders engaged in. Over half of offenders who used the Internet admitted masturbating when viewing the images on screen. In the light of previous research (Taylor and Quayle, 2003), this figure might have been expected to be

**Table 5.2**  Reported behaviours online and off-line by Internet and mixed sexual offenders

|  | Type of sex offender | |
|---|---|---|
|  | Internet | Mixed |
| Masturbating (whilst viewing images on-screen) | 56 % | 60 % |
| Cataloguing (on- or off-line) | 50 % | 30 % |
| Networking – trading / swapping images on-line | 19 % | 20 % |
| Role-playing | 6 % | 20 % |
| Downloading/writing stories, e.g. incest stories | 6 % | 10 % |
| On-line grooming/seducing child on-line | 0 % | 20 % |
| Taking photographs/videos of victim(s) (mixed only offenders) | — | 40 % |
| Distributing photographs/videos of victim(s) on-line(mixed offenders only) | — | 10 % (1) |

higher. Of course, admitting masturbating to pornography to researchers may not be the easiest of things so there may have been some under-reporting. But there are other reasons which may affect the figures. Using a computer in an Internet café, or even at work, is not conducive to masturbation on the spot. Furthermore, an offender may suffer from a sexual dysfunction which makes ejaculation difficult, for example. Of course, the fantasy generated by the Internet child abuse imagery does not have to be an immediate stimulus to have an effect. The imagery from the Internet may be saved in the offenders memory for later use in solitary masturbation or sexual intercourse with the offenders' adult sexual partners. Furthermore, it is not unknown for Internet offenders to masturbate as an accompaniment to the 'role playing' that they engaged in on the Internet. They talk through their fantasies with another person, perhaps another adult, while masturbating to their thoughts.

A great deal of time is spent by many offenders on their collections of child abuse images. These can be more than mere accumulations of files since often they are carefully sorted and organized. As many as half of the Internet exclusive sex offenders and a third of mixed Internet/contact offenders indicated that they did this either on- or off-line:

> My hard drive... it was very organised there was boys; there was girls... there would be boys posing on their own in a folder; boys in groups; boys soft as I put it; boys with erections... all itemised in various folders [7: Mixed Offender]

> P: It was semi-organised ... I would split it up into pictures of boys, pictures of more than one boy, pictures of boys with girls... separate folders... bb; young boy... bond; bondage... wg; woman with... girl

> I: Did any of that give you a sexual feeling?

> P: Not the action of organising them that was more of a chore... but... I had to look at them in order {he laughs} to decide where... they would go and... that would sexually excite me [18: Internet Offender]

Various researchers have noted these cataloguing behaviours of Internet child pornography users (Quayle and Taylor, 2002b; Taylor and Quayle, 2003; Tate, 1990). However, collections of Internet child pornography images are, as much as anything else, responsible for Internet offenders being arrested and convicted. In this sense, some offenders show little or no forensic awareness in that they fail to destroy the evidence of their crimes though this may not be true of men currently offending on the Internet. There are legitimately available computer programs which destroy a computer's Internet trail beyond the point of recovery. The normal process of deleting files used by most users is not secure since not only is a trail of web sites visited left behind but the so-called deleted file normally remains on the user's hard drive while memory is available. The police, by copying the offender's hard drive, can obtain access to the downloaded files with a little expertise. There are programs such as *Cyber Scrub*, *WipeDrive*, and *DataGone* which can ensure that deleted data is not recoverable and that the trail of sites visited is obliterated.

No satisfactory explanation exists for this cataloguing and collecting behaviour. It could, of course, merely be an extension of collecting behaviour in general though hoarding seems to be a better description of the masses of child pornography that some offenders download. Of course, not all child pornographic images are equally stimulating to Internet child pornography offenders and they do need an opportunity to sort through images to find the ones which suit them. But, then, it is difficult to understand why the offender fails to destroy the material which is of little interest if it is collected for their purposes alone rather than to trade with others. The number of images stored is sometimes so big that they cannot all be required for masturbation purposes:

> 50 % of the stuff I had I never even looked at ... You might look at the first picture and the last picture and you never even look at them pictures again rather it's "I'll have those 'cos they may come in handy with what I want" ... adult-child sex action I use to trade for ... my preference ... none none actual sexual just posing [9: Internet Offender]

One consequence of organizing or cataloguing the images is that the offender spends considerable amounts of time viewing the images to be catalogued. This may serve to increase the sexual arousal that the offender experiences from his collection – and it may create a less direct and more comfortable route to using the pornography in masturbation. Cataloguing may distance the offender from the material by giving a relatively innocuous task to do which is more subtle than merely searching through files looking for suitable material to accompany masturbation. One interesting insight which emerged from the interviews was the fact that a small percentage of men perceived collecting and cataloguing as a way of feeling in control which contrasts markedly with them feeling out of control in other aspects of their lives.

'Trading' or 'swapping' child pornography images was not a common activity among the offenders we studied. Only about 19 to 20 % of Internet only and mixed offenders reported 'trading' or 'swapping'. It is important to note that where a man did trade or swap child pornography images, he was much more likely to engage in cataloguing the material. For example, of those who traded on-line 80 % catalogued or sorted the material. Non-trading offenders generally did not catalogue or sort the material to anywhere near the same degree. Only a third of non-traders sorted or catalogued. This has been noted by other researchers (Taylor and Quayle, 2003).

Collecting child abuse images is illegal but talking about and role-playing fantasies might be inappropriate but it is not necessarily illegal (Quayle, Erooga, Wright, Taylor and Harbinson, 2006). The use of the Internet for sex is not restricted to paedophiles (Quayle, *et al.*, 2006) – cybersex is engaged in by people in general, for example (Cooper, McLoughlin and Campbell, 2000). A number of on-line offenders reported adopting the persona of a child on-line and engaging in Internet conversations with individuals they believed to be adult males. This only applied to about one in eight of the men we interviewed but, nevertheless, it does help us understand the range of activities engaged in on-line;

> I would actually give myself a profile of a young girl...and go into a [child orientated] chat room...within time they'd always be some male, man approaching and start talking to you, invariably somebody in their 30s, 40s, or 50s...I am chatting to these men pretending to be a girl and actually engaging in sexual conversation with them as a girl [11: Mixed Offender]

> P: You'd go to chat room...one would act out the role of the child for example and the other would act out the role of the adult...it would be like "I'm undressing you" kind of thing...the chat rooms would say 100% preteen sex...and you'd just start talking about fantasies basically

> I:...during these role plays, you'd be masturbating?

> P: Well yea during the role playing [22: Mixed Offender]

This is further evidence of the importance of sexual fantasy in the lives of offenders if any more is needed. It is interesting to note that the fantasy seems to be so powerful that the knowledge that it was another adult male on-line did not undermine the experience. For some offenders, at least, the fantasy element was more important than direct sexual contact – that is, for some men, it is all about fantasy though there are other men who both engage in this sort of fantasy and also contact offend against children. For example, the second excerpt quoted above is from an interview with an offender [case study 22] who had been convicted of both raping his 6-year-old daughter as well as Internet offences. His fantasies clearly mapped well onto his contact sexual abuse. He fantasised prior to his offence concerning whether he or his daughter would initiate the sexual contact, what clothes he would dress her in, and what sort of sexual contact would be instigated. These fantasies formed part of his role-playing and his offending behaviour. He would also fantasise about the offence afterwards including masturbating whilst watching the video(s) of the abuse.

A small percentage of Internet-using paedophiles 'groomed' on-line. One offender tried to groom a 15-year-old girl on-line though there was no attempt by him to disguise his persona as that of another young person. He would 'say' things like:

> "Hi...my name's Andy" [not real name]..."I'm...39...I'm 6 foot 4...married...looking for someone to chat to, if you're interested say hi". And I'd...copy and paste it to each of the female names on there and see who come onto you...she claimed to be 15 [11: Mixed Offender]

It is difficult to judge whether this is a case of a man engaging in communications with young people because this allowed him the opportunity to fantasise and masturbate. Some men may merely be sexual fantasizers with no intention of contacting a child in order to abuse them directly. This particular man may have merely been engaging in a cybersex experience since he was caught using an adult-site rather than, say, a chatroom for teenagers. He was, whatever the intention, convicted of grooming a child on-line which involves showing an intention to meet. In any case, despite being aware of the child's age he persisted in engaging her in sexual conversation. This offender described their conversations as sexually stimulating but placed most of the blame with the victim who he describes as promiscuous!

> There was talk in the chat about meeting...I actually found it sexually stimulating to think that this girl was being very promiscuous...and very sexually explicit towards me...she was talking about meeting, what we could do, I never had any intentions whatsoever of meeting...but...as a bit of fantasy thinking about sex...if it was a 15 year old girl or not ...that wasn't so important, it's the fantasy that it could be [11: Mixed Offender]

Another mixed Internet/contact offender we studied attempted to groom a 'child' but was not convicted of such an offence. It transpired that the 'boy' was an FBI law enforcement agent and it was actually part of a sting operation.

Accessing, downloading, collecting and distributing indecent images of children are common behaviours disclosed by Internet using offenders in our work and that of others (Quayle *et al.*, 2000; Quayle and Taylor, 2001; 2003; Sullivan and Beech, 2003). This involvement with like-minded other men may serve to reinforce and justify a man's offending behaviour to himself. Generally, however, the scope for this is limited since most of the activities of the offenders we studied were the solitary ones of masturbation rather than anything involving communication with others online. However, some might point out that the mere fact of knowing that child pornography is out there on the Internet on websites and newsgroups means that the offender knows that there are like-minded men sharing his sexual interest in children (Quayle, 2004). Being aware of other individuals engaged in much the same kind of activities may serve to justify the behaviour to the offender to himself.

How much 'trading' of images goes on is difficult to assess and probably depends on the offenders involved – whether they are solitary users of the Internet or part of a network with others. Our figures are relatively low compared to that of Taylor and Quayle's (2003) sample of w0nderland club members. This club was an Internet paedophile ring so it is not surprising to find individuals swapping or trading images quantities of images with others. There were no examples of web-cams being used as part of the sexual abuse of children by the men we interviewed. Occasionally other researchers mention such activity (e.g. Sullivan and Beech, 2003) but it seems relatively uncommon. This is not to say that it never happens or could not happen, merely that it is not typical of the paedophile activity on the web engaged in by our sample of paedophiles.

## THE FUNCTIONS OF INTERNET CHILD ABUSE IMAGES

Of the various functions that child pornography may fulfil in the lives of offenders, a common concern is that child pornography contributes to the further abuse of children by stimulating fantasies which, when acted out, result in new child victims. Furthermore, researchers suggest that offenders may show their victims child pornography in an attempt to lower the child victim's inhibitions because the pornography indicates that other children find the sexual activities depicted acceptable (Goldstein, 1999; Lanning, 2001). Others suggest that child pornography is used by offenders to sexually stimulate themselves prior to and in preparation for engaging in acts of child sexual abuse (Marshall, 1988). Such uses of the Internet and child pornography relate to premeditated contact offences. Since it seems that a proportion of Internet sex offenders have no history of contact offending (Seto and Eke, 2005), what functions does Internet child pornography serve for them?

Following Taylor and Quayle (2003), we carried out a thematic analysis (Braun and Clarke, 2006; Langdrige, 2004) on the interviews that we conducted with sex offenders. This analysis suggested that there were four dominant themes comparable with those of Taylor and Quayle (2003). These themes we identified as:

- pornography as a means of sexual arousal and aid to fantasy;
- pornography as a way of avoiding real life;
- pornography as a collecting behaviour; and,
- pornography as a way of facilitating social relationships.

### Sexual Arousal

Overwhelmingly the theme of sexual arousal characterised the Internet offender's use of pornography. It was identified in the interviews of 75 % of Internet offenders and 90 % of mixed sexual offenders. Not all of these offenders reported masturbation to ejaculation since only half of each sample did so. As we have seen, offenders often download large amounts of images so they may need to be able to select from the available material suitable imagery. This choice may be a matter of a specific age group, a particular gender of child, a preferred physical type or a particular sort of sexual activity. Take the following examples:

> If I decided that I was going to masturbate this afternoon . . . the images that I would choose to look at tend to be girls . . . 12 to 14 . . . usually on their own, or with another girl but generally they would be masturbating themselves or each other, that was my preference [12: Internet Offender]

In order to maintain that sexual arousal you think...its wrong, both morally and illegally...plus the sexually penetrative act regardless of age is a thrill [13: Internet Offender]

The idea that the taboo and illegal nature of child pornography made it sexually exciting was not just restricted to the previous quotation. Other men spoke of the offending behaviour as 'taboo', 'dirty', seedy', 'forbidden' and the 'Pandora's Box syndrome' which contributed to the sexual thrill.

One surprising suggestion, given the disgust the general public expresses about child pornography, is that offenders impose a moral or ethical code on their selection of material. Quite what that morality is depends on the individual (Taylor and Quayle, 2003). However, there are distinct limits to this morality. Taylor and Quayle found that the moral codes were flexible such as when pictures were being exchanged then moral objections to particular content were overcome or sidelined. The acceptability of an image was sometimes determined by the same factors which determined sexual interest - for instance, the gender of the child or the nature of the sexual acts involved could be the important factor. The next man stressed his sexual interest in females by the emphasis on his claim that he is not homosexual and that he searches for girl images:

No boys...I'm not gay in any way shape or form [2: Internet Offender]

Whereas the following offender seems to have much more of a problem with pictures involving bestiality:

Kids with animals...I always got rid straight away [19: Mixed Offender]

Taylor and Quayle (2003) pointed out that Internet offenders prefer images of children smiling. Presumably the smiling acts as a cue that the child was consenting to and enjoying their sexual abuse. According to some of the men we interviewed, if the picture was not of an apparently happy child the image would be deleted. The abuse is legitimized by the child smiling and is consistent with the view frequently expressed by paedophiles that adult-child sex does 'no harm' to the victim. The following extract shows how the child's enjoyment facilitates the offender's masturbation:

P: What I wanted from an image was the fact that a. the child looked happy with what they were doing and b. it was a situation I would have liked to have been in...a one night stand...essentially wanting sexual intercourse with the child...because all these events ended in masturbation...they [images] would generate sexual fantasies it wasn't a fantasy that I would have and then go and look for something to back it up...I would look through all these various things and then I could fantasise about them

I: What sort of fantasies would the images generate?

P: Someone who was...innocent...that I could give a good time too, teach them how to enjoy themselves sexually...so what they would be doing would be a pleasurable thing...And they would want to do it [5: Internet Offender]

This offender here minimises the offence – a rape – by stressing that the child's enjoyment is important. This is redolent of the cognitive distortion 'children are sexual beings' (Ward and Keenan, 1999) and the associated view that children can benefit from sexual contact with offenders who help them to become the sexual beings paedophiles believe them to be.

Men who admitted to masturbating to child pornography mentioned that they rarely referred back to a child pornography image once they had used it for this purpose despite the material remaining on their hard drives. Instead, they usually sought new material from the Internet despite having a veritable catalogue of stored images. Greater sexual excitement came from searching for and viewing new pictures:

Looked at them...masturbated...saved them, not referred back to...I think the activity of...seeing new material and searching for it was of far greater sexual excitement than looking at stuff that I'd looked at before [5: Internet Offender]

Some images are chosen because they fit with an offender's pre-existing fantasies some of which relate to earlier behaviour:

Girls got dressed up in school uniforms at University [disco revivals] which was a turn on so I started to look for school uniforms, school girls on the Internet [10: Internet Offender]

Of course, there is a satiation effect to pornography which was demonstrated long ago for adult pornography (Barron and Kimmel, 2000; Reifler, Howard, Lipton, Liptzin, and Widman, 1971). Gradually, repeated exposure to the same pornographic material results in satiation whereby the user eventually ceases to be aroused by previously highly stimulating images. If new pornographic material is introduced then sexual arousal to this is likely to occur. However, whether the offenders we interviewed were describing this process of satiation is not clear especially since material was discarded after one use, whereas the process of satiation implies something more gradual. There is a related notion that sexual fantasy loses it ability to arouse after time and so fantasies need to become more extreme and explicit (Gee, Ward and Eccleston, 2003, Gresswell and Hollin, 1997) or the offender may move onto contact abuse. Taylor and Quayle (2003) found evidence that most of the offenders they studied gradually accessed increasingly extreme material. This progression might involve a move to younger children or toward such themes as bestiality. Because of the way that the Internet works, a user is faced with numerous hyperlinks to other sites - some with the label 'illegal' – it is easy for accomplished Internet users to access ever more extreme material. Habituation may be especially strong on the Internet because of the sheer amount of material available and the amount of time individuals spend downloading and cataloguing the pornography (Taylor and Quayle, 2003).

The number of pictures seized during an arrest is often focused on by the media and law enforcement agencies and used as an index of the severity of the crime or deviancy of the individual. Given the nature of the material this is not surprising. The size of an offender's child pornography collection may be indicative of the degree to which he is involved in collecting material or indeed how much he has become absorbed in the paedophile community. Alternatively, having large numbers of child pornography pictures may simply indicate 'how successful a person is in collecting deviant material, rather than an index of deviance itself' (Taylor and Quayle, 2003, p. 86). Time spent on a computer has been lead to gains in technical knowledge and skill at finding material (Quayle, Holland, Linehan, and Taylor, 2000; Taylor and Quayle, 2003).

We have seen that a substantial number of offenders gave no indication that they used child pornography as part of or as a stimulus to masturbation. This may be a truthful response since, for example, the fantasy generated might be used in their sexual relations with an adult partner (Howitt, 1995a). One Internet offender denied masturbating to child pornography because he accessed the Internet in a public place. Nevertheless, the strong feelings and physical reactions that viewing these images generated in him acted as a form of 'foreplay' prior to sexual intercourse with his adult partner:

> My heart was pounding faster . . . I was flushed . . . your head . . . heavy, your temples were buzzing . . . I felt hot and your eyes would stand out of your head . . . I was not fully erect, but I felt a bulge in my trousers . . . I never masturbated because it was in a public place [but] . . . the child pornography was like foreplay. I wouldn't be having sex with the images in my head. I'd see [girlfriend] and I'd want to jump into bed with her. I was in a state of . . . mental arousal [10: Internet Offender]

While masturbation may accompany viewing of an image on the computer screen, sometimes an offender would describe how he would use the image as a starting point to generate new images which may be more stimulating for him. The following offender, when his offending was at its peak, would masturbate most days both on- and off-line. He manipulates the images in ways which Howitt (1995b) noted that paedophiles did even for innocuous material. The images were 'morphed' such that they fitted with his personal fantasies:

> I'd be masturbating . . . most, but not every day . . . whilst on screen usually, sometimes off screen I would masturbate to what I had seen . . . but usually I would be fantasising something different than what was on the screen . . . fantasise something different from what she was doing . . . instead of her just posing and naked I'd perhaps imagine her moving around or watching me masturbate . . . generally that would be it . . . I'd watch the image and imagine what I liked [4: Mixed Offender]

This man masturbated to Internet child abuse imagery but stopped short of progressing to ejaculation. In order to climax sexually he would revert to imagery of his contact victims:

> I did on occasion masturbate while I was looking at those [Internet] pictures but more often than not what would happen ... I would look at the pictures and get an erection and maintain the erection for a length of time but then to actually ejaculate I would revert to the [naked] pictures of [step daughter] and use that as the release [31: Mixed Offender]

He added:

> I asked her if she would be willing to let me take pictures. She agreed ... [I used them] for masturbating ... no publishing or distributing the images [31: Mixed Offender]

It was much more likely that an offender who had both Internet and contact offences would take photographs of their contact victims (40 % did) whereas only 16 % of the contact only offenders did though this does not necessarily mean that all of the photographs were of illegal subject matter. As Howitt (1995b) indicated, perfectly legal child images may stimulate the offender and possibly aid masturbation. Another perpetrator with both Internet and contact [case 22] offences admitted producing photographs and videos of his daughter not for his own sexual satisfaction alone. He photographed her in order to trade with a chat-room contact who promised to reciprocate with images of his daughter. This provided the offender, he claimed, with 'pleasure' from sharing images but also 'sexual reward' from getting additional images in exchange which he found enjoyable. It also helped establish status and trust within the Internet communities he engaged with. Other studies have found that producers of abusive material do distribute the images both on- and/or off line, but again not always (Wolak, Finkelhor and Mitchell, 2005). This offender was the only perpetrator we studied who distributed the images he produced to others.

## Emotional Avoidance

The Internet is a world which is very unproblematic compared with the real world with all of its difficulties. This distinctive nature of the world of the Internet is one of its attractions:

> It's just coping with life, because I escaped, it's a, it was a form of escapism because I wanted to get out of my dilemma ... and the dilemma was ... worried about debt, can't get out of it, nobody to talk to, no relationships, hatred of [wife] ... when I went on the net ... that was ... swept away ... I was in ... me own little world [3: Mixed Offender]

But when I was on line it was a completely discreet and isolated world [12 Internet Offender]

When interviewing paedophiles, one cannot avoid the impression that in many ways they experience their lives as unsatisfactory. Not surprisingly, to the extent that this impression is accurate, sizeable proportions of Internet using offenders used child pornography and the Internet as means by which they could deal with or avoid their 'real-world' dissatisfactions. Fifty percent of Internet and 40 % of mixed sexual perpetrators spoke in terms which suggest that their Internet activity was part of the way that they avoided problems of their daily reality. In this way, we can regard Internet sex as a coping strategy. They indicated to us that they experienced a 'buzz' or 'high' or, paradoxically, a tranquilizing feeling of 'escape' or 'numbing'. For example, one Internet contact offender used the Internet and child pornography in order to help with a range of problems including a difficult relationship, his son's health problems, and debt. While using the Internet, he could shut himself emotionally away from his real-life situation which was producing escalating levels of distress in him. Positive feelings could be achieved through the sexual gratification he found in masturbation. Indeed, he escaped his difficulties by physically removing himself to another room where he could access material;

> I can...compare it to like...you know that feel good factor of you buy yourself something and you feel a lot better? Well it was the same on the Internet...you'd go and...download a whole lot of music or pornography and...you'd feel better...the double edge thing with the pornography was the masturbation...you're obviously getting the...gratification from the masturbation that went with that...the fantasy and this kind of alternate world I'm using...for gratification and...as a coping strategies...when things are going wrong in the real world...my avoidance strategies of locking myself away and I'm using this as a tool to try and cope with stress, stressors and strains...certainly as the problems got worse...and things could get really bad in the relationship to the point where...I would shut myself away well I'd physically move out of, for example the bedroom and totally isolate myself for long periods of time, we are talking weeks and weeks [22: Mixed Offender]

This same offender identified computer use as a major coping tool that originated in childhood. As a child he played on the computer as a way of dealing with bullying, general unhappiness, and isolation. The feelings that he associated with the computer, either as a child or during adulthood, were positive. He mentioned things like *'protection'*, *'contentment'*, *'security'*, *'happy'* feelings of *'control and power'*, *'emotional escapism'* *'a world where everything made sense'* and *'acceptance'*. Away from the computer, he experienced feelings such as *'felt like the underdog'* *'unsettling'*, *'quite unhappy'*, *'didn't get much support at home'*, and *'quite a difficult period'*.

The idea of controllability was not confined to this offender alone. It contrasts with how they see their real-lives which they experience as unsatisfactory and unmanageable. On-line, these men felt in greater control than they did in real life. They felt in control of the children they abused and had perfect control over their sexual satisfaction:

I think a large part of that was I'd been in control of my life...and that particular period I'd felt there was no control at all...I felt out of control with the situation and in control over the children as well as me, it gave me something to try and hang onto [4: Mixed Offender]

However, for some the feeling of regaining control through offending was later reversed and they felt out of control:

Originally it was something I had a bit of control over...but then I lost control as I lost control of work [49: Internet Offender]

The use of child pornography was very entrenched for some offenders who showed some of the characteristics reminiscent of addiction such as tolerance, salience, conflict, and relapse (Griffiths, 2000; Hodge *et al.*, 1997; McGregor and Howells, 1997). In terms of tolerance, much as the addict needs greater and greater levels of drugs, there was a need for more extreme child pornography in order to achieve the same mood modification effects previously produced by 'milder' imagery:

The sort of fantasies and the images that I was looking at were becoming more depraved...more sexual...younger children...certainly there was a desire in me, to, a need to look at more of these depraved images...to feel as aroused [22: Mixed Offender]

Gresswell and Hollin (1997) have also pointed out that as offenders continue to use a fantasy theme to induce or enhance sexual arousal, its ability to produce the desired feelings decreases. This is very much a stereotype of the nature of addictive drugs. The Internet allows the user rapid and varied access to massive amounts of material. This speed and sheer quantity might facilitate the quick satiation of sexual images such that they cease to produce as much sexual response as they did formerly (Taylor and Quayle, 2003):

The sexual excitement was for me...maintained by...clicking on an image looking at that for a few seconds then clicking on another image...it was quantity rather than quality...You look at one and you think well there are others out there or I wonder what that's like...and then you get saturated with it and in the end you think well...forget it I'm not interested in that anymore [5: Internet Offender]

In research of addiction, the concept of salience refers to the situation in which the addictive behaviour becomes the paramount activity in the addict's life – it dominates their thinking, feelings and behaviour (Griffiths, 2000). Internet child pornography offenders, despite increasing serious negative consequences, continue using child pornography. They also seem to be unable to respond to the excessive nature of their pornography use (Quayle and Taylor, 2002b). In some cases, the process of locating, downloading and masturbating to the images is all-engrossing. Other activities become excluded to the point of being problematic. Caring for children, leisure time and maintaining social relationships become secondary. The offending behaviour has absorbed their lives. Not surprisingly, this may bring them into conflict with members of their family and social network simply because their time is spent on the Internet and the computer. When blocked from using the Internet, they experience frustration or unpleasant feelings:

> Hours and hours, several hours per night...most days, at the weekends so I didn't do any social activities, I stopped playing...football...stopped going to church...stopped evening activities, home groups, bible studies...I just concentrated on...warding myself off in my little room and downloading the images...I was masturbating every day...in the evenings...several times at the weekends [15: Internet Offender]

> I'd come home from work I'd have...my tea and I'd go and sit up on my computer and that would be it till 4 o' clock in the morning and no contact with anybody else...that become...my main goal in life...and I got very angry and frustrated if...my wife would interrupt my...time [22: Mixed Offender]

Relapse is common when addicts try to go cold turkey with drugs. Sometimes the Internet child pornography user made attempts to stop this behaviour. Thirty one percent of Internet and 40% of mixed Internet-Contact offenders tried, in some way, to stop but rarely with any long-term success. The following Internet offender physically cut himself off from the Internet but this lasted for just one week. Internet cold turkey just did not work for him or most of the others:

> I...damaged the cables...and for about a week I didn't log on...Then I fixed them...I was logging on again but ten times as bad...it...was every spare moment [20: Internet Offender]

Whether this level of involvement with child pornography can be described as addictive behaviour is a moot point. It is equally unclear whether or not other terms such as compulsive behaviour can be applied either. There is some debate about the extent to which the concept of addiction can be stretched in order to allow us to speak of 'addiction to crime' (Hodge et al., 1997; McGregor and Howells, 1997). The addiction would be to the process of doing crime. Evidence of addiction to crime is difficult to provide and researchers differ in the extent to which they consider it to be a useful idea. At best, the addiction notion should perhaps be regarded as a metaphor which provides an interesting way of conceptualizing the intense commitment to this form of offending behaviour. It certainly characterizes substantial numbers of users of child pornography on the Internet. But to understand this we cannot rely on notions that child pornography has addictive properties or ideas that sex offenders have addictive personalities, for example. It is probably easier to see the roots of their obsessional commitment to the Internet and child pornography in fundamental inadequacies in the lives of these offenders which stretch back into childhood and which are exacerbated by events in their lives. But even this has to be predicated on the fundamental fact that these men are sexually interested in children.

## Collecting

As we have seen, researchers have highlighted that paedophiles do not passively 'view' child pornography but are much more active in that 'they collect, catalogue and index it as well' (Tate, 1990, p. 112). Indeed, the COPINE interviews identified that users saw their child pornography material as 'collectibles' (Quayle and Taylor, 2002b; Taylor and Quayle, 2003). They quote the following comment from one of their research participants:
   'And there was the thrill in collecting them. You wanted to get complete sets so it . . . was a bit like stamp collecting as well' (Taylor and Quayle, 2003, p. 81).
   A similar point of view was expressed by some of the men we studied:

Particularly when the images were getting younger and I noticed . . . you would get sets of images as well and that played quite a big part as well . . . to get complete sets of things [22: Mixed Offender]

Taylor and Quayle point out that their group of offenders gained pleasure from collecting pornography which is part of a themed series of pictures. The men would find enjoyment in tracking down and obtaining pictures which were missing from a series that they were collecting. Some of the men gained pleasure from spending time offline cataloguing their pornography collections. The complexity of this cataloguing depended upon the function of the material for them. Cataloguing was more extensive where it was to be exchanged and the men tended to use more discriminating subcategories of folders on their computers. Sometimes, if the material was totally for personal use, then all of the images might be put into one computer folder containing all of the images. Other men reported activities such as editing the images to ensure that they fitted the computer screen properly or they reviewed the file names to ensure that they identified the man's particular preferences properly. There is reason to believe that permanency, constancy and organization are characteristic of Internet pornography collections (Lanning, 1992; 2001; Quayle, Holland, Linehan, and Taylor, 2000).

References of huge collections of child pornography are not uncommon in news reports from trials of Internet sex offenders. Of our current sample of Internet and mixed sexual perpetrators, 37 % and 20 %, accordingly, referred to the process of 'collecting' in relation to their offending behaviour or described the material they had as 'collections'. This tendency perhaps does not readily fit with Lanning's (1992) comment that situational child molesters might collect child pornography but not with the high degree of predictability of preferential child molesters (p. 23). This distinction harks back to the idea of fixated versus regressed paedophiles (Chapter 3). The preferential offender is the fixated offender more-or-less. However, Internet-only offenders by defini-tion have not engaged sexually with real children and, apart from masturba-tion to child imagery, any sexual relations they had would involve other adults. So, despite being the group likely to collect child pornography, the Internet-only offender cannot be construed as a preferential child molester.

Some of the men that we interviewed compared their collections to other types of collection including 'cigarette cards' or 'book matches'. This possibly serves to normalise the activity and distance the offender from his deviance. At the same time they tend to make very little reference to the fact that the collections are of sexually abused children. In other words, they are denying the nature of the collections. The men's collecting behaviour was not solely confined to child pornography. Many participants collected adult pornogra-phy before they moved on to child pornography. Indeed, 75 % of the Internet and 80 % of the mixed Internet-contact offenders collected adult as well as child pornography on-line. This pattern of more general collecting behaviour was also noted by the COPINE researchers. They also found that collecting was not always confined to child pornography but appeared part of a progression from collecting other forms of pornography mainly adult porno-graphy (Taylor and Quayle, 2003). A small minority of Internet collected a variety of bizarre material of which child pornography was just a part:

> Quite a big collection…some freakish, mutilations, torture, necrophi-lia…bestiality… imagery of child abuse was part of the overall thing [11: Mixed Offender]

For some offenders, collecting child pornography appeared to be an exten-sion of general collecting behaviour off-line. Over a third of the Internet offenders that we studied had a pattern of collecting behaviour off-line which sometimes combined with their on-line collecting. The figure for mixed Internet-contact offenders was rather lower at about one in ten. One man told us that the intrinsic value of his collections appeared not to be the nature of the objects – that to some extent was inconsequential - but that collecting was perceived as helping him fill a void in his life. The void was a lack of an adult relationship. So in a sense, the collecting relates to the issue of emotional avoidance (Muensterberg, 1994):

> I had half a million of these wretched things…I was going through this compulsive obsessive stage and I'd brought thousands of CD's…LP's

when they were around... videos of American sports... hundreds of videos with thousands of games recorded on them... DVDs... because I needed to fill that gap in my life which was not being filled with a proper relationship [15: Internet Offender]

Taylor and Quayle (2003) point out that the extent to which offenders spend time sorting and organising may serve as a crude indicator of the offender's involvement in, and the amount of time spent 'off-line' engaging with, child pornography. The detail of the pornography collection may, to an expert eye, suggest the extent to which an offender is integrated into a circle of offenders. Offenders whose collections include the most recently produced pornography rather than just material which has been circulating for decades probably have access to child pornography producers. It may also indicate the type of paedophile social networks through which the new material circulates (Taylor et al., 2001b).

## Facilitating Social Relationships

Although much of the behaviour of the men in relation to child pornography seems to be isolated and insular, nevertheless almost a quarter of Internet only and Mixed Internet/Contact offenders referred to the important social benefits afforded them by involvement in child pornography. For example, one man felt on the 'inside' as a consequence of being able to obtain special photographs and as a result he felt valued:

You'd talk about... "have you seen such and such?" so it become a kind of place to meet people and to talk about similar fantasies... I'm getting an element of feeling that I'm wanted... I got a thrill out of being a part of being accepted by the group [22: Mixed Offender]

Not only did this offender enjoy engaging with others on-line but he used child pornography as a way of increasing his credibility with other people. He almost describes it as if child pornography was the small-talk of interaction;

I was more interested in the conversations I was getting, the friendship I was getting... the images... provided me with a form of communication... that was my pleasure... I was very lonely... to prove that they were genuine they sent me the indecent stuff... I had to prove myself that I were genuine by doing the same to them [50: Internet Offender]

As we have seen, one concern relating to the exchange of pornographic images and the use of chat rooms is that, inevitably, other offenders may be a powerful influence by reinforcing and validating the offender's views (Durkin and Bryant, 1999; Lanning, 2001; Tate 1990). There was a degree to which their cognitive distortions were externally reinforced through discussions with others on-line:

The issues wasn't just fantasies that were talked about in the chat rooms there was a lot of the legality of the whole situation...we were all trying to self-justify..."well if you were in any other country it would be acceptable"...I was introduced to this other world where you were talking to other people which have similar fantasies...I can all of a sudden share similar feelings...that I couldn't do before for fear of the repercussions...these fantasies they'd become more acceptable...to me because other people were having them...this is where I started justifying...what I was doing...and...role playing out fantasies become a way of again fuelling the fantasies in me and acting them out in a sense [22: Mixed Offender]

## CONCLUDING COMMENTS

It is clear that, like adult pornography, the primary uses of Internet child pornography is sexual arousal and sexual gratification through, typically, masturbation. Further, Internet child pornography enables fantasizing. But at the same time, the usable 'life' of a pornographic image seems to be short before it loses it ability to stimulate sexually. Offenders are highly selective in their choice of material for sexual gratification – despite offenders sometimes appearing to be indiscriminate hoarders of child pornography. Only certain material is highly arousing to individual Internet pornography users and, to a certain extent, the stimulating material is that which fits into their individual fantasies. Researchers such as Howitt (1995b) and Seto, Maric and Barbaree (2001) have made similar claims. However, Seto et al.'s argument that there is little evidence that pornography users become sexually aroused and mastur-bate while viewing child pornography material is contradicted by our evidence. Many most certainly do. The Internet, for the user, provides a sort of pseudo-privacy and immediacy of access which may be conducive to or facilitate sexual behaviour (Taylor and Quayle, 2003). We should also note that despite the fact that the Internet offenders viewed and masturbated to child pornography over many months, and in some cases many years, their sexual fantasies did not drive them onto hands-on offences (at least as far as can be established). This contradicts the consensus that sexual fantasy drives, guides or energizes offending in some way (Daleiden, Kaufman, Hilliker, and O'Neil, 1998; Gee et al., 2004; Looman, 1995; Pithers et al., 1988; Prentky et al., 1989; Turvey, 1995). It is, therefore, theoretically and practically important to identify what factors Internet offenders assigned to desisting (at least temporarily) from directly molesting children (see Chapter 12).

We have no doubt that some offenders use child pornography to normalise adult-child sex in the eyes of potential victims as other researcher have found (e.g. Goldstein, 1999). Nevertheless, there were few signs of this sort of use of the Internet in the activities of the offenders we studied. But sex offenders differ markedly in their characteristics. Many of the offenders we studied did not seem to stray beyond the Internet for their paedophilic activities. Such offenders are unlikely to seek victims directly and to use pornography to help them recruit their victims. In some ways, certain Internet offenders are similar to the 'closet collectors' described by Hartman, Burgess, and Lanning (1984). That is, individuals who acquire material from commercial and other sources but keep this collection a secret and are not thought to be actively molesting children. We can add to this that some men, although not actively molesting children, did trade their collected images and held discussions with other men. A considerably smaller number of men could be described as 'isolated collectors' (3 mixed offenders) – men who were molesting children and producing photographs but not actively sharing this material online. Their own pornography was an aid to masturbation. Only one offender distributed the images he produced online. He actively molested his daughter and exchanged those photographs and videos with others online for several reasons - as a way of validating his behavior, to gain other images and as an aid to masturbation. There was no evidence to suggest that any pornography was intentionally produced or used for commercial profit by the men we studied.

Sexual fantasy has been consistently linked with regulating negative feelings (Gee et al., 2003; Proulx, McKibben and Lusignan, 1996; Ward, Fon, Hudson and McCormack, 1998). The Internet is also thought to be able to provide an attractive alternative to a mundane or otherwise unhappy life and it can be used to deal with negative moods such as depression, anxiety, and isolation (Morahan-Martin and Schumacher, 2000). Certainly for some of our interviewees, pleasure was gained from the Internet images in terms of helping them avoid their real-life problems. In addition, positive feelings could be achieved through the sexual gratification found in masturbation. For others the Internet gave them a sense of being in control (Taylor and Quayle, 2003).

Social relationships over the Internet involving child pornography do occur though our sample revealed these to be less important than did previous studies (Quayle, 2004; Taylor and Quayle, 2003). One obvious reason for this difference is that previous research was based on Internet pornographers who were 'community' oriented since they were members of the w0nderland club. The fact that our offenders tended to trade images to a lesser extent and entered chat rooms relatively infrequently is consonant with this interpretation. Our sample were often individual offenders sending another individual requested material with no relationship further than this implies. Some of the men in our sample simply did not wish to be part of a 'community' since they were concerned about 'doing wrong' or feared for their personal security on the Internet.

# CHAPTER 6

# The Childhood Histories of Paedophiles

Adult characteristics often originate in childhood. Out-and-out rejections of the thesis are not to be found in discussions of paedophilia but it is equally rare to find enthusiastic support for the idea. There is a reluctance to acknowledge anything that might exonerate sex offenders in any way. Offenders are responsible for their actions, we would argue, yet why they are the way they are is not the result of some perverse decision on their part alone. Early ideas about paedophilia are more likely to emphasise the early experiences of offenders in the development of paedophilia than more recent ones. Psychodynamic models proposed that disruptions to psycho-sexual development may lead to failures to inhibit the expression of infantile sexual interests (Cohen, Seghorn and Calmas, 1969). Conditioning and social learning models identified particular developmental events related to deviant sexual interests as problematic (Laws and Marshall, 1990). Others blamed childhood masturbation in that it reinforces learned associations between deviant sexual imagery and sexual arousal (McGuire, Carlisle and Young, 1965). Even the prominent multifactorial model (Finkelhor, 1984) held childhood experiences to be important elements in the preconditions for offending. More recently attachment behaviour in sex offenders has received consideration by theorists (for example, Rich, 2006). Adverse events seem to characterise the early lives of sex offenders. Among them, are the following:

- events associated with the emergence of insecure attachment styles to others such as the death of caregivers, loss of caregivers through divorce and separation (Ryan and Lane, 1991);
- problematic paternal relationships (Lisak, 1994);
- physical abuse (Williams and Finkelhor, 1990);
- unstable and inconsistent relationships with caregivers (Prentky, Knight, Sims-Knight, Straus, Rokous and Cerce, 1989).

The question for this chapter to address is simple: just how do the early experiences of Internet sex offenders compare with those of paedophiles? Are the developmental histories of contact sex offenders against children different from those of Internet sex offenders? Both, it is clear, have a sexual interest in children. Despite this, the Internet sex offender seems for the most part to have the sexual interest in children but without the motivation to directly offend against children. How can this be explained? There is another important consideration. Childhood risk factors such as neglect, family instability and problematic parenting are commonly associated with histories of childhood sexual abuse in sexual offenders (Smallbone and McCabe, 2003). Nevertheless, the role of childhood sexual abuse in the paedophilia's development has been, and remains, a somewhat controversial issue especially with regard to sexual abuse. It is fairly frequent for researchers to find that sexual abuse is commoner in sex offenders than non-offenders and offenders who have not committed sexual offences (see, for example, Cohen *et al.*, 2002; Craissati and McClurg, 1996; Glasser *et al.*, 2001). Sexual abuse is associated with the tendency for offenders-to-be to begin masturbating at a younger age (Small-bone and McCabe, 2003). Despite all of this, it is generally argued that cycles of sexual abuse in offenders' childhoods are insufficient, in themselves, to explain all sexual offending against children. This is because not all sex offenders against children disclose childhood sexual abuse (Cohen *et al.*, 2002; Howitt, 2002). Furthermore, not everyone who is sexually abused in childhood goes on to be an abuser themselves. A history of sexual abuse does not seem to characterise all offenders against children.

So what about other sexual experiences in childhood? It is possible that child-child sexual activity (peer sex) may have a distinct role to play. There is nothing to suggest that child-child experiences do not influence the development of sexually abusive behaviour (see, for example, Howitt, 1995a). As noted in Chapter 3, significant amounts of sexual abuse against children are committed by juveniles (Anderson *et al.*, 1993; Davis and Leitenberg, 1987; Finkelhor, 1980; Flanagan and Hayman-White, 2000; James and Neil, 1996; O'Shaughnessy, 2006; Synder, 2000; Veneziano, Veneziano and LeGrand, 2000). This is in keeping with the view that the roots of sex offending may emerge in childhood and adolescence and continue, almost careerwise, into adulthood (Howitt, 1995a).

Very little has been firmly established about the sexual development of adult sex offenders, particularly during adolescence (Cortoni and Marshall, 2001). This lack of information is particularly acute, of course, for Internet sex offenders.

## DEVELOPMENTAL HISTORIES OF SEX OFFENDERS AGAINST CHILDREN

It is difficult to express how complex and problematic the early lives of many sex offenders against children are. Simply to give counts of the numbers physically abused or living in care, for example, is only partially informative and tends to ignore the interplay of different childhood adversities. Statistical data are, of course, vitally important, but they need to be set in context. For this reason, three case-histories of sexual offenders against children follow to give a fuller picture to the dry statistics. We have chosen to describe one of each of the three types of offender – Internet-only, contact-only and mixed contact/Internet offenders. In each of these case studies, there is clear evidence that their childhoods were significantly stressed and they experienced suboptimal parenting and other factors which commonly occur in these offender groups.

## CASE STUDY 1: 64-YEAR-OLD INTERNET SEX OFFENDER [16]

As a consequence of the Operation Ore police investigation (see Chapter 2), George was convicted for possession and making of Internet child pornography. A previous conviction for theft was noted on his probation files although he adamantly refused to discuss this conviction. His eventual career was as a fairly successful secondary school teacher although in his youth he spent some time in the hotel industry and worked for an international car-rental company. He strongly disputed that his childhood was in any way linked to his offending behaviour. We could find no evidence that he had been sexually abused; nevertheless, there were a number of adverse aspects to his childhood. These included the loss of caregivers as his mother died when he was three years old and his father was engaged in an Army career. After 18 months in the care of his grandparents, he spent about ten years in an institution from the age of five years. He was separated from his only sibling who was sent to a different care home.

George superficially described his childhood in idyllic language but his positive statements referred exclusively to the *facilities* he grew up in. This contrasts markedly with a total lack of evidence of emotional closeness with adults. He did not identify any important adult relationships or even significant others even in response to a direct question:

Interviewer: Who would you have had close relationships with when you were growing up?

Participant: A very wide circle of friends...there was staff looking after us...some were okay and some weren't...but the environment was superb, it was a big house on the edge of the lake with all the facilities like holiday camp really...middle of the countryside, total freedom

Although questioned in various ways about interpersonal relationships in childhood, overall a rather detached view of other people pervaded his comments. A similar sense of remoteness applied when he discussed important childhood events in his relationship history. For example, when questioned about the separation from his sister he claimed that he felt 'Nothing really...Not a lot.' Similarly he felt that he had not been affected by the lack of a close relationship with his father – a relationship that he described as *civil* and *friendly*. This lack of any elaboration and absence of introspection may reflect a lack of secure childhood attachment to parents or parent substitutes. Conversely, defensiveness did pervade parts of the interview and may be the basis of the restricted information he provided. However, he generally seemed very open about most matters except the few he adamantly refused to address. It is important to note that his relationship with his wife was simply described as *'fine'* and *'deep'* – although, by his own admission, George engaged in frequent impersonal sex and affairs. His sexual adventures, in general, seem best described as casual. He travelled abroad and engaged in sex with prostitutes. This may reflect his difficulties in attachment with adult women (especially) which initially began in childhood:

> I've ... used brothels, saunas over the years ... prostitutes ... I thoroughly enjoyed China ... it's this psyche of the man is king ... I do remember hiring a girl who used to be a bunny girl ... that was a big turn on for me ... had a relationship [with her] ... I had some relationships [across the country] which have gone on over a number of years without us being a couple, girls who I met through work ... hotels I use to stay in, the receptionist ... could have been somebody else.

Listening to this offender in interview, one is presented with a picture of a man engaging in numerous short-term sexual episodes with very little distinction made between paid-for sex and (possibly) longer term relationships while away from home. Furthermore, episodes at school when he was a teacher involved 'friendships' with children as well as perceiving young girls as almost offering themselves to him 'on a plate'. He describes himself almost as 'doing the right thing' and kindly dissuading them:

> Participant: Over the years of teaching, lots of children gravitate towards particular teachers and towards me it becomes ... a bit more than a child-teacher relationship ... they confide their problems to you ... I've got my son's friends ... some of them want to go and have a pint with me when I come out, you know and they're only seventeen, eighteen

> Interviewer: Have any of them ever expressed a sexual interest in you?

> Participant: No ... I've had girls from time to time ... whose ... relationship with me has been threatening towards that erm ... You know, tended to be over the, you know going beyond ... normality when I've had to ... dissuade them kindly ... I mean forty year olds don't have ... romantic romantic relationships with girls of that age ... but girls that age can, do come onto you ... decide they like you ...

## CASE STUDY 2: 42 YEAR OLD CONTACT SEX OFFENDER [28]

Eddie was convicted of indecent assault (fellatio on him) against the five-year-old daughter of his second long-term partner. Among a range of previous convictions he had non-sexual ones including theft, driving and criminal damage. A history of non-sexual previous convictions is a common pattern among paedophile offenders (Greenberg *et al.*, 2000). His developmental history reveals many of the aspects of a severely neglectful childhood.

He had a history of local social services interventions and multiple transfers to child care institutions, which began in infancy (around four years of age) but continued until, as he remembers, he was 15 or 16 years of age. Eddie described to us how he was severely beaten at these institutions as well as being the victim of sexual assaults. Researchers have long recognised the high levels of physical abuse that took place in some care homes (Hobbs, Hobbs and Wynne, 1999). He also spent time in a Borstal. Borstals were institutions that attempted to reform delinquent boys between the ages of 16 and 21 years. Their regimes emphasised and enforced education, discipline, regular work and respect for authority. Acts of violence perpetrated in Borstals could result in the officially allowed punishment of being hit with a birch 'whip'. The Borstal system was abolished in 1982. Eddie's first consistent experience of family life was when he lived at the parental home of his first girlfriend.

> I got transferred to [children's home] and from there I went to [care home] and from there I went to another care home . . . I wasn't wanted . . . I met my first girlfriend [about 16], and her family took me in basically . . . I stayed with her for 20 odd years.

During childhood, Eddie experienced inconsistent and, sometimes, unwarranted punishment. Feeling unwanted and unloved, this sense of his unworthiness coloured even his adult relationships. He believes that he is not the sort of person to whom others are likely to respond in a positive way:

> A lot of my problem is based on being unloved as a child . . . and as an adult, that's a big problem for me, feeling not wanted, not needed, always being punished for something I haven't done . . . I know no one cares about me . . . and it's something I have to live with.

His childhood was one of confusion and anxiety. Eddie had no information of, or understanding about, why he was so regularly separated from his family. Feelings of uncertainty and rejection would worsen and develop into what he deems 'crises' when he was later separated from other significant family members. One important event, around puberty, occurred when his step brother was removed by his step brother's natural father to live at home. Eddie remained in care. This was followed by him running away from care, fighting and criminal activities:

> I blamed myself . . . then . . . his real father took [step-brother] out of care when he was 11 and just left me there which . . . made me worse because I started retaliating having . . . little crises . . . running away . . . fighting.

Interaction with his parents was limited and that which he described to us emphasised disregard, abandonment and a lack of physical warmth:

> It's as if I'm not there, I'm a ghost.

Sexual victimisation was, of course, quite a common experience for youngsters brought up in institutions and foster care, both in the UK and US (Hobbs *et al.*, 1999; Rabb and Rindfleisch, 1985; Rindfleisch and Rabb, 1984; Rosenthal *et al.*, 1991; Spencer and Knudsen, 1992; Utting, 1991). At the age of six, Eddie had oral sex performed on him by an older boy. He experienced this as both frightening and comforting – and felt almost helpless in relation to these sexual experiences. There was a lack of satisfactory interactions with any adult who might have acted as an effective substitute for his absent parents. One female care home staff member who might have provided such a relationship instead sexually abused him by fondling, kissing and performing oral sex on him when he was about seven or eight years of age. However, he presents this abusive experience almost exclusively as a positive one. This is common in the case histories of offenders (Howitt, 1995a). Sexual victimisation becomes construed almost as a substitute for maternal warmth and responsiveness. His actions towards his victimiser include signalling behaviours such as crying, and actively seeking out her company. It is notable that as the interview progresses he refers to his victimiser as a 'mother figure':

> I'd have turned to anybody, if anybody had have showed me one slight bit of affection . . . To me it was love and affection . . . she was always there. And I looked for her all the time. And I'd cry to her . . . she'd always comfort me . . . maybe being a child of that age and . . . you've got nothing . . . if someone approaches you like that, you've got to take it. And cling on to that. I enjoyed, loved what she done and I suppose in lots of ways I've carried on looking for that because it was love, it was comfort and I felt warm and I felt wanted . . . she wouldn't punch me or physically beat me . . . she showed me something that a child deserves which is love and affection and care and understanding . . . she [abuser] was a mother figure to me . . .

In this sort of circumstance, the vulnerability of some children to the approaches of their abusers is obvious. Eddie's female abuser is consistently accessible to him and responsive to his actions and emotional needs. Close bodily contact was possible though in a sexualised context. He hints that anyone would have sufficed at that time to meet his needs – so long as they were responsive to him.

There is evidence that Eddie's understanding of the world as reflected in his cognitive distortions may be based on more enduring schema developed at this time in his childhood (for example, Howitt, 1995a; Ward and Siegert, 2002) and built on the basis of his experiences at that time. For instance, Eddie felt that he had not been harmed by his abuse so, in this way, why should his victim have been harmed by him?

> I was saying to [victim] I'm here to comfort you, to protect, to love you . . . maybe because that's how someone showed me love and comfort when I was a child, by abusing me.

It is possible to see links between Eddie's childhood and his offending behaviour. In the following comments, he seems to suggest that his offending behaviour involves, in part, a recreation of his childhood experiences and behaviour. Specifically, when he experiences feelings of humiliation and rejection during adulthood as a consequence of conflicts in his relationships, he resorts to sexually abusive behaviour for comfort. That is to say, his equating of love and affection with sex (which developed as a child) persists into adulthood:

> When...she just treated me like dirt [having an affair], that's what triggered it off. She humiliated me, ripping me off...it was bringing back memories of my childhood...humiliation...rejection, feeling unloved...so I would hold comfort with [victim] and [victim's brother] as I would when I was trying to comfort another child when I was young, so was this. It wasn't an adult clinging to them it's like I was a child.

Eddie's thinking and behaviour reveal a substantial degree of emotional congruence with children. Adults do not provide him with what he needs emotionally. This offender's victim was only five-years of age but he talks of her as if she were an adult. The young victim is bestowed abilities that typify much older children and adults including perspective taking, understanding and compassion. These capacities are considered absent in adult behaviour towards him, including his two long-term partners:

> [Victim] was the only one there...she just showed me 'don't worry'...I couldn't believe that at least somebody in my life, but of all people a child, can see the pain, and...could actually experience how I was feeling. It's like she's been there before...I think a lot of children really understand life.

This emotional congruence involves attributing adult characteristics to his victim. Attributing adultlike qualities to children reappears again when he describes his victim and her mother. He perceives their interaction as flirtatious behaviour much as might be demonstrated, he believes, by two women competing over a potential sexual partner:

> To me it was flirting...they...would bitch at each other...each day she'd [victim] be in the mirror doing herself...she would think 'yea I'm better looking than you mum!' [Victim] was always clinging to me...she was, trying to maybe, get my attention? Using her make-up...and her mother would have none of it, why?...well if [victim] had have been capable of saying it she would have said 'Why? What you afraid of mum in case Eddie takes me instead of you?' She was jealous of her own daughter.

Despite conceptualising children as if they were adults, Eddie also takes the opportunity to behave in a childlike manner. He describes being 'entitled' to behave in this way because he missed out on a proper childhood. This may appear paradoxical but it is also an opportunity to be physical with children:

> I don't want to grow up...I'm entitled to a child's good life I haven't had one yet...if I want to ride my BMX and do wheelies...climb a tree...leave me and let me do it...being with [victim] and having pillow fights with her and fighting on the floor and mucking around and whipping her ear holes that's just me being a child.

It is common to find that an offender's abusive behaviour reflects his early experience of sexual abuse. This seems to be the case with this offender since his offending behaviour involved him masturbating his penis in the victim's mouth – the sort of behaviours he had been victim to as a child. This is almost a reenactment of the behaviours (Cohen *et al.*, 2002; Haaspasalo, Puupponen and Crittenden, 1999; Hilton and Mezey, 1996; Howitt, 1995a) perpetrated on him by the older boy.

## CASE STUDY 3: 49-YEAR-OLD MIXED INTERNET CONTACT SEX OFFENDER [51]

Steve was convicted of two indecent assaults against an 11-year-old boy as well as downloading Internet pornographic images of children. The images included level 3 as categorised by the Sentencing Advisory Panel (2002) (see Chapter 2). Level 3 images consist of non-penetrative sexual activity between adults and children. The majority of the images he had obtained depicted boys – the gender of his target victim. There was no record of any previous convictions, sexual or otherwise.

Like the other sex offenders, adverse interpersonal experiences characterised his life. One of the most striking features in his history was the extent of his religious institutionalisation. He grew up in a family with a strong Catholic ethos and was heavily involved in the Catholic Church from about the age of eight years until he went to a Catholic boarding school when aged 11 years. At the age of 16 years, he entered a monastery where he stayed until early adulthood. These experiences went along with the loss of his father when he was three years of age. Both home and primary school involved high levels of conflict as well as physical abuse. This record of physical abuse continued at boarding school. However, in addition, at boarding school he was exposed to and participated in extreme sexual abuse as well as sex play with other boys. On several occasions during his interview he described the difficulties he had in adjusting to the boarding school's strict regime.

Steve's childhood was either at boarding school or at home unsupervised by his mother who was largely unavailable for various reasons. He found his mother unresponsive to his needs and periodically controlling and violent. She also seemed to lack the ability to express love and affection. This latter characteristic seems to have become a model for his later adult behaviour:

> The only other adult in my life...was my older brother who assumed my father's role...I was regularly physically battered by him...and

increasingly over the years I was being seen only during holiday times, the family drifted apart but the aggression still carried on...I have got no relationship with my older brother other than intimidation. I do have vague memories of...male friends of hers calling to the house...and one of them taking me to a football match...and never going again basically...My mum physically assaulted me and punished me...that wasn't unusual...it happened in school anyway...in primary school the brother...used the window pole...the cane was part and parcel of everyday life...whipping lads...My mom was quite selective about who she would allow me to play with...I've no memories of hugs or...cuddling up next to my mom...there were many times when I come home from school and she would have been in the ironing cupboard crying...the result of that was I became more and more...an expert...at internalising things

Relationships with almost every family member were strained. For instance, he was estranged from his grandfather who, he claims, refused to see or speak to him when Steve was asked to leave the monastery because of 'depraved' behaviour – he says that he was found smoking. Beyond the primary care giver, there was an acute lack of substitute positive and constructive inter-personal experiences. For example, prior to boarding school and during home visits he spent 'incalculable' amounts of time alone or staying at friend's homes. The only relationship he presented positively during the interview involved a stepfather with whom he developed a strong bond for a short period of time, when he was a young adult of 21 years. When this man died shortly afterwards, this was a traumatic experience for Steve.

This lack of proximity to his mother through her unavailability and rejection possibly led to several negative outcomes. It obviously facilitated a detachment from his mother and the family in general. Further, the lack of close parental supervision and protection and placement in an institutional context increased his vulnerability to predatory offenders and also his psychological 'openness' to sexual abuse. Indeed, there were few reliable adults around him to offer a base for security and support. Furthermore, as can happen, among the adults who should have been protecting him there were some physical and sexual abusers. The following illustrates one of several occasions described where the religious staff were sexually abusing (penetrative sex) one of the young boys:

It was...as sure as you'd get up in the morning and have porridge...I knocked on the door and opened it, it was this guy's private room he had a young lad in bed with him...and I didn't bat an eye lid...it was sort of oh I see...it never occurred to me to question it.

His ambivalence towards being a regular witness to such sexual victimisa-tion of other teenage boys is reiterated again when he described to us his adult offending:

[Victim] was actually stark naked and masturbating...I remember looking at him and I remember he looked back up at me...I remember at the time...feeling very ambivalent.

The inadequate relationships Steve had with his caregivers may have led to his failure to develop psychological resources with which he could use to deal with, and resist the sexual abuser(s). For instance, the lack of support may have made him vulnerable to abuse but may also have increased the probability that he would seek attention in maladaptive ways, including through other vulnerable children. He presents himself as an unhappy and solitary child prone to seeking physical comfort from anyone who responds to him in a positive way – that is, his peers. For example, the following comments show that he uses peers as emotional crutches for the abuse and difficulties he was enduring during boarding school. In a sense, comfort lies in sexual activity:

> There were one or two priests that you could go and talk...but the approach was always pray about it...[Mother] visited I'd say about three times...I was bullied extensively at boarding school...physical bullying with sexual undertones...you learnt there was no escape from it so you learnt to accept it, to internalise it...and in a lot of ways you began to look for, to turn to other kids who were also lonely and who were isolated for comfort in the same way they turn to you...cuddles in bed.

Physical interactions with other vulnerable boys included mutual embracing, genital contact and fondling, face-to-face contact and kissing. Later as an adult, faced with a difficult and distressing relationship and work related problems, he again turned to young teenage boys (in images and in person) much as he did when he was a boy.

The offending behaviour with his victim mirrors that of his childhood sex-play with other boys – he was even a school teacher much as his early adult abusers were:

> My relationship with my wife was...becoming strained...the stress of my work...I was already viewing the Internet...I ended up having a break-down...and that went on for three years...[then] I started giving him [victim] tuition on a one-to-one...I could see a lot of similarities between this lad and myself...He enjoyed my coming round to the house and I enjoyed going round there...a friendship started to grow...I was being welcomed with open arms, accepted...both of us genital contact it was in bunk beds...gentle fondling...above and below clothing.

Generally, contact, Internet and mixed sex offenders reported similar childhood upbringings including early experiences of parental non-supervision, violence and institutional care. All of these are hallmarks of disorganised childhood attachment behaviour. But what begins to emerge is how commonly sexual victimisation, present in the lives of contact and mixed sexual offenders, acts as a substitute for absent parental warmth. To some extent, sex play with peers also functioned as a means of succour, and emotional congruence with children seems common. At certain times, this emotional affiliation is greater to young people than adults.

## THE FAMILY BACKGROUNDS OF OFFENDERS IN STATISTICAL DETAIL

Just as nature abhors a vacuum, researchers often abhor a lack of differences. The similarities between clearly identifiable and distinguishable groups should be as informative as any statistically reliable differences. And this is our main conclusion and message about Internet sex offenders – they are in many crucial ways little different from the men who carry out direct sexual crimes against children. In the same way, this is also true of the family backgrounds of Internet offenders – they are distinguishable in very few respects from contact offending paedophiles. Nevertheless, despite the homogeneity in the offenders backgrounds, they do show a few differences which are worthy of note (see table 6.1).

Rates of physical abuse by adults were exceptionally high in each of the three groups of offenders we studied. But the highest rate was for contact sex offenders (72 %), followed by mixed offenders (60 %) and with the lowest rate being identified in Internet only offenders (44 %). The offenders, in general, reported unprovoked or excessively disproportionate physical punishment when they had committed some misdemeanour as a child. For instance, the following contact offender (aged 40) reported a lengthy childhood history of violent victimisation. Consequently, he used violence as a way of coping with the feelings he was enduring as a child and as a way of 'survival'. He was convicted of sexual assaults against two girls aged 15 years and one against his infant son but his prior convictions also included grievous and actual bodily harm (including against children) as well as a variety of criminal damage, theft and burglary offences. These prior violent offences indicate how violence became a normal way of interacting with people from childhood through to adulthood – for example, as a means of disciplining his children, resolving marital conflicts, and dealing with general frustrations;

> At around seven I went into care, my mom left took my elder brother and left me . . . haven't seen mam since . . . I was in and out of temporary foster care until I was about 18, I was sexually assaulted by one lot of foster parents who was recently convicted . . . but it was very abusive [care], from staff and other boys, so I become very aggressive, very nasty, very violent in my mind . . . as time went on I felt more let down, felt even more bitter with adults . . . I use to do things like that [self harm scars] I would cry about how, how, how I was feeling, how I was hurting and what was going on in the home . . . I wasn't a child self-harming just for attention, I was self-harming because I was trying to . . . cry and scream out this is what's going on . . . would someone take notice? No . . . I had been let down by, by adults . . . I would fight, not only . . . psychologically I was fighting physically so I would hurt people . . . I didn't like hurting people but it was the only in care it was the only way . . . I could survive was through violence . . . this frustration carried on into adulthood . . . if I got frustrated . . . the first thing I'd do was smack a wall, smack a window, or whatever . . . early to late twenties if somebody got in my face I wouldn't hesitate I'd smack

him I'd put him in hospital . . . anytime we had an argument, I grabbed her by the throat . . . . . . went to punch her . . . I didn't punch her but went smack straight past her ear and straight through the window I said 'you wanna be lucky that's not your face.'

The offender also reports childhood physical violence in combination with sexual abuse. The use of violence seems to represent a way of gaining control in his life especially as he felt out of control in terms of what was happening to him sexually:

With the sexual abuse . . . I could never show emotions because if I cried while they were doing it [anal sex with male friends of the family] I'd get battered more . . . I always use to blame myself, I felt that I could have stopped it? So I started to become controlling . . . and I started controlling everybody else . . . if you didn't toe the line with me bang . . . [hit them] it was a way of feeling in control.

Similarly the following mixed contact-Internet offender also reported violence during his early teens. He was convicted of a variety of indecent sexual assaults and Internet child pornography offences. His previous convictions included violence, fraud and handling stolen goods.

Physically I was [abused] . . . I didn't go into children's home till I was 13 but . . . I'd have been about 11 when me dad remarried . . . it was after that the physical stuff started 'cos I was with me stepmother . . . and she use to beat me black and bloody blue . . . I was a bloody nervous wreak, I use to wet the bed . . . me dad was hen-pecked, he never got involved in telling her about the beatings, but the only time he really got involved was when he . . . saw her going overboard . . . he was coming off the 2 till 10 shift, I run out the bloody house and she chased me with a broom stick and belted me over the back with it . . . but instead they put me in care . . . apparently I was unruly . . . my step brothers and sisters never went into care. [case study 17]

Such violence was not unique in the descriptions given by the men we interviewed and was often in reaction to minor misdemeanours. Others, such as the following mixed-contact-Internet offender, reported that their parents had a variety of frustrations and problems, which were expressed through violence taken out on the children:

Participant: My father was distant, strict . . . handy with the whackings

Interviewer: Is that how he'd discipline you?

Participant: Yea but whenever really, you didn't have to do anything wrong, usually what happened was he'd come home completely drunk, gambling all the money away, as a result he'd be taking it out . . . on someone, you, hitting me mother. [case study 3]

Parental pathology, in the form of substance misuse, was not a major aspect of any of the three groups of offenders but our interview data showed that the quality of parent-child relationships was consistently poor and it was common to hear that the fathers of many of these sex offenders were relatively insignificant in their domestic roles or the men reported not being close to them at all, as clearly demonstrated by this following 49-year old Internet-only offender [Case Study 9]:

> Dad was...very strict...never really see a lot of him because he was always working...he never really had a lot of time for me or me older sister...he was controlling...he did use to take me fishing now and again but...he spent nearly four years on his back through TB and other illnesses...he was frustrated, he couldn't do anything because of the illness so perhaps he took it out on us...? then as soon as he was able to work again all he done was work, work, work, work, and it...felt like 'oh who's that man who comes in on a Friday?'...yea we very rarely wanted for anything...but lovey-dovey son and dad...sharing things, no we had none of that.

Similarly the following mixed offender [case study 22] highlighted the lack of emotional closeness with his father;

> Dad...his role was more he took a backseat, he wasn't really there much, he was working long hours...he wasn't there to talk to...he was more the disciplinarian...I didn't really get to connect with him emotionally because he wouldn't really spend much time with us finding out what we wanted.

Sadly, what was rarely described was the presence of a positive mediating interaction and there appears to be very few positive adult relationships in the lives of all three groups of men.

Sexual abuse was common in the contact-only (56%) and mixed contact/ Internet (50%). Sexual abuse was significantly less common in the upbringings of the Internet group at 20%. The cooccurrence of both physical and sexual abuse was extremely common at 68% of the entire sample. This is not a new finding since physical abuse and discipline are noticeably high in sex offenders against children according to previous studies (Morris *et al.*, 1997; Seghorn, Prentky, and Boucher, 1987; Tingle *et al.*, 1986; Williams and Finkelhor, 1990).

Behavioural or emotional difficulties were also found in a substantial minority of all the sex offender groups. Approximately 40% of all groups demonstrated at least two such characteristics. These characteristics included truancy, running away, criminal activities, substance abuse, deliberate self-harm, aggression towards others, feeling miserable a lot, bullying others and risk-taking behaviours (for example, promiscuous behaviour). These behaviours are typically associated with sexually abused children (Browne and Finkelhor, 1986; Craissati, McClurg and Browne, 2002; Thompson, Authier, and Ruma, 1994) and up to half of the offenders described incidents of

**Table 6.1**  Childhood characteristics of Internet, contact and mixed sex offenders

| Childhood characteristic | Type of sex offender | | |
| --- | --- | --- | --- |
| | Internet (%) | Contact (%) | Mixed (%) |
| Substance abuse by parent(s) | 12 | 16 | 10 |
| Parent/s in military | 9 | 20 | 10 |
| Religious upbringing | 19 | 16 | 20 |
| Death of significant other | 37 | 16 | 10 |
| Witness to domestic violence (parent-parent) | 0 | 8 | 20 |
| Separated/divorced parents | 12 | 16 | 10 |
| Physical (non-sexual) abuse | 44 | 72 | 60 |
| Sexual abuse | 19 | 56 | 50 |
| Two or more behavioural/ emotional problems | 37 | 40 | 40 |
| Absent parents or caregivers/seclusion | 37 | 28 | 40 |
| Period(s) in institution(s) | 19 | 32 | 50 |

* One mixed offender declined to offer further details of his childhood sexual abuse other than to confirm its occurrence, his age and the age of the perpetrator.

childhood sexual victimisation. However, given that some contact and mixed sexual offenders described their sexual abuse as pleasurable and consensual, these difficulties may conceivably be a response to their more general situations. As observed, both contact and mixed groups report high levels of physical abuse and experiences of institutionalisation are frequently described in less than favourable terms. For some offenders their 'acting out' behaviours may well be attributed to these conditions rather than the sexual abuse per se. Furthermore, sexual abuse was not a predominant feature for Internet offenders yet over a third were coded as engaging in similar 'acting out' behaviours. Acting out cannot be attributed to sexual abuse in these cases and seems rather more to be linked to their experiences of parental caretaking, e.g. physical abuse or loss of caregivers. The latter variable was not significant in the lives of contact offenders.

Many of the offenders experienced childhoods in which parents or caregivers were absent or they experienced periods of seclusion. The rates scarcely differed with 37 % of Internet, 32 % of contact, and 40 % of mixed offenders reporting this feature in their childhoods. Essentially, then, a substantial minority of offenders experienced long or frequent periods either alone or with siblings, at home or outdoors, in which they were largely expected to take care of themselves. In many of these cases such seclusion or unsupervised care was the consequence of parental inability or disinterest, demands of parents work, parental mental instability and being a difficult or demanding child. In terms of being placed in a foster home or institutional care, there was once again evidence that a substantial minority spent at least some time in these settings. This was especially the case for contact offenders (32 %) and mixed contact/Internet offenders (50 %). Of course, such placements may signal that they were problematic children rather than that the placements caused their later problems although it was just a small proportion who seem to have been taken away from home as a result of their disruptive behaviour. A smaller percentage of Internet sex offenders (19%) reported such placements away from home.

These figures can be expressed even more graphically because almost half of each offender group grew up in circumstances where they were spending long periods of time unsupervised or in an institution away from their parents. This may be because the parent is physically or psychological unavailable due to a variety of factors. These factors could be deliberate choices by the parents or factors beyond their control (such as excessive work demands or alcoholism). Whichever circumstance applies, to some extent caregivers are not appropriately available or responsive to the offender as a child and this may influence the development of an inappropriate attachment style – say to other children. The case studies showed troubled efforts to become 'connected' to someone through sexual contact with other peers and adults

## CONCLUDING COMMENTS

In conclusion, it is clear that, in general, contact, Internet and mixed sex offenders report similar childhood upbringings including early experiences of parental non-supervision, violence and institutional care. These are hallmarks of sex offender's childhood histories. What also begins to emerge is that sexual victimisation, especially present in the lives of contact and mixed sexual offenders, can act as a substitute for absent parental warmth in some cases. Certainly, we have seen that sex-play with peers can equally function as a means of succour, and emotional congruence with children is clearly illustrated. This emotional affiliation is greater with young people than with adults.

The whole question of the psychosexual development of sex offenders against children is complex. As a result the following chapter will explore further the psychosexual development of the three types of sex offenders in order to help understand better what other features of sexualisation and childhood experiences may be conducive to the development of Internet sex offending and paedophilia.

# CHAPTER 7

# Sexual Abuse and Sexualisation in the Childhoods of Paedophiles

When talking freely in interviews, many offenders describe childhoods full of sexual episodes. Assuming that these accounts are not merely fantasy, this early sexual milieu needs to be better understood. This is not solely an issue of adult-child sex abuse but also involves peer-peer sexual activity. Childhood sexually abusive victimisation is a characteristic of the childhoods of some paedophiles (see Chapter 6) though the rates are too low to identify childhood sexual abuse as a crucial factor in all paedophiles. Sexual abuse is limited as an explanation of paedophilia for the following reasons:

- *Not all sexual abuse victims become abusers.* Surveys of adults in general result in estimates of rates of sexual abuse in childhood which are quite substantial. Reported sexual abuse rates for women, for example, have ranged from 8% to 32% in retrospective general population samples, whereas the rates for men range from 1% to 16% (Finkelhor, 1994b). Overall figures in the 10% to 20% range would not be uncommon (Finkelhor, 1994b). If sexual abuse led to paedophilia in all cases, this would imply that there are many millions of paedophiles around the world. While figures for the actual rates of paedophilia are difficult to obtain, if all sexual victimisation in childhood turned the victim into an adult abuser then there should be something in the order of 5 to 10 million paedophiles in the UK and three or four times that number in the US. The only 'official' estimates in the UK put the figure much lower, at less than half a million, although the basis for this is unknown (Foreign and Commonwealth Office, 2004).
- *Female victims of sexual abuse in childhood appear to outnumber male victims.* Although female molesters of children exist, they appear to be relatively infrequent compared to male offenders. For instance official data obtained from criminal records indicate that somewhere between 1–5% of all sexual offences are committed by women (Tomlinson *et al.*, 1991; Travin, Cullen

and Protter, 1990). Some retrospective studies conducted on sexually abused victims suggest that between 3 % and 5 % are abused by women (Dube and Hebert, 1988; Kendall-Tackett and Simon, 1987). In contrast, other retrospective studies suggest the figures for female sex offenders are higher at somewhere between 13 % and 22 % (Finkelhor and Russel, 1984; Ryan *et al.*, 1996). Overall, the bulk of research indicates that females are responsible for a relatively small number of sex offences against children and that men constitute the vast majority of perpetrators (Banning, 1989; Grayson and De Luca, 1999; Green and Kaplan, 1994; Snyder, 2000; Tomlinson *et al.*, 1991). Consequently, there is a problem; if child sexual abuse can result in paedophilia, why does the process result in few female sexual abusers? Because many victims of sexual abuse do not grow up to be abusers themselves, then claims by offenders about their childhood abuse appear to be self-serving excuses or pro-paedophile rhetoric. After all, most victims avoid becoming adult victimisers, so why not everyone?

- *How to identify sexual abuse in offenders' childhoods?* Childhood sexual abuse is more characteristic of contact paedophiles or child molesters than it is of Internet offenders (see Chapter 6). The prevalence of sexual abuse in the childhoods of the contact offenders we studied was around 50 %. This is comparable to figures from previous research (for example, Cohen *et al.*, 2002; Craissati and McClurg, 1996; Craissati, McClurg and Browne, 2002). This means that sexually abusive childhoods are not a universal feature of sexual abusers. Of course, some methodological issues may be partly responsible for the lack of a perfect relationship (such as reluctance to report victimisation even to a researcher). One way of circumventing this difficulty is not to use terms such as 'sexual abuse' but to ask about childhood sexual experiences. In this way, the researcher can classify these sexual experiences as abuse or not. The study by Burgess *et al.* (1988) that used this method found that the figures among sex offenders for sexual abuse in childhood were 75 % whereas few revealed their abuse if questioned about sexual abuse directly. There are many reasons for this difference, one of which is that some paedophiles fail to recognise their own sexual abuse as such and construe it as sexual activity that they desired themselves or freely consented to.

- *Is all sexual abuse equally damaging?* Research in this area has a tendency to regard all sexual abuse as equally serious in its effects. This idea is partly the consequence of the influence of feminist writers who, correctly, point out that for some victims relatively innocuous sexual acts can be distressing and damaging (see, for example, Kelly, 1988). However, it is clearly wrong to conclude from this that all forms of sexual abuse are equally distressing and damaging for children in general. In other words, there may be certain patterns of sexual abuse that are more likely to be related to paedophilia (Howitt, 1995a, 1998b).

Despite the superficial appeal of explanations of paedophilia based on victim-offender cycles, we have already seen that sexual abuse is less of a feature of

Internet sex offender's backgrounds than contact offenders (Chapter 6). It occurred quite frequently in the childhoods of those who contact offended against children (contact only = 56 % mixed contact/Internet = 50 %) but was far less common in the childhoods of Internet-only offenders (20 %). The co-occurrence of both physical and sexual abuse was found in a third of the sample (30 %). Three-quarters (75 %) of our entire sample experienced either sexual or physical abuse.

What is typical of all of these men is that when they suffered sexual abuse in their childhood, they seldom disclosed it to say a trusted adult or to the authorities. In fact only one contact offender had disclosed his own sexual abuse history to his mother who took no action. It was his perception that he had annoyed his mother by disclosing information about his abuse of which she was already fully aware. Some offenders mentioned embarrassment and shame as the reasons for non-disclosure but others said that non-disclosure was the result of a lack of closeness with parents, being unable to talk to their parents about sexual matters and because sex was a taboo topic. We need to add to this the co-occurrence of sexual abuse and physical abuse in the childhood's of these men. This has important implications in terms of resilience. A child from a highly nurturing home who is sexually assaulted or even approached by a stranger is more likely to have the internal coping mechanisms as well as external supports to manage the situation (Seghorn, Prentky and Boucher, 1987). Such a child would be more likely to view such an experience as inconsistent with his prior experiences with adults.

Friendships and social support may also act as buffering factors in the victim-offender cycle. Receiving verbal as well as physical displays of affection and high levels of emotional support during times of crisis enhance a child's self-esteem and decrease their social isolation following abuse. However, the effects of sexual assault can only be magnified if the victim is in a deprived and abusive home or one where there is a lack of communication. Alexander (1992) argued that the negative consequences of sexual abuse for children with insecure attachment relationships with their parents are likely to be more severe than for children with secure attachment relationships with their parents (see Chapter 9). In addition, Alexander suggests that insecure children will have a less functional family support system available to them. Support for abused children requires that they disclose what has happened to them and that they are in an environment where this will be appropriately responded to. It may be that poor childhood attachment relationships may increase both the risk of being sexually abused and lead to more negative outcomes (Alexander, 1992). Chapter 6 revealed nearly a third (31 %) of the men we studied had some experience of institutional care. Some would have entered into care having already been harmed psychologically or emotionally and thus may have developed behavioural difficulties. As such these children may form a group at risk of being further abused and neglected within the institution or placement (Hobbs et al., 1999). Many of the confirmed reports of abuse in out-of-home placements are serious in nature (Rosenthal et al., 1991).

## PSYCHOSEXUAL DEVELOPMENT IN INTERNET AND CONTACT OFFENDERS

Victim-to-offender cycles have not featured in research and theory concerning Internet child pornography offending. It might be expected that, if sexual abuse is important in the process of becoming a sexual abuser, then it would also be a common feature of the childhoods of Internet sex offenders. This makes some assumptions that may or may not be valid. In particular, it is to assume that Internet and contact offences are similar in terms of their aetiology. This may not be entirely the case; sexual victimisation may be associated with becoming a contact offender in adulthood since about half of the offenders in the contact categories showed evidence of sexual abuse in their childhoods. This is a level that is commensurate with findings of some past research (for example, Cohen *et al.*, 2002; Craissati and McClurg, 1996; Craissati, McClurg and Browne, 2002).

### Childhood Sexual Victimisation

Of course, the term 'sexual abuse' covers a wide variety of acts, frequencies of acts, and perpetrators of acts. This, naturally, offers the possibility that the experience of abuse can be radically different and raises the question of whether some forms of sexual abuse are more prone to lead some victims to abuse children themselves. Howitt (1998b) made this argument and suggested that not all forms of sexual abuse are implicated in the cycles of abuse thesis – the more extreme forms of abuse are more likely to involved. Although it is difficult to define precisely what is meant by 'extreme' forms of abuse, there are indications from research that abuse by female abusers and repeated penetrative acts of abuse are more likely to typify the victims who enter the cycles of abuse process (Howitt, 1998b). It might be expected that, because the contact offenders were committing more serious and more damaging offences, they should reveal more extreme sexual abuse in childhood. In the light of this, it is important not merely to code for the presence of sexual abuse in the offenders' childhoods but to employ indicators of the severity and extremity of the abuse. Certain characteristics of abuse seem to be associated with the circumstances in which it can be damaging:

- A young child will generally have fewer psychological resources to deal with abuse than an older child. Even simply at the level of sexual knowledge, the young child might be more vulnerable because his or her understanding of sexual matters is more rudimentary. Consequently, one of the more notable findings to emerge in our research was that the different offender groups first experienced abuse at different ages. Contact-only offenders, if they report being abused at all, tended to be first abused at a substantially younger age than the two Internet groups. For those who revealed that they had been sexually abused, the average age of the contact offender's first sexual abusive experience was 7.6 years; the average age for first abuse for the mixed Internet/contact group was 12.0 years and the average for the Internet-only offenders was 9.3 years.

- Most of the abused offenders we studied were abused by men in childhood. This was highest was for contact (79 %) and Internet sex offenders (67 %). Half of the mixed offender group were victimised by males. While the numbers of female abusers was small in absolute terms, they were more common than has generally been suggested by previous research (Dube and Hebert, 1988; Kendall-Tackett and Simon, 1987; Tomlinson et al., 1991; Travin, et al., 1990). Of our sample who had been sexually abused, 29 % of the men had been abused, at least once, by a female perpetrator including their mothers. Of course, women are generally not seen as sexually abusive (Hetherton, 1999; Tardif, Auclair, Jacob, Carpentier, 2005). So if women are not seen as sexually abusive, what are the psychological consequences of being sexually abused by one's mother Kelly, et al., 2002? It is probably more difficult for a child victim to deal with a female victimiser simply because the cultural expectations of men and women are quite different in this regard as are expectations about nurturance. A child who is abused by a female may not perceive what happened as a sexual act, perhaps because it is more likely that the behaviour is seen as affectionate (Banning, 1989). Some researchers suggest that mother-son incest is likely to be subtle involving behaviours that may be difficult to distinguish from normal care-giving (for example, genital touching) (Kelly et al., 2002). Professionals such as police workers tend to have more positive attitudes towards female than male sex offenders (Hetherton and Breadsall, 1988). One assumption is that sexual abuse by females is regarded as less traumatic than that perpetrated by males basically because boys involved with women sexually are seen as willing and benefiting accomplices rather than victims (Hetherton, 1999). However, sexual abuse by females may have an even greater detrimental effect on the victims because the care-giving relationship can engender a sense of betrayal when it is breached by sexual abuse (Finkelhor, 1979; Saradjian, 1996). Kelly et al. (2002) found that men who reported mother-son incest endorsed more trauma symptoms than did other sexually abused men. Furthermore, the men who were abused by their mothers and recalled positive or mixed initial perceptions of this abuse reported more adjustment problems later in life than men who recalled purely negative perceptions.
- For the offenders we studied who had been sexually abused in childhood, penetrative sexual activities (oral and anal) are common experiences. About two-thirds of the contact offenders and the Internet-only offenders experienced such penetrative sexual activities although the figures were slightly lower at 50 % for the mixed-contact-Internet offenders who had been sexually abused.
- Single experiences of sexual abuse in childhood were relatively uncommon. The abuse tended to be repeated on more than one occasion. About three-quarters of all of the sex offenders who had been sexually victimised in childhood claimed that this happened on more than one occasion. The

co-occurrence of two or more abusers was 50 % for the abused contact and mixed sex offenders but slightly higher at 67 % for the Internet-only offenders.

- Extrafamilial abuse was a typical characteristic of the sexual abuse. This refers to abuse carried out by an acquaintance, stranger, or person in a position of trust such as a teacher. None of the Internet-only offenders had been sexually abused by a family member. This was not true of the other types of offender although extrafamilial abuse was typical – for example, three-quarters of the mixed Internet/contact offenders had experienced extrafamilial abuse. However, it is important to note that half of the contact offenders had been sexually abused both within the family and outside of the family. By 'familial' sexual victimisation we mean abuse perpetrated by a relative such as parent, sibling, stepparent or uncle.

When considering these trends, it is important to bear in mind that the frequencies of sexual abuse in childhood were generally lower in Internet-only offenders. This means that the contact offenders experienced multiple abuse more commonly since a greater proportion of them report being sexually abused in childhood. In general, for much the same reason, contact offenders tended to experience these more extreme forms of abuse more commonly than Internet offenders.

The idea that some forms of abuse are more extreme than others is inextricably linked to the idea that some forms of abuse are more damaging than others. Of course, what is damaging depends on more characteristics than we have mentioned. It is likely to vary between children and according to other characteristics such as the quality of parenting. It also implies that children can have a degree of resilience to the damaging consequences of abuse. Intrafamilial abuse, because it impinges in many ways on family dynamics, may be more damaging than extrafamilial abuse. For one thing, it is likely that the abuser will remain in the proximity of the child unless the abuse is disclosed and action taken. The high rates of experiencing both intrafamilial and extrafamilial abuse in the contact offender group may, of course, be the result of a number of different factors. For example, intrafamilial abuse may make the child more vulnerable to extrafamilial abuse but equally it may be regarded as symptomatic of a family negligent of the needs of the child in general.

## Sex-play with Peers

There is a tendency to regard child-child or peer sexual activity as relatively benign. Sexual activity between children is seen as common and a normal and innocuous part of growing up (Sperry and Gilbert, 2005). Indeed, legislation very clearly makes this distinction (Sexual Offences Act 2003). While it may be true that much peer sexual activity in childhood is 'natural' and harmless, it does not follow from this that all peer sexual activity in childhood is without adverse consequences. There is a substantial body of literature evolving that documents the existence and seriousness of the problem of sexually aggressive children (for example, Araji, 1997; Cantwell, 1988; Friedrich, 2000; Masson and Erooga, 1999; Shaw, 2000). Furthermore, it is now generally recognised that sexual offending by children accounts for a substantial proportion of sexual offences (Anderson *et al.*, 1993; Davis and Leitenberg, 1987; Finkelhor, 1980; Flanagan and Hayman-White, 2000; James and Neil, 1996; O'Shaughnessy, 2006; Snyder, 2000; Veneziano, Veneziano and LeGrand, 2000). Consequently, a simple assumption that peer sexual activity is necessarily benign fails to recognise the social reality of sex offending. Furthermore, Howitt (1995a) argued that rather than dwell solely on sexual abuse as the key to later adult sexual offending, researchers should consider the contribution of other aspects of early sexualisation, which includes sexual activities with other children. This, of course, raises the difficult question of when child-child sexual activity should be regarded as abusive. For practical purposes, we simply defined abusive sexual acts as those involving another child five or more years older than the offender at the time and adults. Sex-play between two children involved acts like fondling, exposure, mutual masturbation, oral sex and sexual intercourse. It should also be recognised that peer sex activity could include abusive experiences at the hands of another child.

If this early sexualisation is an important in the development of sexual offending against children, then peer sex should be common, if not universal in the lives of offenders (Howitt, 1995a). At a minimum, peer sex should account for more offenders than sexual abuse by adults alone would in the cycle-of-sexual-abuse perspective. Indeed, if we explore whether there are any offenders who report no sexual experiences as a child our findings are remarkable; only 12 % of offenders suffered *no* sexual abuse or reported *no* sex-play experiences with females (at any age) during childhood. That is to say, 88 % of sex offenders against children experienced early sexualisation either through abuse and/or through sexual contact with another similar-aged female peer. This early sexualisation might be influential in the development of sexual fantasies of some offenders. The figures were not so conclusive for homosexual childhood experiences: 45 % experienced *no* sexual abuse and *no* sex-play experimentation with males (at any age) during childhood. Yet that still leaves over half of the sample sexualised through abuse and/or through willing sexual contact with another similar-aged male peer. Of the entire sample, 14 % experienced sexual abuse *and* sex play with males and females (at any age). Combining all these things together, 92 % of offenders had experienced one or more of the following: sexual abuse by an adult, sexual play with a female in childhood or sex play with a male in childhood.

The child-child sex play experiences of contact and Internet offenders were very similar. Sex play with girls was typical of the vast majority of the offender childhoods – the lowest percentage was 75 % for the Internet-only offenders but 80 % for both types of contact offenders. In one aspect there was a difference between the offender groups because few (16 %) of the contact offenders had engaged in heterosexual experimentation prior to puberty. On the other hand, 31 % of Internet offenders and 60 % of the mixed contact/Internet offenders did so. Of course, some of the offenders engaged with sexual behaviours with boys when they were under 12 years of age – the figures were 19 % of Internet offenders, 20 % of contact only offenders, and 10 % of mixed contact/Internet offenders. There was a noteworthy level of homosexual experimentation at any age during childhood because 40 % of the contact offenders reported such activity – the figures were 25 % for the Internet sample and 20 % of the mixed contact/Internet group.

### Sex Play in Sexually Abused Offenders

Sexual abuse seems to be a precursor of sexual play with other boys in childhood though not with girls. Offenders who had been sexually abused in childhood engaged more in male-male sex play at some point during their childhood – 45 % compared with only 21 % of those who had not been abused. Moreover, those who were sexually abused were more likely to engage in male-male sex play when they were aged 12 or older (36 %) than those who were not sexually abused, for whom the figure was 10 %. The figures for sex play with females at some stage in childhood did not seem to be affected by sexually abusive experiences in childhood; 77 % of the abused offenders engaged in sexual activity with girls as against 79 % of those who were not sexually abused. It made virtually no difference if the sexual abuse took place before or after puberty.

## CASE STUDY ACCOUNTS OF CHILDHOOD SEXUALISATION

No matter how useful statistical data are for understanding Internet and contact offending, they usually lack a degree of resonance with our ordinary understanding of things. They are, after all, abstractions. While we believe that these statistics paint a reasonably comprehensive picture of sex in the early lives of offenders, inevitably we found ourselves referring back to the interview material when trying to put a total picture together. It is easier to see complex interactions between events in case study material so we will describe in some detail the lives of examples of three different types of offender. Many things already have discussed in this chapter emerge quite clearly in the offenders' accounts.

## CASE STUDY 1: 35-YEAR-OLD INTERNET SEX OFFENDER [49]

Crucially, Internet-only sex offenders were much less likely to have been sexually abused in childhood than those who contact offended against children. However, the childhoods of the Internet-only offenders characteristically involved sex play with other children. The sex-play began before the age of 12 years in a third of the cases. Three-quarters of Internet-only offenders reported childhood sex-play with girls and a quarter had engaged in childhood sex-play with other boys.

This case is of a 35-year-old offender, Tom, who was convicted of possession and downloading 500,000 Internet pornographic images – including paedophilic, heterosexual, homosexual and bestiality. His own personal sexual practices have included urophilia and bestiality. His sexual experiences from early teens onwards are varied, initially involving same-aged and slightly older girls. These relationships seem largely to be short-lived encounters for purely sexual purposes. Indeed the term 'relationships' seems to be generally a gross misnomer. Exceptionally, he had two close female friends who he discusses in terms of a need for intimacy but by this he did not mean sexual intimacy:

I had too much sex when I was young lad, too many relationships that didn't mean anything ... the first time I'd actually probably made love [was] at 20, but I'd been having sex since I was 12 ... when I was 12 I was having sex with 12, 13, 14, 15 years old, older ... They were my two closest female friends and I didn't end up having a sexual relationship with ... they were what I wanted in a relationship ... but I couldn't make it work ... that was the frustrating thing in that I felt I wanted to be close to girls like I was close to them but couldn't be you know.

Tom not only reported extensive sexual contact as a child with peers but also contact with adult women:

And I use to go have sex with older women ... anywhere between 17 and 35 ... because I look older anyway ... we use to hang around in a group and there was a big age group ... women who were 35, 40 when I was about from 13 ... to 16 ... the oldest difference was when I was 17 and she was 42 ... my mate's mum ... so anyone really I didn't mind ... see when I was that age, 12, you know we didn't think we were doing anything wrong I never ever thought anyone used me I mean I slept with older women, had sex I enjoyed it ... everyone was having sex.

He does not construe his sexual contacts with women as abusive. Nevertheless, he is classed as abused according to the criterion that there is a five-year age gap between the underage person and the adult sexual partner. However, his situation reflects one of the many anomalies in terms of the way we deal with adult-child sex, especially for boys. Tom clearly regarded these sexual contacts with adult woman as both desirable and pleasurable. So, in a sense, here is a young man gaining sexual experiences with older women and, in some people's minds, this might be regarded as good fortune rather than sexual abuse. But this is to apply a double standard because it is less likely to be applied to a girl of the same age experiencing adult male sex partners. However, if the problem with sexual abuse is the damage that it causes young people in the future we cannot gloss over the fact that quite substantial proportions of paedophiles report childhood sexual abuse involving adult women. There is evidence of the damage in that fact that this offender struggles to understand the idea that childhood sex with older persons is harmful. Such cognitions may facilitate his Internet offending and makes it difficult for him to regard child pornography as wrong. In other words, since he regards what happened to him in childhood as positive with little or no adverse consequences for his general well-being, then where is the harm for his 'victims'? As in other instances, this is evidence that the cognitive errors related to children as 'sexual beings' are developed in childhood and do not always seem to be a response to the guilt engendered by his adult offending. The following illustrates how he believes that children under 16 years of age are, in general, not 'innocent' because he was not and neither were the people he sexually engaged with:

> There's this media thing you know all under 16s are innocent . . . its ridiculous . . . everyone's a virgin until they're 16 . . . but they're not . . . they will have sexual relationships with other people, other children, adults . . . See when I was that age, 12, you know we didn't think we were doing anything wrong I never ever thought anyone used me, I slept with older women, had sex I enjoyed it . . . everyone was having sex . . . there was one point when I was 13, 14, [I had] 3 or 4 girls a week probably.

Sexual contact served his needs at least *partially*. However, the sexual activities at the time serve attachment needs for emotional closeness to other people in a fundamentally flawed way:

> [I have had] about two-, three-, four-, 500 [sexually intimate relationships] since I was 12 till now . . . maybe I used the girls when I was younger to get that love that I didn't get from my parents . . . I never have really had that togetherness the warmth side from my parents; maybe I used the girls when I was younger to get that love that I didn't get from my parents . . . no, I knew they loved me . . . they didn't treat me badly or anything . . . but there was no warmth so eventually I use to get the feeling of being wanted, of being close by being with the girls, sexually and the women. I wanted just a feeling of being wanted, being close.

The physically gratifying sexual act as well as the 'pseudo-intimacy' provided by the sexual act may have helped him to feel cognitively and emotionally secure. Also given the pleasure of the sexual act and its intimacy, coupled with the lack of intervention by a responsible adult to curtail the behaviour, it is perhaps no surprise that the behaviour would be repeated on many future occasions.

The account of his childhood provided by this offender is replete with sexual encounters although he specifically mentions that he did not 'make love' until he was about 20 years of age. He describes his parents as strict which does not seem to tally with the general freedom and 'sexual freedom' that he had to, for example, organise parties with a male friend:

> They [parents] weren't in your life in that respect they were strict but they didn't know what you were doing . . . when I went to university I'd been there for a year and dad said 'what you doing at university?' He didn't

know; they were very much focused on what they were doing ... I went to house parties and we were having sex in the rooms and the parents didn't mind ... someone came in and said anyone want any birthday cake ... you could see we were all having sex ... and in high school we use to organise parties between us.

## CASE STUDY 2: 29 YEAR OLD CONTACT SEX OFFENDER [43]

This contact offender, Sam, had a previous conviction for gross indecency against a nine-year-old (familial) girl and his current index offence was against a six-year-old (familial) girl. His earliest recollections of sexual experiences were of his own extrafamilial abuse by two male abusers together. They performed both oral and anal penetrative sex acts on him. Irrespective of his initial response to his abuse, he gained some comfort and pleasure from these experiences. Sex was equated in his mind with love and affection.

> I used sex quite a lot as affection I liked the feeling of somebody inside me.

At about the age of nine or 10 years, things begin to change as he ceased to regard himself as a victim and he started actively seeking adult men for sexual purposes. He describes himself as being a 'rent boy'. No matter how he personally labels these activities, they clearly should be regarded as sexual abuse by his customers notwithstanding the extent to which he claims that he sought the men out himself. This sort of sexual activity continued through until the age of about 17 years. Numerous episodes of (sometimes) paid for anal sex and reciprocal oral sex were involved. His partners were almost all adult men. However, his range of sexual partners began to involve a small number of girls inside and outside of the family. As an older teenager, his partners included adult women although these were not episodes for which he was paid:

> Lots of one night stands ... I've put it around ... many men, hundreds ... few girls ... I had sex with a woman when I was about 13 ... she was late 30s ... my mom's friend ... my mom caught us, she went up the wall ... I would just go round [to this lady] and have sex occasionally ... if I couldn't get it anyway else I'd just go there.

Sometimes Sam was sexually involved with vulnerable children of a similar age to himself. He describes growing up in a family where other children (sometimes sexually victimised) would be fostered. The progression was from sexual victim to sexual victimiser though some of the time he was both. The first episode described below refers to an incident when he was a young teenager and was engaging in sexual activities with a family member. The second episode relates to an offence:

> There was a boy [about 10] ... he'd been sexually abused ... that's why he was in our care ... I was still a child at the time [about 12] I was with [female

child] in my bedroom and he walked in on me [having sex?] ... yea ... he took down his trousers and tried to ... join in ... that kind of clicked in my head oh ... maybe he is like me, because I ... was willing, even though I was a child I was still willing to have sex.

She [about 9 years old] started taking off her clothes ... and was just about to take down her knickers ... whoah! she wants sex basically ... thought I'd be better off talking to her and explaining what sex is ... but I got turned on ... got an erection ... I showed her my penis ... I ended up masturbating.

The seemingly endless variety of sexual partners is a pattern that often emerges when interviewing paedophiles. The continuity of sexual contacts from childhood to early adulthood is another feature that characterises the childhoods of at least some paedophiles. The transition from victim to victimiser in Sam's case can almost be described as seamless. There is no clear thematic connection between his early victimisation and his behaviours as a victimiser – his offences were against prepubescent girls within the family and involved indecent exposure, fondling and digital penetration. This appears to be quite different from the early oral and anal abuse he experienced at the hands of men. He makes links between his own abuse and that of his abusive adult behaviour arguing that it was the 'relationship' part of the abuse that was a comfort to him:

[When I was offending] I wanted an immediate relationship ... being with a child was maybe like a relationship ... I think most of my offending was because of the void I had in my life ... and that's probably why another reason I was taking the drugs ... just trying to fill that void with anything and ... I saw sex as another way of filling that void ... the emptiness, a longing for something.

Like some other offenders (Howitt, 1995a), he recreates in fantasy himself as a child. That is, rather than being the abuser he imagines himself as the child victim of his abuse:

I made believe in my head that she was ... older and I was ... younger, which brought our ages similar ... I made myself about 12, a 10 and a 12 year old.

Throughout his interview, he presents his childhood as a period of sexual awareness. The following comment he made illustrates a possible direct bearing of early child-child sexual experiences on adult thoughts and behaviour. Specifically, he believes that children are knowledgeable and willing sexual beings just as he was made to be. Children, especially himself, are viewed as if they are sexually predatory. He was pursuing sexual activity as a child and children in general are painted in much the same way. Adult-child sexual activity was the norm in his life so why should he not construe adult-child sex as a normal activity? Indeed, we can describe these as cognitive distortions in the professional lexicon but such distortions existed in this offender, among others, from childhood – they do not seem to be post-offending justifications to protect him from guilt:

> I started to tickle her [6 year old victim] to make her laugh ... and as she pushed my hand away it brushed against her ... vagina, she said oh tickle me there ... I was ... thinking ... she might be like how I was as a child ... looking for it ... as a rent boy ... A child can't obviously put about that ... they want sex but what they can do they can make themselves more vulnerable than most children and that way they can get sex ... Flirting ... without anybody else noticing ... especially with the eyes ... they'd like be very ... sly ... they might come up to you ... and say 'oh I was raped when I was little' and then like smile if you know what I mean ... or say if you were alone with them then like ... they'd make it obvious ... children are speaking with their eyes.

Family life, for him as a child, involved a number of children who were fostered at the family home. Very little time was spent together as a family and his parents failed to (or were unable to) see the sexual abuse and other sexual activities he was involved in even where it occurred at home. This feature goes some way to expose the dynamics of his family. The contrasts between the mother and father were striking and he describes them in terms that indicate that they were poles apart in their characters. The mother was authoritarian and incapable but the father was loving, capable and thoughtful but nevertheless led by the mother. As a young teenager of 12 or 13 years Sam was frequently locked out for arriving home after midnight. The gang of children of which he was a member he described to us as 'the only family that I really ... respected'.

## CASE STUDY 3: 35 YEAR OLD MIXED SEX OFFENDER [31]

Paul's contact offences were gross indecency and indecent assaults on his 14-year-old step daughter and her friend of the same age. His Internet offences involved making indecent images of his victims, possession and making of indecent images from the Internet (prepubscent and postpubescent females). He was also convicted of supplying a controlled substance (cannabis) to a minor. His abuse began at about the age of eight years when his female babysitter of about 16 years of age fondled him. This abuse had always, he claimed, seemed harmless and even pleasurable to him. However, since his incarceration he had become aware that professionals working in the prison regard such events as exploitative:

> Earlier on in my life when I was 8, 9, 10 ... I was abused I guess by my [female] baby sitter ... but because of the way that it was done ... there wasn't force ... she would dare me to touch my penis on her breasts, or

suck her breasts ... I never touch[ed] her genitals ... by the way it was
handled I did enjoy what was going on because it was treated as a game.

For Paul, sexual experiences in childhood also included numerous interactions with same aged peers. More significantly, perhaps, there were episodes
with older women in their thirties. This happened particularly when he was
fourteen years of age. He describes many of these relationships as 'non-
sexual', which seems to mean not involving penetrative sex:

There were ... [victim's] friends that did fancy me ... who did particularly
have quite a big crush on me ... I didn't necessarily judge them as children
they   were ... 12,   13,   14,   15 ... so   I   was   looking   at   them
as ... mature ... knowing their own mind ... in some respects this relates
back to my childhood ... the fact that at that age I felt that I knew what I
was doing ... because I had non-sexual relationships with older women
from about the age of 14 ... kissing, cuddles, fondling ... one was a close
friend of the family when I was 14, she told me on her 34th birthday that
she fancied me ... I also had a similar type of relationship with one of her
friends ... also at 14 with my German teacher who ... left suddenly when
we were discovered by another teacher kissing in the classroom ... I don't
think... she deserved the grief that she got ... Again I lost my virginity
when I was 14 to an older woman ... I had again flirted with this person for
quite a while ... I said 'when are you going to take me to bed and teach me
everything you know?' ... I wasn't manipulated into that situation by her. I
approached her. I asked her. I actually spent the morning at my friend's
house ... watching his dad's pornographic video before I went round and
had sex with her ... it was consensual and mutual.

Most of us would perhaps find it difficult to believe that such extensive
contact, both socially and sexually, with so many older women would be
possible in normal family life. However, he seemed to have been largely
'unsupervised' by his parents as his father worked days and his mother worked
shifts so there was extensive use of a baby sitter who was herself a young girl
(16 years old) and who had abused him. When he was not at school, he would
have to find his own entertainment which was, of course, unsupervised. He also
needed to avoid disturbing his mother if she was sleeping during the day. So he
describes himself as being isolated and spending long periods of time playing
outside and walking just with his own company. In this sense, freedom and
independence were encouraged. He claimed that he met some of his women
sexual 'partners' whilst unsupervised at a local 'conservative' type club.

Furthermore, his parents' responses to sexual matters tended to be inconsistent. They approached sex by explaining 'basic terms' but their response to
matters of a sexual nature could be physically abusive:

I was singing this daft song ... 'are you a woman, no, how do you know?
Because I don't get tummy ache once a month' ... dad actually belted me
for saying that ... that was big part of the learning curve for me'

His parents were thus unapproachable about sexual matters whereas, in contrast, the adult women he contacted allowed him freedom to explore sexual issues.

Paul did not label these experiences with adult women as abusive. As noted elsewhere, sexual behaviour by women may be perceived as affection (Banning, 1989) rather than abusive or the abuse is seen as an 'initiation' (Condy et al., 1987; Holmes, Offen and Waller, 1997; Saradjian, 1996). He wanted the contact with them and he was happy to go along with it. There is no indication that he recognised any harm done to him as a consequence of the abuse. There was an important consequence of these early sexual experiences with adult women in terms of his cognitions. He feels that his experiences as an adolescent with adult women – the things he felt then – reflect the way that children in general and his own victims in particular felt about being sexually involved with adults. As an adolescent, he felt mature enough to decide to engage sexually with these adult women so why shouldn't young girls nowadays also feel this way towards having sexual contact with him? This is a cognitive distortion but again it does not function to protect him from guilt 'post offending'. The distortion existed before offending.

## THE CONSEQUENCES OF CHILDHOOD SEXUALISATION

If early childhood experiences influence later adult behaviour it might be expected that offenders reproduce in their own abusive behaviour things which had happened to them in their own childhood (Haapasalo et al., 1999; Hilton and Mezey, 1996; Howitt, 1995a, 2002). There was evidence in favour of this. For instance, those who were abused by an extrafamilial adult as a child had convictions against only extrafamilial victims (86 %). Furthermore, 67 % of intrafamilial abused offenders had a history of child convictions which were confined to only intrafamilial children. Moreover, those who were abused at age 12 or older tended to choose children aged 12 or older (67 %); and those who were abused at age 11 or below tended to have offences against victims who were also aged 11 years or younger (59 %). From the interview data, we can illustrate how important childhood experiences can be in determining adult offending behaviours. The following contact offender illustrates the homology between the feelings he experienced when he was abused and those feelings felt during the offending and the similarities between acts:

My father would say ... that you are the most special in the family, all the other times I would be like the outcast in my father eyes ... but during the abuse I felt loved ... wanted ... needed ... and those are the same feelings when I committed my offence ... My offences that were committed against me as a child took place in the bathroom and were focused on oral sex only. My crime that I committed against [sons] was in the bathroom and was oral sex only ... that comfortability stems back to what I had to do, the words that were spoken and the environment I was in ... the bathroom. [29: contact offender]

Reproducing childhood experiences is presented as reinstating the feelings of safety and security experienced during his own abuse when otherwise he was experiencing rejection. Of course there are other explanations for any behaviour but no alternative seems to fit fully what we know of the relationship between childhood experiences and adult offending behaviour. For example, in this case the alternative explanations might include the expedience of intrafamilial offending where the victim was available or the possibility that sexual preferences develop independently during adulthood rather than being a sort of re-enactment of childhood experiences in order to help deal with confusion and stress.

Another example of the unity between childhood behaviour and later adult offending can be observed in case study 24. This contact offender abused very young (four years old and older) male and female victims. He describes his offending as taking place within the context of babysitting and 'caring' for the children. The abusive behaviour with his victims is very much the same irrespective of their sex - fondling, digital penetration and oral sex during toileting, bathing and un/dressing children. Other styles of abuse were not central to his *modus operandum*. It is notable that his pattern of abusive behaviour occurred in very much the same sort of situation in which he was sexualised with younger peers during his institutional care. As a young adolescence, he engaged in sexual contact with young prepubescent peers within a context of caring. The sexual contact was fondling, digital penetration and oral sex. In fact, it is difficult to separate his adult abuse of children from what he was doing with other children during adolescence. He also repeats the behaviours on his victim (oral sex) that were performed on him by other adults (oral sex) as a child:

> Participant: In the [care] home I was also looking after an 8 year old boy … I would more or less dress him … wash his hair … bath … happiest memory would be looking after [him] … he would get into bed with me … Sometimes he was wet so I use to make him take his trousers off put them by the radiator … It was touching and oral sex on [victim] … for [victims] it happened where I'd been baby sitting them … espeespecially [name] because she was the youngest … bathing them, nappy on and … getting them ready for bed and all that … I would touch them, digital penetration, oral sex on the boys.

> Interviewer: Is that what you wanted to do to [victim] or did you want to do more?

> Participant: No it was just life experiences that I'd had. That had been done to me. But obviously then I was a child so the oral sex was on me, I was on him. [24: Contact Offender]

If early sexualisation has an influence on the development of paedophilia, one might also expect thematically close parallels between early childhood experiences and contents of offenders' fantasies (Howitt, 1995a). The study conducted by Kirkendall and McBride (1990) is of relevance here. The researchers presented data to suggest that fantasies alter behaviours but in turn experiences could alter fantasies, furthermore, 59 % of their participants indicated that their earliest fantasy was also their favourite or most frequently occurring fantasy. They provide an example of one participant who experienced his first same-sex encounter during adolescence and who reported restructuring his subsequent fantasies to include homosexual components. Our interviews revealed examples of imagery being used by offenders for masturbation during adulthood where the imagery was associated with early sexual abuse and/or peer-sex experiences. For instance:

My childhood fantasy has stayed the same ... a very promiscuous Lolita ... a 12 year old nude with small breasts, thimbles for breasts, no hips or waist, no hair ... the image is actually of a 12 year play mate I had when I was 14 ... I dared her to take her clothes off and she took everything off ... I would masturbate to that image of her even now, particularly when things start falling apart. [2: Internet offender]

My mother and I slept in the same bed ... as a 6, 7, 8 year old I had a liking to touch my mother when she went to sleep ... her breasts and stroking her ... and feeling very lustful ... she would stop me, but ... I very soon came to realise that she had a drink on ... a Saturday night and a Friday night and I'd know she went into a deeper sleep ... then she wouldn't stop me obviously ... I very definitely started having sex when I was 12 ... when I was 10 I was caught in bed with three girls [11–16 year olds] ... and very definitely that feeling never went away ... I was a very precocious sexually active child ... from that developed a kind of flavour for illicit sex ... and that followed into adulthood. [37: Contact offender]

I found it quite a pleasant experience, [abuser] fondled my genitalia, his hands over my naked body ... he did perform oral sex ... and I would think about that ... then as a teenager I use to buy a magazine called *Health and Efficiency* [nudist magazine containing nude pictures], which featured not only pictures of adults but pictures of children too ... I would masturbate to these ... as I've grown older I have not got those interests out of my system ... the interest was ... to ... boys. [7: mixed offender]

There are some indications of how family systems and sexual experiences might coalesce in adults who sexually offend against children. Specifically, where the child is exposed to disorganised and at times violent (albeit intact) family systems (or to separation away from parents or even to nonexistent parenting), this seems to result in the now-vulnerable child seeking closeness and attention in maladaptive ways. Sometimes these contacts were outside of the home with same-age and older peers but, in other cases, with adults. Sexual offending may represent to the offender a repetition of the strategies that he used as a child to achieve basic feelings of safety and security (Howitt, 2006a). Sometimes peers provided what the to-be paedophile experienced as love and warmth. Sexual experiences, in contexts such as these, become perceived as emotional and physical closeness. One can easily understand that a child who feels lonely, isolated, unloved, physically abused may turn to other possibly vulnerable children for comfort or to adults who may sexually exploit this situation. In this way, the at-risk child may identify closeness with sexual activity. Indeed, emotional congruence with children, viewing children as friends and identifying strongly with children seem to be widespread characteristics of sexual offenders against children.

Quite commonly, offenders reported sex play with peers as enjoyable experiences (and in some cases so were their experiences with abusers). If such activity is pleasurable then it is reasonable to assume that such activities are more likely to be repeated in the future (Howitt, 1995a). However, some sex-play experiences may not be the result of choice and although peer experiences were generally portrayed positively there were one or two occasions where peer-sex was traumatic and might have the same adverse effects as abuse by an adult. Some offenders remarked on the confusion and lack of understanding concerning mutual masturbation and sexual talk with same-sex peers and the mechanics of sex. Added to this, one common response to the question 'how did you learn about sex as a child?' was one of limited, if any, sex education or opportunity to discuss their developing sexuality. The family environment did not always effectively address a child's developing sexuality. In some cases experimentation is ignored, occasionally encouraged and at other times punished by the family which was generally ineffective in managing such occurrences, as the following illustrates:

> When I was about 5 or 6 playing doctors and nurses and there was two girls ... they'd be 4 or 5 ... and I use to be the doctor ... obviously with operating you've got to take your clothes off ... I can remember the feeling of softness of the belly ... [They] told their dad and my dad absolutely beat the crap out of me. [20: Internet offender]

## PREDICTION OF SEXUAL OFFENDING FROM CHILDHOOD EXPERIENCES

To what extent is it possible to discriminate between the different types of offender using childhood characteristics? There are statistical techniques which use various predictors in order to assess whether different groups can be discriminated from each other. The 11 childhood adversities listed in Chapter 6 (which include the variable 'sexual abuse') and the four sex-play variables (sex-play with male peers when 11 years of age or younger; sex-play with female peers of 11 years of age or younger; sex-play with male peers of 12 years or older; and sex-play with female peers of 12 years of age or older) were entered into a multinomial logistic regression analysis (Howitt and Cramer, 2005).

Two outcomes were identified:

- one that compares Internet sex offenders with contact and mixed sex offenders; and
- another pattern that compares contact offenders with Internet and mixed.

**Table 7.1**  Classification table of sex offenders according to childhood adversities and childhood sex-play experiences

| Actual | Predicted Internet | Contact | Mixed | Percentage correct |
|---|---|---|---|---|
| Internet | 9 | 4 | 3 | 56 |
| Contact | 2 | 23 | 0 | 92 |
| Mixed | 0 | 2 | 8 | 80 |
| Overall Percentage | 22 % | 57 % | 22 % | 78 |

Internet sex offenders were differentiated from the other two groups by not having witnessed domestic violence to the extent that the other two groups had. Contact sex offenders were differentiated from Internet and mixed sex offenders by not having engaged in heterosexual sex-play prepuberty and not spending frequent periods of time alone/unsupervised but nevertheless having been sexually abused as a child.

Overall, as can be seen from Table 7.1, the predicted classification of the offenders was accurate at 78 %. The accuracy, however, varies according to the type of offender. Contact-offenders were overwhelmingly accurately classified with a 92 % 'hit' rate. Childhood adversity and sex variables identify contact offenders with quite a high degree of accuracy. If a misclassification occurred then the contact offender was mistakenly placed in the Internet-only category. The accuracy of prediction was also good for the mixed offenders at 80 %. If an error was made it was to classify them as the contact offenders whcih they also were. However, the identification of those who were Internet-only offenders was substantially poorer at 56 % accuracy – Internet-only offenders tended to be misclassified as contact offenders or mixed contact/Internet offenders. Perhaps the misclassified Internet-only offenders are the ones most at risk of progressing to contact offending.

## CONCLUDING COMMENTS

Not every sexual offender against children experienced sexual abuse in childhood and sexualisation by peers. However, most of them do report one of these or both. Just 12 % of the offenders we studied reported neither of these things. As with previous research, the men we studied reported the more extreme forms of sexual abuse including abuse by females (for example, Howitt, 1998b). Contact offenders, when they had been abused, tended to have been victimised at an early age – the average being seven years. They were also more likely to engage in sex-play with other boys. For some children, childhood and early adolescent sexual experiences may be part of a developmental pathway in which they become increasingly engaged in sexual activities with peers which may be or may become inappropriate and coercive but also may involve sexual activity with adults. Offenders as children are often immersed in a highly sexual and sexualised environment. Thus there may be a development process that begins with abuse or peer sex-play and eventually ends in paedophilia (Howitt, 1995a).

Compared to any of the offenders whose offences included contact offences against children, Internet-only offenders, by and large, were less likely to have been sexually abused as children. Nevertheless, Internet only offenders do seem to have other experiences in early childhood conducive to the development of a sexual preference for young people. Among these important experiences is sex-play with girls, particularly when the offender was younger than 12 years of age. However, Internet offenders generally do not act out their sexual interest by offending directly against children. It could be argued, therefore, that particular sexual scripts are learnt during psychological development and present a framework for guiding the individual's behaviour. One possible scenario is that sexual experiences that occur before a child is fully able to deal with them cognitively and emotionally may have a long term impact. As such there are distortions in offenders' sexual scripts which include inappropriate partners, inappropriate contexts and inappropriate behaviours (Ward and Siegert, 2002).

Mixed Internet-contact offenders were abused at the average age of twelve years of age. They also engaged in early sex-play with girls especially before the age of twelve years. Again this suggests that their sexual attraction to children begins early and may remain into adulthood; that the origins of their sexual interest is in childhood. Of course, a sexual interest in children does not preclude sexual involvements with adults.

Having been sexually abused as a child may be the risk factor most predictive of the acting out of a man's sexual interest in children. Certainly, the Internet-only offenders, who by definition do not sexually act out directly against children were the least likely to have been sexually abused in childhood. Furthermore, the rates of sexual abuse experienced by Internet-only offenders seem to be closest to the rates that researchers have claimed in the general population. If we add to this the relatively low levels of the more extreme forms of abuse in the childhoods of Internet-only offenders, then we may have hints as to why some men grow up with a sexual interest in children but do not contact offend against them.

One reason why childhood is important in understanding paedophilia is that paedophiles can identify their sexual identity from quite an early age. Indeed, one could argue that paedophilia is a sexual orientation just as heterosexuality and homosexuality are (Howitt, 1995a). Heterosexual and homosexual orientation emerges quite early in life and even before the onset of puberty (Herdt and McClintock, 2000). Children's developing awareness of their sexual interest in same or opposite sex persons involves a progression in their sexual behaviour towards others, typically (Seto, 2004). It has been found that paedophiles were aware of their sexual interest in children at a young age, in some cases as young as 7 to 10 years old (Abel *et al.*, 1987; Bernard, 1975; Freund and Kuban 1993). They remember developing a sexual interest or curiosity towards other children and a desire to see children in the nude which was present in them as young adolescents. Non-offenders, although they may share such a curiosity in other children, lose this curiosity by the age of puberty. As Seto (2004) suggests, this raises the intriguing possibility that boys in general are sexually curious about children but paedophiles-to-be remain fixed at a pre-pubertal stage and their sexual interest does not progress to older age groups as they get older like it does in other people. One possible explanation of this is that paedophiles-to-be are sexually fixated on children because their emotional needs have been served by other children. Unable to have their emotional needs satisfied by other adults, their sexualised emotional dependency on children remains fixed.

# CHAPTER 8

# Coping with Life through Abuse and Child Pornography

Much of the time, most paedophiles are capable of coping with their everyday lives. But this is not true of all paedophiles all of the time. They frequently identify life's stresses as factors in their offending behaviour. Many of us would regard many of the stressors that they describe as run-of-the-mill – problems at work, financial problems, relationship problems, family problems and so forth. In themselves they hardly seem to constitute sufficient to lead to sexual assaults on children. One of the reasons why paedophiles may respond to stressful situations differently from other men is because they may use sex as a coping strategy; paedophiles turn to children because children are their sexual interest and they feel comfortable with children psychologically. Paedophiles often feel rejected by other adults and also harbour a mistrust of them. Their cognitions are dominated by ideas that children are much safer than adults and are a psychological comfort zone (see Chapter 11). They are drawn to children who they see as more trustworthy and accepting than adults. Children, to them, are more accepting of them and more trustworthy. Equally unrealistically, paedophiles see in children partners who will provide the sort of support that most of us would expect from adult partners and close friends. Paedophiles will attempt to cultivate 'safe' relationships by engaging children in ways that are very different from the unsatisfactory nature of their relationships with other adults. Child molesters have been described as displaying an exaggerated affiliation with children and childhood which has been labelled 'emotional congruence' (Wilson, 1999). Of course, the developmental histories of sex offenders against children described in Chapter 6 suggest that this lack of trust in adults is fostered in childhood. In some of the case histories of these men, it is easy to see that adverse family situations encouraged these paedophiles-to-be to use other children as substitutes for parental warmth. This emotional congruence with other children in childhood, if it continues into adulthood, becomes dysfunctional and may lead to offending behaviour.

## POSSIBLE PRECURSORS TO OFFENDING

### Self-identified Triggers

Offenders against children, both Internet and contact, identify a similar variety of stressors as the 'triggers' for their offending behaviour. In the case of the offenders we studied, for instance, the following were the main factors that, they claim, led to offending:

- *Interpersonal problems* (for example, marital discord, loneliness or divorce) were frequently cited (contact offenders 76%, mixed offenders 70%, and Internet-only offenders 56%).
- *Health-related problems* (for example, long-term illnesses or injuries, mental health problems, substance abuse) were also commonly cited are precursors to sexual offending (Internet offenders 50%, contact offenders 40% and mixed offenders 40%).
- *Sexual factors such as sexual frustration or dissatisfaction* (e.g. lack of quantity, not able to live out preferred fantasies, not feeling close to their partner during sex) were fairly common among the mixed offenders (40%) and contact offenders (32%) but were much less common among Internet only offenders (13%).
- *Work-related problems* (including redundancy, unemployment, overwork, financial difficulties and bullying) were much more frequently cited by mixed offenders (50%) and Internet-only offenders (44%) than by contact-only offenders (12%).
- *Self-esteem problems* were not commonly mentioned (Internet offenders 19%) mixed offenders 10%, and contact offenders 8%).

Overall, the different types of child sexual offenders shared much the same range of triggers to their offending. In a sense, this extends previous research findings of an association between negative emotional states and the instigation of sexual aggression (Pithers, 1990). But there were some differences. In particular, Internet offenders mentioned work-related problems more frequently as an offence trigger. This might reflect little more than the trend for Internet offenders to be in professional and skilled occupations (e.g. teaching, management) whereas contact offenders were more likely to have unskilled manual occupations. The higher status occupations of Internet offenders might place increased pressure or stress on these offenders, perhaps because of bigger demands on their time, which adversely affects their ability to cope:

> I was made redundant...worried about money...so we started our own company...but I was working an 18 hour day just to try and get by...things started...getting stressful...And that in turn places a lot of strain on the marriage and family life. [23: Internet Offender]

## Other Adult Difficulties

Although these were not factors that offenders identified as triggers to their offending behaviour, it is notable that offenders talked about a range of difficulties which they experienced as adults. While the offenders did not make any connection of these to their offending behaviour, they do amount to general problems which may increase stress levels:

- *Substance abuse.* This included expressions of circumstances such as regular binge drinking, drug rehabilitation, substance related previous offences, periods of time [i.e. days] lost and financial difficulties and/or loss of employment/relationships as a consequence of substance misuse: 'Drinking it's a problem solver ... I try and blank everything out with it ... since I was about 17, 18. I ... drink until I'm comatose' [33: Contact Offender]. This was rather more common in contact (56 %) and Mixed offenders (50 %) than Internet-only (25 %) offenders.
- *Social intimacy problems.* These are basically difficulties in establishing, maintaining or using friendships and/or developing a social support network. Examples of this includes suggestions that the offender never had close friends to which to turn: 'Don't really have any, never had many close friends' [2: Internet Offender]. This was moderately to very common in all groups (mixed offenders 70 %, Internet-only offenders 56 % and contact offenders 36 %).
- *Using sex as an escape from problems*: Substantial numbers of offenders raised, as a difficulty, their use of deviant and non-deviant pornography, masturbation and sexual intercourse as means of escaping from, coping with, or relieving feelings or problems such as helplessness, boredom, or loneliness, for example: 'Being a professional and seen as an upright model citizen I felt was an enormous strain and stress upon me and on a daily basis I would feel the need to masturbate [to adult women and girls] to relieve the tension' [15: Internet offender]. 'In times of stress ... I masturbated and fantasised about boys' [51: mixed offender]. Fifty-six per cent of Internet-only offenders, 32 % of contact-only offenders and 50 % of mixed offenders reported this problematic sexual response to stress.
- *Self-esteem problems.* These included a variety of issues related to the offender's personality, abilities or body image: 'I have never thought much of myself' [13: Internet offender]. 'I have always thought of myself as stupid and fat' [20: Internet offender]. About a quarter to a third of all of the groups mentioned self-esteem related problems (Internet only 25 %, contact only 32 %, and mixed Internet/contact 30 %).
- *Mental health problems* including self-harm. Such problems were exemplified by revelations such as the offender had in the past received medication for depression or some other form of psychiatric treatment or mentioned that they had made a suicide attempt. The extent of such problems broken down by group was Internet-only offenders 19 %, contact-only offenders 36 %, and mixed Internet/contact offenders 20 %.

There seems to be little doubt that many sex offenders against children experience long-term life stressors whether or not they regard these as factors in their offending behaviour. To what extent do such stressors account for offending?

## COPING BEHAVIOUR

Particularly stressful periods of life make many sex offenders more vulnerable to sexual offending. When faced with periods of greater than normal stress, according to many offenders, they become driven towards children and offending. Many report loneliness or losing a job as pre-offence stressors (Pithers, 1990). Relapse prevention strategies incorporated into sex offender treatment programmes acknowledge this sort of enhanced risk due to stress among other things (Laws, Hudson and Ward, 2000). Such strategies emphasise that effective coping is important in preventing offending. The inability of sex offenders to cope appropriately with high-risk situations (specifically negative moods) puts them at greater risk of reoffending largely because their coping behaviour involves turning to children, with whom they feel psychologically more comfortable than adults. It is the way in which they try to cope with the effects of stress – the nature of their coping strategies – which fails to address their problems (Serran and Marshall, 2006). Despite this being generally accepted in treatment programmes, there is very little research that examines this notion (Serran and Marshall, 2006). It would seem that sex-crime perpetrators experience frequent stressors, although this, in itself, is insufficient to explain their offending. Alcohol abuse is among the problematic behaviours of child molesters and rapists (Looman *et al.*, 2004) although whether this is a consequence of their relationship or other problems is not known. Nevertheless, it might be assumed that alcohol abuse is to some extent symptomatic of difficulties.

Adverse childhood experiences may lead to the offenders' insecurity in adult relationships and their commensurate rejection by other adults. But that is not all. It is thought that these early experiences may also lead to inadequate coping strategies (Marshall, Serran and Cortoni, 2000). The usual view is that negative personal situations and emotional states tend to be precursors of sexual offending among those so inclined (Pithers, 1990). According to relapse prevention theorists, a critical deficit in sexual offenders is their inability to cope (Marshall, Serran and Cortoni, 2000). Coping is a response that attempts to ameliorate the negative impact of stress generated by problems. Effective coping strategies are thought to play a major role in any individual's well-being when faced with negative and/or stressful situations (Endler and Parker, 1989). The term 'coping styles' refers to the typical ways of confronting stressful situations and dealing with them (Folkman and Lazarus, 1985). There are three consistently identified styles – task-focused, emotion-focused and avoidance-focused (Endler and Parker, 1990):

• Task-focused coping strategies tackle the stressful situation(s) and emphasise problem solving skills.

- Emotion-focused strategies are aimed at emotional separation from the stressor. Such strategies would include fantasising and self-preoccupation.
- Avoidance-focused strategies involve techniques designed to escape or avoid the problem, which can be either distraction techniques or social diversion activities.

Research suggests that sex offenders tend to choose ineffective coping strategies. Using a standard measure known as *The Coping Inventory for Stressful Situations* (Endler and Parker, 1990), it has been found that child molesters typically make use of emotion-focused strategies such as 'blaming oneself' or 'worrying about what to do' (Feelgood, Cortoni and Thompson, 2005; Marshall, Cripps, Anderson and Cortoni, 1999; Marshall, Serran and Cortoni, 2000). Neidigh and Tomiko (1991) found that sex offenders used self-denigrating and avoidance coping responses when attempting to deal with stress.

A distinction should be made between having the specific skills to cope with particular stressful situations and the more general ability to cope with a wide variety of stressful situations. This is important because treatment programmes, for example, characteristically help sex offenders deal with specific situations that are believed to be involved in their offending behaviour yet offenders also need help to develop a general and effective coping style given the range of difficulties they are vulnerable to (Serran and Marshall, 2006).

There is a special role for fantasy in coping behaviour. Fantasy can be part of the coping strategy of emotionally distancing oneself from a stressful situation. There is research which indicates that, for some sex offenders, sexual activity and sexual fantasy are involved in coping as well as when dealing with depression, anger, marital arguments and feelings of rejection. These fantasies may be within the range of most people's sexual fantasies but they may also feature deviant sexual activities (Cortoni and Marshall, 2001; Looman, 1995). As we described in Chapter 6, the use of sex to cope with stressful situations develops quite early in the lives of sex offenders (Marshall and Marshall, 2000). This is motivated by a lack of perceived self-worth and deficiencies in love and affection that would normally be provided by a child's parents. This is amply illustrated in offenders' accounts of how sex with other children or adults was comforting to them in childhood; sex was a substitute for the affection that normally parents supply. This would imply that coping would be related to self-esteem and cognitive distortions but Marshall *et al.* (2003) found little evidence for this.

A major criticism of research examining mood and emotions in sexual offending is that the focus has been almost exclusively on negative mood states and emotions (see, for example, Hanson and Harris, 2000). Furthermore, just how emotional states and poor coping lead to sexual offending is not adequately explained. For instance, Serran and Marshall (2006) make two proposals:

- the negative affect results in the person seeking sexual relief from whoever is accessible as a way of reducing the negative feeling which is similar to Cortoni and Marshall's (2001) concept of 'sex as a coping strategy' or;

- negative affect serves as a motivator to offend, similar to Groth's (1979) model of rapists.

The emphasis on negative mood states is inadequate in the light of Ward *et al.*'s (1995) work. There appear to be two pathways to offending: a negative and a positive emotion pathway. The negative pathway involves negative moods, substance abuse and implicit planning over a short duration. The positive affect pathway involves positive emotions, explicit planning, distorted thinking, deviant sexual fantasies and high arousal over a longer duration.

Just what relevance do such ideas about coping and offending have to Internet sex offenders? Do Internet sex offenders have much the same inappropriate coping styles as contact offenders? The idea that the Internet provides an alternative to the mundane aspects of life and some respite when one is unhappy is familiar. Like any other form of entertainment, the Internet has been associated with altering mood and avoiding negative emotional states such as boredom, depression or anxiety (Quayle, Vaughan and Taylor, 2006). Consequently, it might be a reasonable assumption to suppose that Internet offenders use the Internet, and specifically fantasies concerning children, to relieve negative states. Quayle *et al.* (2006) argue that some negative feelings such as loneliness may produce situational suppression of empathy for children and may adversely affect decision making. When they were experiencing negative mood states, Internet pornography offenders engaged in more risk taking and tended to tell themselves that the child pornography images they were looking at did not involve the sexual abuse of children (Quayle and Taylor, 2002b). Taylor and Quayle (2003) argue that child pornography is used by Internet child pornography offenders in order to cope with unpleasant circumstances in real life and unsatisfactory relationships.

## EMOTIONAL CONGRUENCE

For most adults, turning to their partner, relatives and friends is a natural response to stressful events. So if this were true of paedophiles, why would they turn to children at times of trouble? Paedophiles have feelings of congruence with children who they regard as, for example, supportive and not a threat unlike other adults. During the course of our interviews with sex offenders against children, we explored this notion of the emotional congruence that offenders felt with children. Two questions were asked which specifically aimed to gain information on this:

- Some men enjoy being in the company of children, not necessarily looking for sexual opportunities, but enjoy their company. How much can you relate to that?
- What, if anything, do you see, or gain, from friendships or relationships with children that you could not perceive or obtain from adults closer to your own age?

Substantial numbers of the offenders clearly demonstrated emotional congruence with children. In excess of half of the contact and mixed offenders and over a third of Internet offenders showed emotional congruence or attachment to children. By this we mean indications that they felt most satisfied in the company of a child or assigned qualities to children that they felt were not to be found in adults. Emotional congruence was most tangible in the contact and mixed offender groups as can be illustrated by the following excerpts from the interviews:

[Children] they're just a lot easier to please. They give as much back as what you give them. It winds me up when you see adults, they either talking about somebody else, criticising them, slagging them off ... if they didn't like you ... they'd be pissing all over you, no loyalty. [24: contact offender]

I feel ... more contented with myself ... more joyous with boys than adults ... Boys ... they are more trusting ... thoughtful, and give more unconditional love. [25: contact offender]

An adult tells you that they love you because they want something ... a child doesn't. [29: contact offender]

[Compared to an adult] ... [children] never seem to question they just accept you for what ... and who you are ... I am very untrusting of adults, from my life experiences the only people I have ever found have hurt me have been adults and I have never known a child hurt me ... I've opened up to people ... it's been thrown back in my face ... once they think they have your confidence ... stabbed me in the foot ... children ... I know what they want ... I have that vibe ... I've never really had problems communicating with young children ... unlike adults. [27: contact offender]

To a child you don't have to tell them your problem, they come and talk, they can see you're sad. [19: mixed offender]

I always got on better with kids ... 11 year olds ... I found it easier to relate to children than to adults ... more comfortable ... [They] tend to gravitate towards me for some reason ... it's an empathy. [51: Mixed Offender]

These illustrate how paedophiles' conceptions of children hold them to be trustworthy, affectionate and perceptive. Children respond positively and provide a feeling of physical closeness in the minds of sex offenders against children. These offenders have a 'desire' to be psychologically close to children. Paedophiles frequently allude to the idea that children are 'easier' to be with and that it is more comfortable to be near children than adults. Remarkably, even children of six years of age or so are perceived as being able to empathise with the paedophile's deepest feelings. Children than are less of a responsibility than adults and lack the sort of emotional baggage that paedophiles characterise adults as having. Children embody the fine qualities that are absent in the make-up of adults. For paedophiles, relationships with children are 'safe' and they are described in ways that contrast markedly with the rejection, disloyalty, deceitfulness, selfishness and manipulation that, for paedophiles, typify relationships with other adults. Anyone who spends time professionally with paedophiles will note that some of them, at least, describe their relationships with their child victims in terms which are age inappropriate – much like men in courtship relationships with adult women would use.

Although this sort of emotional commitment to children is less frequent in Internet offenders than in contact offenders, nevertheless it was still present in the thinking of a substantial number of Internet offenders. A factor high-lighted by other research (Middleton, Beech and Mandeville-Norden, 2005). Some of our sample of Internet offenders, like contact offenders, speak of child-adult intimacy or closeness as more satisfying than adult-adult relation-ships. For example, the following Internet pornographers identify qualities in children they feel are missing in adults:

> I didn't trust adults . . . because I've had so many knock backs . . . children you can trust . . . can give more acceptance and love than other adults. [5: Internet offender]

> Things attractive about children . . . innocence and charm . . . naïve and eager, trying . . . committed . . . caring . . . they have lots of qualities that adults lose as they grow up. [16: Internet offender]

Emotional congruence means that offenders may find comfort from children that they are incapable of getting from adults.

## COPING IN STRESSFUL SITUATIONS

In order to understand the coping behaviour of the sex offenders against children, we employed the *Coping Inventory for Stressful Situations* measure (Endler and Parker, 1999). This helps to assess the means by which individuals cope with stressful experiences (Endler and Parker, 1990). The measure asks respondents to indicate how much they engaged in various types of activities (for example, getting angry, or going out to buy a snack) when they encountered a difficult, stressful, or upsetting situation. In general, this measure indicated little or no difference between any type of offender – Internet or contact – in terms of how they coped with stressful situations. Three different coping strategies were measured:

- *Task oriented methods of coping* (analysing the problem before taking action, determining a course of action to follow, outlining and adjusting priorities, trying to be organised so as to be on the top of the situation, and using the situation to prove that one is able to sort it out). The three offender groups we studied had similar scores on the measure. Internet offenders had the highest average scores and the mixed Internet/contact offenders the lowest. These differences were of no importance and were not statistically significant.

- *Emotion-focused methods of coping* (the management, palliation, or expression of emotion such as anger, worry or self-pity) (Folkman and Lazarus, 1986). Emotion-based responses to stress include becoming very upset, blaming oneself or 'freezing' because one does not know what to do to cope in the situation, pretending that the situation is not really happening or becoming extremely tense. Again there were no substantial differences. Contact offenders engaged in more emotional coping responses than did mixed offenders.

- *The avoidance oriented strategies for coping with stressful situations*. This includes two separate elements: (a) the use of distraction and (b) the use of social diversion. Distraction methods include 'shopping therapy', treating oneself to a favourite food or snack, and watching television or a movie. Once again there was nothing that effectively differentiated the three groups of offenders. Social diversion was not particularly common since those who offend sexually against children have rather restricted social networks, in general. So, consequently, social ways of coping with stress are not readily available to the offenders. Thus only a minority mentioned that they frequently or very frequently took it out on other people (12 %), went to a party (6 %), tried to be with other people (33 %), or phoned (33 %) or visited a friend (39 %). This is more-or-less what would be expected given the emotional congruence offenders have for children rather than for adults.

A frequently adopted coping strategy was the negative one of 'blaming oneself for getting into the stressful situation' (72 %). Other fairly common negative responses were 'tension' (55 %), 'worry' (45 %) and 'anxiety' (45 %). Uncommon strategies included 'telling oneself that it was not really happening' (12 %), 'freeze and not know what to do' (12 %), 'window shopping' (14 %) and 'seeing a movie' (12 %). On the other hand, among the coping strategies regularly used by offenders were several positive and problem-focused ones. High proportions of offenders mentioned frequently or very frequently engaging in such positive strategies as 'think about the event and learn from my mistakes' (69 %), focusing on the problem (67 %), and making an effort to get things done (67 %).

One 57-year-old contact sexual offender was asked to elaborate on the comment that he gets 'stressed over problems'. He provided the following explanation, which is a clear and distinctive example of the extended use of emotionally focused strategies for this group of perpetrators:

It's mainly life itself . . . or something I cannot handle, or I get too much to do . . . I am afraid . . . to put it to one side . . . I have to try and do it, and then it stresses you up . . . I'll immediately ask somebody to . . . help me . . . I find it a bit annoying when . . . people say 'well I can't help you today because I'm busy' you think 'I...will struggle on'...but then I get worked up...you feel tired, you feel like crying...you tend to lose your appetite...fed up of people being around you...you don't pick up on what people say, you tend to panic...you want to ask them but you cannot because you are so tensed up, nothing will come out...I feel angry...I try and push the bad things away from me...I try to ignore it but the problem is there...I can't get it out of my system and I try and talk to somebody...but the problem is in my head and I can't throw it out...it stays in me, its like a bottle...put the cork on and more pressure builds up and then it explodes. [35: Contact Offender]

To some extent he attempts to solve his problems by turning to other people although this is thwarted with generally negative consequences. He is not emotionally congruent with adults. Consequently his response does not alleviate his stress and he becomes more emotional and self-orientated. The offender reacts very strongly – or perhaps overreacts. He speaks of anxiety and autonomic experiences that exacerbate the stress. He persistently uses activities or makes cognitive changes aimed at simply avoiding the situation. These do nothing to alleviate the problem and generally lead to greater distress as the persistence of the problem is recognised. This offender is in regular treatment for depression. Coping plays an important role in mediating between stressful events and outcomes such as anxiety and depression (Billings and Moss, 1982, 1984). Emotion-focused coping is found to be related to depression and neuroticism (Serran and Marshall, 2006) and tend to dominate when the person feels that the stress is something to be endured. For offenders who use children sexually as a way of escaping negative feelings, the use of emotional coping strategies is problematic. Emotional coping strategies can induce further negative feelings which may have the consequence of enhancing the likelihood of reoffending (Serran and Marshall, 2006):

When I'm stressed, I go home sometimes and pick up a woman's magazine [adult porn]...and fantasise about having sex and masturbate. You tend to feel...better afterwards...you've opened up a plug...and its all drained out...but then you find because the stress gets harder that it doesn't happen...you can't get rid of this stress [by masturbating]...you're trying to find other ways of doing it...having depression tablets but...that doesn't work...that's where...you find yourself losing control...you feel...I've got to get sex from somewhere, the tablets are overriding this for a bit...at that same time you're losing control...then all of a sudden it just clicks...you find yourself trying to have sex with somebody else... anyone, a child, either trying to have sexual with them...or getting close to them.

Presumably, he does not offend every time he experiences a negative mood, but when he does the moods are often similar – the predominant feelings are negative and he is receiving medication for depression. Indeed, he attempts to actively deal with stress through pornography and medication although they appear, paradoxically, to increase the risk of offending. He also appears to lose control of his behaviour and lacks effective coping strategies. His offending always occurred during access to children through his voluntary work as a church helper and youth band organiser and this indicates a level of planning to his behaviour together with distorted beliefs about the sexual willingness of children. This offender's sexual activities are, however, wide-ranging. He describes using sex in the past to deal with boredom, using casual sex to help deal with relationship conflicts, and masturbating to deviant fantasies during what he terms '*normal*' affective periods, as illustrated here: 'I fantasise about children...asleep, sometimes awake...all times, stressed but also normal...[in the fantasy] you capture them and you put them in your own laboratory...and then you're exploring their bodies.'

## CONCLUDING COMMENTS

Our findings reflect earlier work on Internet sex offenders, which found that Internet offenders use Internet and child pornography as a way of avoiding unpleasant states in real life (Taylor and Quayle, 2003). There is also support for the findings of Middleton *et al.* (2006). Of the Internet offenders they studied, 33 % reported major problems in dealing with negative emotions (like anger, rejection, stress) as indicated by elevated scores on the Personal Distress scale of the Interpersonal Reactivity Index (Davis, 1983). Importantly, Middleton *et al.* argued that this group of Internet offenders were capable of making and sustaining intimate relationships but would be unable to gain support within the relationship and so would not be able to deal with emotional stressors.

It has been suggested that if the childhood experiences of sex offenders against children are disturbed and involve abuse such as neglect, then they will not only show insecure adult attachment but will also develop inadequate coping strategies (Marshall, Serran and Cortoni, 2000). However, there was a general lack of association between such adverse childhood factors and coping strategies in our research. That is, the sex offenders show problems in coping irrespective of particular adverse factors in their background. So those offenders who had been physically abused in childhood did not differ from other offenders in terms of their coping strategies; the men who had engaged in sex-play in childhood did not differ in their coping strategies from those who had not engaged in sex-play; there were no differences in coping strategies between abused and non-abused men; and there was no relationship between childhood attachment and the broad types of coping strategies an offender employed.

All types of sex offenders against children experience a variety of adult difficulties, which may be considered alongside the idea that sex offenders use fantasy sex as well as sexual activity as part of coping (Cortoni and Marshall, 2001). This implies a clear link between stress and fantasy sex and sexual activity.

Researchers have argued that child molesters make greater use of emotion-focused coping methods than other offenders (Marshall, Cripps, Anderson and Cortoni, 1999; Marshall, Serran and Cortoni, 2000). Generally there were no differences between the different offender groups in terms of coping behaviour. Interestingly, though, one small difference we found between contact and mixed Internet-contact offenders involved emotion-focused coping strategies.

A final important question is whether the sorts of coping strategies and the extent of their use by Internet and contact sex offenders against children are within the normal range for the general population or whether they are abnormal in some way. Endler and Parker's (1990) standardisation data suggest that the mixed offenders in our study scored outside of the normal range on task-orientated coping; that is they reported less frequent use of task-orientated strategies compared to the general population. Contact offenders also scored outside of the normal range for the general male population on emotional-focused coping; that is, self-orientated and emotional methods. This is significant because they are indications that the coping strategies of these offenders are not particularly effective ones, which, taken along with their other proclivities, pushes them towards offending.

# CHAPTER 9

# Relationships in Childhood and Adulthood: Security and Attachment

The idea that the quality of childhood attachment to parents or an adequate parent substitute is vital to the lifelong wellbeing of people is well established in psychological, psychiatric, social work and educational thinking. Despite numerous refinements, attachment has survived as a core idea since the psychiatrist John Bowlby alluded to it in 1944. Bowlby's seminal work 'Forty-four thieves' (1944) compared a group of juvenile thieves who had been referred to a child-guidance clinic with a matched group of children who were also attending the clinic but with no reports of thieving. Those in the 'thieving' group were found to have much higher rates of separation from their mothers for six months or more in the first five years of life (Bowlby, 1944). This led Bowlby to conclude that a close and unbroken relationship with a mother or another care-giving figure was crucial for well-adjusted mental health and that separation was responsible for many of the cases of serious delinquency. A later, larger study (Bowlby *et al.*, 1956) failed to provide the evidence for the theory and it came under heavy criticism (Coleman and Norris, 2000). Nevertheless, his ideas stimulated research on the role of the family background focusing first on broken homes and later on a whole range of factors such as those affecting the quality of upbringing and its impact of delinquency and anti-social behaviour (Blackburn, 1993; Feldman, 1993).

Not only is satisfactory attachment to parents important in childhood but Bowlby also argued that it affects the ways in which we, as adults, relate to significant others as spouses and partners. Consequently, lacking satisfactory attachment with our parents, we may fail to develop satisfactory adult relationships (Bowlby, 1977, 1979). Different styles of attachment have been proposed, some of which tend to be dysfunctional in relationships and so lead to relationship problems.

The main childhood attachment styles are seen in the child's behaviour in relationship to parents and others. *Secure attachment* implies that the child is able to separate from his or her parent without distress, will seek comfort from the parent if distressed, will demonstrate a preference for the parent over strangers, and is comfortable when a parent returns after a period of separation from the child. A *dismissing attachment* style is indicated when a child seems not to prefer to be with its parent rather than strangers, does not seek out the parent when in a distressing situation, and even avoids the parent. An *ambivalent attachment* style is demonstrated by a child who cannot separate from its parent without manifesting distress although the child is not apparently comforted by the return of its parents. They also show a wariness of strangers. Finally, a *disorganised attachment* style is characterised by a mixture of the secure attachment behaviour and the insecure attachments behaviours. The style that dominates varies but not really in any sort of consistent way.

Four adult attachment styles have been suggested. These are *secure, dismissing, preoccupied* and *unresolved/disorganised*. Each one appears to relate to the four main childhood attachment styles: *secure, avoidant, ambivalent, disorganised* respectively (Ainsworth *et al.*, 1978). Ward *et al.* (2006) describe how each adult attachment style maps onto childhood attachment styles. A secure infant attachment would lead to a *secure adult attachment style* in which individuals view themselves and others positively and manifest high levels of intimacy in close adult relationships. Those with an avoidant infant attachment style may go on to develop a *dismissive adult attachment style* in which they have a positive regard for themselves but view others negatively. They are also likely to endorse the idea that sex without love is pleasurable. A *preoccupied adult attachment style* is the product of an ambivalent infant attachment style. Such individuals view themselves negatively but others positively and seek approval from others. They reveal possessiveness in *relationships*. Finally, those with a disorganised infant attachment style grow up to manifest a *disorganised adult attachment style*. They view themselves and others negatively. This attachment style is characterised by the fear of intimacy in relationships and the avoidance of closeness with other people. Hence they will seek impersonal sex.

Bartholomew and Horowitz (1991) offered a framework for understanding how adult attachment styles affect a person's view of themselves and others. They propose a model of 'self'; loveable (positive self) versus unlovable (negative self). They also provide a model of 'others' in which those capable of giving love and viewing other people positively are contrasted with those incapable of giving love and having a negative view of other people in general.

## CHILDHOOD ATTACHMENT TO PARENTS IN SEX OFFENDERS

In a variety of ways, sex offenders against children often have childhoods that warrant the description 'less than optimal' (see Chapter 6). Sometimes questioning offenders about their childhood and parents can be unproductive because they may become defensive or distressed. They may occasionally paint a very rosy picture of their childhood that is not warranted in the light of other things that they say. But the question is how such poor relationships can lead to future sex offending. Insecure attachment is, in itself, not thought to be the direct cause of future offending behaviour but it enhances the chance that a youngster will become a sex-offending adult (Marshall and Marshall, 2000; Marshall, Serran and Cortoni, 2000). Other factors must come into play too. We have seen how offenders describe their childhood sexual experiences in ways suggestive of poor monitoring of their activities by their parents (Chapter 7). They may have to seek the warmth they fail to receive from their parents by forming emotional relationships with peers or even paedophiles. In this way, problems of attachment may be a pathway leading towards offending as an adult. Attachment difficulties can thus result in the increased likelihood of damaging early sexual experiences (Marshall, 1989; Marshall and Marshall, 2000), possibly leading to eventual offending against children in adulthood. Consequently, sexualised coping, early masturbation and sex acts with others may later develop into sexually abusive behaviour in adulthood.

Sex offending may occur because adult sexual offenders experience an overlap between the attachment, care giving and sexual systems of their childhood and early adolescence (Smallbone and Dadds, 1998, 2000). Children who experience child sexual abuse might develop a disorganised attachment style that results in sexual behaviour during periods of high subjective feelings of stress. According to Smallbone and Dadds, such early disorganisation of the childhood attachment system can reduce the 'functional separation' between the adult attachment, sexual and parenting behavioural systems. For example, in intrafamilial abuse the proximity to a child (which would normally set off the parenting behaviour system) when the offender is distressed (which would normally set off the attachment behaviour system) may result in inappropriate activation of the sexual behaviour system resulting in sexualised parent-child interactions.

More directly to the point is the proposal that a child's relationship with its parents, whether positive or negative, provides a model or template for *future* personal and intimate adult relationships (Beech and Mitchell, 2005). Interpersonal attachment styles especially in relation to women may be associated with sex offending. Ward, Hudson and Marshall (1996) drew attention to various ways in which insecure adult attachment styles may relate to distinct types of sexual behaviour: *dismissive* individuals would be hostile and likely to offend violently against women; *preoccupied* individuals would tend to seek approval from others and sexualise attachment relationships. *Disorganised* individuals would seek intimacy through impersonal sexual encounters. Burk and Burkhart (2003) noted that men with a disorganised attachment style are likely to use sexual offending as a possible strategy to cope with negative mood states.

Research has not entirely supported these ideas and findings are inconsistent in certain respects. For example, Marshall, Serran and Cortoni (2000) found no significant differences in attachment styles between child molesters, non-sexual offenders, and non-offenders. They concluded that participants in all three groups 'reported greater security in their attachments to their mothers than to their fathers' (Marshall, Serran and Cortoni, 2000, p. 17). They add that insecure attachment may be a risk factor for criminality in general, rather than sexual offending specifically.

Nevertheless, in the first of an important series of studies, Smallbone and Dadds (1998) found that sex offenders are significantly less secure than non-offenders in terms of their childhood attachment. On the other hand, they were similar in attachment to the non-sexual criminal offenders. Various sex offender groups showed much the same levels of secure and insecure attachment. However, intrafamilial child molesters were more likely to regard their mothers as unloving, inconsistent and abusive whereas rapists were more likely to regard their fathers as uncaring and abusive towards them. Another study in the series involved a sample of male undergraduate students (Smallbone and Dadds, 2000). Insecure maternal attachment style in childhood did not predict their adult style of attachment to other adults. Much the same was found for childhood paternal attachment though childhood avoidant paternal attachment seemed to influence the development of aggression and anti-social behaviour.

This was, however, contradicted by their subsequent study (Smallbone and Dadds, 2001), which showed that avoidant maternal attachment was related to coercive sexual behaviour in undergraduates. Finally, Smallbone and McCabe (2003) found that between 31 % and 40 % of their sex offenders (intrafamilial and extrafamilial child molesters and rapists) experienced insecure maternal attachment. However, they suggest that the numbers of these in offender populations are comparable to rates in the general population experiencing insecure attachment (which they put at 33 % to 38 %). Interestingly, insecure paternal attachment was associated with being sexually abused by an adult. Sexually victimised offenders also tended to have an early onset of masturbation. Again this is evidence that early sexualisation leads to earlier sexual behaviour (Chapter 7).

On the face of things, these findings are somewhat disappointing in that they provide, at best, only very limited support for the idea that attachment problems form a specific and important mechanism in the development of sexual offending (Rich, 2006). If anything, attachment deficits seem to be overrepresented in anti-social/criminal offenders, in general, rather than sex offenders in particular. However, some studies have concluded differently. Lyn and Burton's (2004) investigation of incarcerated adult sex offenders and incarcerated non-sexual criminals found stronger support for the idea. They found that insecurely attached sexual offenders were nearly six times more likely to be found in the sex offender group than securely attached ones. In particular, fearful attachment was significantly related to having a history of sexual offending. There was no relationship between either preoccupied or dismissive attachments and being a sex offender. However, overall even this fails to support the more specific idea that different types of attachment are related to different types of sexual offences.

It should not be forgotten that attachment style is formed through a complex interpersonal process starting within the family at first but eventually going beyond that. As such, attachment style is best regarded as an abstraction rather than a clear-cut psychological disposition. Early patterns of experience will not affect a child's development in a single, invariant way. In keeping with this, Smallbone and Dadds (1998) suggested that early insecure attachment experiences place some men at risk of sexual offending if other factors in their lives drive in the same direction. This can be seen in the work of Craissati, McGlurg and Browne (2002) who found that childhood neglect and emotional abuse were associated with sexual abuse. This was particularly the case for child molesters. Offenders who had been sexually abused in childhood tended to have a wider range of psychosocial difficulties, such as persistent truanting, bullying, and prolonged difficulties with peer friendships. However, many sexual offenders do not sexually offend until they reach adulthood, although they may have criminal records for other crimes (Smallbone and Wortley, 2004). This might suggest that attachment is not the significant feature of offending if we accept that attachment style is established by adolescence and largely fixed in the psychology of the offender thereafter. The evidence that attachment style remains constant throughout life, irrespective of circumstances, is mixed (Scharfe, 2003). Stability over time implies a deterministic nature to attachment and overlooks the possibility that changes in personal circumstances, such as losing a partner, may modify an individual's attachment style (Hazan and Shaver, 1994) or make it more salient.

Of course, contradictions between the findings of different studies may be the consequence of important differences in the measuring instruments used and the research design employed. There is greater consistency in attachment measurement in non-clinical populations where the well-validated and supported Adult Attachment Interview is used (George, Kaplan and Main, 1996; Ward et al., 2006). However, its use is time consuming because of the process of administration and interpretation and it requires extensive training to use effectively. In research on sex offenders, retrospective self-reports tend to be used to assess attachment and this, potentially, may provide less reliable data (Rich, 2006). Even the self-report methods used vary across studies, which also makes comparisons across studies difficult. Furthermore, inconsistencies in the findings of research studies may be due to the heterogeneity of the samples used; that sexual offenders vary greatly in their personal attributes and qualities.

## INTERNET OFFENDERS AND ATTACHMENT

Internet offenders afford another possibility to explore the role of attachment in encouraging sexually abusive behaviour. Two main possibilities might be identified. First, if it is assumed that attachment problems are specific to sexual offending rather than criminality then Internet sex offenders should not differ from contact sex offenders against children in terms of their attachment patterns. Secondly, if (a) attachment problems are more conducive to criminality and (b) sex offenders against children are less inclined to anti-social/ criminal behaviour (Seto and Eke, 2005), then Internet offenders should show different attachment patterns from contact offenders who tend to manifest generalised patterns of anti-social behaviour.

We saw in Chapter 6 that the childhoods of both Internet and contact sex offenders against children were frequently problematic. Periods of separation from parents, for example, were fairly common. Although things did vary between offender groups, the overwhelming conclusion from Chapter 6 was that contact, Internet and mixed sex offenders frequently report similarly problematic childhoods. Parental non-supervision of the offender as a child and parental violence were fairly general. Some things were not so typical of the Internet-only offenders – in particular being cared for at some stage in an institution and being sexually abused were more characteristic of the child-hoods of contact offenders against children. One characteristic which was more typical of Internet-only offenders was the 'loss of significant others' in childhood. Not surprisingly there was evidence of 'acting out' behaviours in offenders' childhoods. These are possibly the response of the child to the unstable, disturbed family background and the seeming lack of parental nurturance. Childhood tensions and difficulties were also bound up with other issues. In particular, sexual victimisation was common in the lives of contact and mixed offenders and seems to substitute for the longed-for parental warmth that was lacking. Such adverse characteristics are associated with the disorganised childhood attachment style.

Typically, the Internet sex offenders lack previous convictions for any type of crime. So, in a sense, they can be construed as a group free from a general background of criminality. Consequently, if they are affected by attachment difficulties then these must be responsible for their sexual offending. This raises the question of whether attachment serves as a *specific* cause of sex crime or is it a *general* risk factor in the development of antisocial tendencies? Based on this, Internet offenders might show different attachment patterns from contact offenders, who are more likely to exhibit generalised patterns of antisocial/offending behaviour. There is evidence, which links attachment problems in childhood to behavioural problems (Rich, 2006). The difficulty, though, is to explain why there is any exclusive relationship between child-hood attachment deficits and sex offending rather than offending in general (Rich, 2006; Smallbone and Dadds, 1998).

The *Parental Bonding Inventory* (PBI) (Parker, Tupling and Brown, 1979) is a retrospective measure of how childhood bonding with parents is remembered over the first 16 years of life. Both parents are assessed separately. It is regarded as a measure of perceptions of parental characteristics rather than actual characteristics although it is claimed to have good validity as a measure of the latter (Parker, 1983). Its internal reliability is good and, importantly, it does not seem to be affected by the individual's mood when completing the scale (Gotlib *et al.*, 1988). It consists of two separate subscales:

- The *care scale* measures the amount of care that the child received from its parents, for example items include 'Could make me feel better when I was upset', 'Appeared to understand my problems and worries', 'Frequently smiled at me', and 'Enjoyed talking things over with me'.
- The *overprotection scale* indicates the extent to which the child experienced controlling behaviours from its parents. Example items include 'Did not want me to grow up, 'Tried to control everything I did', 'Invaded my privacy' and 'Tried to make me feel dependent on him/her'.

We found no differences between Internet, contact and mixed offenders in terms of either of these aspects of parental boding. However, the parental bonding measures can be used to identify four different categories of parental bonding on the basis of the pattern of scores on the care and overprotection scales:

- 'Optimal parenting' = high care and low protection scores.
- 'Affectionate constraint' = high care and high protection scores.
- 'Affectionless control' = high protection and low care scores.
- 'Weak bonding' = low care and low protection scores.

This way of conceiving attachment produced more exciting findings. Perhaps consistent with expectations, the offender groups were most strongly represented in the suboptimal maternal bonding categories. Indeed, only about one in five offenders were in the category of 'optimal parenting'. For the entire group of sex offenders that we studied, the commonest category was that of 'affectionless control'. This means that the majority of paedophiles studied had experienced neglectful and indifferent maternal care combined with intrusive, rejecting and abusive control. Weak bonding was the second most common unsatisfactory boding style. Mostly, the trends were the same for both maternal and paternal bonding. However, mixed sex offenders showed a different pattern for paternal care in that their most common category involved low levels of paternal care together with a low levels of paternal overprotection – in other words, weak bonding.

While our belief, based on interviews, that paedophiles experienced poor bonding with their parents is confirmed by these findings, we found it somewhat frustrating to find that Internet and contact offenders were fairly similar in this respect. Despite trying a variety of different analyses (for example, factor analysis) of the parental bonding data in an attempt to refine our understanding, nothing changed the picture that parental bonding styles, although generally far from optimal, were not particularly different between contact, Internet and mixed sex offenders against children.

As has previously emerged in research, there was evidence that some of the factors associated with sex offending were also associated with having a more general criminal history. For example, having a cold mother and an over-protective father was related to having a criminal history, irrespective of the sort of crime. Men with criminal histories prior to their current offence indicated that their mothers did not give them praise, failed to understand their needs and wants, and were emotionally cold to them. At the same time, their fathers were reported as being overprotective and tending to 'baby' them. They simply did not want their son to grow up. Men with a previous history of convictions for sexual offences against children tended to describe their mother has exhibiting overprotective maternal behaviours such as encouraging dependency on the mother and babying the offender.

The findings of previous research are redolent of ours in that difficulties in attachment in early childhood lead to later difficulties such as sexually abusive behaviour. For instance, the pattern that low levels of parental care and high levels of overprotection had been found in previous research such as that of

Craissati, McClurg and Browne (2002). Furthermore, the pattern is substantially more extreme than that found in the general population (for example, Parker, Tupling and Brown, 1979). Most important, in this context, is the general lack of differences between Internet offenders and contact offenders in this regard. It seems that our findings from the parental bonding scale agrees with the findings based on our interviews with sex offenders against children; that is, adverse and suboptimal parenting epitomises the childhoods of all types of sex offenders against children.

## ADULT ATTACHMENT

In summary, early childhood attachment is thought to serve as the 'template' for relationships in adulthood. Suboptimal childhood experiences increase the risk that the child will go on to adopt an insecure attachment style that dominates their adult relationships (Marshall, 1989; Marshall and Marshall, 2000). They may fail to learn the necessary interpersonal skills to develop and maintain close relationships including romantic ones. In offenders, deficits in the ability to form attachment may result in the use of coercive sexual behaviour in order to satisfy their emotional need for closeness. There are claims, as we have seen, that insecurity in adult attachment is associated with sex offending (Ward *et al.*, 1996). According to Ward *et al.*, their child abusers demonstrated either a preoccupied attachment style or a fearful attachment style. Preoccupied attachment style offenders sought immature victims through a process of grooming over time and developed a pseudo-relationship with them. Fearful attachment style offenders used short-term, impersonal contacts.

  Paedophiles are frequently involved in relationships with other adults, notwithstanding their sexual interest in children. At the time of their index offences, 69 % of Internet, 64 % of contact and 70 % of mixed sexual offenders in our research were in a sexual relationship with another adult (married, girlfriend, boyfriend, cohabiting or long-term partner including any gay relationships). These figures were much the same across the different offender groups. And relationship problems were frequently blamed by offenders for their offending against children. Thus 56 % of Internet offenders, 70 % of mixed Internet/contact offenders and 76 % of contact-only offenders placed the blame – partially or entirely – on relationship problems though this was significantly less in Internet offenders. Thus many offenders were in long-term adult relationships (although it is known that some contact offenders pursue adult relationships simply to obtain contact with the child in a family).

  Nevertheless, what was notable was the approach of offenders to and the quality of some of these relationships. It is notable that offenders in all groups seemed to engage in interpersonal sex to a substantial extent. The levels of casual or promiscuous sex were notable although comparative data on normal populations does not seem to be available. Forty-four per cent of Internet offenders reported using prostitutes, described themselves as promiscuous or reported frequent one-night stands or sex with a stranger. The equivalent figure for contact-only offenders was 48 % and for mixed contact/Internet offenders 40 %. There are several explanations for this. One is that such men persist in impersonal sex since it produces sexual pleasure and offers the promise of intimacy (Marshall, 1989). The problems that the offenders have in achieving intimacy in adult relationships may contribute to their promiscuous behaviours and, possibly, encourage inappropriate ways of pursuing intimacy such as through casual sex, child pornography or with inappropriate sexual partners such as children (Marshall, 1989). Of course, impersonal sex might imply that they were dissatisfied with sex with their adult partner or it might simply reflect the somewhat chaotic lifestyles of offenders in their youth.

Many of these things are reflected in the following excerpt in which an offender talks about impersonal sex. As his relationships fail they are quickly replaced by new ones:

> I am a bit promiscuous . . . snogging, dating whatever . . . I had relationships with people my own age but I call a long-term relationship for me over six months . . . there was one person who I went out with for three months . . . whenever I seem to get to know anybody and I'd start getting comfortable with them something would change and they'd bugger off . . . so I've been hurt too many times and so I was a tart . . . lots of girls. Then I went to university and . . . they were all 18 year olds and I was . . . the older man I liked that because it was a way of getting girls . . . I moved into a student house and P. [girls name] . . . we hit it off straight away . . . we went out for 10 months, so serious for me . . . we got engaged . . . I was still going out with the lads . . . and sleeping around . . . often it was a case of I got drunk with the lads I come back home she'd be in bed we'd have sex, I'd take that for granted . . . I was what you'd call a power and control partner . . . but then P. [girls name] wanted her independence so she left and I had one night stands again here there and everywhere . . . Then I meet M. [girls name] . . . quite an intense relationship we were living with each other after a couple of weeks . . . then after a while she was getting boring . . . I wanted to go out and enjoy myself and I found life boring with her . . . we split up, got back together again and . . . I ended up moving back in . . . then I started teacher training course . . . things were going okay but she wasn't being fully supportive . . . and that's when I met H. [girls name] . . . hit it off straight away I finished with M. [girls name] and next day I moved into H.'s [girls name] place to live . . . and it finished after about . . . two months . . . I went back to going out . . . one night stands as before . . . I have experimented with homosexuality, kissed blokes . . . I've had a blow job from a bloke and . . . I've given a hand job to a bloke . . . it was a phase, I wasn't seeing anybody at the time and I was working with a bunch of lads . . . couple of them were gay went to a gay club one night . . . and . . . got drunk and went to bed with one of them. [10: Internet offender]

The next man tried to convince the interviewer that monogamous relationships are unhealthy and he promotes the idea of communal living – though he seems to be referring to extramarital affairs. He describes the reality of his two long-term relationships as not living up to what he wanted from a partnership, and emphases that he ended up as the carer of the child. What is not apparent is that his wives were very young when they met him. Perhaps they lost their sexual attraction for him as they grew older. There appeared to be domestic violence against both his wife and his children:

> The relationships I've had, in reality turn out to be different from what I thought was gonna happen...the [relationships] weren't what I could accommodate very readily because it wasn't what I wanted from a relationship, and it wasn't what I, what I went into for...for instance I was the one who ended up looking after the child I didn't want that. It's also part of society's attitude to relationships, especially females, they feel they've, you've got to be exclusive...you know you can hit a bad patch, you can go off someone for a while some, they do something to upset you but you learn to cope with it and the relationship is back on tap...and for me for somebody else to become more important for a while is not unhealthy to my relationship...it's the automatic exclusivity that helps destroy some relationships, my relationships...but if you just let things flow there are some societies living quite happily in communal relationships...plus my first wife she cited me being violent but she wasn't afraid of violence...she claimed custody because I was violent towards the children, I've never hurt them...but in some senses, it's difficult to avoid it but I've never intentionally hurt children...my first two wives they were young when I became attracted to them...14 and 15. [6: Internet offender]

Men who engaged in impersonal sex seemed less anxious about adult relationships and did not worry about being abandoned by their partner. They felt uncomfortable opening up to partners or when trying to become emotionally close. Impersonal relationships provide sex but avoid the undesired emotional intimacy, which risks being withdrawn. Short-term relationships meet their needs very well. They do not have to fear abandonment and short-term relationships do not arouse concern about whether their partner cares for them. Such relationships leave the offender in control. They may not feel comfortable opening-up to their sexual partners and prefer physical sex without the need to do this. Physical intimacy may be equated with emotional intimacy (Marshall, 1989). Theirs is fleeting sexual satisfaction that leaves them to seek closeness elsewhere – and they only know how to achieve this through sexual contact.

One way of measuring adult attachment is the self-report *Experiences in Close Relationships* (Brennan, Clark and Shaver, 1998), which assesses two distinct dimensions:

- *Anxiety*. This is the extent to which individuals worry about losing their partner, worry that their partner does not have equally strong feelings for them, and need reassurance that they are loved.
- *Avoidance of closeness*: This is the extent to which individuals feel uncomfortable about opening up to intimate partners or when an intimate partner wants to get close, even when this is what they want.

Taken separately, there were no reliable differences between Internet only, contact, and mixed Internet/contact groups. Nevertheless, these two dimensions can be used to identify four different attachment styles in adulthood and a different picture emerges by doing so:

- *Secure*: individuals are not anxious about losing their partner and enjoy closeness with intimate partners.
- *Dismissing-avoidant*: although individuals avoid closeness with intimate partners they are not anxious about the feelings of their partners for them.
- *Fearful-avoidant*: such individuals avoid closeness in relationships but are concerned about the feelings of their partner for them – their fear of rejection may encourage the short-term relationships, which characterise this group.
- *Preoccupied*: such an individual is distrusting of relationships with other adults. Such offenders typically would view children as more reliable and less threatening than adults. They are approval-seekers, see themselves as unworthy and are anxious about the other person in the relationship. They are comfortable with closeness.

Using this scheme, contact-only offenders were rarely found to have a secure adult attachment style. Indeed, 88 % of this group was to be found in one or other of the three insecure adult-attachment categories. Forty-four per cent were in the preoccupied category, 25 % in the fearful-avoidant category, and 20 % in the dismissive avoidant category. It is notable that the least common insecure category – dismissive avoidant – is the one that is more likely to characterise rapists (Ward *et al.* 1996). In contrast, the groups of offenders who engaged in Internet offending showed much more secure attachment. Fifty per cent of Internet-only and 30 % of the mixed contact/ Internet group were classified as having a secure attachment style. The tendency of Internet offenders to be securely attached in relationships was statistically reliable. The strong presence of contact offenders in the preoccupied category supports the notion that they are characterised by seeking immature partners, grooming them over a lengthy period of time and developing a pseudo relationship (Ward *et al.*, 1996). This corresponds with our finding that some perpetrators experience feelings of rejection or mistrust in relation to adults and consequently are drawn to children (Chapters 6 and 7). They see children as accepting and trustworthy individuals who, in a relationship, will provide the offender with support and encouragement.

## ATTACHMENT DEFICITS IN OFFENDERS' LIVES

Of course, the notion of attachment deficit is a creation of researchers and theorists, it is not a concept that the offenders use. Since attachment deficit is an abstraction, it may be helpful to understand just how these deficits are manifested in the lives of offenders or, at least, in the words that offenders use when describing adult relationships. The insecurity that is at the foundation of their adult relationships pervades much of the interview material that we gathered about their intimate relationships with adults. For example, the following offender provides almost a succinct vignette of how anxiety and avoidance may dominate relationships:

> Participant: Worry a lot...about being in relationships...about losing partner...a big worrier...I've always felt like I've been alone ...
>
> Interviewer: How about significant intimate adult relationships?
>
> Participant: I've not really had any...I won't let people get close...I've got this fear of people getting close...what I use to do in a relationship with somebody if I lost me temper...I would grab them and that was frustrating as well...not being able to communicate properly with them, not being able to let them in, because...a lot of the girls that I've been out with, don't really want me. [26; Contact Offender]

The following 35-year-old contact offender was married but acknowledged that he liked and regularly engaged in homosexual relationships, which was a cause of problems in his marriage. He sees his childhood sexual abuse as being responsible for his distrust of adults. He describes having a loving homosexual relationship while incarcerated in which there was a mutual sharing of interests as well as physical attraction. Although he appeared to be describing a long-term intimate relationship, in actual fact it lasted just one week:

> Interviewer: What do you think partners have gained from being in an adult relationship with you?
>
> Participant: I don't know about what people get from me...someone should be dominant as in the dominant person in the relationship, someone should stay at home brings up the kids, has your dinner on the table when you walk through the door, puts your slippers on your feet, makes you a cup of tea when you tell them to that's what I like...or did like, I met and fell in love with a guy in here...he liked the things I liked, curl up on the sofa with a good DVD, a nice glass of wine and a meal...and on an intellectual level...he [also] found me attractive...and not fat, useless, or ugly...he was what I wanted...he was only in for a week but...when he left, I didn't want to go and kill myself which is brilliant because that means that I did take the positive from the relationship, often I would have said in a relationship 'oh god it's the end' 'they didn't really like me, they were just saying that'...but I haven't trusted people since I was small, I've just never trusted people, I was abused as a child myself...well, well several times and quite severely so why should I trust people? [32: contact offender]

Characteristically, offenders describe adult relationships in ways that suggest that they have unrealistic expectations of what they entail. The offenders' high expectation of intimacy and closeness from their partners meant that they were not prepared, or perhaps were unable, to offer affection and support in return. By having such high expectations, their partners could only fail to meet what was expected and came to be viewed as unreliable or insufficiently supportive and available. As a consequence, the offenders often felt that had been taken advantage of in what for them seemed to be a one-sided relationship. They view adults as untrustworthy and likely to let them down. In some cases, this seems to reflect their childhood experiences with emotionally inconsistent or emotionally rejecting parents. As children they sometimes sought their emotional warmth from other children. Children, in contrast to adults, are perceived as offering ample and unconditional affection. The following two offenders, who demonstrate rather remarkable approaches to conducting adult relationships, amply illustrate this. They believe that they invest more into the relationship than their partner(s).

Participant: I put 110 % into a relationship sometimes I only get 70 % in return

Interviewer: What do you mean?

Participant: I don't think they take interest...she said 'you did put me through a lot of hell by reoffending [offender had 23 prior sex offences] I lost a lot of friendships'...but I think ooh hang on its not me it's her! You see she didn't put as much in it as me [42: Contact Offender]

Participant: I have a tendency [to] give so much to a relationship and I get very disappointed and hurt quickly if that starts to fail, if the relationship doesn't give back what I give, I tend to think that the person perhaps doesn't like me or I shouldn't be in the relationship, I start getting depressed and I...turn to somebody who does appreciate me...a child ... because they've never shown anything but love and affection and needed me...every time once the initial buzz has gone out of the relationship and you start settling down to family life...you start getting mundane, people start to be...complacent in their attitude towards you

Interviewer: What do you mean?

Participant: They get too comfortable, it starts to bother me then I start getting worried...instead of sitting on the settee when I walked in the house in the dressing gown she had on that morning...she could have perhaps cooked. She knows I am coming home, have the children ready perhaps for me...and it just seemed to be me ploughing everything in and getting nothing in return...all my adult relationships have been people being complacent and allow me to do all the work and they just sit back and reap the rewards. [27: contact offender]

Offenders provide only weak reasons for why they lack trust in adult relationships despite the strength of the feeling they express about the issue. This is precisely what one would expect if the root of the distrust lay in attachment problems rather than the partner. The offender above simply identifies domestic and routine chores as evidence for the lack of trust. The offender fails to recognise the significance of the fact that his partner had remained with him for many years. When adult relationships 'fail' in his eyes he turns to children, who are viewed as 'appreciating' him.

One noteworthy feature of the offenders' interviews is their responses to two questions – 'what did you gain from your current or past relationship(s)?' and 'what did your partner(s) gain from a relationship with you?' Some offenders had some difficulty in providing much by way of answers to these questions whereas others did manage to supply longer descriptions. The following 31-year-old contact offender provided quite a remarkable description in which there is generally a lack of positive attributes assigned to his adult relationships. What his partners gain seems to be confined to financial support and physical intimacy from him. There is little or nothing to suggest that he is able to recognise positive aspects to being in a relationship. Many of his relationships seem to be merely about sex. During one long-term relationship substantial health difficulties of his wife seemed only to irritate him, as she was unable or unwilling to provide him with support:

Interviewer: What do your partners gain from being in a relationship with you?

Participant: . . . Provide money . . . physical intimacy . . . I like to please most of the time . . . unless I think it's completely irrational and then I wont please them . . . if I don't think it is rational

Interviewer: Generally what have your relationships been like? Can you describe them for me?

Participant: In almost every relationship I've had . . . jealously and obsession . . . I've ended relationships on that . . . the rules are simple . . . don't make an effort to fall in love with anybody . . . I was very promiscuous between 17 and 19 . . . I had two or three partners a night . . . even from 12 . . . girls go down on me, I would go down on girls . . . I mean I started quite young at school . . . the younger you are, I do actually think it gives you a good grounding doesn't it? I've had three marriages . . . my wife who had my second child . . . she had postnatal depression for a while but she came out of it but she didn't get back into the relationship at all . . . well she had to spend months in hospital in the run up, I'd been visiting her once a week . . . so I'd spent a lot of time trying to be a perfect husband and looked after her and God knows what else, and gone through all that hell . . . [but after the baby was born] she just didn't get back into the relationship . . . she was pretty detached, she wouldn't do anything for me . . . everything was an effort. So I went off and had an affair.

Interviewer: What do you gain from your relationships then?

Participant: I like clean, I like them to look after their house, have their own jobs for what they are suppose to do . . . you probably think it is very old fashioned [but] you are quite welcome to study or to have a job . . . but for me it's a hobby it doesn't matter how important it is to you that's not an issue...but its spending money...I'm there to earn money and she's there to look after the kids...you've got to be there for them most of the time...I'm certainly not doing it. [47: contact offender]

## CONCLUDING COMMENTS

Attachment difficulties in both childhood and adulthood pervade the lives of many paedophiles. Their bonding with their parents may be regarded as less than satisfactory and they are frequently insecure in their attachment as adults. The two things are related, of course, which further confirms that in order to understand paedophilia we need to know a great deal about offenders' childhoods. Unfortunately, this is dependent on their adult recollections of biographical information about themselves, which may be less than perfect and partly lost through the passage of time. Nevertheless, what information we have seems to suggest that attachment problems are characteristic. This seem less so for many Internet offenders who often seem to be in more stable relationships than the typical contact offender. It is not our suggestion that there is a direct link between attachment difficulties and offending against children. Many adults will have similar difficulties yet not turn to children. What we are suggesting, however, is that attachment difficulties reflect a complex process by which the child may become an offender if the circumstances facilitate this. We suspect that attachment difficulties are much more likely to lead to offending against children as an adult if attachment deficits in childhood lead to sexualised emotional involvements with other children or sexual abuse by an adult.

Nevertheless, it is abundantly clear that adult relationship problems such as conflict are often seen by offenders as the immediate precursors of offending behaviour. This was true of the index offence of the Internet-only offenders (56 %), the mixed offenders (70 %) and the contact offenders (76 %). These are high figures given that not all offenders were in adult relationships at the time of the offence. Thus there is something to be said for a model of offending behaviour that links current offending behaviour to current attachment problems. This is further supported by research that indicates that sexual recidivism is associated with conflicts in current intimate relationships (Hanson and Morton-Bourgon, 2004 cited in Rich, 2006).

But, of course, much of this chapter has revealed attachment deficiencies to be more characteristic of contact offenders than of Internet offenders. So, in that sense, attachment deficiencies do not have a particular relevance to Internet offenders. However, some Internet offenders do have attachment deficits which may make the issue pertinent to our understanding of at least some Internet offenders. Since one of the issues concerning Internet offenders is the possibility that some, probably a small minority, will go on to contact offend, we should ask what factors might encourage this progression. One possibility is obvious – that the Internet offenders with attachment difficulties are the men most at risk of going on to contact offend. Naturally, we have no direct evidence of this as we did not follow-up our offenders after a period of time to discover which Internet offenders (if any) went on to contact abuse. On the other hand, we do have information about the mixed Internet/contact offender group that suggests that they are more likely to have an insecure adult attachment style. So attachment style is potentially an important factor in trying to identify which Internet offenders may proceed on to contact offend. Gathering evidence about this is clearly difficult because, inevitably, we are dependent on men convicted for offending who, on release, will be monitored as effectively as other offenders on the sex offenders register. That is to say, there will be considerable limitations on them in terms of their freedom to reoffend as we saw in Chapter 4.

Finally, it should be added that we know very little about the extent to which childhood attachment difficulties may be ameliorated following satis-factory adult intimate relationships. Do some men whose childhood back-grounds appear to be suboptimal in this respect manage to overcome these problems and form satisfactory adult close relationships? If they do, then this may be one reason why our offender groups were more similar in childhood in terms of attachment than in adulthood.

# CHAPTER 10

# Sexual Fantasy and Paedophile Offenders

It is a common belief that sexual fantasy plays a role in sex offending (Daleiden *et al.*, 1998; Howells, Day, and Wright, 2004; Marshall *et al.*, 1999). Despite this, Swaffer *et al.* (2000) argued that more needs to be known about the linkage between sexual fantasies, masturbation and offences against children. Originally, the idea of the connection between *sexual* fantasy and deviant sexual behaviour was put forward many years earlier by McGuire, Carlisle and Young (1965) who believed that deviant sexual responses could be conditioned by the pairing of deviant sexual fantasies with orgasm, as in masturbation. They regarded early sexual experiences, for example with adults, as possible sources of sexual fantasy; a preference for deviant sexual fantasies they saw as a reflection of the offenders social inadequacies. Their idea that sexual deviancy can be conditioned by combining fantasy and masturbation was taken up by other researchers such as Abel and Blanchard (1974) who similarly argued that repeated pairings of deviant fantasy content and masturbatory arousal or orgasm leads to acquired sexual preferences that are subsequently acted out in sexual offending. One of the most influential early studies promoting the idea of an association between fantasy and offending behaviour concentrated on fantasy in violent psychiatric patients rather than sex offenders (MacCulloch, Snowden, Wood, and Mills, 1983).

Another quite distinct research tradition highlighting the role of sexual fantasy in offending also originated in the 1960s. This is the substantial body of research on the influence of pornography on sexual behaviour including deviant sexual behaviour (for example, Baron and Straus, 1984, 1989; Condron and Nutter, 1988; Court, 1977; 1984; Howitt and Cumberbatch, 1990; Kutchinsky, 1970, 1973). Much of the research in this field concentrated on the behavioural outcomes of exposure to pornography on sexual violence rather than pornography's impact on sexual fantasy prior to offending (see, for example, Donnerstein and Berkowitz, 1981). This research tradition tended to present pornography's content as a blueprint for deviant sexual behaviour and any intermediary role of sexual fantasy tended to be ignored. Nevertheless this has been a highly controversial field which has not yielded a totally consensual interpretation (see Howitt, 1998b). Curiously, research on sex offenders is relatively scant in this tradition despite concerns about the effects of pornography on sexual violence.

A third route by which sexual fantasy entered professional thinking was the research and writings of the Federal Bureau of Investigation's offender profilers (for example, Burgess *et al.*, 1986). They, perhaps, more than anyone else, encouraged the view that sexual fantasy is common in the mental life of serial sexual murderers and probably begins to develop in early life. Meloy *et al.* (2001) found that substantial numbers of their sample of adolescent mass murderers exhibited a preoccupation with violent fantasy. Furthermore, fantasy is a common element in sexual homicide (Meloy, 2000). However, Meloy expresses the caution that it is an extremely problematic matter to identify the factors that lead the fantasiser to act out the fantasy as a crime. This is because some potential offenders may confine their fantasy to masturbation or even merely daydream about offending. Sexual fantasy has value to the offender in a number of ways that are different from the sexual arousal value of sexual fantasies to most people (Turvey, 1995). Fantasy may serve as a means of control in that it is alterable by the offender and clearly expresses the offender's power over his victim-to-be. For example, by fantasising about the victim's willingness to engage in degrading sexual acts the offender feels in control of the victim. Turvey describes cases in which fantasy helps dissociate the outward veneer of social respectability of the offender's everyday life from his offending behaviour. By objectifying the victim the conflict between his everyday behaviour (perhaps as a family man) and his extreme offending behaviour is neutralised because the objectified victim is not regarded as part of decent life. Finally, there is a sense in which fantasy is a sort of mental archive for the offender in which each offence and each experience of a different victim is used as a resource in future offending. The accumulated fantasy, at least partly based on experience, serves as the plan for eventual re-enactment of the offending behaviour against new victims. This, in its turn, further fuels the fantasy of the offender.

One of the important features of sexual fantasy within the FBI offender-profiling tradition is once again the notion that fantasy serves as a 'blueprint' for offending behaviour. A corollary of this thinking is that information found at the crime scene can provide a picture of what the offender's fantasy might be. For example, Britton (1997) created a profile of the killer of Rachel Nickell who was murdered on Wimbledon Common, London, in 1992. His profile suggested that the killer's sexual fantasy involved the woman being frightened and submissive, assault on her vagina and anus, and the fantasy culminates in a sexual frenzy and murder of the woman. This fantasy profile is little more than a straight reading of the crime scene. Rachel Nickell was left with her buttocks prominently displayed and an object inserted into her anus with a massive number of different types of injury to her body. Such an assumed correspondence between fantasy and criminal acting out is common to both the FBI and MacCulloch *et al.* approaches. Sexual fantasy guides, drives and energises offending in these models.

However, the offences of the serial killers studied by the FBI profilers and MacCulloch *et al.*, for example, are so extreme that one cannot assume that they tell us a great deal about the typical sex offender against children who does not exhibit this gross violence. Thus, the argument that sexual fantasy is a key element in the offending behaviour of sex offenders against children is something of an untested assumption.

Fantasy has been regarded as an important thing for sex offender treatment programmes to deal with. Behavioural modification techniques were employed by some to recondition fantasy and effectively neutralise it (Howitt, 1995a). Fantasy modification is one of the cornerstones of contemporary UK cognitive-behavioural programmes (Beech, Fisher, and Beckett, 1999). But as programmes assume that sex offending is multidetermined (to include cognitive distortions, victim empathy, social skills and so on), it is the overall effectiveness of the entire cognitive-behavioural programme that is studied; the *independent* effectiveness of the therapy aimed at reducing deviant fantasy is difficult to establish (Howitt, 2004). In other words, little or no effort has been devoted, for example, to examining how changes in fantasy lead to reductions in offending behaviour.

Sexual thoughts are commonplace among both men and women in the non-offender population (Jones and Barlow, 1990). Some of these thoughts reflect themes of an unacceptable nature such as sex with children (Langevin, Lang and Curnoe, 1998) and images of force (Kirkendall and McBride, 1990). One should also consider the obvious question of the relevance of what we know about normal sexual fantasies to those of sex offenders. Ideas from studies of normal people's sexual fantasies contrast markedly with those from studies of sex offenders. Few, if any, have argued that there is an invariant relationship between sexual fantasy and sexual behaviour in normal populations whereas such an implication is quite common for offenders (Cramer and Howitt, 1998; Howitt, 2004). While it is acknowledged that sexual fantasy and sexual behaviour may sometimes correspond in general population samples, strikingly this link is not regarded as inevitable. In normal samples, sexual fantasy is often viewed as a cognitive stimulus, which results in sexual arousal – this is quite different from it being regarded as the blueprint for sexual behaviour. There have been quite extensive studies, for example, of the sexual fantasies of normal women, which largely dismiss the link between fantasy and a desire to act it out (Friday, 1973). In other words these sexual fantasies are regarded as just that – fantasies and not as behavioural templates. The women may even insist that it would be a sexual turn-off if these fantasies actually became incorporated into their real-life sexual behaviour (Friday, 1973). This begs the question of why some sexual fantasies should be acted out whereas others, apparently, are not.

There is a lack of clarity about the role of fantasy in sexual behaviour and a range of different roles that fantasy may play in sexual behaviour and sexual offending has been suggested (Howitt, 2004). Apart from the idea that fantasy is a blueprint for offending in which fantasy is acted out through the offence, among a number of other important roles that have been suggested for fantasy in offending are:

- *Rehearsal of offending in fantasy.* This is the planning of the offending in imagination (Gee *et al.*, 2004). In this sense fantasy provides the offender with the opportunity to visualise, plan and test out the offence-to-be (Pithers *et al.*, 1988; Turvey, 1995). Through mental simulations an offender could test out a variety of scenarios and anticipated experiences and prepare himself for alternatives. In other words, if he replayed a scenario several times he can prepare himself and develop contingency plans and better ideas of what to do should any difficulties arise (Turvey, 1995). For example, what would the offender do if the child threatens to disclose the abuse to a parent or teacher or if the child simply takes flight from the situation? The offender is therefore planning the offence in imagination or 'practising' his paedophilia (Meloy, 2000). This supports Hazelwood and Warren's (1995) conclusion that the behaviour manifested during a sexual crime is often a representation of the offender's fantasies. It is also the sort of fantasy that Gee *et al.* (2003) refer to as offence-specific fantasy. This seems to be a distinctive meaning of sexual fantasy as it is not clear that it is, in itself, involved in sexual arousal and masturbation.

- *Fantasy as a stimulus for inducing or enhancing sexual arousal.* Early researchers concluded that sexual fantasy was a means of heightening, or maintaining, sexual arousal psychologically and/or physiologically (Malamuth, 1981b). Fantasy content can be used as part of masturbation when a partner is not available (Brody, 2003; Friday, 1973; Hunt, 1974) and many men and women fantasise while engaging in sexual intercourse (Crepault and Couture, 1980; Davidson and Hoffman, 1986; Hariton and Singer, 1974; Lunde *et al.*, 1991; Sue, 1979). Fantasies are considered an important part of the 'sexual response cycle' (Masters and Johnson, 1966). That is, for some individuals, fantasy facilitates the initiation of sexual activity; for others it moves them from a low level of arousal to a heightened level; and for still others it moves them from high levels of arousal to orgasm (Masters, Johnson and Kolodny, 1992). There is very little research exploring the arousal function of fantasy for sex offenders but that which does exist suggests it serves similar arousal functions to that of non-offender populations (Gee *et al.*, 2003). For instance, for at least some offenders sexual fantasy can heighten sexual arousal (Polaschek *et al.*, 2001); for others fantasy may be used to replace a 'non-arousing offence reality' with an alternative situation which is more arousing – for instance perceiving the abuse victim as a willing partner (Gee *et al.*, 2003).

- *Shared common origins of fantasy and offending.* Here the assumption is that there is actually no causal relationship whereby fantasy is the cause of the offending. This is the case despite the possibility that the sexual fantasy and the offending behaviour are similar in terms of their content. For example, perhaps an offender suffered sexual abuse in childhood and that this led directly both to fantasies that reflected his abuse but also to offending behaviour in an attempt to deal with the psychological aftermath of his own abuse. The shared origins notion, of course, poses one difficulty theoretically since it is dependent on us knowing what that shared cause is for the fantasy and the offending. Perhaps the study of the efficacy of fantasy reduction in therapy might help us to understand this better. Thus therapeutic reduction of fantasy might be expected to have no impact on offending behaviour because it is not the fantasy that is the cause of the offending (Howitt, 2004).

- *Fantasy enhancement/renewal.* This emphasises that fantasy generation is actually an important consequence of offending rather than fantasy driving the offence. In other words, one of the consequences of offending is that it provides material for sexual fantasies which the offender uses in, for example, masturbation at a later stage or while engaging in sexual intercourse with a partner (Howitt, 2004). An example of this is provided by Gee *et al.* (2003, p. 53): 'I was using fantasies of what I had done to the victims to masturbate to.' Ward and Hudson (2000) suggest that offence scripts with mental simulation of the offence behaviour might provide the offender with a goal-directed action plan and this partially facilitates subsequent offending behaviour. The offender uses fantasies to relive past experiences and repetition and rehearsal reinforce these themes. These fantasies are rehearsed before, during, and after, sexual activity and allow the offender to relive the mental and sexual 'buzz' or 'high' associated with the actual offence.

Others have provided partially different conceptions of the functions of fantasy in offending and it should not be assumed that fantasy serves the same purposes in all offenders or all types of offenders. Gee, Ward and Eccleston (2003) proposed a model of fantasy in sexual offending based on interview material which suggests four different themes in how offenders discussed fantasy. Thus fantasy may be used:

- *To regulate the offender's mood.* The offender may be in a negative mood state such as feeling down or depressed because of the consequence of problems in everyday life such as at work or relationship difficulties. It can also be used to elevate an ambivalent mood such as boredom. Cortoni and Marshall (2001) found that sex offenders used both deviant and non-deviant sexual activities to cope with negative moods. Equally it can be used to regulate or enhance a pre-existing positive mood – to make things even more exciting.
- *To regulate sexual arousal.* The offender may use the sexual fantasy in the context of masturbation where it may serve to arouse the offender sexually. It is known, for example, that masturbation is normally and frequently accompanied by sexual fantasy in normal adults, especially men (Jones and Barlow, 1990; Leitenberg and Henning, 1995).
- *As a coping mechanism.* This may be either (a) to deal with the need to escape reality or to (b) feel in control over threats. This form of fantasy may involve, for example, fantasy control of others in imagined situations such as when abusing a child sexually. Alternatively, it could merely be part of a general tendency to employ fantasy as relief from or to escape from the painful and distressing realities in the offender's life.
- *As a mental mechanism to relive past experiences (i.e. rehearsal) or as a way of creating new experiences in a process of simulation.* In other words, offenders can live fantasy experiences either by drawing on past experiences or synthesising new experiences in fantasy.

The idea that fantasy may be generated from the offence to be used later in masturbation or intercourse with an adult partner is a direct reversal of the idea that fantasy causes offending. This does not mean that offending is never driven by fantasy. Nevertheless, it does help to understand some of the otherwise perplexing characteristics of child sexual abuse. Many paedophile offences do not seem to lead directly to orgasm (Howitt, 1995a). That is to say, fairly high proportions of paedophile offences involve acts that are not penetrative and/or do not involve immediate masturbation to orgasm. Thus the offending is not to achieve sexual climax at that time but is a means of generating fantasy, which the offender could then use in masturbation or sexual intercourse later (Sheldon and Howitt, 2005) though an alternative may be that the offending could lead to sexual arousal and later masturbation without fantasy. There is some evidence in our interviews with offenders to support the assertion that offending generates fantasy for later masturbation. The following three examples are a fairly precise statement of this process:

- 'It was very much a case of almost...the offences become the fantasy afterwards...I would masturbate to the fantasy' [37: Contact Offender].
- 'I think about what is clearly my life and what I've seen in reality, I can't make things up, I'm not turned on by making things up...when I am fantasising about [things] I am remembering what me and [victim] did' [3: Mixed offender].
- 'It [masturbating] was to what had just happened [abuse of 6 year old] and...as...I am masturbating to me touching her but it, the fantasies would progress to lowering of the pants, it would go all the way...to actual intercourse with a child...I know a child can't have sex...Although me sexual fantasies have been with children' [19: Mixed offender].

Whereas it is possible that the following offender, in terms of his pornography offences, is describing a process in which he is sexually aroused by the pornography rather than the pornography generating fantasy:

- 'I'd think about that [abuse]...certainly watch the videos [of perpetrator abusing his daughter] and the excitement came from what had happened and the contact that was there' [22: mixed offender].

It is, therefore, of some importance to note the findings of Dandescu and Wolfe (2003). They showed in their research that child molesters were much more likely to report masturbatory fantasies after their first offence than prior to their first offence. The frequencies were nine times more common following offending than before offending. This is commensurate with the idea that many sex offences generate sexual fantasy for later masturbation. Certainly the figures may suggest that sexually deviant fantasies are not as important as sometimes suggested in terms of *driving* deviant sexual behaviour. However, Dandescu and Wolfe indicate that that fantasy may be increasingly important in the maintenance of offending behaviour once the offending has begun.

What about Internet sex offending? Fantasy does have a role in a number of models of Internet sex offending against children according to Sullivan and

Beech (2003). They generally concentrate on the role of fantasy rehearsal of the offence, which may not be the same thing as sexual fantasy about children as we have already discussed. Fantasy rehearsal is about planning the execution of a crime and is thus offence directed. Fantasy itself does not necessarily involve this element of rehearsal. The 'spiral of sexual abuse' model offered by Sullivan and Beech conceptualises sexual fantasy about children as part of an escalating process of sexual abuse. The first response an offender has to sexual fantasies involving children is guilt which is dealt with by various cognitive distortions. By using appropriate cognitive distortions, masturbating to sexual fantasies about children becomes guilt free and so can serve to reinforce the fantasy behaviour. As a consequence, and we stress that this is according to Sullivan and Beech's clinical experience, the offender can psychologically move on to actual contact offending.

## THE SEXUAL FANTASIES OF PAEDOPHILE OFFENDERS

The greatest imperative, of course, is the concern that sexual fantasy may contribute directly to sexual offending against children (Looman, 1995; Prentky et al., 1989). Whatever the role of sexual fantasy in extreme cases, attention needs to be paid to its role in the activities of more typical sex offenders. Basic information is required about the nature of paedophile sexual fantasies before we can understand their role in offending. Just what are the typical sexual fantasies of paedophiles? Which fantasies do they have most often? There are few systematic accounts of the sexual fantasies of sex offenders. Thus it is difficult to say how common different sorts of fantasy are experienced by paedophile offenders. Basic data on the major types of fantasy that sex offenders experience is welcome as it helps to fill this void. We provided a fantasy questionnaire where offenders gave a rating for each fantasy to indicate how frequently they had experienced such a fantasy. For instance they gave a rating of 1 if they had never experienced that fantasy, a rating of 2 if they had experienced it at least once in their lives, and a rating of 3 if they had experienced it at least once a week. The offenders were also interviewed about their fantasies as appropriate.

From this, a number of important characteristics of the fantasies of sex offenders against children were noted. Perhaps most significant is that many of their fantasies are run-of-the-mill adult male ones about, in particular, adult women. In other words, the dominant fantasies that a paedophilic offender reports are unlikely to strike one as unusual. The most common fantasies (that is, those which on average the sex offenders claim to have had more than once in their lives) were as follows starting with the most frequent:

- having vaginal intercourse with a willing female adult;
- giving oral sex to a willing female adult;
- receiving oral sex from willing female adult;
- masturbating a willing female adult.

Each of these fantasies refers to consensual sexual activity with an adult female. These would seem to be reasonably 'normal' fantasies in that they contain no truly deviant acts and seem not atypical of the findings of surveys of the fantasies of normal adult males (see, for example, Crepault and Couture, 1980; Sue, 1979). How frequent the fantasies are is not so important as their dominant themes. Particularly interesting is that none of the common fantasies involved children at all, which, if fantasy is seen as being paramount in offending, is unexpected. Indeed, it is striking that deviant content is missing from the top fantasies of these offender groups. Perhaps to expect anything else would be a misleading interpretation of the psychosexual characteristics of sex offenders. Many of them had previously been in sexual relationships with adult females (and less frequently males) (Chapter 9). This was particularly the case with Internet-only offenders. Even granted the erratic and problematic nature of some of their relationships with women, it is hardly surprising that the commonest fantasies involve women given their (in some cases) numerous sexual involvements.

Nevertheless, child oriented fantasies were fairly common - though at a lower level of incidence than for the adult female fantasies. In terms of girl fantasies, starting with the most frequent, these included:

• looking at pictures, or films, of naked girls
• fondling girls' breasts
• fondling a girl's genitals
• receiving oral sex from a girl
• having vaginal sex with a girl
• looking at pictures, or films, of girls in sexual acts
• giving oral sex to a girl
• watching a girl(s) in secret when they are naked or undressing

Generally speaking, none of these fantasies contain any deviant element other than the underage object of the fantasies. It is a revealing set of fantasies in a number of ways. Perhaps it is not surprising, given the number of Internet pornography offenders in the sample, that looking at visual depictions of nude girls tops the list of child fantasies. If this is expected then less expected is the lower frequency of looking at visual material featuring girls in sexual acts. In other words, some offenders may have far less interest in pictures that are basically contact abuse and explicit sexual behaviour than in pictures which simply feature nudity. Furthermore, it is also noteworthy that bottom of the list of these fantasies are ones in which the girl is watched secretly or voyeuristically. Similarly, penetrative sexual intercourse is lower down the list of fantasies than fondling breasts and genitals. That is to say, penetrative sex with a girl was less important, as a fantasy, than sexual touching.

The fantasies featuring boys tended to involve looking at pictures of naked boys or looking at boys involved in sexual acts. Another fantasy (carrying out oral sex on a boy) was just as common. The three fantasies were:

• looking at pictures, or films, of naked boys;
• looking at pictures, or films, of boys in sexual acts;
• giving oral sex to boy.

In this case, the issue of nudity versus sexual acts made little or no difference in terms of the frequency of the fantasy.

The *least* likely fantasies to have been experienced consist mostly of those with some form of deviant element other than the involvement of a child. Forcible sexual activity generally was infrequent or non-existent in the fantasies of offenders. So among the fantasies very unlikely to have been experienced by sex offenders against children were:

- overpowering a woman and forcing her to give me oral sex;
- overpowering a woman and forcing her to have vaginal sex with me;
- overpowering a woman and forcibly masturbating her;
- overpowering a woman and forcing her to have anal sex;
- overpowering a woman and forcing her to masturbate me;
- overpowering a man and giving him oral sex forcibly;
- overpowering a man and forcing him to give me oral sex;
- overpowering a man and forcing him to have sex with me.

Necrophilic, sadistic/masochistic fantasy, humiliation, and cross-dressing fantasy was also extremely rare:

- having sexual contact with a dead body;
- being physically hurt during sexual activities, for example being whipped;
- physically hurting someone during sexual activities, for example whipping them;
- being humiliated during sexual activities;
- humiliating an adult during sexual activities;
- being sexually excited when crossdressing (wearing female clothing).

Fetishistic fantasy was also virtually non-existent:

- touching or rubbing against a non-consenting person in a sexual manner (for example on a bus);
- being excited by non-living objects (for example, shoes, leather).

Bestiality was also uncommon:

- having sex with an animal.

Some paedophilic fantasies were also infrequently reported – for instance anal sex with a female child, anal sex with a boy and exposing one's genitals to a boy.

So non-deviant heterosexual fantasies are the most typical of child sex offenders. Paedophilic fantasies, although quite frequent, are certainly not the most common fantasies among the offenders. The finding that the commonest fantasies are typical male fantasies should not be regarded as unexpected. Neither is it an entirely new finding because Looman (1995) found evidence that child molesters were no different from rapists in that adult women dominated their fantasies. Interestingly, Looman pointed out that there are studies that show that child molesters are aroused by pictures of adult women to much the same extent as other men are (for example, Baxter *et al.*, 1984).

Another crucial point is the very low level of fantasy involving force, violence and rape. Such fantasies were virtually absent from the cognitions of our sample although the evidence is that these fantasies are apparently quite common in normal adult males. For instance, Crepault and Couture (1980) and Grendlinger and Byrne (1987) reported that 33 % and 54 % of men, respectively, had fantasies of forcing sex on women.

The question is whether sex offenders against children differ in any of these respects from other men. Few studies include a 'normal' control group or even a non-sexual offender control group (Leitenberg and Henning, 1995). One exception to this investigated incarcerated adolescent sex offenders, incarcerated sex offenders, incarcerated non-sex offenders and undergraduates (Daleiden *et al.*, 1998). It showed that deviant fantasy levels were not markedly different between offenders and non-offenders. Nevertheless, non-deviant fantasies were lacking to some extent in the incarcerated sex offenders. O'Donohue, Letourneau and Dowling (1997) found greater levels of sexual fantasies involving children among child molesters than a convenience sample of non-offenders.

There seems to be little to support in our research for the finding of Daleiden *et al.* (1998), which suggested that the deficit of 'normal' adult sexual fantasies rather than greater levels of child fantasies may be responsible for offending against children. It is clear that the most commonly reported sexual fantasies in our sample of offenders, despite their sexual interest in children, were essentially 'conventional' sexual fantasies involving adult women.

## PATTERNS OF SEXUAL FANTASY IN INTERNET OFFENDERS

Does sexual fantasy differentiate Internet Offenders from Contact offenders? Two main possibilities may be considered. The first is that Internet offenders are fantasists who regularly employ child sexual abuse images in masturbation fantasy or sexual intercourse. This might suggest that Internet offenders are more likely to use sexual fantasy than contact paedophiles. The second, very different point of view, is that if fantasy is indeed a blueprint for contact sexual offending against children then contact offenders should show very different fantasy patterns from those of Internet offenders. Perhaps contact offenders have more deviant fantasies or more fantasies of a particular type compared to Internet offenders.

What are the typical patterns of sexual fantasies in sex offenders? In order to answer this question, complex statistical methods were employed (factor analysis). This is described in Howitt and Sheldon ( in press). Among our list of sexual fantasies are some that were not experienced by any of the offenders so could not be included in this particular analysis. Eight different types of fantasy are found which account for 73 % of the reliable variation in the replies to the fantasy questions. These groups of fantasies are as follows:

1. *Girl fantasies.* These involved girls of 15 years of age or lower. Examples of fantasies include:
   - fondling a girl's genitals;
   - looking at pictures or films of girls in sexual acts.
2. *Boy fantasies.* This group is similar to the *girl fantasies* except in so far as they involve boys:
   - fondling a boy's genitals;
   - looking at pictures or films of naked boys.
3. *Humiliation of others fantasies.* Both the giving and receiving of humiliation in a sexual context are involved in this group of fantasies:
   - being humiliated during sexual activities;
   - humiliating an adult during sexual activities.
4. *Force-against-others fantasies.* These fantasies involve forcing or overpowering other adults into sexual activities. Representative items include the following and refer to women (the fantasies involving overpowering a man did not closely belong to this group):
   - overpowering a woman and forcing her to masturbate me;
   - overpowering a woman and forcing her to have anal sex.
5. *Adult homosexual fantasies.* These are consensual sex fantasies involving men:
   - giving oral sex to a willing male adult;
   - having sexual intercourse with a willing male adult.
6. *Adult heterosexual fantasies.* While other groups feature adult women as the participants in the sexual acts, this group of fantasies involve more fantastical elements such as multiple partners. There are no indications of any force or violence in these fantasies:
   - intercourse with multiple female adult partners;
   - giving oral sex to a willing female adult;
   - willingly being tied up or handcuffed.
7. *Confrontational/non-contact fantasies.* These fantasies do not involve sexual contact or even actual physical contact. However, they directly involve the response of another person. For this reason they seem to be confrontational although they are not forceful or violent in nature. Examples include:
   - exposing my genitals to an unsuspecting adult or adults;
   - exposing my genitals to an unsuspecting girl or girls;
   - making obscene phone calls.
8. *Bestiality fantasies.* This hardly constitutes a group since it is only strongly represented by one fantasy:
   - sex with an animal.

These groups of fantasies range quite widely from the clearly deviant (sex with animals; force against others) to the non-deviant (adult heterosexual fantasies). *Girl fantasies* and *boy fantasies* are distinct groupings in the fantasies of paedophiles and there is little relationship between the two. This means that some will have girl fantasies only, some boy fantasies only and others both sorts of fantasy. There is a similar gender specificity to be found in *adult heterosexual fantasies* and *adult homosexual fantasies*. Many of the fantasy patterns confirm that the typical fantasies of normal adult males dominate those of paedophiles. These include having sex with multiple partners (Davidson, 1985; Ellis and Symons, 1990; Hunt, 1974; Knafo and Jaffe, 1984; Sue, 1979; Wilson, 1987), forcing someone to have sex (Arndt, Foehl and Good, 1985; Crepault and Couture, 1980; Grendlinger and Byrne, 1987; Hunt, 1974; Kirkendall and McBride, 1990; Miller and Simon, 1980; Sue, 1979), sexually initiating 'a young girl' (Crepault and Couture, 1980), having sex with girls under 15 years (Templeman and Stinnett, 1991) or feeling sexually attracted to young children (Briere and Runtz, 1989; Langevin *et al.*, 1998).

There are also differences between the three groups of sex offenders on these different groupings of fantasies. Overwhelmingly, however, contact offenders and Internet offenders tend to be more similar than dissimilar. The important differences across the groups can be summarised as follows:

- *Contact-only offenders.* These report fewer *girl fantasies* than the other two groups. In contrast, they did not report having more *boy fantasies*. Of great importance is that contact only offenders report higher numbers of *confrontational/non-contact fantasies* than the Internet offenders. In summary, they less commonly show girl fantasies and have more fantasies involving confrontation with a victim, which do not involve contact.
- *Internet-only offenders.* These offenders are more likely to have sexual fantasies involving girls than the contact offenders. They report fewer *adult homosexual fantasies* than the mixed sex offenders and fewer confrontational/non-contact fantasies than the contact offenders.
- *Mixed contact/Internet offenders.* This group of offenders have the highest level of girl fantasies. Notably, this went along with reporting the highest levels of *adult homosexual fantasies*. In terms of *confrontational/non-contact* fantasy they score in the middle of the three groups and are not statistically different from the other two groups.

One of the intriguing findings is that contact sex offenders had the least number of girl fantasies. Indeed, they also had the least number of boy fantasies, though not to a statistically reliable extent. There was, however, a distinct association between the gender of the victim(s) of the index offence (the one that they were currently convicted for) and the gender of the object of the sexual fantasy. For instance, taking boy and girl fantasies only, offenders with only boy victims are relatively high on boy fantasy and low on girl fantasy whereas offenders with girl index victims show the reverse pattern. That is, they have greater levels of girl fantasy and lower levels of boy fantasy. Equally, those with mixed gender victims are by far the highest scorers on the girl and boy fantasies. This is to be expected given their pattern of offending.

There does seem to be a relationship between the victim's gender and the offender's fantasy but this does not demonstrate that offending behaviour follows a simple link with sexual fantasy. Quite simply, if it is correct that fantasy drives the acting-out of behaviour, Internet offenders should report the lowest levels of paedophilic fantasy as they have no reported acts against children. Yet this is not the case. These findings have some support from a study by Seto, Cantor and Blanchard (2006). Measuring erectile responses to child pornography images using phallometry, child pornography offenders with no history of contact offending were almost three times more likely to be identified as paedophiles compared to contact-only child sex offenders (and sex offenders against adults). Thus, a higher sexual response to child images was not necessarily an indicator of their contact offending against children. Indeed, offenders convicted of child pornography offences were more-or-less equally responsive to child images regardless of whether they had previous contact child sexual offences or not. Therefore, there does *not* appear to be a relationship between a high level of sexual arousal to pornography and the propensity to directly commit sexual offences against children. The reverse seems closer to the truth. Of course, it could be argued that Internet pornography offenders are driven by their responsiveness to child pornography to seek this material on the Internet. However, this does not undermine the finding that contact offenders are not particularly high on sexual fantasies involving children.

This, of course, applies only to the sexual fantasies involving children. We did find that contact offenders tended to report more *confrontational/non-contact* fantasies than the Internet-only offenders. The offending of Internet pornography users involves no confrontation with the victim and their fantasy is low on such elements. This seems to suggest that there is an element in the offending of contact offenders in which the direct experience of the response of the victim is important. This is not in terms of physical contact because the fantasies are not ones in which direct contact is involved – the contact offenders reported more fantasies involving indecent phone calls or flashing. Certainly this sort of fantasy may encourage contact offending though, of course, it may merely reflect something that the offender needs which is supplied by contact offending and which is a component of their fantasy life.

Furthermore, one might expect men with a previous criminal history for sex offences against children to show distinct patterns of fantasy and, especially, greater levels of fantasy than those without previous convictions. This, however, is not the case. This further undermines the idea that paedophilic sexual fantasies, by themselves, are either a sufficient or a necessary condition for committing a sexual offence. Indeed, we find no indication that any sort of criminal history is associated with greater or lesser levels of any sort of sexual fantasy. As previously noted, many men who have never committed a sexual assault have fantasies of forcing sex on someone (Crepault and Couture, 1980; Grendlinger and Byrne, 1987; Hunt, 1974; Sue, 1979).

It might be speculated that a history of sexual abuse in childhood might make the offender more susceptible to sexual fantasies of various sorts in adulthood. This has been suggested and seemingly accepted since the 1960s (McGuire, Carlisle and Young, 1965). More recently it has been argued that there is a link between an offender's early sexual experiences and their own abusive acts (Howitt, 1995a). Over our entire sample, 43 % had experience of sexual abuse determined by us. However, there are no differences between the abused and non-abused offenders in the types of sexual fantasies they report having. As we saw in Chapter 6, sexual abuse in childhood is just one form of childhood sexualisation. Sex-play with peers was common in the childhoods of our offenders and their self-reported sex-play experiences included fondling, genital exposure, mutual masturbation, oral sex and sexual penetrative intercourse. Such sex play with male peers was found in 31 % of interviews whereas 78 % mentioned sex play with a female peer at some stage during their childhood. Unlike sexual abuse, there were quite a number of important relationships between peer sex experiences and sexual fantasies in adulthood:

- *Sex play with girl peers.* The offenders who engaged in sex play experiences with girl(s), when they were aged under 12 years, reported more girl paedophilic fantasies as adults. Similarly, heterosexual adult fantasies are commoner in those who had sex play with girl peers when the offender was 15 years of age or younger. There is also a tendency for fantasies involving forced sex to be less common in those offenders who report sex play with girls at some stage in childhood.
- *Sex play with boy peers.* Those who engaged in sex play with boy peers when they were aged under 12 years were less likely to have heterosexual adult fantasies and were also more likely to indicate that they had boy fantasies. This is also true of offenders who reported sex play with other boys at any stage of childhood.

This is important since it shows that sexual activity in childhood may influence at least some adult sexual fantasies. However, it was peer sex and *not* sexual abuse by an adult that was related to fantasy. Furthermore, the fantasy depends on the sex of the child partner. Broadly speaking, sex play with a girl is predictive of heterosexual fantasy in adulthood (involving both women and girls); sex play with boys is indicative of boy fantasies in adulthood but it makes no difference to homosexual adult fantasies and seems to reduce the number of adult heterosexual fantasies. This is suggestive of one mechanism by which child-child sex could be important in the development of abusive behaviour in adults.

## THE FANTASY NEEDS OF INTERNET AND CONTACT OFFENDERS

The idea that, in general, Internet pornography offenders tend to have more fantasy involving children than the men who physically contact abuse children needs some explanation. Sheldon and Howitt (in press) put forward an argument based on their finding that Internet sex offenders tend to be better educated; that is, they have spent more years in education than contact offenders. This is the case despite the fact that the average ages of all three groups of offenders are virtually identical.

With this in mind, one possible explanation is that this is indicative of the higher intelligence of Internet offenders. They were much more likely to be in professional and other occupations requiring qualifications than contact offenders. It is argued that those with more educational achievements are likely to be more intelligent (see, for example, Atkinson *et al.*, 1993) so perhaps Internet offenders have a greater ability to create, manipulate and otherwise deal with fantasy than contact offenders. Since masturbation seems to be the most likely consumatory behaviour of both contact and Internet offenders, then it could be said that Internet offenders are better resourced in this regard. Perhaps the contact offender needs the extra stimulus of the 'contact' to arouse him. Maybe Internet offenders, because of their intellectual advantage, are more able to generate fantasy efficiently and effectively. There is some evidence that intelligence and creativity correlate (for example, Dunn, Corn and Morelock, 2004) so perhaps Internet offenders are less in need of sexual contact with children since they can generate sufficient fantasy in their imaginations. Sex offenders have been described as concrete and/or unimaginative in their thinking (Langevin *et al.*, 1998) and, if this is the case, maybe contact offenders simply do not generate fantasy sufficient to meet their needs without offending.

One needs to be very careful when using the word 'fantasy' since many of the sexual fantasies of sex offenders are simply not the complex, visionary, creative and abstract creations that the term 'fantasy' may imply. Often 'mundane' is the most apt description. Howitt (1995b) described how paedophiles use a range of sources of fantasy to generate child-sex fantasy, including Walt Disney films featuring children, television advertisements for baby products and adult heterosexual pornography. Many of these contained no explicit pictures of children. However, these otherwise innocuous sources of fantasy might be mentally manipulated to generate a more explicit fantasy. Such acts of imagination might be easier for those of higher intelligence. One difficulty with this argument is that it suggests that contact offenders would be lowest in terms of levels of all sorts for fantasy. For the most part this was true irrespective of the sort of fantasy contact. Nevertheless it was not true for *confrontational/non-contact* fantasies.

A further caution is appropriate. The idea that offenders ought to have high levels of fantasy if they are indeed driven by fantasy is questionable. Daleiden *et al.'s* (1998) study may have something to offer here. In this study, the difference between offenders and non-offenders was not the presence of deviant sexual fantasy, which was not markedly different between the two groups, but that the offenders reported fewer normal fantasies. We have found something different in that our sample of contact offenders actually had lower levels of all types of fantasy – deviant and non-deviant – with the exception of confrontational fantasies.

## CONCLUDING COMMENTS

There is a common assumption that Internet child pornography offences constitute stepping-stones that finally lead to direct sex offending against children. This idea is common but is most systematically covered by Sullivan and Beech (2003). Despite this belief, the evidence is not strong in its favour. Many Internet child pornography offenders lack a history of contact sex offences against children (Burke *et al.*, 2001; Carr, 2003; Quayle *et al.*, 2000; Seto and Eke, 2005; Taylor and Quayle, 2003) and lack any previous contact with law enforcement or social services, prior to their Internet conviction (Carr, 2003; Jewkes and Andrews, 2005; Silverman and Wilson, 2002). Equally, few Internet offenders have been found to reoffend subsequently with a hands-on offence (Seto and Eke, 2005). Some offenders do, of course, have a mixed pattern of Internet and contact offences against children. According to Calder (2004), we will continue to see men whose crimes are about pornography downloading only and not to do with contact offending. Many Internet child pornography offenders clearly demonstrate a strong sexual interest in children but, all the same, do not directly sexually assault them (at least in the medium term). In the literature on paedophilia, the idea that there are men with a paedophile orientation but who do not contact offend against children has largely been ignored (Howitt, 1995a). Evidence for the existence of such a group has been confined to a single published paper that highlighted the situation of men who despite seeking help for their paedophilia have refrained from sexual offending directly against children (Righton, 1981). There is considerable evidence that recidivism for child sex offences is generally at low levels (Howitt, 2006a; b) and especially in comparison to such offences as burglary, theft, handing stolen goods, violence and drug offences (Home Office, 2001). Moreover, once released back into the community, sex offenders are more likely to commit new non-sex offences than they are to commit new sexual offences (Firestone *et al.*, 1998). Of course, some paedophiles are frequent sexual re-offenders. In addition, sexual offenders are more likely to have previous convictions for non-sexual offences than for sexual ones (Greenberg *et al.*, 2000). This is important as it suggests that paedophile orientation does not necessarily lead to repetitive offending against children and this is precisely what the patterns of fantasy of Internet offenders suggest. The Internet offender seems to have generally the highest levels of sexual fantasy involving children but the least likelihood of offending against children.

Interest is developing in the role and nature of sexual fantasy at various stages of the offending process (Gee *et al.*, 2004). This has only, to date, been formally researched in the case of contact offenders. The general indications are that sexual fantasy changes during the course of the offending cycle. Early on the men's sexual fantasies seem to be typical of adult male fantasies, in general. They are generalised fantasies that lack elements related to the offence. Later in the cycle the offender begins to have offence relevant fantasy. This is fantasy that is of a fairly generic nature but contains themes that are related to the offence-to-be. Thus, the paedophile may have more fantasy that is thematically about children. The final stage of fantasy in the offending cycle is offence-specific in the sense that the offender may fantasise about a specific child and engage in planning the offence. The fantasy may rehearse different possible eventualities during the course of the offending behaviour. For example, the offender may fantasise about what he would do if the child resists his sexual grooming or threatens to tell her parents.

So what is the role of sexual fantasy in offending? We do not believe that there is a simple direct relationship between sexual fantasy and the need to carry out, or the activity of carrying out, that fantasy in most offenders. Sexual fantasy is primarily of importance in sex offenders against children because it facilitates arousal in the course of masturbation or sex with an adult partner. This is clearly the case with Internet pornography users but also fits well with the lack of immediate orgasmic behaviour in sex of much paedophile sex offending. One of the curiosities is that many offenders confine their contact offences against children to touching and fondling rather than activities involving ejaculation and sexual climax. Having sexual fantasies involving children is clearly indicative of a capacity to be sexually aroused by children and it is partially indicative of the risk that the individual may seek a child to offend against. But there is no certainty in this, despite what is repeatedly asserted by professionals in the field. Quite simply, there are offenders who have these fantasies and are capable of being sexually aroused by the fantasies but do not contact offend against children. Chapter 12 deals with this process of desisting from direct abusive offending by Internet pornography users. At the same time, we need to know more about which offenders move from being an Internet only offender to actually sexually abusing children.

It is clear that sexual fantasies about children are learned, as many have argued. However, it seems unlikely to us that fantasy is merely learnt as a consequence of the reinforcement of the fantasy or as a consequence of masturbating to it. The process seems more complex than that. Neither is it learnt solely from sexual abuse in childhood and seems more of a consequence of a variety of sexual experiences with peers in childhood (cf. Howitt, 1995a).

There seems to be a degree of unity between the characteristics of childhood abuse and later adult behaviour. For instance there are links between the age at which an offender was abused in childhood and the age of the victim he himself eventually acts against. Specifically, those who were abused at age 12 or older tend to choose children aged 12 or older (67 %); and those who were abused at age 11 or below tend to have offences against victims who were also aged 11 years or younger (59 %). In addition, 67 % of intrafamilialy abused offenders report a history of child convictions that are against only intrafamilial children. Similarly, those who were abused by an extrafamilial adult as a child report convictions against only extrafamilial victims (86 %). This tendency of offenders to replicate their own experience of abuse has been noted by other researchers (for example, Cohen et al., 2002; Haaspasalo, Puupponen and Crittenden, 1999; Hilton and Mezey, 1996; Howitt, 1995a). Further, we have already noted the relationship between the gender of early sex-play partners and the gender of the object of their fantasies. If early sexualisation has an influence on the development of paedophilia we would expect there to be thematically close parallels between early childhood experiences and the fantasies of offenders (Howitt, 1995a). The study conducted by Kirkendall and McBride (1990) is of relevance here. These researchers present data to suggest that fantasies alter behaviours but, in turn, experiences can also alter fantasies. Our interviews provide us with examples where the images associated with early peer-sex experiences were introduced into early masturbatory fantasies and how these fantasies continued into adulthood, as the following extract from a Mixed Internet/Contact offender clearly demonstrates:

> There was another incident at a junior school [9–10 years old] . . . a young girl . . . she come in class and asked everybody all lads who wants to see my pee hole? I do! Later she took me to back of class and says lay on floor there she pulled her pants one side as I looked up her skirt and she says 'touch me with your hand' . . . there was feather on floor . . . I used that and she says 'now use your hand'. I did. I remember that well. I didn't get sexually excited 'cos my body wasn't quite ready then, but yes I did enjoy it . . . I still think of that memory and use it [now as an adult?] yea, and other proper girlfriends . . . younger than me, long, blond hair . . . that's my taste but yea girlfriends, 13, 14 [years old] I bring that up to me mind us having sex and I'd masturbate over them. [19: Mixed offender]

# CHAPTER 11

# Distorted Thinking

Cognitive distortion is a crucial concept in current theories of sex offending. The seminal theorising of Abel, Becker and Cunningham-Rathner (1984) is generally held to be responsible for introducing the concept. They argued that child sexual abuse is socially regarded as so heinous that offenders cognitively adapt in order to justify and excuse their offending. Accounts vary but currently it seems to be assumed that this cognitive adaptation occurs prior to and following the commissioning of the offence. Previously, however, Burt (1980) formulated a not dissimilar idea in relation to rape. She proposed rape myths as an explanation of that crime. Rape myths are beliefs that explain, justify and condone rape crime. For example, the idea that women feign resistance to sex and when they say 'no' they mean yes, or that if a woman dresses provocatively she is 'asking for it'. The radical feminist perspective (for example, Breckenridge, 1992) argues that rape myths and cognitive distortions pervade society. All men are potentially sexual offenders because of the beliefs and attitudes they hold concerning sex, women and children. These rape myths are learnt partly through gender socialisation and directly facilitate offending (Ward *et al.*, 2006). Cognitive distortions, however, are not regarded as normative in this way as they describe a way in which sex offenders are different from other men.

Rape myths and the more general concept of cognitive distortions have been accepted far beyond the research community as possible explanations of sex offending. Sex offender treatment programmes tackle them both in order to reduce offender recidivism. The sex offender treatment employed throughout the UK prison service (Beech, Fisher and Beckett, 1999) is just one example of this and little, if any, current therapy for sex offenders, fails to address them. Despite this, it should be recognised that the two concepts are distinct with distinct aetiologies.

The idea of cognitive distortions is important in cognitive behavioural therapy for sex offenders. This is highly dependent on Finkelhor's multi-factorial theory of sex offending (Finkelhor, 1984). A number of his 'preconditions' reflect cognitions. For instance, the second of the four preconditions suggested by Finkelhor (1984) includes 'overcoming internal inhibitions' which incorporates excusing or justifying one's intended actions. Indeed, most (or all) of the multifactor models of sexual offending identify cognitive distortions as a key theoretical building block. The influence of Finkelhor's theory cannot be overestimated in terms of its impact on both research and the work of practitioners (Ward and Hudson, 2001). Remarkably, however, it is hard to find any empirical evidence which supports the theory (Howitt, 2002). Challenging cognitive distortions forms an integral part of current sex-offender treatment programmes (Marshall, Anderson and Fernandez, 1999). However, evaluations of the effectiveness of cognitive behaviour therapy invariably evaluate the effectiveness of the package (Beech *et al.*, 1999) so leaving the impact of its components unknown (Howitt, 2004). Thus evidence as to whether reducing cognitive distortions effectively prevents recidivism is unavailable (Ward, Polaschek and Beech, 2006).

Howitt and Sheldon (in press) claimed 'In strictly research terms, arguably the concept of cognitive distortion has achieved a centrality exceeding its demonstrated importance.' We believe that there is every reason to accept that cognitive distortions in many ways characterise clinicians' experience with sex offenders against children. Clinicians and researchers hear a whole raft of different cognitive distortions during interviews with offenders. There seems little doubt that child molesters manifest attitudes and beliefs which justify sex between an adult and child, for example that children enjoy sexual contact with adults (Hanson and Morton-Bourgon, 2005; Neidigh and Krop, 1992; Sheldon, 2004). Lengthy examples of this are available (Howitt, 1995a) and Neidigh and Krop (1992) and Pollack and Hashmall (1991) describe different types of cognitive distortions. Accepting the apparent universality of cognitive distortions among sex offenders does not tell us a great deal about what cognitive distortions are, what functions they serve and how they affect offending behaviour. Ward *et al.* (2006) in their extensive review of theories of sex offending, suggest a lack of clarity and some confusion in the way the concept of cognitive distortions is addressed. For instance, the term is often used to refer to offence-supportive attitudes (Hanson and Morton-Bourgon, 2005), cognitive processing during an offence sequence (Maruna and Mann, 2006), as well as post-hoc neutralisations (Sykes and Matza, 1957), rationalisations (Neidigh and Krop, 1992), justifications (Murphy, 1990), or excuses for offending (Pollock and Hashmall, 1991). In this sense, cognitive distortions are defined as both products and processes (Ward *et al.*, 2006).

Not surprisingly, the concept of cognitive distortion can be seen from various perspectives. Among the most unexpected is Auburn's (2005, p. 699–700) claim that:

> the notion of cognitive distortions is a practice which reinforces the identification, separation and pathologisation of those to whom it is applied. Furthermore, the focus on underlying cognitions ensures attention on the individual offender and his pathology and shifts attention away from the morality of his actions. The idea of cognitive distortions, therefore, provides a means for the technical specification of an abnormality that has been identified by the courts or other institutional body and the means for specifying and measuring one of the arenas of change required of the individual.

This criticism is, in a sense, a version of a somewhat elderly view that categories of mental illness (such as schizophrenia) are means of labelling individuals as pathological – which then justifies whatever the mental health system subjects them to. Cognitive distortions are essentially construed as internal pathological psychological structures that neglect the social nature of the phenomenon. Auburn can only make such a claim on the basis of a limited reading of research on cognitive distortions. Thus he confuses the concept with a particular viewpoint on their psychological status by drawing too heavily on the work of Ward *et al.* (1997) who he cites as the source of the following viewpoint:

> Cognitive distortions are regarded as maladaptive beliefs and processes of distorted thinking arising from cognitive structures (beliefs, schemata), cognitive operations (biased information processing) and cognitive products (self statements, attributions) (as cited by Auburn, 2005, pp. 688–9).

Despite this, it has to be stressed that these is simply not this degree of clarity in writings about cognitive distortions. For example, there are at least three distinct views on the nature of cognitive distortions not all of which reflect the above.

- *Cognitive distortions are enduring beliefs that support the abuse of children.* This is based on the notion that cognitive distortions arise when the offender is already contemplating offending and is aware of how morally reprehensible his behaviour is (Abel, Rouleau and Cunningham-Rathner, 1986). They protect the offender's self-image from condemnation while he continues to experience the external reinforcement of offending, for example masturbation. Abel *et al* (1986) also suggested that cognitive distortions gradually become more entrenched over time. It is argued that Abel viewed cognitive distortions as maintaining or facilitating offending, rather than causing sexual offending (Ward *et al.*, 2006). Others have also interpreted his theory this way (for example, Murphy, 1990). This makes Abel's view inconsistent with current theories of sexual offending, which see cognitive distortions as cognitive vulnerability factors (for example, Ward and Siegert, 2002). Abel's theory presupposes the motivation to engage with children (Finkelhor, 1984) and suggests that distortions develop as part of the preparation for offending.
- *Cognitive distortions can be thought of as 'transient post-offence justifications and excuses'* (Gannon and Polaschek, 2005, p. 184). In other words, distortions are not significant in the aetiology of offending but are simply generated to excuse one's actions when required to explain or account for one's behaviour to police officers, psychologists or treatment workers. This means that cognitive distortions do not motivate or facilitate sexual crimes since they emerge when the offender is put to account for his actions. One example of an excuse for sexually assaulting a child might be 'I was just being affectionate' (Pollock and Hashmall, 1991, p. 57). Thus, chronologically, this conceptualisation of cognitive distortions suggest that they originate after offending almost in mitigation of the offending in conversations with

professionals. Cognitive distortions may also be considered as a special case of neutralisation theory (Sykes and Matza, 1957). Some techniques of neutralisation theory are similar to some cognitive distortions and processes of denial attributed to sex offenders, for instance denial of responsibility, denial of injury and denial of victim. The theory is criticised because it is unclear whether the neutralisation process comes before or after offending – an issue which is pertinent to cognitive distortions. Research has produced mixed results concerning whether neutralisations precede deviant behaviour (Maruna and Copes, 2005). Maruna and Copes (2005) insist that conceptually it can only apply post-offence and that this cannot explain the aetiology of offending. In contrast, Hartley (1998, p. 36) describes cognitive distortions as rationalisations used by offenders not *just* after disclosure but as a way to overcome their internal inhibitions 'throughout the history of sexual contact.'

- *Cognitive distortions reflect the distorted experiences of the offender or are 'narrative accounts' of the offender's early childhood experiences* (Howitt, 1995a). In this sense they do not reflect altered or distorted cognitions but ideas, experiences and beliefs that develop out of the offender's distorted experiences. Thus they are essentially narrative accounts of the offender's childhood experiences especially those of sexual abuse or sexual play with other children (Howitt, 1995a). This conceptualisation of cognitive distortions gives them a possible role to play in offending. They are assumed to pre-exist offending but are closely linked to the offending. Offenders' accounts of their childhoods are invariably somewhat skeletal and subject to all of the problems of remembering back so far. Their accounts, as we saw in Chapters 6 and 7, frequently describe a great deal of significant sexual behaviour including histories of sexual abuse or sexualised play with other children. To illustrate this, cognitive distortions which suggest that *children are sexual beings* may reflect that the offender as a child was sexualised at an early age and sexually active. Gross distortions of normal childhood experiences become represented as the standard of behaviour of children in general. It is thus a misnomer to use the phrase cognitive distortion since that are not created to justify the offence but reflect more enduring schemas which were developing in childhood. This conceptualisation places the origins of cognitive distortions well before the offence chronologically.

Every one of the above explanations though seemingly different may be partially correct – each explanation merely reflecting different aspects of what offenders think and say which we classify as cognitive distortions. These different approaches also indicate some of the difficulties of defining the concept of cognitive distortion.

## WHAT WE KNOW ABOUT COGNITIVE DISTORTIONS

If cognitive distortions facilitate sexual abuse then child molesters should obtain higher (more distorted) scores on standard cognitive distortion questionnaires than other prisoners and controls groups. These questionnaires include the Cognitions Scale (Abel, Becker, and Cunningham-Rathner, 1984; Abel *et al.*, 1989); MOLEST and RAPE inventories (Bumby, 1996); the Multiphasic Sex Inventory (Nichols and Molinder, 1984); the Rape Myth Acceptance Scale (Burt, 1980) and the Hanson Sex Attitudes Questionnaire (Hanson, Gizzarelli and Scott, 1994). Research, however, has not consistently shown that paedophiles differ from other men in terms of their use and acceptance of cognitive distortions on these measures. Some empirical studies report child molesters scoring significantly higher than controls (Arkowitz and Vess, 2003; Marshall *et al.*, 2003; Stermac and Segal, 1990) whereas others report no differences (Gannon and Polaschek, 2005; Tierney and McCabe, 2001). An examination of individual responses reveals only occasional agreement with cognitive distortion items; a much lower rate of responding than would be expected from Abel's theory for instance (Ward *et al.*, 2006), leading some researchers to question the notion that cognitive distortions facilitate offending (for example, Gannon, 2006). Some researchers claim that sex offenders against children tend not to agree with cognitive distortions but, instead, they reject cognitive distortions less strongly than other men (for example, Arkowitz and Vess, 2003; Marshall *et al.*, 2003). Put another way, sex offenders are more likely to *disagree* with cognitive distortions rather than *strongly disagree*.

The most frequent explanation for such contradictory findings is that child molesters avoid revealing their distorted beliefs to psychologists and researchers. Facilitated by the apparent transparent nature of the questionnaires (Langevin, 1991; Murphy, 1990), offenders exhibit little effort to work out what the questionnaires are measuring and give socially desirable answers (McGrath, Cann and Konopasky, 1998; Tierney and McCabe, 2001) or 'fake good'. In other words, they reject the distortion while secretly holding that belief. This fits in with the idea that sex offenders are manipulative (Wyre, 1987). Quite plausibly, researchers have built in separate social desirability responses but, unexpectedly, some have found that sex offenders' replies to cognitive distortion questionnaires are unrelated to their social desirability response set (for instance, Blumenthal, Gudjonsson and Burns, 1999). This explanation is undermined by experimental work with sex offenders, which found no relationship between their cognitive distortion scores and measures of their tendency to respond socially desirably in general (Gannon and Polaschek, 2005). Similarly, Gannon (2006) found that child molesters were not deliberately trying to hide their offence-supportive attitudes when attached to a fake lie detector, which they believed could detect lies. Gannon (2006) told some child molesters they were being connected to lie-detecting apparatus and the offenders accepted this. Nevertheless, when connected up to this lie-detecting apparatus offenders did not report greater numbers of cognitive distortions compared to control conditions.

In another study, Gannon and Polaschek (2005) employed an information processing paradigm to much the same effect. The study drew on personality-related research methods, which suggests that when participants deliberately respond on the basis of social desirability they respond more quickly to questions than when they are being honest (for example, Hsu *et al.*, 1989).

Gannon and Polaschek found that responses to a computerised cognitive distortion questionnaire were the same for non-treated sex offenders and offender controls. However, there was one unexpected finding. Child molesters who had undergone treatment displayed the faking-good (socially desirable) pattern of responding faster to the cognitive distortions than relevant controls. In other words, it would appear that treatment led to socially desirable behaviour. This is much what those who suggest that cognitive distortions are generated in the context of interaction between professionals and offenders would expect. All groups of offenders disagreed on average with the cognitive distortion items. The researchers suggest that these findings are important since 'we are puzzled by the pervasiveness of both the cognitive distortion hypothesis and its social desirability hypothesis given the lack of convincing scientific tests of either explanation' (Gannon and Polaschek, 2005, p. 197).

This, in essence, is an argument to suggest that cognitive distortions are rare among child molesters but that this is not because of social desirability effects in general. Howitt and Sheldon (in press) argue that the low levels of cognitive distortions may be an artefact of the particular cognitive distortion questionnaire used in these studies. When the cognitive distortions questions used by Gannon and Polaschek (2005) are examined they include such items as 'Some children are mature enough to enjoy sex with adults' and 'A person should have sex whenever they feel it is needed.' Howitt and Sheldon (in press) argue from their findings that such items do not typify the cognitive distortions accepted by sex offenders against children. In other words, Gannon and Polaschek (2005) assessed cognitive distortions using items the content of which offenders are unlikely to accept anyway. A measure using commoner cognitive distortions would have been more likely to generate higher levels of cognitive distortions from the offenders. So Gannon and Polaschek (2005) may be dubious about the role of cognitive distortions in offending simply because they used low-frequency-of-occurrence cognitive distortions.

Whatever the methodological problems, we need to establish more clearly even simple information such as the extent to which offenders accept the range of cognitive distortions that can emerge in clinical work with sex offenders. The contrast between clinical experience and the findings of research seem to place the research base on an uncomfortable footing. Clinical interviews uncover many instances in offenders' discourse of things such as the denial of the offence, minimisation of the seriousness of the offence, and beliefs about children and sex which constitute what is generally meant by cognitive distortions. But this is not to argue that all sex offenders have much the same cognitive distortions as all other sex offenders. That is to say, cognitive distortions may be to some extent specific to an individual offender.

Work in other areas of cognitive psychopathology has offered the concept of 'schemas' as a way of organising and explaining offence supportive statements (Polaschek, Ward and Hudson, 1997; Ward et al., 2006; Ward, Keenan and Hudson, 2000). A schema contains core beliefs about the self and the relationship between the self and the outside world, as well as related attitudes about external objects and ideas (Huesmann, 1988; McFall, 1990). We all have these schemas, which help us to interpret and make predictions about the world around us. The schema of sex offenders, however, is argued to be maladaptive. Ward and Keenan (1999) hypothesised five 'implicit theories' or 'schemas' that guide the interactions of paedophiles (generated mainly from existing psychometric scales). These implicit theories are (a) children as sexual objects; (b) entitlement; (c) the nature of harm; (d) the world is a dangerous place and (d) the world is uncontrollable. Sheldon (2004) identified examples of many of these implicit theories in the cognitive distortions of a mixed group of offenders against children:

- *Children as sexual objects.* Children are inherently sexual creatures who enjoy and even seek out sex with adults, for example 'I see very little difference between children and adults...children have feelings, emotions, knowledge, desires... to put a blanket label on everything, everything under 14 is immature and everything over 14 is mature is too simplistic' (Sheldon, 2004, p. 27).
- *Entitlement:* The offender is inherently superior to others and therefore entitled to have his needs (including sexual needs) met by inferior others (such as children), for example: 'I like the Chinese approach, they [women] tend to treat you as, the psyche is the man is King in everything and not just sex, looking after you without it being any badge of shame, it is not an oppressive thing, it's just a natural thing' (Sheldon, 2004, p. 28).
- *Dangerous world.* There are two variants – either the world is a 'dangerous' place and the only way to deal with it is to dominate others (including children) or children are perceived as reliable and a safe haven compared to adults, for example: 'I find two things attractive about children: their appearance...innocence and charm...the other thing is they are at the dawn of their life... naïve, eager, trying, committed, caring, they have lots of qualities adults lose as they grow up' (Sheldon, 2004, p. 28).
- *Uncontrollable.* The offender is not in control of his actions but driven by external factors. For example: 'It was accidental' (Sheldon, 2004, p. 28).
- *Nature of harm.* Not all sexual activity with children is harmful and children can benefit from sexual activity with adults, for example: 'If it's a relationships that's giving him [father] pleasure and comfort and support and giving her pleasure and comfort and support [daughter] then what harm is it doing?' (Sheldon, 2004, p. 29).

Similar schema have been found in other studies of contact offenders. For instance, Polaschek and Gannon (2004) showed that three implicit theories, *women are dangerous, women as sex objects* and *entitlement* were prevalent in two-thirds of rapist's accounts. Further, the presence, or absence, of *dangerous world* and *male sex drive is uncontrollable* produced three types of sexual murderers who differed in their motivations – motivated by urges to rape and kill; motivated by resentment/grievance; motivated to sexually offend but prepared to kill to avoid detection (Beech, Fisher and Ward, 2005). The implicit theory approach, however, suffers from a number of weaknesses. For example, the mechanism for how implicit theories come to *cause* sexual offending has not been discussed (Ward *et al.*, 2006). It is proposed that implicit theories mainly develop early in childhood and so initially they are adaptive. Then as the offender becomes more sexually active they come to apply to the sexual domain (Ward, 2000). Yet some of the implicit theories are clearly not sexual in nature (for example, *entitlement*). Why do they not affect some offenders until adulthood when some late onset offending begins (Ward and Keenan, 1999; Ward *et al.*, 2006)?

If a single schema (implicit theory) can generate many different cognitive distortions, the implication is that treatment should focus on the modification of these 'core' implicit theories rather than on individual cognitive statements (Ward and Keenan, 1999). Thus, treatment would seek primarily to help the offender to understand his characteristic thinking patterns that may have contributed to him choosing antisocial behaviour as his response to a situation. Ignoring stable underlying cognitive structures such as schemas would leave clients open to future processing errors (Maruna and Mann, 2006). Drake *et al.*(2001) set about documenting a therapeutic intervention approach based on the implicit theories of child molesters. Likewise, Beech and Mann (2002) describe a schema-based treatment programme which focuses not just on offence-justifying attitudes but also on underlying self-understandings, motivations and implicit beliefs.

One theory of paedophilia proposes distinct pathways that lead to offending sexually against children (Ward and Siegert, 2002) (see Chapter 3). These are identified as (a) intimacy and social skills deficits, (b) deviant sexual scripts, (c) emotional dysregulation, and (d) cognitive distortions. There is a fifth pathway, which typifies the 'pure paedophile'. This combines the first four pathways in almost equal measure. Although the various pathways involve a variety of factors, cognitive schema and their associated cognitions are most important in this theory. These schema were identified using a qualitative analysis of offender's interviews. As yet, there is no evidence from other research that they constitute distinct schema or that they characterise different groups of sex offenders.

## COGNITIVE DISTORTIONS IN INTERNET SEX OFFENDERS

It is not possible to assess the cognitive distortions of Internet sex offenders using measures previously employed by researchers because these questionnaires mostly assume that the offender is a contact offender. Consequently, we drew together a range of cognitive distortions on the basis of our experience working with sex offenders including Internet sex offenders but also taking ideas from previous questionnaires and adapting them. We started with 60 very diverse cognitive distortions. In each case, it was clear that the distortions were about children being sexually involved with adults. Questions in which peer with peer sexual activity could be mistaken for abusive behaviour were avoided.

Because of the theoretical significance of Ward and Keenan's (1999) core implicit theories or schemas, we included items that, in our judgement, seemed to reflect the five categories of Ward and Keenan's taxonomy:

- *Children are sexual objects*, which included items such as 'Sometimes children don't say no to sexual activity with an adult because they are curious about sex or enjoy it' and 'Sometimes a child instigates sexual activity with an adult.'
- *Uncontrollability*, which included items such as: 'For many men their sex offences involving children were the result of stress and the offending behaviour helped to relieve that stress' and 'A lot of the time men do not plan their sex offences involving children – they just happen.'
- *Entitlement*, which included: 'Children are supposed to do what adults want and this might include serving their sexual needs' and 'A person should have sex whenever it is needed.'
- *Nature of harm*, which included two types of item since this schema is made up of different cognitions labelled 'levels of harm' and 'sex is beneficial for children' by Ward and Keenan. Examples of items assessing these included 'Just looking at a naked child is not as bad as touching and will probably not affect the child as much' and 'Sexual activities involving adults and children can help the child learn about sex.'
- *Dangerous world*, which included, once again, two subdivisions, which can be termed 'the world is hostile' and 'children are reliable' subscales. Illustrative items include 'Professionals pursue some people involved in sexual activities with children to make themselves look good' and 'children can give adults more acceptance and love than other adults.'

Having allocated the items to Ward and Keenan's categories, we checked the reliability of our classification by having an independent rater also sort the items into Ward and Keenan's schema. There was complete agreement between that rater's coding and our original categorisation. The questionnaire was called *Children and Sexual Activities* (C&SA). The items were responded to by participating offenders on a simple scale of 1 for 'strongly disagree' to 4 for 'strongly agree'. No midpoint was provided to discourage offenders from choosing moderate neutral responses. Some items were reversed scored. The maximum possible score on our 39 item scale was 156 with high scores indicating more acceptance of cognitive distortions. The average score was 76.4. Items on which there was agreement or strong agreement (allowing for reverse scoring) are regarded as being endorsed by the offender. What is clear is that that some cognitive distortions are strongly endorsed by offenders whereas others received no endorsement although there were no cognitive distortions with which all offenders *strongly disagreed*.

Highly endorsed cognitive distortions included:

- 'Children are more reliable and more trusting than adults' (92 %).
- 'Many men commit sex offences involving children because they were sexually abused as a child' (63 %).

- 'Some people turn to sexual activities involving children because they were deprived of sex from adult partners' (57 %).
- 'Some people who have sex offences involving children are not true 'sex offenders' - they are just out of control and make a mistake' (53 %).
- 'Some children act seductively towards adults' (49 %).

Much less frequently endorsed were cognitive distortions such as:

- 'Some sexual relations with children are a lot like adult sexual relationships' (9 %).
- 'If a child looks at an adult's genitals, the child is probably interested in sex' (6 %).
- 'Children are supposed to do what adults want and this might include serving their sexual needs' (2 %).
- A man should be able to have sex with whomever he wants' (2 %).
- 'Involving children in sexual activities with, or for adults, can be an acceptable way of controlling and punishing the child' (0 %).

Quite clearly, there are certain cognitive distortions accepted by the majority of sex offenders against children and some that are accepted by a substantial minority. Overall, the offenders agreed with many offence-conducive statements reflecting cognitive distortions. This runs counter to the claims that offenders are reluctant to agree with cognitive distortions (see, for example, Arkowitz and Vess, 2003; Marshall *et al.*, 2003). Our offenders seem to admit to many more cognitive distortions than this earlier research showed. There seems to be no support for the claim by Gannon and Polashek (2005) that 'distorted cognition seems to be about disagreeing slightly less than non-child molesters, not about agreement' (p. 184) – certainly as far as our research is concerned.

It is notable that the most frequently endorsed cognitive distortions lack the sort of bizarre and extreme elements that the phrase 'cognitive distortion' seems to imply. The most common cognitive distortions consist of ideas which professionals such as social workers might have used in the past (Howitt, 1992b). For instance, the cognitive distortion 'Some people turn to sexual activities involving children because they were deprived of sex from adult partners' might seem to the unguarded to possess a superficial reasonableness that disguises the dangerousness of the view. On the other hand, when the cognitive distortions that were not commonly endorsed are examined, we find distortions such as 'Involving children in sexual activities with, or for adults, can be an acceptable way of controlling and punishing the child.' This does contain bizarre elements. None of the sex offenders endorsed this item. It would seem reasonable to argue that cognitive distortions have a role in offending behaviour because of, and not despite, their superficial ordinariness and acceptability. With this in mind, a better way of describing them is as 'cognitions conducive to offending' rather than cognitive distortions. This is more than a matter of mere semantics because the idea that some offenders develop cognitions very different from ordinary men is problematic as it implies a degree of abnormality in sex offenders beyond what we know from research. Offenders endorse cognitions that conceive of the sexual abuse of children as almost a rational and reasoned consequence of exceptional circumstances. It is also significant that many sex offenders against children live largely ordinary lives – for example, some of them have successful careers as schoolteachers. Just how would it be possible to harbour bizarre cognitive distortions and function well in the real world? Indeed, it would be difficult for sex offenders against children to live in many ways ordinary lives if their cognitions were so different from other people as the acceptance of certain bizarre cognitive distortions would imply.

In view of the importance of the five different cognitive schemas suggested by Ward and Keenan (1999), average responses were calculated on each of our five schemas scales. This ensured that responses to the different schema were comparable. The offenders, as a whole, were most likely to agree to the *Dangerous World* scale and especially the *Children are Reliable* subscale, and to the *Uncontrollability* scale. The offenders tended to endorse most strongly items on the 'children are reliable' subscale for which the mean rating was 2.8. The other highly endorsed schemas included 'uncontrollable' (mean = 2.3), 'dangerous world' (mean = 2.3), and 'children as sexual objects' (mean = 2.2). The schema scale with the lowest endorsement related to 'entitlement to sex' for which the average endorsement was only 1.4. Similarly, the average score for the 'sex is beneficial for children' schema was also low at 1.7. There is more than a strong suggestion in this pattern that it is the offenders' empathy for children which tends to dominate their thinking about offending. The idea that children are reliable and can be trusted compared to adults presents offenders as not merely emotionally committed to children but also as socially committed to them. The idea that the world is otherwise dangerous is also dominant in the thinking of paedophiles.

## OFFENCE TYPES AND PATTERNS IN COGNITIVE DISTORTIONS

Internet sex offenders cannot be differentiated from those who commit contact offences simply on the basis of their overall agreement with cognitive distortions. The mean scores for the three groups were as follows: Internet offenders = 79.6, contact offenders = 74.2 and mixed offenders = 77.0. Consequently, each individual cognitive distortion was examined to see whether Internet offenders differed from contact offenders. Although, in general, there were no differences between the Internet and contact offenders in terms of their cognitive distortions, this was not quite universally the case. There were four cognitive distortions that differentiated Internet from contact offenders and these were all endorsed more strongly by the Internet-only offenders than the contact-only offenders:

- 'Having sexual thoughts and fantasies about a child isn't all that bad because at least it is not really hurting the child.'

- 'Just looking at a naked child is not as bad as touching and will not affect the child as much.'
- 'A child can make their own decision as to whether to have sexual activities with an adult or not.'
- 'Some children are willing and eager to be involved in sexual activities that are with, and for, adults.'

Of course, this is only a small number of significant findings out of the total number of items.

One might regard the fact that Internet offenders agree more than contact offenders on the first two cognitive distortions as reflecting self-serving excuses on the part of the Internet-only offenders. What is surprising then is that they are also more likely to agree with the final two items which, on the face of it, would appear to be ones which contact offenders would be more likely to endorse if self interest underlay endorsement. But they did not and it was again the Internet offender who was more likely to endorse these items.

When the Ward and Keenan schema are considered, there were few statistically reliable differences. Despite having committed rather different crimes, the three offender groups were much the same in terms of their cognitive schema. One significant difference was found. This was for the 'children as sexual objects' schema. Perhaps contrary to expectations, the highest endorsement for this schema was found for the Internet pornographers not the contact offenders. This is much what was found for the analysis of individual items where we found that two items relating to children as sexual beings were endorsed more strongly.

Of course, part of the problem in finding differences may lie in the schema typology employed. So almost as a final attempt to tease differences out of the data, the cognitive distortion data were factor analysed in a search for empirically derived patterns of cognitive distortions, which tend to co-occur. This is clearly different from the original theory-led analysis of Ward and Keenan. The data met minimal standards for factor analysis though there are no universally accepted standards for data to be factor analysed (SAS Library, 1995) and recommendations start (and escalate from) a lower number of 50 cases for the analysis to be stable. If only a small number of factors are found in the analysis, fewer cases are needed for stability (Pedhazur and Schmelkin, 1991). Furthermore, interpretability is one of the more important signs of a satisfactory analysis. Using the standard criteria (Cramer and Howitt, 2004; Howitt and Cramer, 2005), our analysis suggested that there were two important groups or 'clusters' of cognitive distortions.

The first 'cluster' of items contained those cognitions which assumed that children have sexual feelings towards adults and are capable of enjoying and desiring sex with them. This corresponds to Ward and Keenan's (1999) schema of 'children as sexual objects'. Thus, we have borrowed that phrase to describe this cluster of items. Typical high-loading items included the following:

- 'Sometimes children don't say no to sexual activity with adults because they are curious about sex or enjoy it.'

- 'Some children are mature enough to enjoy sexual activities with, and for, adults.'
- 'Some children are willing and eager to be involved in sexual activities that are with, and for, adults.'
- 'Some time in the future our society will realise that sex between a child and adult is alright.'
- 'Sometimes the child instigates the sexual activity with the adult.'
- 'Children don't tell others about sexual activities involving adults probably because they liked it or weren't bothered by it.'

This first group of cognitive distortions concerning *children as sexual beings* merely confirmed much of what we have already seen from the earlier analyses – that Internet offenders tended to score higher than contact offenders on this sort of cognitive distortions. What was new was the finding that the mixed group of offenders had a higher mean score than the contact-only offender group.

The second factor or cluster of items contained items that seem to excuse offending against children in some way. This cluster seems to reflect *justifications for offending* as the most characteristic items on this cluster were:

- 'Children are supposed to do what adults want and this might include serving their sexual needs.'
- 'The only way to do harm to a child when involving them in sexual activities would be to use physical force to get them to do it.'
- 'Children, who have been involved in sexual activities with, and for, adults, will eventually get over it and get on with their lives.'
- 'Sometimes touching a child sexually can be a way to show them love and affection.'

On the assumption that cognitive distortions facilitate offending, one might expect that *justifications for offending* would be commoner in the offenders committing the most serious offences. For instance, those who committed the most serious crimes (for example, indecent assault, rape of a child and so on) might need to develop more extensive excuses for their actions. Thus, contact (and to some extent mixed offenders) would be expected to report the most *justifications* and Internet offenders the least. Yet this was not the case. There were no reliable differences according to the type of sex offender in terms of their justifications for offending.

Nevertheless, we did find that certain offender characteristics were associated with higher levels of *justifications for offending*. The question is what sort of offender might need more justifications for offending? One answer is that men with previous histories of child sex offences may need to resort to cognitive distortions more in order to justify their repeat offences. Indeed this is what we found since offenders with previous criminal records and those who had previous records for sex crime had higher levels of *justifications for offending*. It is very difficult to justify repeat offending as reflecting a one-off and uncharacteristic situation. Repeat offending means that the offending is characteristic and not uncharacteristic of that man. In this argument, *justifica-tions for offending* are not about facilitating offending but are cognitive mechanisms seeking to avoid defining oneself as deviant (Sheldon and Howitt, 2005). However, if cognitive distortions serve as excuses, why are some commonly endorsed and not others? Also, if we examine the items contained within the 'justifications' factor, it is difficult to see how items such as *'children are supposed to do what adults want and this might include serving their sexual needs'* would be viewed as a reasonable argument, or justification, for one's behaviour. If the offender thinks this argument is a convincing justifica-tion to provide to criminal justice professionals, this implies that the offender believes this distorted point of view rather than simply exploits it. As such offenders with previous convictions and more justifications may be more 'committed' paedophiles. In contrast, the cognitive distortions that *children are sexual beings* were not associated with having a previous criminal record including previous sex offences against children.

It is sometimes believed that offenders who target boys are among the most persistent and intransigent sex criminals. If this rationale is correct, then the highest levels of cognitive distortions ought to be found in association with offenders whose index offence(s) were committed against boys. Yet, this was not necessarily the case. Those men with offences against *both* girls and boys had the highest score for 'children are sexual beings'. Interestingly, the group who targeted both genders is actually composed mainly of the Internet offenders, not the contact offenders. Again this seems to reflect our basic findings that the Internet-only offenders tend to have the highest levels of agreement with the *children are sexual beings* cognitive distortions. Those who offended against boy victims tended to agree with the *justifications for offending* groups. This group consisted mainly of contact-only offenders.

## CONCLUDING COMMENTS

There seems little doubt that sex offenders, in appropriate circumstances, endorse a considerable number of cognitive distortions. But it is also evident that the more endorsed cognitive distortions were not particularly bizarre and abnormal. While it cannot be claimed with absolute certainty that social desirability does not affect disclosure of cognitive distortions, nevertheless the offenders we studied were willing to endorse them much more frequently than other researchers have implied. This leads us to the view that cognitive distortions are commonly part of the cognitive worlds of sex offenders much as clinical experience would suggest. The commonly endorsed cognitive distortions superficially had a sense of 'reasonableness', which possibly makes them more dangerous. It may be that sex offenders have difficulty in recognising the social unacceptability of some of the cognitive distortions we asked them about and so do not reject such cognitive distortions. Of course, this begs the query of how an offender can have a cognitive distortion, recognise that the majority of people would not accept it, and yet use that cognitive distortion as an excuse for his offending behaviour? To us this implies that by-and-large they do not see their cognitions as socially undesirable and that they believe much of the cognitions they express. Furthermore, we do have some doubts as to whether cognitive distortions are as general as attempts to capture them using cognitive distortion scales and scores would imply. Experience of interviewing these men pushes us towards the view that in many cases the contents of their distorted thinking is to a degree specific to that offender. They do not always appear to be simply 'off-the-peg' excuses made up on the spot.

Sometimes, as we have seen, cognitive distortions do seem to be self serving excuses but in many cases they seem to be more deeply held than that. In this context, it is important to note that the cognitive distortions which are more characteristic of the Internet-only offenders were 'Having sexual thoughts and fantasies about a child isn't all that bad because at least it is not really hurting the child' and 'Just looking at a naked child is not as bad as touching and will not affect the child as much.' These would seem to be self-serving excuses by the Internet-only offenders to justify their offences. Nevertheless, it is difficult to maintain the view that all cognitive distortions may function as self-serving excuses. Internet-only offenders were also more likely to accept the cognitive distortions 'A child can make their own decision as to whether to have sexual activities with an adult or not' and 'Some children are willing and eager to be involved in sexual activities that are with, and for, adults.' These cognitive distortions could be self-serving for contact offenders who were actually the least likely to endorse these distortions.

In terms of Ward and Keenan's schemas, the schemas most endorsed were those which superficially seem normal rather than distorted. Entitlement to sex with children (the least endorsed of the schema) is far from socially normative, thinking that children are trustworthy and reliable seems to be superficially an acceptable sentiment. Indeed, it would not be unexpected that offenders regard offending behaviour as out of control behaviour on the basis of social psychological attribution theory. That is, the tendency not to see the origins of our own unacceptable behaviour in our own character and personality but as the consequence of external influences. If these cognitions are conducive to offending, then their lack of bizarre or unacceptable content may make them not only resistant to reality monitoring but consequently not amenable to change.

The pattern of cognitive distortions of Internet sex offenders tell us that we should be wary of any models that imply a simple, direct relationship between the contents of cognitive distortions and the contact sexual abuse of children. Such simple models would predict that contact-only offenders should endorse more cognitive distortions conducive to offending. Actually, this should be the case irrespective of the role of cognitive distortions in offending. If cognitive distortions merely excuse offending rather than motivate it then those committing the worst crimes should have the most cognitive distortions and hold them most strongly. It emerged that contact-only offenders endorsed the fewest cognitive distortions of the *children are sexual beings* group. The same is problematic for the idea that cognitive distortions actually direct offending behaviour because, once again, the more extreme cognitive distortions should be associated with the worst crimes against children. Internet-only offenders do have a sexual interest in children (Taylor and Quayle, 2003) but their sexual interest is primarily in terms of fantasy for masturbation rather than a drive to behave sexually with a child. This may partially explain why they have higher levels of such cognitions. Contact offenders have engaged children sexually and, as a consequence, some of them may have recognised the reality that children are not sexual beings in the sense required by these cognitive distortions. This is to assume that experience may change cognitive distortions in some circumstances. This is a very different perspective on cognitive distortions from the one usually employed though Ward *et al.* (Ward, 2000; Ward and Keenan, 1999; Ward and Siegert, 2002) appear to recognise this when they suggested that schema may change with experience, just as any other cognitive schema does.

The issue of whether or not paedophiles believe the cognitive distortions they express is a moot point in the research literature. It is, of course, very difficult to obtain valid evidence on this. However, some cognitive distortions we identified loosely as *justifications for offending* and these might be expected to be the most likely to be used in a face-saving way. This pattern of cognitive distortions was related to previous criminal history. It might be suggested, then that this may lend support to the notion that cognitive distortions are, partially at least, motivated by the need to provide justifications for one's offences within the criminal justice system. Nevertheless, we should return to the point that it is difficult to understand how an offender could believe that psychologists, probation workers, and other professionals would share the views embedded in the cognitive distortion. For example, 'Sometimes touching a child sexually can be a way to show them love and affection' does not strike one as being a remotely convincing explanation of or justification for offending. We would suggest that if an offender believes this cognitive distortion is convincing to others then he must fundamentally believe this distorted point of view himself. For this reason, the alternative explanation that offenders with previous convictions are simply more committed paedophiles who have greater levels of offending may be the preferred one. Persistent offending may demand that the offender accepts certain cognitive distortions in order to justify the offending to himself and in the eyes of others.

What of the idea that cognitive distortions substantially reflect the offender's early experiences? This means that cognitive distortions are narrative accounts that link together the offender's early experiences with their subsequent offending behaviour as adults. Thus, cognitive distortions are not distortions in a meaningful sense but the product of difficulties in childhood. Ward *et al*'s idea that sex offender's cognitive schema are learnt in childhood and can, to a degree, change is very similar when put this way (Ward, 2000; Ward and Keenan, 1999; Ward and Siegert, 2002). There were many instances in our interviews with offenders where the men drew links between their sexual crimes against children and their own childhood experiences. We can see in the following quotation from an Internet offender, ideas that equate to the 'children-are-sexual-beings' cognitive distortion pattern. The source of this rather broad view – or schema - seems to have derived from his experiences of his foster sister:

> [Name] was my ... foster sister a real 'promiscuous Lolita' ... and what I saw, and the way she was sexually she was a Lolita, as they're called it, it isn't a phase that a girl goes through she's that for life I'm convinced of that and it starts from childhood ... she was about 10, 11 yea, promiscuous but with older men, flirting with them, sexually teasing them, that sort of thing. [2: Internet offender]

There were further examples from interviews with other offenders that cognitive distortions might reflect accounts of early sexual experiences. These following examples essentially contain what would be a 'children-are-sexual-beings' distortion. Children are viewed as sexual beings simply because as a child this offender was sexually active with peers and adults;

> When I was 14 ... I did have sex willingly with other boys, with men ... I knew what I was doing, what I wanted, no man apart from the times I've told you about, no man abused me, but I went and had sex with men ... but, here [prison] you get this blanket no children don't go out and have sex, but I know that's wrong, I did it myself and I know I wasn't the only one that was doing it ... there are people out there, 14, 15 that are mature enough to decide that they want sex ... with other people. [32: contact offender]

In this example we see the offender's difficulty in establishing victim empathy because in his perceptions his sexual activities as a child and his abuse by a baby-sitter were enjoyable experiences:

> Very heavy petting with female cousins I was a nightmare ... the family would become concerned if I went off into the countryside with cousins and things like that because I was so sexually precocious ... fondling, yea, whatever ... I remember I was very sexually active with my peer group ... I was always a big lad ... and all my girlfriends were at least two years older than me ... I was having relationships with adult women by the time I was a young teenager ... as a result I have a problem with victim empathy ... because I remember sexual contact as being a nice thing when I was a child ... I have a distinct memory of a neighbour's daughter who would be about 16 and I would be about 10 getting me to come into the house and kiss her breasts and playing with her down there ... I don't remember that as abuse, I remember that as being something I enjoyed very much ... it has been a massive problem for me to overcome that in the last 3 years ... in a sense of are children curious about sex? Well yes I think they are because I was [37: contact offender]

# CHAPTER 12

# Desisting from Child Abuse

Why is it that some men who are clearly aroused by child pornography and risk imprisonment to get it yet do not sexually abuse children directly? Just what factors stop them from acting out their paedophilic interests? One reason given why Internet pornography downloaders should be punished is that they pose the serious risk of their sexual interest in children escalating to levels at which they will be driven to seek out children to sexually abuse; their sexual fantasies are fuelled by child pornography to a point beyond the offenders control. Hammond (2004. p. 95) makes a crucial point: 'The fundamental question of whether such offenders may be qualitatively distinct from contact offenders, and the degree of overlap there is between them, depends upon the collection and collation of data.' The problem is where to look for the vital differences. One possibility is, of course, to simply ask offenders why they desist from offending directly against children.

Numerous studies show that sexual arousal to images of children as assessed by the size of a man's erection (phallometry) is a strong predictor of contact sexual offences against children (Hanson and Bussiere, 1998). Nevertheless, the strongest sexual response to sexual images of children is among child pornography offenders with no history of contact offending (Seto, Cantor and Blanchard, 2006); these offenders had greater increases in their erections to child images than did contact child molesters with one to two victims. Not only this – they also showed more response to such material than sex offenders against adult victims. Child pornography offenders had similar levels of sexual response to child pornography as child molesters with three or more victims!

Contact offenders seem to have fewer fantasies in general, relevant to their pattern of offending than do Internet-only offenders (Sheldon and Howitt, 2005; Sheldon and Howitt, in press). No simple fantasy-causes-sexual-abuse model is capable of explaining the existence of Internet offenders with no history of sexually abusing children directly (Burke *et al.*, 2001; Carr, 2003; Quayle *et al.*, 2000; Seto and Eke, 2005; Taylor and Quayle, 2003). We are simply wrong to assume that sexual fantasies are invariably acted out in reality as if they were blueprints for offending. The neglect of the body of research on the sexual fantasy of normal people is partly responsible for the lack of subtlety of theorists about the role of sexual fantasy in sexual crime. It is a mistake to disregard the possibility that fantasy is just that – fantasy – rather than the key to action. There are some similarities between fantasy and the offending behaviour of contact sexual abusers but there may be reasons for this other than the putative driving force of fantasy.

Desistance from contact offending in men otherwise paedophilically inclined is a research opportunity presented by Internet child pornography offenders. It seems less than satisfactory to merely regard all Internet sex offenders as contact offenders in waiting. Quite clearly, as we have demonstrated in this book, there are some factors that appear to differentiate contact offenders from Internet offenders but, as yet, they do not explain desistance. So why do Internet-only offenders not contact offend? The offenders we studied were interviewed about this and their explanations subjected to a thematic analysis to draw out overarching themes or ideas in their 'accounts' (Braun and Clarke, 2006; Langdridge, 2004). The dominant themes that we identified were (a) focus on fantasy-contact, (b) moral/ethical reasoning and (c) fear of consequences.

## FOCUS ON FANTASY-CONTACT

The evidence that contact-only offenders need to offend against children as a means of generating fantasy is somewhat conjectural. Although some offenders are known to have penetrative intercourse with children, many paedophile offences do not directly result in the offender's orgasm. The offences may involve sexual touching, photographing, flashing and similar activities in which orgasm is not achieved or may not even be the intention. One reason why the paedophile may engage in such behaviours is that their preference is actually to use the stimulation and fantasy generated by their contact offence in later masturbation or during intercourse with an adult partner. In a sense, fantasy and masturbation may be more closely linked than fantasy and orgasmic child sexual abuse. Internet offenders generally seem to be a group of men whose primary interest is indeed sexual fantasy; most of the Internet offenders we studied (56 %) claimed that their paedophile interest was solely fantasy-focused. Theirs is a fantasy world driven by child pornography.

There are instances of Internet offenders who, although presented with opportunities to sexually assault children, do not do so. The following man attempts to use his decision to not touch children sexually as demonstrating the 'responsible' way in which he deals with his 'problem'. Repeatedly, during the interview, he was emphatic that he would not assault a child sexually in his comments such as 'Definitely. No. No.' Rather he speaks of his sexual needs being fulfilled from viewing the images – 'looking at the images is enough' and, using the discourse of addiction, he refers to his 'fix'. This discourse allows him to present himself as someone who, in some aspects, is not in control of what he does. It is not clear from what he says whether if he did not receive his Internet 'fix' he would have pursued other avenues to deal with his 'addiction'. He appears to be suggesting that by viewing images of child abuse he is protected from carrying out sexual assaults on children. The pornography offers him the opportunity to explore and express his strong sexual interest in children harmlessly, in his view, in fantasy. Rather he used a 'surrogate' victim who would not be harmed in the same way as a real child. There is a possibility that his contacts with children, although non-sexual, might stimulate fantasy, of course. This man is a 50-year-old offender with one previous Internet offence but no convictions for direct sexual assaults. He has biological children but there was no suggestion that he had ever assaulted them:

> I have been in the position shall I say if I'd wanted to I could have done . . . on many, many occasions, but I always drew the line of actually touching [a child] I got to the point where if I was looking at something that to me was my, like a drug addict, that was my fix for the day . . . my end release was looking at the pictures. I never got to the point where I would want to touch . . . looking at the images is enough, though a lot of people will disagree . . . I mean I've meet people in prisons . . . who are in for the same thing and . . . their talk was never of actual sexual contact. Definitely. No. No. I would never. [9: Internet offender]

Another offender recognised that there is a common assumption that there is a link between 'thinking' and 'doing'. He raised the point that because he was arrested for his Internet offending then this broke the link to possible contact offending:

> Because I never in a serious sense considered actually physically involving myself . . . which is bizarre in the sense of . . . logically for any other purpose you would progress through things . . . and yet that thought process never accumulated whether that was because . . . my offending was 'nipped in the bud' before it progressed I honestly can't answer that . . . but going back to the times when I sat on the computer by myself and you're sexually aroused . . . there was no actual thought of 'I wish I was doing that' rather it was 'I find that sexually exciting' that's . . . a true representation of the way that I felt during that offending period . . . It isn't so much wanting to be a part of the picture as being excited by what the images represented, sexual images [13: Internet offender]

There is little indication that contact offending would be satisfying to him because he expresses the view that he did not want to touch a child. However, he does acknowledge how fantasy was a source of sexual stimulation and pleasure; it was the images that were sexually exciting, not the thought of contact offending.

For some offenders sexual activity with real children risked what they achieved through fantasy – that is, for them, reality would not live up to fantasy. For example, the following Internet offender reflected on his thoughts about one of the young trainees at work:

> We had a trainee at work . . . Very pretty but when I spoke to her you soon realised that she is 14, 15 even though she told me that she was sexually

active . . . If I'd seen an image of her . . . naked . . . you'd still be sexually attracted to her until you speak to her, she's a child . . . there's a difference between someone I find sexually attractive and actually doing anything about it . . . basically when you speak to them you think oh too young . . . it puts me off . . . she is no longer attractive. [49: Internet offender]

This is quite a remarkable set of ideas. A man sexually interested in underage people meets an attractive youngster but her immaturity 'puts him off'. On-screen and in fantasy, an underage person can be manipulated into a representation of an experienced, willing, and receptive individual. Off-screen, however, she is definitely a child – indeed she sounds like a child. Thus the reality and the fantasy are incompatible and the illusion in the fantasy essentially shattered. If the offender wanted sex with an underage person primarily, then his comments make little sense. On the other hand, if the sexual aim of the offender is masturbation to fantasy then his comments fall into place perfectly. His behaviour (viewing) is performed in order to provide suitable masturbatory fantasy that fits in with his preferred sexual script.

Other offenders similarly expressed the importance of the fantasy contact when asked why they would not molest a child directly:

I have had . . . sexual thoughts about pubescent children . . . I honestly don't think that those thoughts are any more or any stronger than any other normal heterosexual . . . its not just a question of laws either I mean . . . when you're actually talking to . . . young girls face to face . . . when a 13, 14, 15 year old girl opens her mouth it's painfully obvious she's a 13, 14, 15 year old girl . . . but when you're just looking at an image . . . you can use your imagination more about the sort of person that she is, or how experienced they are, or how mature they are, it's just the fact that . . . young teenage bodies are, are the most beautiful, are the most flawless and so that's what I find . . . attractive to look at . . . and to masturbate to [12: Internet offender]

This is another indication that, on screen, the images or fantasy can be manipulated to the offender's own sexual preferences and desires. The idea is of a 'willing' child who can be sexually experienced in fantasy just as the offender wishes. The offender can initiate and participate in whatever sexual activities arouse him. Most importantly, there are no repercussions or consequences. In contrast, acting out such sexual thoughts risks coming face-to-face with the 'painful' reality that child is behaving as a child, unable to participate in sexual activity in the informed and knowing way that a fantasy child would. A real child would challenge the offender's fantasy that children are inherently sexual and, as a consequence, the real child would not be sexually attractive.

Another offender pointed out that his sexual preference was for voyeurism. Acting out fantasies again would clash with this sexual preference and 'touching' for him simply 'wouldn't work':

Direct offence? Never come across to me, it was simply the act of masturbating . . . I never actually fantasised about me self being involved in that photograph ... I'm a voyeur ... its [like] looking through somebody's living room window and seeing the women naked ... looking through the bedroom window and seeing the girl naked in the bedroom ... I love the visual, I couldn't touch them because that wouldn't work [20: Internet offender]

Sometimes offenders would suggest that child pornography had the positive function of dealing with their deviant sexual needs and that this might prevent sexual abuse. One man reported a clear and constant interest in paedophilic material since he began visiting Amsterdam at the age of 16 or 17 years. He described how he managed this interest, for about thirty years, until the time of his index offences using 'teenage' pornography videos and personal fantasies. There is disappointment that before the Internet he was unable to obtain child pornography. Clearly he exemplifies men with deviant interests who nevertheless are able to desist from physical contact with children. He became aware of the availability of child pornography from the Internet after seeing a BBC TV programme, *Hunt for Britain's Paedophiles*:

I've always had an interest ... I'd never done anything about it physically at all and I wouldn't but if you asked me what kind of pornography I prefer it's that kind [child] ... [Prior to the Internet] there wasn't anything out there, what I use to do was get ... videos with teenage sex, 18s ... you couldn't get this material to buy prior to the Internet, some people could but I'm blowed if I knew where they got it from so ... I never went out and actively did anything about this interest ... I just found another way, fantasising and I use to be, quite happy with videos of teenage sex ... when when the BBC showed that programme it was like a bloody advert to me ... child pornography is an outlet for my, those fantasies and without it you'd have more nutters doing ... horrible things ... it's no point denying it in your own head because you go mad ... you have to make sure you don't give an indication of it. [30: Internet offender]

These extracts show that many Internet offenders expressed a lack of aspiration in pursuing actual direct assaults, for example 'I just don't want to' [30: Internet offender]. This is, to some extent, due to their interest in masturbatory fantasy with children rather than actual contact. The reverse pattern was true for contact and mixed child molesters where intentionality in their contact offending was evident. When contact and mixed child molesters were asked about why they contact abused then frequently the notion 'I wanted to do it' [8: mixed offender] was offered. More importantly, contact and mixed offenders emphasise the importance of touching as the key to sexual gratification. In a sense, such a statement as 'I did it because I wanted to' is an internal, stable attribution of cause. It gives the impression that sexual offending is part of the individual's 'core self'.

One child molester referred to the need for the children (boys in this case) to be 'in the flesh', which suggests that for him they need to be naked and/or involve contact. Pornography can serve as an aid to assist him in maintaining his masturbatory fantasies. However, actual touching has greater impact:

The attraction is towards prepubescent boys that's always been there and it is ... mostly in the flesh. I sought out imagery of pre-pubescent boys ... sexually interacting with each other ... mutual masturbation, oral sex, anal sex, digitally, with boys ... naturist videos of boys but anything like that is no substitute for the real thing [25: contact offender].

Similarly, taking photographs and videoing the abuse were important to another contact offender. No matter how much pornography he has, he would seek the next step which, to his mind, is direct sexual contact with a child. He had tried to satiate his deviant attraction through home-made pornography of the abuse, but, rather disappointingly for him, this was ineffective. Greater sexual satisfaction came from actual physical contact with his victim:

[Internet pornography?] You'll eventually want the real thing ... like me ... I would say even if I'd got a house full of that I would be looking for the next thing ... The video was ... just an ego thing but it didn't work out ... how I wanted ... it wasn't quite as real, I didn't get as much ... out of it as I thought I would have done ... I didn't get that much ... sexual gratification ... the images not really either ... not like touching. [1: contact offender]

Further examples from contact offenders carry on with much the same theme:

But I've never thought ... computers before ... because I am a touchy man rather than looking. [27: contact offender]

I was never into porn ... frankly I'm not interested ... my danger is doing it, I live my fantasies. [37: contact offender]

Visuals are not that good really to me. [39: contact offender]

Similar comments to those of contact offenders were made by the mixed-contact-internet offenders:

These children I abused represented the [Internet] images that I'd been seeing, and that other adults were doing ... I wanted to try it, see if I felt I enjoyed it, or I got some satisfaction from it ... I felt like I would ... initially just like to, to see her naked. [3: mixed offender]

What satisfaction can a male get out of looking at something on a bloody picture for Christ sake? I'm a performer, I want to go out there and do it ... what kicks can you get out of seeing it on bloody screen?' if not it'd do your own 'ead in ... and get on with it but do it right. [17: mixed offender]

Both extracts are what might be described by therapists as 'active' rather than 'passive' accounts. For example, in the former extract the offender takes at least partial responsibility for his behaviour represented in the frequent use of the personal pronoun 'I', although we do not know truly what the offender did; there is no mention of actual acts. The final sentence strikes one as a fallacy – his abuse involved more than seeing her naked. Moreover, the Internet material seems to serve two purposes. First, as 'permission giving' – the offender is given more courage and ideas from what he sees on the computer especially regarding the escalation of his offending behaviour. Second, as 'imitation' as he replays with a victim what he has witnessed on the computer. Overall, his cognitions support contact abuse.

In contrast, the last extract above communicates rather an aggressive tone and the offender overtly states his intentions. Indeed, he is almost surprised at the suggestion of not engaging in sexual contact and there is a sense of entitlement. The use of the word 'performer' is remarkable for its many connotations. On the one hand, it indicates an interest in engaging directly with a sexual partner – in this case a child – but it also suggests an underlying 'sexual prowess'. He gives the impression of exhibitionism – a so-called porn actor would perform in movies; he is there 'to do a job' and there is no interpersonal aspect to it. Further, the comment reflects a large ego, indicating that perhaps he considers himself the most important person in the sexual 'partnership'. There appears to be no collaborative aspect to it – he is there to perform and his partner is there to enjoy it. In this sense it is almost predetermined that his partner will enjoy it. He also implies that by not acting out his fantasies he would be adversely affected psychologically: 'if not it'd do your own 'ead in'. It is not clear what the phrase 'but do it right' means. It could be a reference to ensuring he is not caught, a reference to not 'harming' the sexual partner or, if the previous comments are considered, a reference to sexual performance or prowess. It should be noted that this offender had both Internet pornography as well as indecent assaults offences and alleged rape charges.

The notion that Internet offenders may prefer fantasy contact through the use of pornography is further supported by the importance of pornography in their lives. Eighty one per cent of Internet offenders admitted to using adult pornography whereas only 40 % of contact offenders and 50 % of mixed offenders did so. This would fit in well with the view that Internet offenders generally show a preference for visual fantasy materials rather than contact abuse. The lower levels of interest of contact offenders in pornography may fit in with the idea that they are less likely to be aroused by pornography than Internet only offenders (cf. Seto *et al.*, 2006).

## MORAL/ETHICAL REASONING:

A majority of the Internet-only offenders (56 %) gave reasons for not expressing their fantasies through direct assault, which had a paradoxical 'moral' or 'ethical' basis. This was expressed in a variety of ways, not all of which seem to reflect the nature of what they been convicted for. One offender said:

Because I have very strong sense of duty and loyalty and what's proper. [12: Internet offender]

The offenders did not appear to simply wish to avoid punishment by concentrating on fantasy; they claim to consider the harm and damage that a direct sexual assault on a child would do to the victim:

> Because it's harmful . . . to innocent people . . . I wouldn't want to harm adults; I don't want to harm children. [30: Internet offender]

> No . . . because as an adult you've got to be thinking for the child . . . they've got to live with it for the rest of their life. [50: Internet offender]

They appear not to notice the paradox that their offending is justified morally by not having done another sort of crime. Instead, they present their position as that of empathy for a real-life child whom they should not harm. It is not surprising that child pornographers in general tend to prefer photos of children appearing to enjoy themselves. Images involving signs of distress, such as crying, tend to be avoided and would immediately signal harm being done to the child. Nevertheless, despite stipulating that they would not harm any child their actions ignore the common argument that child pornography users contribute to the exploitation of children. The position of the Internet offenders about direct child sexual molestation is summarised by the simple comment:

> Having sex with a girl . . . *that is really wrong.* [15: Internet offender (emphasis added)]

Quite simply, Internet-only offenders judge their own criminal behaviour as less damaging, less illegal, less 'unhealthy' and less 'immoral' than touching a child. Quayle *et al.* (2005) point out that there is no research to date exploring empathy in Internet offenders. They point out that some practitioners find it difficult to understand how traditional empathy training (for example, viewing videotapes of victims, writing an apology letter) is of relevance to Internet offenders who have in some cases collected thousands of images. The concern is that the children are merely seen as objects rather than as people, which may impact on their willingness to control their Internet behaviour. Quayle *et al.* point to the research by Hanson *et al.*, (1995) who argue that empathy is threatened when there is an indifferent relationship between the abuser and the victim. Quayle *et al.* continue by arguing that the Internet images offer no context concerning the child and their circumstances that would enable the offender to empathise better with the victim.

## FEAR OF CONSEQUENCES

Howitt (1995b) suggested that among the reasons why some paedophiles do not use pornography is because of the risks it poses in terms of discovery, say, by the police. The adverse consequences of contact offending, such as violence, appear to act as a deterrent to a small minority (19 %) of Internet offenders:

> Partly because I wouldn't want the guy to go "Ahh! This man's trying to grope me!" ... and I'd have his big brothers' mates coming with baseball bats. [18: Internet offender]

> One of the things that held me back from doing that [touching a child sexually] was that ... I was very conscious of not telling anybody that I was thinking these things ... what would they think of me? My professional status. [15: Internet offender]

The emphasis is on the consequences for the individual. This theme also incorporated fearing interpersonal consequences that would result when being convicted of sexual assault, for example, the negative effect on one's reputation, how others would view him, disapproval from significant others, and loss of loved ones. They also feared physical reprisals, especially vigilantism. What is interesting is that some offenders assumed that there was a much greater chance of being caught for a sexual assault on a child than being caught for downloading Internet pornography. The Internet had some level of anonymity, which contact offending did not despite high levels of media and public attention directed towards major national and international police operations. The implication is that authorities need to raise the profile of 'policing' on the Web. 'Perceived' anonymity is thought to be one factor of the Internet that makes it an attractive venue for online, and disinhibited, sexual behaviour (Barak and Fisher, 2001; Cooper, 1998; Cooper, McLoughlin and Campbell, 2000; Cooper and Sportolari, 1997; McKenna and Bargh, 1999, 2000) with little embarrassment and with at times an inflated sense of security (Quayle et al., 2005). The Internet allows paedophiles to operate, from their point of view, very safely (Brookes, 2003), as illustrated here:

> I'm anonymous, I'm in England they're in Russian or wherever ... you always feel safe in your own walls ... don't matter where you are you feel that's your cocoon ... no matter what I do in here nobody can ... touch me now. [5: Internet offender]

This situation is in sharp contrast to announcing one's sexual intentions with a child to a group of people face-to-face. The effects of anonymity have long been known (for example, Zimbardo, 1969). The comment from Internet offender 5 corresponds with respondents in surveys who have admitted to an interest in sexual contact with children – if this was unknown to other people and they were not punished (Briere and Runtz, 1989). Furthermore, it is known that the link between anonymity and deviant behaviour is likely to be strongest when there are personal or material rewards for the individual (Postmes and Spears, 1998) such as stealing or, in this case, sexual gratification. The following offender assumed that touching a child was easy to detect compared to Internet offences. He had been collecting child pornography for approximately 10 years, which would reinforce his belief that such offending can go undetected for a long period of time:

> Well nobody's found out therefore it doesn't matter keep going . . . touching a child is much easier to be found out about, being caught you know, but Internet stuff well no one had found out so far [15: Internet offender]

This Internet offender had been a teacher at a boarding school. He was using perfectly normal day-to-day experiences with the children at his school as a basis for fantasy content, e.g. playground activities, sports events, conversations. He had been a teacher for over 25 years and in that time did not engage in any long-term adult relationships – the more time he spent with the children the more he felt he was 'imposing his sexual fantasies upon them' and the less he 'tried to build decent relationships with women'.

## CONCLUDING COMMENTS

Downloading Internet child pornography is a focused and planned activity. It involves time and effort and the accumulation of skills if it is to be done effectively. There is clear evidence that the majority of offenders masturbated to the images they downloaded. The primary function of child pornography is as a means of sexual arousal and fantasy. Offenders are discriminating in their choice of material, searching for content that is personally arousing and integral to existing fantasies or useful for generating new ones. At the same time, substantial numbers of them collect child pornography images without much consideration of the specific image. Clearly, Internet child pornography offenders have a strong sexual interest in children which warrants the description paedophilic. However, most of the Internet offenders either had no interest in, or avoided for some other reason, sexual contacts with children. One offender (case study 5) we interviewed claimed that he could imagine sexual activity with a child if an adolescent child 'showed some interest in him' and there was a sexual 'come on'. The remainder, however, spoke of the barriers which hindered them from directly expressing their sexual fantasies; including moral reasoning and fear of the consequences. However, the most important factor was that they simply had a greater interest in deviant fantasy than in actual contact with children. So what does this mean in terms of how we understand child pornography in relation to contact offending? As we know, there are men whose index offences included both direct assaults against children and Internet offending behaviour. In our study, 80 % of the mixed contact/ Internet offending cases revealed clear evidence that the Internet downloading of abusive images occurred prior to any contact abuse (10 % were unclear which action started first and 10 % indicated that the contact offending came first). Such evidence is compatible with the idea that fantasy/pornography may lead to sexual behaviour and sexual aggression. This is illustrated by the following offender:

It did start off with adult pornography . . . a good two-and-a-half, three years before moving onto child imagery and eventually contact. [22: mixed offender]

Of course, this does not necessarily mean that the fantasy caused the behaviour. Indeed, it is difficult to establish whether the pornography viewing caused the offending given that of those 80 % of cases, all acknowledged at least one of the following:

- a sexual attraction to children *prior* to any Internet offending;
- engaged in sex play with female girls when under the age of 12 years;
- sex play with boys when under the age of 16 years;
- had been sexually abused as a child.

This suggests that their offending was an extension of their *already* established sexual attraction to children or their previous sexual experiences with children. Naturally, it is not known how many of these mixed offenders would have offended if the Internet had not been available. But understanding the risk that these men pose to the public is complicated by their lack of criminal (sexual or non-sexual) histories.

On the other hand, there are Internet-only sex offenders with no *apparent* history of contact offending against children who, nevertheless, have higher levels of paedophilic fantasies than do contact offenders against children. Nevertheless, their paedophilic fantasies were not related to their choice of victims in the sense that they often had convictions for images of both boys and girls but, say, their true interest was in girls. This lends no support to the common assumption that a simple, direct model links sexual fantasy to contact offending. Few of these men suggest that they have any intention of directly molesting children yet, at the same time, they have had sexual fantasies involving minors both before and after access to the Internet. This tends to negate the argument that fantasy from pornography drives offending and clearly demonstrates that men with paedophilic thoughts seem able to desist from acting out their deviant sexual impulses in many cases.

To further complicate the issue, there are contact offenders who, if the fantasy-behaviour hypothesis is accepted, should be demonstrating levels of paedophilic fantasy that are at least higher than those of Internet offenders. They offend against children so ought to be high on fantasy if fantasy does fuel behaviour. However, contact offenders scored the lowest on paedophilic fantasies. There are several possible explanations of why Internet offenders might report higher rates of sexual thoughts compared to contact-only molesters. These include lower levels of denial as well as expediency concerning their Internet behaviour.

More importantly, contact offenders may need contact in order to generate fantasy whereas Internet offenders do not. In support of this is the fact that over half of the Internet offenders spoke of their interest, or preference, for fantasy contact with children over actual contact. They may be described as 'fantasy voyeurs'. Internet offenders may be able to generate rewarding and complex fantasies and may achieve 'satisfaction' by masturbating to orgasm. The fact that they were better educated than contact-only molesters may mean that they may be able to generate more fantasies as a consequence. Contact offenders were 'fantasy performers'. They spoke of favouring physical contact over pornographic material, which would simply fail to provide sufficient sexual stimulation. Contact offenders had fewer paedophilic fantasies than Internet offenders, and a fantasy deficit relevant to their victim targets (girls). If fantasy drives behaviour then this is remarkable. Contact-only offenders may have difficulty generating fantasy about children, which they can then use in masturbation. Thus they need to offend directly against a child in order to generate fantasy. Further credence to this comes from the fact that contact offenders report more confrontational non-contact fantasies. Thus, the response of the child may be crucial as offenders indicated with comments such as 'a picture it doesn't do anything for me', or 'I need to be with them'. These comments make sense if masturbatory-fantasy is what is important for offenders. Contact-only molesters need simulation for their fantasies, which, for them, is provided by physically engaging with children which consequently provides imagery for later masturbation or for use in sex with their adult partner. Further, contact offenders were less educated than Internet offenders again suggesting that they may lack the cognitive resources to derive fantasy from pictures. Concrete experiences are needed by them on which to develop sexual thoughts.

A substantially bigger proportion of Internet child pornography offenders used adult pornography compared to contact and mixed offenders. Internet offenders seem to be more experienced users of pornography in general. In contrast, contact offenders, perhaps because of their inability to use the material as well as a lack of interest in it, were less likely to have used adult pornography.

On the basis of this evidence and the limited literature in this area (for example, Quayle et al., 2000), there is reason to propose that there is a group of offenders whose focus is on fantasy and not on engaging children directly for sexual purposes. Making inferences in this area is difficult especially since Internet sex offender research is solely confined to convicted offenders and we know nothing about men who may fantasise about children but have not been involved with Internet child pornography or contact sex offending. Of course, the men we interviewed in prison were aware of the limits of confidentiality and that the interviewer was required to disclose previously unrecorded offences. So they may have withheld any contact offences they may have committed. Sullivan and Beech (2003) argue that most Internet offenders will deny that they are ever likely to commit contact sexual offences. Sex offenders are frequently presented as lying and manipulative though careful evidence evaluating this assertion is rare. Whilst this is clearly a possibility, there is recent evidence to suggest that sex offenders against children are generally honest in their replies to questions (Gannon, 2006; Gannon and Polaschek, 2005). This supports the argument that Internet-only offenders are unlikely to have unrecorded contact offences in significant numbers. Further, half of the current Internet offenders were fathers and there was no evidence from social services or the police that the men had pursued their deviant interests with their own children.

# CHAPTER 13

# Epilogue: What has been Learnt and What shall we Do?

Ideas about paedophiles are political with both a capital and a small 'p'. There is a seeming consensus about paedophiles, which can be seen as dominating the agendas of the criminal justice system, the work of professionals involved in the management of sex offenders, treatments of sex offenders, and the researchers who venture into the field. This constitutes a virtual hegemony that may hamper our understanding of what can be done to deal with sex offenders against children. That consensus essentially holds that paedophiles are among the most dangerous offenders; they lie, cheat and deceive in order to gratify their vile needs; and they cannot stop offending which is likely to escalate in frequency and intensity. To question this hegemony in any way is to risk censure and the accusation of being an apologist for paedophiles. Scarcely a day goes by when paedophiles do not feature in the news in some way. As this is being written, today's news is that a children's charity is calling for polygraphy (lie detector tests) for sex offenders against children. Yesterday it was the lack of supervision of registered sex offenders in hostels. Tomorrow it may a different headline still. Paedophilia is remarkably central to the modern political agenda; it is a crucial part of the current ideology surrounding crime in a way that it was not even ten years ago. Our ideas about paedophilia are socially constructed by government, child protection agencies, experts on sex offending, psychologists and so forth. The input of research into this process, where it supports the agenda makers, is welcomed.

In a sense, we are all experts on paedophiles. We all know what we would do with them. It is easy to clash with the sensibilities and knowledge of a great many people. Thus a serious book of paedophilia may be described as 'a dangerous apologia for child sexual abuse' probably without being read carefully. The sexual abuse of children is unacceptable yet how can it be stopped? In part, we would argue that only by questioning our own understanding of paedophilia can we tackle offenders more effectively. This involves asking ourselves difficult questions about how we know what we believe we know and the extent to which we have evidence on our side. We would like to see the end of the sexual abuse of children as well as other forms of exploitation but suspect that cut-and-dried, black-and-white explanations of sexual abusive behaviour and how to deal with it sometimes may do more harm than good.

## HOW SHOULD WE KNOW ABOUT PAEDOPHILES?

Just what should we make of research based on the word of paedophiles? All of our findings – and those of many other researchers – rely on self-reported childhood and adulthood experiences. The validity of such data is not clear and is difficult to assess. Adults' retrospective accounts of their childhood are particularly vulnerable. They are, irrespective of anything else, current constructions of past events and cannot be entirely guaranteed as accurate biographical accounts of offenders' childhoods. Nevertheless, it is possible to overestimate the unreliability of retrospective accounts of childhood events (Brewin, Andrews and Gotlib, 1993). For instance, when adults are asked to recall salient factual details of their own childhood they are generally accurate, especially when these experiences are unique, consequential and unexpected (Brewin, Andrews and Gotlib, 1993). Two prospective controlled studies that examined the recollections of childhood physical and sexual abuse have indicated a reasonable degree of reliability (approximately 60 % accuracy) in retrospective reports of childhood maltreatment (Widom and Morris, 1997; Widom and Shepard, 1996).

Even studying the current experiences of *offenders* poses potential problems. That is, do they distort or fabricate their experiences to elicit sympathy or even to cover up humiliating and painful early trauma? Moreover, the conventional image of the 'sex offender' as a skilful and practised liar seems to be emphasised in recent demands for the polygraphic testing of offenders – 'sex offenders may face lie detector tests' (Travis, 2004). This image of deceitfulness is reinforced by the idea that sex offenders should be tagged – '500 paedophiles to be tracked by satellite tags' (Doward, 2003). This is something of a quandary because, for instance, amongst the best available evidence that there is a link between childhood abuse and later adult offending against children are the very retrospective reports that some researchers view negatively (Herman, 1990).

Hindman's (1988) study, in particular, is quoted as evidence of the tendency of sex offenders to fake a history of childhood sexual abuse. Two groups of sex offenders (pre-1982 and post-1982) were interviewed but only the post-1982 were warned that they would be subject to a polygraph examination concerning whether their reports of childhood sexual abuse were truthful. The offenders were warned that they would be returned to prison should they fail this lie detector examination. Only 29 % of offenders threatened with reimprisonment reported childhood abuse; in contrast, 67 % of offenders who were not threatened in this way claimed to have been abused in childhood. Since the threatened group reported less childhood abuse this has been interpreted as evidence that offenders fake their responses to questioning (Freund, Watson and Dickey, 1990). Howitt (1995a) further suggested that, on the one hand, reporting childhood abuse may be a self-serving excuse but, equally, the sex offender group may have denied a history of childhood abuse as the safest way to avoid re-imprisonment and

> Given that the lie-detector is a controversial instrument, it might well be the safest course of action since no-one would take action against them if they had denied the abuse, despite it having occurred' (Howitt, 1995a: p. 58)

Furthermore, the two sex offender groups differed in terms of the nature of their offences and their democratic characteristics (Lee *et al.*, 2002).

The institutional contexts in which much sex-offender research takes place may inhibit disclosure and encourage or motivate distortions. For example, clinicians sometimes find sex offenders reluctant to discuss sexual fantasy. Furthermore, offenders may be inclined to overreport what they perceive to be socially acceptable fantasies. Whilst this reticence was apparent in some of the interviews we conducted, generally this was not a major factor; there were spontaneous comments during the interviews indicating the ease that some of the men felt. The question of the validity of their reports must be considered in terms of the recruitment process we employed and the motivation of the participants in taking part. All participants had freely consented to participate which may indicate that they were willing to be honest. The men had no indication that any particular response would be advantageous to them and they were aware that they were participating in academic research and nothing else. So all participants were reminded that the research was not part of their treatment or any decision-making process, for example in terms of parole, and thus they had nothing tangible to gain by being interviewed. Time was spent discussing the role of a researcher to reduce any assumptions being made concerning interrelationships between researchers and management.

On a somewhat different methodological issue, superficially, there is every reason for wanting a 'normal' control group in studies of sex offenders. However, there are equally good reasons for not including one. Put simply, it is an extremely complex judgement to decide what is an appropriate control group for sex offender studies. In what ways should the control group be similar to the offender groups? Should any differences be merely the fact of having committed a sexual offence? Despite the burgeoning research literature on sex offenders, there is no consensus as to what control factors should be included. And the practicalities of obtaining an appropriate control group can be enormously difficult.

There is also a risk of wringing all meaning out of offender research if we concentrate solely on 'things' that make offenders different from the rest of us. Frequently, it would seem that it is not the presence or absence of 'factors' that differentiate offenders from other people but the complex way in which these factors operate. For example, perhaps the need for closeness and affection is simply a human characteristic and therefore should we be surprised that offenders share this with the rest of us? However, it is the way in which this need for closeness interplays with other aspects of the lives of offenders which we must understand in paedophiles. It does not all boil down to there being a few different factors which distinguish paedophiles from the rest of us. Understanding paedophilia is not a matter of identifying a few ways in which they are different but identifying the complex process which blends various aspects together to create the sexual offence.

The lack of a 'normal' control group or even a non-sexual offender control group is typical of studies of sex offending. Take, for instance, sexual fantasy which was extensively reviewed by Leitenberg and Henning (1995). One exception to the no-control group rule in this field is Daleiden, Kaufman, Hilliker and O'Neil's (1998) study of incarcerated adolescent sex offenders, incarcerated sex offenders, incarcerated non-sex offenders and undergraduates. Interestingly, this study showed that deviant fantasy levels were not markedly different between offender and non-offenders and noted that there was a lack of fantasies with non-deviant content for the incarcerated sex offenders. Another study found greater levels of sexual fantasies involving children among child molesters than a convenience sample of non-offenders (O'Donohue, Letourneau and Dowling, 1997). Finally, Crepault and Couture (1980) found that a third of the general male population report sexual fantasies about raping a woman. Each of these studies makes us think again about how we understand fantasy in sex offenders but they do not, in themselves, completely address the processes by which sexual fantasy may become part of a process leading to offending. Normal control-group studies need to be exacting in terms of how controls are matched with offenders for the purposes of comparison. This, of course, is problematic when we note that Internet sex offenders are not typical of all sex offenders in many ways, such as their lack of a previous offence history, their age and their educational backgrounds. Furthermore, contact sex offenders tend not to have engaged with their victims violently. Hence, just how meaningful is it to compare the Internet sex offender, say, with rapists?

## WHAT WE HAVE LEARNT?

When we began to research Internet sex offenders, the driving force was the simple observation that those professionally involved with sex offenders simply did not know how to deal with the Internet sex offenders who were arriving for treatment, for example, in the probation services (Sheldon, 2004). Middleton (2004: 109) put the situation this way:

> Treatment for offenders who use the Internet to access abusive images of children are currently dependent on adapting generic treatment programmes for sexual offenders which have been developed over the last thirty years.

There was confusion as to whether such men were different from the more familiar stream of contact abusers entering treatment. The Internet offenders, of course, would deny that they would ever harm a young person and would insist, for example, that they have no place alongside the perverts who molest children. We have a simple message about this. Men who look at child pornography on the Internet are overwhelmingly paedophilic in their nature. Finding child pornography on the Internet is not accidental but the result of considerable investment of time and energy. When it is revealed that these men masturbate at their computers to this imagery of sexual abuse then our view that they are paedophiles is reinforced. But this is not all. Although there are some differences between Internet sex offenders and contact paedophiles, these pale into relative insignificance compared to the similarities they share – characteristics that are generally held to explain paedophilia such as cognitive distortions, sexual fantasies and the like.

If Internet paedophiles are so similar to contact paedophiles, this begs theoretical and practical questions as to why some 'contact offend' and others find what they want in child pornography. The ways in which they are the same cannot be the reasons why they differ in their offending behaviours. This is of importance because many of our current ways of understanding paedophile behaviour are brought into question by this. Offenders are frequently characterised as being inexorably driven to ever more serious and frequent sexual assaults on children. This is, of course, a caricature: some exhibit patterns similar to this but others seem to be one-time offenders who are unlikely to reoffend. A one-size-fits-all model does not work very well.

## BACKGROUND FACTORS

### Basic Demographics

Sexual offenders against children – contact or Internet – are similar in terms of being in a relationship at the time of their offending and likely to have dependents. They are not generally the isolated loners who fail in, or who are simply not interested in, adult relationships. We would not suggest that they experience their adult relationships in the same way as the rest of us. There are signs that theirs are fundamentally inadequate or troubled relationships. This is not surprising given their sexual responsiveness to and interest in children yet it is something that needs exploration.

For what it is worth, there were no differences in the average ages of the three types of offenders at the time of their current offence. Internet-only offenders tended to have spent more time in education than contact offenders and, perhaps as a consequence, were more likely to have been in professional occupations whereas contact offenders were more likely to be manual workers. In terms of the victims of their offences, contact molesters tended to offend against their stepchildren and children of their adult partners whereas the mixed Internet-contact offenders targeted victims outside of their family. Like Internet-only offenders, mixed offenders reported relatively few previous convictions. Their prison sentences were the longest of all on average perhaps reflecting the dual nature of their offending.

### The Online Behaviour of Internet Paedophiles

Online behaviour involves considerable effort and computer skills; there is no meaningful sense in which offenders 'accidentally' come across child pornography. The process involves intent: Internet offenders subscribe to Web sites, take part in newsgroups geared towards child pornography and other forms of online sex and use sites which distribute MP3 music files and the like, which can contain child pornography. Frequently they build up digital collections of child pornography. There seems to be no doubt that Internet pornography offenders have a strong sexual interest in children just like traditional paedophiles. Nevertheless, they can curb their sexual desires in that they do not directly molest children. This desistance is not unexpected because, as Mair (1995) pointed out, sexual desire is not curable but sexual behaviour is. Many heterosexual males, despite finding women highly sexually stimulating, do not assault or regularly approach them sexually. And, homosexual and heterosexual celibacy is possible, after all (Howitt, 2006b). If one group of paedophiles can desist, what stops contact offenders from doing so?

## Offline Behaviour of Internet Paedophiles

The proportion of downloaders of child pornography who actually engage in contact offences should not be overstated (Taylor and Quayle, 2003). According to Taylor and Quayle, producers of child pornography are rare and this is much as we also found. Only one man we studied took photographs for distribution via the Internet. However, four offenders we studied took photographs or videos of their victims but for personal consumption alone. There are no indications that substantial numbers of men commissioned the production of child abuse photographs or direct sexual assaults on children in order to videoconference pictures or stream the assaults on live Web cams. Furthermore, only two of the offenders we studied had attempted to groom a child for sexual purposes on the Internet.

Small proportions of offenders engage in these more extreme forms of Internet crime, which contrasts with the substantially larger numbers who access the Internet in order to access child pornography. In this context, it is worth recalling Seto and Eke's (2005) finding that despite the fact that 17 % of child pornography offenders had re-offended in some way within 30 months, only 4 % of them reoffended by committing a contact sexual offence. The Internet offenders most likely to reoffend were those who had committed either a previous or concurrent contact sexual offence. These are very much like our group of mixed Internet/contact offenders. This suggests that among the major challenges for practitioners working with sex offenders in the future will be the development of assessment tools, which effectively discriminate between those who are little or no threat to children and those who may present a chronic problem by going on to abuse children directly.

## Childhood Adversity

Adverse and neglectful experiences in childhood have been implicated in paedophile development. However, Internet sex offenders seem to experience much the same sorts of neglect in their childhoods. Internet and contact offenders of all sorts frequently described experiences of parenting in childhood that were at best inconsistent or which pushed them towards independence. At worst, they had experienced physically abusive, cold and rejecting parenting. Both types of offender shared a pattern of insecure childhood attachment to their parents. They differed in just one regard – contact-only offenders reported that their mothers were less protective; their mothers encouraged them to be prematurely independent, which may have put them at a greater risk of being a victim of sexual abuse (cf. Marshall, 1989; Marshall and Marshall, 2000). Contact and mixed sex offenders describe how, in childhood, they sought substitutes in peers and adult abusers for the parental warmth that was lacking in their lives (Alexander, 1992; Rich, 2006). The consequences of their less-than-optimal parenting can be found in some of their childhood sexual experiences. Most importantly, the offenders whose mothers were low on control and protection tended to have engaged in sexual play with peers before the age of 12 years of age – especially in the cases of the Internet and mixed Internet/contact offenders. The lack of control and protection by their parents perhaps facilitates and encourages these early sexual experiences. Furthermore, these sexual experiences were not simply sexual explorations; it was common that the offender, as a child, was seeking warmth and affection from peers. This sexual play is different from mere youthful sexual exploration because of its emotional features, which may partially explain paedophiles' emotional and sexual commitment to children.

## Childhood Attachment

A crucial concept in child psychology is Bowlby's idea of childhood attachment, which essentially identifies problems of interpersonal security and early bonding with separation from the key caregiver, usually the mother, at a crucial point in the child's life. The research evidence indicates that sex offenders have problems of attachment in childhood but it is not conclusive that these differ from the problems of offenders in general. In other words, attachment deficits are linked to criminality and not sex offending in particular (Marshall, Serran and Cortoni, 2000; Rich, 2006; Smallbone and Dadds, 1998; Smallbone and McCabe, 2003). The offenders we studied generally had suboptimal attachment with their parents. Nevertheless, the three offender groups essentially did not differ in their childhood attachment styles.

## Sexualisation in Childhood

Paedophiles frequently describe childhoods replete with sexual encounters. Some of their accounts are so routinely filled with sexual episodes that, at times, they might almost be an extension of the offenders' sexual fantasies. While we cannot dismiss this possibility entirely, taken at their face value, these accounts of early sexual experiences often set the scene for later offending. Childhood sexual abuse is not universal in paedophiles despite what a 'cycles of abuse' explanation of paedophilia might demand and sexual abuse is less common for Internet offenders. However, we would stress the role that peer sex and similar early sexualisation experiences may play in the development of paedophilia. All three groups we studied shared characteristically sexualised upbringings. Extensive histories of sex with peers were a more distinctive feature of offenders' childhoods than sexual abuse. In the sexual abuse research literature and in law, sexual abuse of children by adults is regarded as damaging and having greater effects than peer sex, which is viewed as relatively benign and a natural thing rather than the perversion of sexual abuse. This is not a view for which our findings lend support. We found that sex play with peers was extensive in the childhoods of the men we studied – especially those whose sexual crimes involved the Internet.

One might expect relationships between childhood sexualisation experiences (both abuse and peer sex) and the cognitive and behavioural characteristics of offenders. We observed some remarkable links between childhood sexualisation and things relevant to offending. Those who engaged in sexualised play with peers when under the age of 12 years tended to have higher levels of paedophilic fantasy and there were many examples in our interviews with offenders of what can be described as 'children-are-sexual-beings' distortions. There were also thematic parallels between early childhood sexual experiences and the sexual fantasies of offenders. For example, sometimes a concordance was found between the characteristics of the offender's own childhood abuse and his offending both in terms of the familial relationship to the victim and age of the victim. This may imply that sexual fantasy is grounded in the early experience of offenders rather than being the creative product of a fertile imagination.

## Factors in Adulthood

### Adult Relationships

Early attachment is important in that this is a template for attachment in future adult relationships (Bowlby, 1977, 1979). Because the early experiences of sex offenders are adverse in terms of attachment, offenders-as-children are at risk of adopting insecure adult relationships styles (Marshall, 1989; Marshall and Marshall, 2000). There are suggestions that different types of sex offender have different types of attachment as adults (Ward et al., 1996). We found that Internet sex offenders were most commonly in the secure adult attachment category whereas contact and mixed offenders were fearful or preoccupied in their relationship styles. Not only are paedophiles likely to be insecure in adult relationships but they also have an idealised view of children and evidence more emotional commitment to them. This is the result of childhood experiences resulting in the dual consequences of (a) encouraging the view of children as supportive and warm and at the same time, (b) leading to the perception of adults as rejecting (Wilson, 1999). Internet offenders seem more secure in their adult relationships than other offender groups, which may help to explain why they have less need to seek out the proximity of children with its attendant risk of sexual offending in men who equate intimacy with sex.

### Coping with Stress

Negative situations accompanied by negative moods were present prior to and/or during their sexual offending for all types of offender that we studied, including Internet offenders. The men spoke of long-term difficulties including substance abuse and social intimacy problems. Yet, in contrast, all types described using a range of seemingly adaptive coping strategies in relation to their problems though this may be misleading. Consequently, just what made the situation prior to the offending so stressful that effective coping strategies could not be employed thereby preventing offending. Just one coping strategy seems to differentiate contact and mixed offenders from the Internet-only group; that was that they used ineffective emotional coping strategies for stress. So, for example, the contact and mixed contact-Internet offenders were more likely to respond to stress by getting angry, feeling anxious and being preoccupied with aches and pains.

## COGNITIONS AND PAEDOPHILIA

Although numerous factors have been offered as explanations of paedophilia, only a few have been systematically researched in depth. Factors that can be modified in therapy constitute the 'cognitive basis' of paedophile offending and, thus, are particularly important in thinking about paedophilia (Beech et al., 1999; Brown, 2005). Such cognitive factors include sexual fantasy and cognitive distortions *inter alia*. For whatever reason, Internet sexual offenders are generally put through the same treatment programmes as contact offenders (Middleton, 2004), which implies that Internet offenders can benefit from cognitive behaviour therapy and that, by and large, they have the same therapeutic needs as contact offenders. Otherwise, the use of cognitive behavioural therapies with such offenders might be counterproductive.

### Sexual Fantasy and Paedophilia

The sexual fantasies of sex offenders are frequently regarded as blueprints guiding their offending. Thus, the generation of fantasy through Internet child pornography is held to lead to offending behaviour. This view of sexual fantasy is not only simplistic but it is also inadequate in the light of our findings and what is generally known about sexual fantasy in non-offender groups. Internet sex offenders have the highest levels of sexual fantasies of a paedophilic nature. This is not surprising if it is assumed that they are fantasists whose main paedophilic activity is masturbating to child pornography images or fantasising during sex with an adult partner. On the other hand, if it is assumed that fantasy is the vehicle to the eventual sexual abuse of children, then why should Internet-only offenders have more sexual fantasy? Recent research, which is in keeping with the idea that Internet offenders are fantasists, has found that child pornography offenders show greater sexual arousal to child images than to adults. Comparison groups such as contact sex offenders against children, sex offenders against adults and general sexology patients did not show this pattern to this extent (Seto et al., 2006).

Internet offenders report a wide range of normal and deviant sexual fantasies. Nevertheless, there is a lack of one-to-one relationships between sexual fantasy content and offending behaviour. That is, there is no clear link between an offender's characteristic victims and the characteristics of the children in their sexual fantasies (though this is not true for contact offenders). For example, Internet offenders 'targeted' both boys and girls in terms of the material that they downloaded yet reported low levels of fantasy involving boys. Now there may be a big difference in this case between the mass downloading of material, which led to their convictions, and their preference for girls rather than boys in terms of sexual stimulation and fantasy. Possibly their interest in both sexes may be confined to their collecting behaviour and may be as much a consequence of their mass file-downloading collecting strategies as any proclivity for both genders sexually. Internet offenders select from their collections suitable child pornography images to accompany their masturbation, which further suggests that their collecting needs to be differentiated from their sexual needs.

Contact offenders tended to target only female victims yet they reported the lowest levels of girl fantasies. One possibility is that contact offenders have problems generating fantasy compared to Internet offenders (Sheldon and Howitt, in press). Interviews with offenders sometimes provided evidence that the function of offending may actually be to generate fantasy not vice versa. One problem with this, though, is that contact offenders tended to have more confrontational sexual fantasies.

The fact that the contact offenders tended to have lower levels of paedophilic ('normal') adult and force fantasies needs to be considered alongside the fact that non-offenders may have similar fantasies (Briere and Runtz, 1989; Crepault and Couture, 1980; Greendlinger and Byrne, 1987; Leitenberg and Henning, 1995). Of particular relevance is Hall et al.'s (1995) meta-analysis of studies of the effectiveness of sex offender treatments on recidivism. One important finding was that there was a negative effect size for therapies directed mainly at fantasy reduction. Assuming that therapy had indeed reduced fantasy, then the implication of the negative effect size is that decreasing fantasy actually increases the risk of reoffending! This might encourage the view that sexual fantasy, rather than being a stimulus for sexual offending has a 'cathartic' or 'safety valve' function, which reduces the risk of offending. Thus, contact offenders lacking such good fantasy-generating resources are at greater risk of offending. One problem with this explanation is that mixed Internet-contact offenders show high levels of homosexual, heterosexual and confrontational non-contact adult fantasies but they did contact offend.

The big gap between expectations about and the realities of sexual fantasy in relation to sexual offending creates difficulties for simplistic explanations of sexual offending against children. It is a common assumption in writings on pornography and sex offending, in general, that pornography encourages sex offending. Such a view is also expressed in terms of the belief that Internet child pornography will eventually drive users to offend sexually against children directly (Sullivan and Beech, 2003). Internet child pornography forms an early stage in an escalating process, which eventually culminates in contact sexual offences against children. This is a difficult issue for research to address and a completely satisfactory evaluation is elusive. Nevertheless, there is clear evidence of a group of sex offenders who view abusive images and then progress onto contact offences on children; this group consists of the men that we identify as mixed Internet/contact offenders. According to their accounts, the contact offence often followed their use of Internet child pornography. On the other hand, there is another group of men who clearly enjoy viewing child pornography images, derive fantasy from this and masturbate to the child images but, nevertheless, have no known history of sexually offending against children directly. What we know about this group seems to challenge the stereotype of the Internet sex offender as an organised paedophile who conspires with others to distribute images of children as part of the more general pattern of sexual interest in children. Of course, media coverage of police operations such as Cathedral would suggest that there are offenders in regular contact with each other (paedophile rings) as part of their extensive pattern of sexual crime. Some Internet offenders may fit this stereotype but others most certainly do not. Some Internet-only offenders appear to be social isolates on the Internet and many of them have no previous sexual offences against children.

## Cognitive Distortions and Offending

Perhaps among the most dramatic revisions of conventional ideas on paedophiles promoted by this book concerns the role of cognitive distortions in offending. Based on the idea that cognitions drive offending behaviour, it might be supposed that contact offenders have more cognitive distortions conducive to contact offending than Internet-only offenders, simply because Internet-only offenders do not act out their sexual interest on children directly. There was no support for this; contact-only offenders had the lowest levels of endorsement of the cognition distortions that regard 'children as sexual beings'. Internet-only and mixed Internet/contact sexual offenders endorsed this type of cognitive distortion more readily. Thus there is a poor fit between our findings and prevalent assumptions that cognitive distortions somehow 'drive' offending behaviour. The explanation of this may relate to the different childhood experiences of Internet and contact offenders (Sheldon and Howitt, 2005). Internet offenders are more likely to report sex-play experiences as a child rather than sexual abuse. Peer-sex may have been experienced in a positive way amid the adverse family circumstances that often applied, which may help create the belief in the offender that children enjoy sex because the offender, as a child, did (Howitt, 1995a). Internet-only offenders have few opportunities to have their cognitions about children as sexual beings tested against reality since they do not sexually offend directly against children–rather they tend to prefer child pornography that presents children as enjoying their abuse.

### Desistance

Internet offenders claim that their reason for not sexually assaulting children was that their sexual interest was in deviant fantasy and not deviant sex. The primary function of pornography in their lives was to stimulate themselves sexually. In other words, the idea that child pornography in some way instigates contact offences (see, for example, Goldstein, 1999) does not apply to these men (in their view). Of course, we know little or nothing about those men who sexually fantasize about children but do not seek child pornography from the Internet or elsewhere. Indeed, it is merely conjecture that such a group exists although there are hints in the research literature that sexual interest in children is commoner than paedophile convictions would suggest.

## WHAT IS TO BE DONE?

By exploring Internet sex offending, perhaps inevitably we have also learnt something about paedophiles in general. Crucially, there are frequent mis-matches between what we appear to know about contact paedophiles and the application of this knowledge to Internet sex offenders. It is probably at least as equally important to refine our views of conventional paedophiles as it is to suggest that Internet sex offenders are different. In this final section, the general issue of what is to be done about Internet sex offenders comes into focus. This is a wide question encompassing the work of many different professions and agencies.

### Policing

Many of the findings arising from the previous chapters pose difficulties for law-enforcement agencies, which are attempting to regulate online content. Law-enforcement agencies worldwide grapple continuously with the number of individuals suspected of Internet-based sex offences. The first profile police operations directed against Internet traded child pornography in the UK and the first arrests of individuals began only in the mid- to late-1990s (Jones, 2003; Renold et al., 2003). The picture is much the same elsewhere. The number of individuals identified from police operations such as Operation Ore also has an impact on police investigations.

There are many policing difficulties ranging from the matter of defining illegal child pornography (including such simple but important issues as the age of a child, which varies internationally in law) to difficulties inherent in the nature of the technology itself such as encryption of images and anonymous remailing. Jewkes and Andrews (2005) discuss a number of implications to the range of policing problems. Not the least of these is the fact that funding is a problem; police priorities are assessed by reference to government-set key performance indicators, which fail to include the effectiveness of policing child pornography. Considerable amounts of time are needed to examine forensically computer hardware that may contain large numbers of files of which only a few may be illegal child pornography. Other policing implications stemming from Internet child pornography include the risk of distress and trauma among police officers exposed to these images in their professional capacity, the police's internal culture which may not willingly embrace technological innovations required to effectively police the Internet for child pornography and the difficulties that the police face in training officers effectively in a field that lacks a sound knowledge base (Jewkes and Andrews, 2005).

Despite considerable policing efforts, few children are ever identified from Internet-mediated child pornography pictures (Holland, 2005). Interpol estimates that a total of 297 victims of child abuse images on the Internet have been identified worldwide (Holland, 2005). (The accuracy of the figure is difficult to establish as Interpol does not receive notification of all identifications.) Yet victim identification is one of the well-publicised cornerstone arguments for directing policing effort towards policing child pornography images on the Internet. Holland (2005) argues that such low figures for victim identification are the result of a number of factors. Firstly, whose problem is it? The Internet has no geographical boundaries. If analysis establishes that a child-abuse image was produced in a particular country then the main onus is on the police in that area to investigate. But what if there is no obvious location for the image, who will investigate then? Secondly, identification is done on an *ad hoc* basis; the strategy is left to various police agencies to choose rather than more embracing overall strategic planning which leaves disparities internationally. Overall, there appears to be a lack of national and international policies relating to victim identification. However, the policing of the Internet can rapidly change and some recent developments are thought to have led to an improvement in positive victim identifications (Holland, 2005). For instance, in 2003 Interpol created the International Victim Identification Group. Twenty investigators across several countries, including the UK, share information across a virtual network. This is thought to have increased victim identification in comparison with previous face-to-face meetings. This highlights the importance of the speedy sharing of information and inter-agency cooperation. International cooperation is important, as Operation Ore illustrated, in the regulation of online content.

Strategies aimed at tackling the problem of Internet pornography can only be welcomed. For example, face recognition computer software has been phased in recently, which can scan the faces of Internet child abuse victims

(Jewkes and Andrews, 2005). The big advantage of this is that it minimises the duplication of work, reduces the extent to which officers need to view distressing pictures and identifies new victims for prioritisation (Jewkes and Andrews, 2005). Furthermore, the police now exploit the anonymous nature of the Internet by posing as children in chat rooms as part of 'sting' operations.

Policing the Internet has become a complex endeavour in which the police are just a part. Instead it involves non-police regulatory bodies such as Internet service providers, government bodies and hotline providers (Jewkes and Andrews, 2005). Increasing emphasis is being placed on self-regulation by the technology industry (Akdeniz, 2006). It could be asked whether Internet offending might be tackled by simply blocking sites which contain offending material. Recently both Vodafone and BT have indicated that they will do this (Howitt, 2006b). Some commentators remain cautious, however, about the value of shutting down illegal Web sites unless there is evidence that the same material would not simply appear elsewhere or be distributed by different means (Howitt, 2006b). Blocking, itself, risks interfering with free commu-nication and, according to Williams (2005), should only be allowed if it is justified. For example, is it right to block all naked pictures of children irrespective of how or for what purpose they were produced? Article 10 of the European Convention on Human Rights sets the standard, which says that blocking is only permissible when it is prescribed by law, prevents a crime, protects morals or protects the rights of others. This is a complex judgement, as we have already seen, and means that material to be blocked would have to be viewed before being released publicly, resulting in an expensive process. The standards for blocking or removing the material would also differ from jurisdiction to jurisdiction. Williams (2005) argues that an alternative is to employ more preventative tools such as placing warnings onto sites in an attempt to dissuade individuals browsing the Internet from viewing the material. The success of warnings has not yet been assessed (Quayle and Taylor, 2005; Quayle et al., 2006; Taylor and Quayle, 2003) but again would require human intervention to analyse the material in order to establish whether it is pornographic, which may make the cost prohibitive (Williams, 2005). Furthermore, such warnings may have a negative impact – indeed some of our interviewees talked of the taboo nature of the material as appealing or stimulating and the attraction of seeing something illegal. The warnings may also become too commonplace and we do not know whether their effective-ness may be reduced by their frequency (Williams, 2005).

Of course, we know from our research and other research that illegal activity on the Internet is conducted in a context of forensic awareness on the part of perpetrators, so there is clearly a question of the extent to which, currently, policing the Internet is merely a chase that offenders will generally win. Resources are finite so the issue is where best to place the resources that are available. Closing down illegal sites and arresting illegal Internet child pornography users is a short-term objective. The major long-term objective is reducing the number of children who are sexually abused in childhood. There is no reason to think that these long-term goals will be substantially facilitated by the short-term goals. Most Internet child pornography offenders will not go on to contact abuse children and there is evidence that those who use Internet child pornography but go on to contact offend against children have such a predilection irrespective of their use of child pornography on the Internet. At the same time, we know that some men use the Internet to contact children for abusive purposes. This is not all men who communicate in chat rooms since some appear to be fantasists rather than perpetrators. Perhaps those most at risk of abusing a child in real life ought to be the primary target for policing; these generally are not the majority of child-pornography downloaders. Furthermore, as damaged childhoods are, in part, responsible for some children growing up to be child molesters then focusing on this may have more significant long-term consequences; we know that youthful sex offenders carry out a high proportion of sex offences so intervention with such damaged young people may be amongst the most effective strategies for preventing future child molestation.

## Clinical Work

Caution must apply to recommendations for clinical practice based on what we now know about Internet offenders. For instance, while it is clear that there are differences in sexual fantasy between Internet and contact offenders, nevertheless their fantasies are similar in many respects and, above all, both groups have sexual fantasies involving children. The most important thing is that attention should be drawn to the similarities between Internet and contact sex offenders against children; Internet offenders must be regarded as paedophile in orientation. The uncertainties that clinicians have in knowing how to deal with Internet offenders (Sheldon, 2004) cannot be fully resolved at this stage but what is abundantly clear is that Internet offenders are psychologically very similar to contact paedophiles. They report deviant sexual fantasies involving children; they masturbate to child pornography images and take time to locate preferred images. Important similarities are found in other ways such as their cognitive distortions; the circumstances that immediately preceded their offending and their general strategies for coping with stressful situations. They report similar adverse upbringings and have sexualised backgrounds either through abuse or through sex play with peers, which may result in them developing sexual scripts involving inappropriate partners.

Hence, any claims made in therapy by some Internet offenders that treatment is irrelevant to them do not stand up to careful examination. The uncertainty of practitioners about how to construe Internet sex offenders simply has not helped. Some Internet offenders are more than aware of this dilemma and check the Internet for evidence supporting their view that they are not paedophiles. Hopefully some of them will read this book, which will, on a proper reading, provide them with no comfort but perhaps a little self-understanding. The message to them is simple – you are a paedophile and need help as you may be dangerous to children. Many contact offenders pose little future risk to children so the low level of risk posed by some Internet offenders cannot be taken as an excuse for their Internet offending.

We are unable, however, to say just how many Internet child pornography offenders will go on to 'contact offend' against children though there is good reason to suspect that they will be the minority. But until it is understood what brings about the progression from Internet child-pornography use to contact offending such information is not very useful. Our research perhaps does offer some clues as to what the process may involve but not with sufficient certainty to allow clinicians to relax about all Internet child pornography offenders. We found that Internet-only offenders could be differentiated from contact offenders on the basis of background adversities and other factors to a degree. This may provide clues to the factors that should be put into a risk assessment of an Internet sex offender's likelihood of proceeding to contact sex offending in the absence of a treatment intervention. In this context, we found that some Internet-only offenders were classified statistically as contact offenders on the basis of background factors and childhood adversities. Are these the men that are most likely to go on to contact offend against children?

It is clinically important, however, that the Internet offenders, despite having similar psychological characteristics to contact offenders, represent a group with a paedophile orientation who desist (at least temporarily) from offending directly against children. Desisting needs to be understood better because it may yield information that helps clinicians facilitate desistance among contact offenders.

Much of the research discussed in this book indicates that simplistic ideas about the role of things like sexual fantasies and cognitive distortions in offending behaviour may need revision. The situation is just not as simple as suggesting that the elimination of deviant sexual fantasy will lead to reductions in offending behaviour directly, for example. Some Internet sex offenders are sexual fantasy users but these fantasies do not push them to being contact offenders against a child victim away from the virtual world. Similarly, the term cognitive distortion seems to refer to several very different processes; the notion that these distortions invariably facilitate the commission of heinous crimes is questionable.

What modern cognitive behavioural therapies for sex offenders seem to fail to handle properly are the roots of paedophile behaviour in the childhoods of offenders. Perhaps confrontation strategies common in modern therapies cause practitioners to overlook the inadequate and damaging childhoods experienced by many offenders for fear of condoning offending. But concern that something needs to be done about the damage done to offenders in their own childhood does not remove the responsibility of offenders for their offending behaviour. It simply implies that therapeutic concentration on wrongful and inadequate cognitions may be insufficient. While cognitive-behavioural therapy may de-emphasise the long-term causes of offending, this risks missing crucial things leading to offending behaviour and new ways of addressing them in therapy. Just what could modern therapies do more to address the deficits in the upbringings of offenders?

# References

ABC News (2001) *An Avalanche of Child Porn*. Retrieved 17 August from http://abcnews.go.com/sections/business/TechTV/TechTV_Avalanche_Porn_011114.html.

Abel, G. G., Becker, J. V. & Cunningham-Rathner, J. (1984) Complications, consent, and cognitions in sex between children and adults. *International Journal of Law and Psychiatry*, **7**, 89–103.

Abel, G. G., Becker, J. V., Mittelman *et al.* (1987) Self-reported sex crimes of non-incarcerated paraphiliacs. *Journal of Interpersonal Violence*, **2**, 3–25.

Abel, G. G. & Blanchard, E. D. (1974) The role of fantasy in the treatment of sexual deviation. *Archives of General Psychiatry*, **30**, 467–475.

Abel, G. G., Gore, D. K., & Holland, C. L. *et al.* (1989) The measurement of the cognitive distortions of child molesters. *Annals of Sex Research*, **2**, 135–153.

Abel, G. G., Rouleau, J. L. & Cunningham-Rathner, B. A. (1986) Sexually aggressive behaviour. In W. Curran, A. L. McGarry & S. A. Shah (eds) *Forensic Psychiatry and Psychology* (pp. 289–314). Philadelphia, PA: Davis.

Adler, A. (2001) The perverse law of child pornography. *Columbia Law Review*, **209**, 1–101.

Ainsworth, M. D. S., Blehar, M. C., Waters, E. & Wall, S. (1978) *Patterns of Attachment: A Psychological Study of the Strange Situation*. Hillsdale, NJ: Lawrence Erlbaum Associates.

Akdeniz, Y. (1997) The regulation of pornography and child pornography on the Internet. *Journal of Information, Law and Technology*. Retrieved from http://www.cyber-rights.org/reports/child.htm.

Akdeniz, Y. (2001a) Internet content regulation: UK government and the control of Internet content. *Computer, Law and Security*, **17** (5), 303–317. Retrieved from http://www.cyber-rights.org/documents/clsr17_5_01.pdf.

Akdeniz, Y. (2001b) Governing pornography and child pornography on the Internet: the UK approach, in cyber-rights, protection, and markets: a symposium. *University of West Los Angeles Law Review*, 247–275. Retrieved 1 March from http://www.cyber-rights.org/documents/us_article.pdf..

Akdeniz, Y. (2001c) *Regulation of Child Pornography on the Internet: Cases and Materials*. Retrieved 9 July 2005 from http://www.cyber-rights.org/reports/child.htm.

Akdeniz, Y. (2006) *Internet Pornography*. Paper presented at the Forensic Psychology and Crime Conference. Forensic Psychology Group/British Psychological Society (NW Branch), Manchester Metropolitan University, 4 February.

Alexander, P. C. (1992) Application of attachment theory to the study of sexual abuse. *Journal of Consulting and Clinical Psychology*, **60** (2), 185–195.

Allison, R. (2000) Doctor driven out of home by vigilantes. *Guardian*, 30 August. Retrieved 28 May 2003 from http://www.guardian.co.uk/child/story/0,,361031,00.html.

American Psychiatric Association (2000) *Diagnostic and Statistical Manual of Mental Disorders*, 4 edn. Arlington, VA: American Psychiatric Publishing.

Anderson, J., Martin, J., Mullen, P. E. *et al.* (1993) Prevalence of childhood sexual abuse experiences in a community sample of women. *Journal of American Academy of Child and Adolescent Psychiatry*, **32**, 911–919.

Anderson, K. (11 July 1997) The remoteness that betrays desire. *Times Literary Supplement Book Review.* Retrieved 4 December 2006 from http://www.wcl.american.edu/faculty/anderson/remoteness.pdf?rd=1./.

Angelides, S. (2005) The Emergence of the paedophile in the late twentieth century. *Australian Historical Studies*, **126**, 272–295.

Araji, S. K. (1997) *Sexually Aggressive Children: Coming to Understand Them.* Thousand Oaks, CA: Sage.

Arkowitz, S. & Vess, J. (2003) An evaluation of the Bumby RAPE and MOLEST scales as measures of cognitive distortions with civilly committed sexual offences. *Sexual Abuse: A Journal of Research and Treatment*, **15**, 237–249.

Arndt, W. B., Foehl, J. C. & Good, F. E. (1985) Specific sexual fantasy themes: a multidimensional study. *Journal of Personality and Social Psychology*, **48**, 472–480.

Atkinson, R. L., Atkinson, R. C., Smith, E. E. & Bem D. J. (1993) *Introduction to Psychology*, 11 edn. Fort Worth TX: Harcourt Brace Jovanovich.

Attorney General's Commission (The Meese Commission) (1986) *Final Report on Pornography*, 2 vols. Washington, DC: US Government Printing Office.

Auburn, T. (2005) Narrative reflexivity as a repair device for discounting 'cognitive distortions' in sex offender treatment. *Discourse and Society*, **16** (5), 697–718. Retrieved 30 December 2006 from http://news.bbc.co.uk/go/pr/fr/-/1/hi/world/europe/4522909.stm.

Baker, A.. W. & Duncan, S. P. (1985) Child sexual abuse; a study of prevalence in Great Britain. *Child Abuse and Neglect*, **9**, 457–467.

Bandura, A. (1977) *Social Learning Theory.* Englewood Cliffs, NJ: Prentice-Hall.

Banning, A. (1989) Mother-son incest: confronting a prejudice. *Child Abuse and Neglect*, **13**, 563–570.

Barak, A. & Fisher, W. A. (2001) Toward an Internet-based, theoretically driven, innovative approach to sex education. *The Journal of Sex Research*, **38** (4), 324–332.

Barak, A. & King, S. A. (2000) The two faces of the Internet: introduction to the special issue on the Internet and sexuality, *CyberPsychology and Behavior*, **3** (4), 517–520.

Barbaree, H. E., Seto, M. C., Langton, C. M. & Peacock, E. J. (2001) Evaluating the predictive accuracy of sex risk assessment instruments for adult sex offenders. *Criminal Justice and Behavior*, **28**, 490–521.

Baron, L. & Straus, M. (1984) Sexual stratification, pornography and rape in the United State. In N. M. Malamuth & E. Donnerstein (eds), *Pornography and Sexual Aggression* (pp. 185–209). New York: Academic Press.

Baron, L. & Straus, M. (1987) Four theories of rape: a micosociological analysis. *Social Problems*, **34**, 467–489.

Baron, L. & Straus, M. (1989) *Four Theories of Rape: A State Level Analysis.* New Haven, CT: Yale University Press.

Barron, M. & Kimmel, M. (2000) Sexual Violence in three pornographic media: toward a sociological explanation. *The Journal of Sex Research*, **37**, 161–168.

Bartholomew, A. A. (1964) Some side effects of thioridazine, *Medical Journal of Australia*, **1**, 57–59.

Bartholomew, K. & Horowitz, L. M. (1991) Attachment styles among young adults: A test of a four-category model. *Journal of Personality and Social Psychology*, **61**, 226–244.

Baxter, D. J., Marshall, W. L., Barbaree, H. E. *et al.* (1984) Deviant sexual behaviour. *Criminal Justice and Behavior*, **11**, 477–501.

BBC News (2005a) *European Police Target Child Porn.* Retrieved 19 April 2007 from http://news.bbc.co.uk/1/hi/world/europe/4522909.stm.

BBC News (2005b) *Sex offenders may face lie detector tests.* Retrieved 27 November 2006 from http://news.bbc.co.uk/1/hi/uk/2208779/stm.

BBC News (2005c) *Child porn campaign winding down.* Retrieved 30 December 2006 from http://news.bbc.co.uk/1/hi/england/norfolk/4522470.stm, 13 December.

BBC News (2006) *Two Jailed for Child Porn Library*, 20 December. Retrieved from http://news.bbc.co.uk/1/hi/england/coventry_warwickshire/619681.stm.

Beard, K. W. & Wolf, E. M. (2001) Modification of the proposed diagnostic criteria for Internet addiction. *CyberPsychology and Behavior*, **4**, 377–383.

Beech, A.. & Mitchell, I. J. (2005) A neurobiological perspective on attachment problems in sexual offenders and the role of serotonin re-uptake inhibitors in the treatment of such problems. *Clinical Psychology Review*, **25**, 153–182.

Beech, A., Fisher, D. & Beckett, R. (1999) *Step 3: An Evaluation of the Prison Sex Offender Treatment Programme. November 1998*. London: Home Office.

Beech, A., Fisher, D. & Thornton, D. (2003) Risk assessment of sex offenders. *Professional Psychology: Research and Practice*, **34**, 339–352.

Beech, A., Fisher, D. & Ward, T. (2005) Sexual murderers' implicit theories. *Journal of Interpersonal Violence*, **20**, 1366–1389.

Beech, A. & Mann, R. (2002) Recent developments in the treatment of sexual offenders. In J. McGuire (ed.) *Offender Rehabilitation: Effective Programs and Policies to Reduce Offending*. Chichester: Wiley.

Bernard, F. (1975) An enquiry among a group of pedophiles. *The Journal of Sex Research*, **11**, 242–255.

Bickley, J. A. & Beech, A. R. (2001) Classifying child abusers: its relevance to theory and clinical practice. *International Journal of Offender Therapy and Comparative Criminology*, **45**, 51–69.

Billings, A. G. & Moss, R. H. (1982) Stressful life events and symptoms: a longitudinal model. *Health Psychology*, **1**, 99–117.

Billings, A. G. & Moos, R. H. (1984) Coping, stress and social resources among adults with unipolar depression. *Journal of Personality and Social Psychology*, **46**, 877–891.

Bingham, J. E. & Piotrowski, C. (1996) On-line sexual addiction: a contemporary enigma. *Psychological Reports*, **79**, 257–258.

Blackburn, R. (1993) *The Psychology of Criminal Conduct: Theory, Research and Practice*. Chichester: John Wiley & Sons.

Blatchford, C. (1996) Internet as pornotopia? *Computers and Security*, **15** (3), 203–210.

Blumenthal, S., Gudjonsson, G. & Burns, J. (1999) Cognitive distortions and blame attribution in sex offenders against adults and children, *Child Abuse and Neglect: The International Journal*, **23** (2), 129–143.

Bonta, J. (1996) Risk-needs assessment and treatment. In A. T. Harland (ed.) *Choosing Correctional Options That Work* (pp. 18–32). Thousand Oaks: Sage.

Bottoms, A. E. (1977) Reflections on the renaissance of dangerousness. *Howard Journal of Criminal Justice*, **16**, 70–96.

Bowlby, J. (1944) Forty-four juvenile thieves, *International Journal of Psychoanalysis*, **25**, 1–57.

Bowlby, J. (1977) The making and breaking of affectional bonds. *British Journal of Psychiatry*, **130**, 201–210.

Bowlby, J. (1979) *The Making and Breaking of Affectional Bonds*. London: Tavistock Publications.

Bowlby, J., Ainsworth, M., Boston, M. & Rosenbluth, D. (1956) The effects of mother-child separation: a follow-up study. *British Journal of Medical Psychology*, **29**, 211–247.

Braun, V. & Clarke, V. (2006), Using thematic analysis in psychology, *Qualitative Research in Psychology*, **3**, 77–101.

Breckenridge, J. (1992) An exotic phenonmeon? Incest and child rape. In J. Breckenridge & M. Carmody (eds) *Crimes of Violence: Australian Responses to Rape and Child Sexual Assault* (pp. 18–37). Sydney: Allen & Unwin.

Bremer, J. (1959) *Asexualisation: A Follow-up of 244 Cases*. New York: Macmillian.

Brennan, K. A., Clark, C. L. & Shaver, P. R. (1998) Self-report measurement of adult attachment: An integrative overview. In J. A. Simpson & W. S. Rholes (eds), *Attachment Theory and Close Relationships* (pp. 46–76). New York: Guilford Press.

Brewin, C. R., Andrews, B., & Gotlib, I. H. (1993) Psychotherapy and early experience: a reappraisal of retrospective reports. *Psychological Bulletin*, **113** (1), 82–98.

Briere, J. & Runtz, M. (1989) University males' sexual interest in children: Predicting potential indices of pedophilia in a non-forensic sample. *Child Abuse and Neglect*, **13**, 65–75.

Bright, M. (2003) Sex offenders let off the hook: Thousands escape cautions because police cannot cope with the flood of child porn offences. *The Observer*, 28 September.

Britton, P. (1997) *The Jigsaw Man*. London: Corgi Books.

Brody, S. (2003) Alexithymia is inversely associated with women's frequency of vaginal intercourse. *Archives of Sexual Behavior*, **32**, 73–77.

Brookes, D. (2003) Investigating child abuse on-line: the interactive approach. In A. MacVean & P. Spindler (eds.) *Policing Paedophiles on the Internet*. John Grieve Centre for Policing and Community Safety (pp. 49–60). Bristol: The New Police Bookshop.

Brooks, A. D. (1996) Megan's Law: Constitutionality and Policy. *Criminal Justice Ethics*, Winter/Spring, 55–66.

Brown, S. (2005) *Treating Sex Offenders: An Introduction to Sex Offender Treatment Programmes*. Cullompton: Willan Publishing.

Browne, A. & Finkelhor, D. (1986) Impact of child sexual abuse: a review of the research, *Psychological Bulletin*, **99**, 66–77.

Budin, L. E. & Johnson, C. F. (1989) Sex abuse prevention programs: offender's attitudes about their efficacy. *Child Abuse and Neglect*, **13**, 77–87.

Bumby, K. M. (1996) Assessing the cognitive distortions of child molesters and rapists. *Sexual Abuse: A Journal of Research and Treatment*, **8**, 37–54.

Bureau of Justice Assistance (2006) *Jacob Wetterling Crimes Against Children and Sexually Violent Offender Registration Act*. Retrieved 27 November 2006 from http://www.ojp.usdoj.gov/BJA/what/2a2jwactbackground.html.

Burgess, A. W. & Hartman, C. (1987) Child abuse aspects of child pornography, *Psychiatric Annals*, 248–253.

Burgess, A. W., Hartman, C. R., Ressler, R. K. *et al*. (1986) Sexual homicide: A motivational model. *Journal of Interpersonal Violence*, **1** (3), 251–272.

Burgess, A. W., Hazelwood, R. R., Rokous, F. E. *et al*. (1988) Serial rapists and their victims: reenactment and repetition. In R. A. Prentky & V. L. Quinsey (eds) *Human Sexual Aggression: Current Perspectives*, Annals of the New York Academy of Science, Vol. 528, 12 August (pp. 277–295). New York: New York Academy of Science.

Burk, L. R. & Burkhart, B. R. (2003) Disorganized attachment as a diathesis for sexual deviance: Developmental experience and the motivation for sexual offending. *Aggression and Violent Behavior*, **8**, 487–511.

Burke, A., Sowerbutts, S., Blundell, B. & Sherry, M. (2001) *Child Pornography and the Internet: Policing and Treatment Issues*. Paper presented at the ANZAPPL conference, Melbourne, Australia.

Burns, E. (2005) *The Year in Search: A 2005 Review*, 21 December. ClickZ Stats. Retrieved 30 December 2006 from http://www.clickz.com/showPage.html?page=3572746.

Burt, M. R. (1980) Cultural myths and supports for rape. *Journal of Personality and Social Psychology*, **38**, 217–230.

Butler Committee (1975) *Report of the Committee on Mentally Abnormal Offenders*. London: Home Office.

Calder, J. (2005) Histories of child abuse. In C. Newnes & N. Radcliffe (eds) *Making and Breaking Children's Lives*. Ross-on-Wye: PCCS Books.

Calder, M. C. (2004) The Internet: potential, problems and pathways to hands-on sexual offending. In M. C. Calder (ed.) *Child Sexual Abuse and the Internet: Tackling the New Frontier* (pp. 1–23). Lyme Regis, Dorset: Russell House Publishing.

Cantwell, H. B. (1988) Child sexual abuse: very young perpetrators. *Child Abuse and Neglect*, **12**, 579–582.

Caplan, S. E. (2002) Problematic Internet use and psychosocial well-being: development of a theory-based cognitive-behavioral measurement instrument. *Computers in Human Behavior*, **18**, 553–575.

Carr, J., (2003) *Child abuse, child pornography and the Internet*. National Children's Home. Retrieved 11 April 2005 from http://www.nch.org.uk..

Carvel, J. (2006) 'Megan's law won't work; Reid warned. *Guardian*, Thursday 22 June.

Cawson, P., Wattam, C., Brooker, S. & Kelly, G. (2000) *Child Maltreatment in the UK: A Study of the Prevalence of Child Abuse and Neglect*. London, NSPCC.

Children's Act (1989) Retrieved 6 February 2007 from http://www.opsi.gov.uk/acts/acts1989/Ukpga_19890041_en_1.htm.

Chou, C., Condon, L. & Belland, J. C. (2005) A review of the research on Internet addiction. *Educational Psychology Review*, **17** (4), 363–388.

Christensen, J. R. & Blake, R. H. (1990) The grooming process in father-daughter incest. In Horton, A. L., Johnson, B. L., Roundy, L. M., Williams, D. (eds) *The Incest Perpetrator: A Family Member No-one Wants to Treat*. London: Sage Publications.

Cleveland Report (1988) *Report of the Inquiry into Child Abuse in Cleveland 1987* (CM 412). London: HMSO.

Clyde Report (1992) *The Report of the Inquiry of the Removal of Children from Orkney in February 1991*. Edinburgh: HMSO.

Cohen, L. J. & Galynker, I. I. (2002) Clinical features of pedophilia and implications for treatment. *Journal of Psychiatric Practice*, **8** (5), 276–289.

Cohen, L. J., McGeoch, P. G., Watras Gans, S. *et al.* (2002) Childhood sexual history of 20 male pedophiles vs 24 healthy control subjects. *Journal of Nervous and Mental Disease*, **190** (11), 1–10.

Cohen, M. L., Seghorn, T. & Calmas, W. (1969) Sociometric study of sex offenders. *Journal of Abnormal Psychology*, **74**, 249–255.

Coleman, C. & Norris, C. (2000) *Introducing Criminology*. Cullompton: Willian.

Coleman, E. (1992) Is your patient suffering from compulsive sexual behaviour. *Psychiatric Annals*, **22** (6), 320–325.

Commission on Obscenity and Pornography (1970) *Report*. New York: Bantam.

Committee on Pornography and Prostitution (1985) *Report*. Ottawa: Supply and Services.

Condron, M. K. & Nutter, D. E. (1988) A preliminary examination of the pornography experience of sex offenders, paraphiliac sexual dysfunction and controls. *Journal of Sex and Marital Therapy*, **14** (4), 285–298.

Condy, B., Templer, D., Brown, R. & Veaco, L. (1987) Parameters of sexual contact of boys with women. *Archives of Sexual Behavior*, **16**, 379–394.

Cooper, A. (1998) Sexuality and the Internet: Surfing into the new millennium. *CyberPsychology and Behavior*, **1** (2), 187–193.

Cooper, A., McLoughlin, I. P. and Campbell, K. M. (2000) Sexuality in cyberspace: Update for the 21st century. *Cyberpsychology and Behaviour*, **3**, 521–536.

Cooper, A., Putnam, D. E., Planchon, L. A. & Boies, S. C. (1999) Online sexual compulsivity: getting tangled in the Net. *Sexual Addiction and Compulsivity: The Journal of Treatment and Prevention*, **6** (2), 79–104.

Cooper, A., Scherer, C. R., Boies, S. C. & Gordon, B. L. (1999) Sexuality on the Internet: from sexual exploration to pathological expression. *Professional Psychology: Research and Practice*, **30**, 154–164.

Cooper, A. & Sportolari, L. (1997) Romance in cyberspace: Understanding online attraction. *Journal of Sex Education and Therapy*, **22** (1), 7–14.

Cortoni, F. & Marshall, W. L. (2001) Sex as a coping strategy and its relationship to juvenile sexual history and intimacy in Sexual Offenders. *Sexual Abuse: A Journal of Research and Treatment*, **13** (1), 27–43.

Council of Europe (1991) *Sexual Exploitation, Pornography and Prostitution of, and Trafficking in, Children and Young Adults. Recommendation R (91) 11*. Strasbourg: Council of Europe.

Council of Europe (1993) *Sexual Exploitation, Pornography and Prostitution of, and Trafficking in, Children and Adults. Recommendation NO. R (91) 11 and Report of the European Committee on Crime Problems*. Strasbourg: Council of Europe.

Court, J. H. (1977) Pornography and sex crimes: a re-evaluation in the light of recent trends around the world. *International Journal of Criminality and Penology*, **5**, 129–157.

Court, J. H. (1984) Sex and violence: a ripple effect. In N. M. Malamuth & E. Donnerstein (eds), *Pornography and Sexual Aggression* (pp. 143–172). Orlando, FL: Academic Press.

Cowburn, M. & Dominelli, L. (2001) Masking Hegemonic Masculinity: Reconstructing the Paedophile as the Dangerous Stranger. *British Journal of Social Work*, **31**, 399–415.

Cowling, M. (1998) *Date Rape and Consent*. Aldershot: Ashgate.

Craissati, J. & McClurg, G. (1996) The challenge project: perpetrators of child sexual abuse in south east London. *Child Abuse and Neglect*, **20** (11), 1067–1077.

Craissati, J., McClurg, G. & Browne, K. (2002) The parental bonding experiences of sex offenders: a comparison between child molesters and rapists. *Child Abuse and Neglect*, **26**, 909–921.

Cramer, D. & Howitt, D. (1998) Romantic love and the psychology of sexual behaviour open and closed secrets. In V. C. de Munck (ed.) *Romantic Love and Sexual Behaviour Perspectives from the Social Sciences* (pp. 113–132). Westport, CT: Praeger.

Cramer, D. & Howitt, D. (2004) *Sage Dictionary of Statistics*. London: Sage.

Crepault, C. & Couture, M. (1980) Men's erotic fantasies. *Archives of Sexual Behavior*, **9**, 565–581.

Daily Telegraph (2004) *Sex offenders register grows by 15 per cent*, 28 July. Retrieved from http://www.telegraph.co.uk/news/main.jhtml?xml=/news/2004/07/28/uoffend.xml&sSheet=/portal/2004/07/28/ixportaltop.html.

Daleiden, E. L., Kaufman, K. L., Hilliker, D. R. & O'Neil, J. N. (1998) The sexual histories and fantasies of youthful males: a comparison of sexual offending, nonsexual offending and non-offending groups. *Sexual Abuse: A Journal of Research and Treatment*, **10** (3), 195–209.

Dandescu, A. & Wolfe, R. (2003) Considerations on fantasy use by child molesters and exhibitionists. *Sexual Abuse: A Journal of Research and Treatment*, **15** (4), 297–305.

Davidson, J. K., (1985) The utilization of sexual fantasies by sexually experienced university students. *Journal of American College Health*, **34**, 24–32.

Davidson, K. & Hoffman, L. (1986) Sexual fantasies and sexual satisfaction: an empirical analysis of erotic thought. *Journal of Sex Research*, **22**, 184–205.

Davis, G. E. & Leitenberg, H. (1987) Adolescent sex offenders, *Psychological Bulletin*, **101**, 417–427.

Davis, M. H. (1983) Measuring individual differences in empathy: evidence for a multidimensional approach. *Journal of Personality and Social Psychology*, **44** (1), 113–126.

Davis, R. A. (2001) A cognitive-behavioral model of pathological Internet use. *Computers in Human Behavior*, **17**, 187–195.

D'Cruze, S. (2004) *Protection, Harm and Social Evil: the Age of Consent since 1885*. Paper presented at the Evil, Law and the State Conference, Oxford, July 2004. Retrieved 18 April 2007 from http://www.wickedness.net/els/els1/dcruze%20paper.pdf.

Demetriou, C. & Silke, A. (2003) A criminological Internet sting; experimental evidence of illegal and deviant visits to a website trap. *British Journal of Criminology*, **43**, 213–222.

Department of Health (1999) *Working Together to Safeguard Children*. London: HMSO.

De Young, M. (1988) The indignant page: techniques of neutralization in the publications of pedophile organizations. *Child Abuse and Neglect*, **12**, 583–591.

De Young, M. (1989) The world according to NAMBLA: Accounting for deviance. *Journal of Sociology and Social Welfare*, **16**, 111–126.

DHSS (Department of Health and Social Security) (1974) *Non-accidental Injury to Children: Area Review Committees*. Circular LASSL (74) 13. London: DHSS.

DHSS (Department of Health and Social Security) (1976) *Non-accidental Injury to Children: The Police and Case Conferences*. Circular LASSL (76) 26. London: DHSS.

Donnerstein, E. & Berkowitz (1981) Victim reactions in aggressive erotic films as a factor in violence against women, *Journal of Personality and Social Psychology*, **41**, 710–724.

Doward, J. (2003) '500 paedophiles to be tracked by satellite tags', *Observer*, 21 September. Retrieved 21 September 2003 from http://www.guardian.co.uk/child/story/0,1046634,00.html.

Dowd, C. (2003) Operation Cathedral Prosecutor's Perspective. In A. MacVean & P. Spindler (eds) *Policing Paedophiles on the Internet*. John Grieve Centre for Policing and Community Safety. Bristol: The New Police Bookshop.

Drake, C. R. & Ward, T. (2003a) Practical and theoretical roles for the formulation based treatment of sexual offenders. *International Journal of Forensic Psychology*, **1**, 71–84.

Drake, C. R. & Ward, T. (2003b) Treatment models of sexual offenders. In T. Ward, D. R. Laws. & S. M. Hudson, (eds) *Sexual Deviance: Issues and Controversies* (pp. 226–43). Thousand Oaks, CA: Sage.

Drake, C. R., Ward, T., Nathan, P. & Lee, J. K. P., (2001) Challenging the cognitive distortions of child molesters: an implicit theory approach. *Journal of Sexual Aggression*, **7** (2), 25–40.

Dube, R. & Hebert, M. (1988) Sexual abuse of children under 12 years of age: a review of 511 cases. *Child Abuse and Neglect*, **12**, 321–330.

Dunn, L. W., Corn, A. L. & Morelock, M. J. (2004) The relationship between scores on the ICMIC and selected talent domains: an investigation with gifted adolescents. *Gifted Child Quarterly* **48** (2), 133–142.

Durkin, K. F. (1997) Misuse of the Internet by paedophiles: implications for law enforcement and probation practice. *Federal Probation*, **61**, 14–18.

Durkin, K. F. & Bryant, C. D., (1995) Log on to Sex: some notes on the carnal computer and erotic cyberspace as an emerging research frontier, *Deviant Behavior: An Interdisciplinary Journal*, **16**, 179–200.

ECPAT (1996) *Child Pornography on the Internet: A position paper for ECPAT International.* Retrieved 23 February 2003 from http://www.crin.org/isac/sedoc11.html.

Edwards, S. (1995) Suffer little children: the government's proposals on child pornography. *Child and Family Law Quarterly*, **7** (2), 49–59.

Edwards, S. S. M. (2000) Prosecuting 'child pornography': possession and taking of indecent photographs of children, *Journal of Social Welfare and Family Law*, **22** (1), 1–21.

Edwards, W. & Hensley C. (2001) Contextualising sex offender management legislation and policy: Evaluating the problem of latent consequence in community notification laws. *International Journal of Offender Therapy and Comparative Criminology*, **45**, 83–101.

Elbogen, E. B., Patry, M. & Scalora, M. J. (2003) The impact of community notification laws on sex offender treatment attitudes. *International Journal of Law and Psychiatry*, **26**, 207–219.

Elliot, A. N. & Carnes, C. N. (2001) Reactions of non-offending parents to the sexual abuse of their child: A review of the literature. *Child Maltreatment*, **6** (4), 314–331.

Elliot, M. (1992) Images of children in the media: 'soft kiddie porn'. In C. Itzin (ed.) *Pornography: Women, Violence and Civil Liberties* (pp. 217–221). Oxford: Oxford University Press.

Elliot, M., Browne, K. and Kilcoyne, J. (1995) Child sexual abuse prevention: what offenders tell us. *Child Abuse and Neglect*, **19** (5), 579–594.

Ellis, B. J. & Symons, D. (1990) Sex differences in sexual fantasy: An evolutionary psychological approach. *Journal of Sex Research*, **27**, 527–555.

Endler, N. S. & Parker, J. D. A. (1989) Coping with frustrations to self-realisation: stress, anxiety, crises, and adjustment. In E. Krau (ed.) *Self-Realisation, Success and Adjustment* (pp. 153–164). New York: Praeger Publishers.

Endler, N. S. & Parker, J. D. A. (1990) Multidimensional assessment of coping: a critical evaluation. *Journal of Personality and Social Psychology*, **58** (5), 844–854.

Europol (2005) *Child Pornography: Legislation within the European Union.* Retrieved 28 December 2006 from http://www.europol.eu.int/publications/Other/Reports% 202005/Legislation%20on%20Child%20Pornography%20Public1.pdf.

Everywoman (1988) *Pornography and Sexual Violence: Evidence of the Links.* London: Everywoman.

Federoff, J. P. and Moran, B. (1997) Myths and misconceptions about sex offenders. *Canadian Journal of Human Sexuality*, **6** (4), 263–276.

Feelgood, S., Cortoni, F. & Thompson, A. (2005) Sexual coping, general coping and cognitive distortions in incarcerated rapists and child molesters, *Journal of Sexual Aggression*, **11** (2), 157–170.

Feldman, P. (1993) *The Psychology of Crime.* Cambridge: Cambridge University Press.

Fields, G. (1998) 12-country raid busts child porn ring Network. *USA Today*, 3 September.

Finkelhor, D. (1979) *Sexually Victimized Children*. New York: Free Press.

Finkelhor, D. (1980) Sex among siblings: a survey on prevalence, variety and effects. *Archives of Sexual Behavior*, **9**, 171–194.

Finkelhor, D. (1984) *Child Sexual Abuse. New Theory and Research*. New York: Free Press.

Finkelhor, D. (1986) *A Source Book on Child Sexual Abuse*. London: Sage.

Finkelhor, D. (1994a) The international epidemiology of child sexual abuse. *Child Abuse and Neglect*, **18**, 409–417.

Finkelhor, D. (1994b) Current information on the scope and nature of child sexual abuse. *Future of Children*, **4** (2), 31–53.

Finkelhor, D., Hotaling, G., Lewis, L. A. & Smith, C. (1990) Sexual abuse in a national sample of adult men and women: prevalence, characteristics, and risk factors. *Child Abuse and Neglect*, **14**, 19–28.

Finkelhor, D. & Lewis, I. A. (1988) An eidemiologic approach to the study of child molesters. In R. A. Quinsey & V. L. Quinsey (eds) *Human Sexual Aggression; Current Perspectives*. Annals of the New York Academy of Sciences. New York: Plenum.

Finkelhor, D. and Russel, D. (1984) Women as perpetrators. In D. Finkelhor (ed.) *Child Sexual Abuse. New Theory and Research*. (pp. 171–187). New York: Free Press.

Finney, A. (2006) *Domestic Violence, Sexual Assault and Stalking. Findings from the 2004/05 British Crime Survey*. Report 12/06. London: Home Office.

Firestone, P., Bradford, J. M., McCoy, M. *et al.* (1998) Recidivism factors in convicted rapists. *Journal of American Academy Psychiatry and Law*, **26** (2), 185–200.

Fisher, D. (1994) Adult sex offenders. Who are they? Why and how do they do it? In Morrison, T., Erooga, M. & Beckett, R. C. (1994) *Sexual Offending Against Children: Assessment and Treatment of Male Abusers*. New York: Routledge.

Fisher, D. & Thornton, D. (1993) Assessing risk of re-offending in sexual offenders. *Journal of Mental Health*, **2**, 105–117.

Fitch, K. (2006) *Megan's Law: Does it protect children? (2) An updated review of evidence on the impact of community notification as legislated by Megan's Law in the United States*. London: NSPCC. Retrieved from http://www.nspcc.org.uk/Inform/NewsAndEvents/InformNews/NewsMegansLaw_ifna31657.html.

Flanagan, K. & Hayman-White, K. (2000) An Australian adolescent sex offender program: program and client description. *Journal of Sexual Aggression*, **5** (1), 59–77.

Floud, J. & Young, W. C. (1981) *Dangerousness and Criminal Justice*. London: Heinemann.

Folkman, S. & Lazarus, R. S. (1985) If it changes it must be a process: study of emotion and coping during three stages of a college examination. *Journal of Personality and Social Psychology*, **48**, 150–170.

Folkman, S. & Lazarus, R. S. (1986) Stress process and depressive symptomatology. *Journal of Abnormal Psychology*, **95**, 107–113.

Foreign and Commonwealth Office (2004) Drugs and international crime: sex offences against children:

Freeman-Longo, R. E. (1996) Feel good legislation: Prevention or calamity. *Child Abuse and Neglect*, **20** (2), 95–101.

Freeman-Longo, R. E. & Blanchard, G. T. (1998) *Sexual abuse in America: Epidemic of the 21st Century*. Brandon, VT: Safer Society Press.

Freund, K. & Kuban, M. (1993) Toward a testable developmental model of pedophilia: the development of erotic age preference. *Child Abuse and Neglect*, **17**, 315–24.

Freund, K. & Watson, R. & Dickey, R. (1990). Does sexual abuse in childhood causes pedophilia? An exploratory study. *Archives of Sexual Behavior*, **19**, 555–568.

Friday, N. (1973) *My Secret Garden*. New York: Trident.

Friday, N. (2001) *My Secret Garden: Women's Sexual Fantasies*. London: Quartet.

Friedrich, W. N. (2000) Children and adolescents who are sexually abusive of others. *Journal of American Academy of Child and Adolescent Psychiatry*, **39** (7), 809.

Friendship, C. & Beech, A. R. (2005) Reconviction of sexual offenders in England and Wales: an overview of research. *Journal of Sexual Aggression*, **11** (2), 209–223.

Friendship, C., Mann, R. E. & Beech, A. R. (2003a) An evaluation of a national prison-based treatment program for sexual offenders in England and Wales, *Journal of Interpersonal Violence*, **18**, 744–759.

Friendship, C., Mann, R. E. & Beech, A. R. (2003b) The prison-based sex offender treatment programme – an evaluation. *Home Office Research, Development and Statistics Directorate Research Findings No 205*. London: Home Office.

Friendship, C. & Thornton, D. (2001) Sexual reconviction for sex offenders discharged from prison in England and Wales: Implications for evaluating treatment. British Journal of Criminology, **41**, 285–292.

Gagnon, J. H. (1965) Female child victims of sex offenses, *Social Problems*, **13**, 176–192.

Gannon, T. (2006) Increasing honest responding on cognitive distortions in child molesters: The bogus pipeline procedure. *Journal of Interpersonal Violence*, **21**, 358–375.

Gannon, T. & Polaschek, D. (2005) Do child molesters deliberately fake good on cognitive distortion questionnaires? An information processing-based investigation. *Sexual Abuse: A Journal of Research and Treatment*, **17** (2), 183–200.

Garland, D, (2001) *The Culture of Control: Crime and Social Order in Contemporary Society*. Oxford: Oxford University Press.

Gee, D., Devilly, G. J. & Ward, T. (2004) The content of sexual fantasies for sexual offenders. *Sexual Abuse: A Journal of Research and Treatment*, **16** (4), 315–331.

Gee, D., Ward, T. & Eccleston, L. (2003) The function of sexual fantasies for sexual offenders: a preliminary model. *Behaviour Change*, **20** (1), 44–60.

General Secretariat (2003) *Interpol Activity Report: Interpol at Work*. Retrieved 5 June 2005 from http://www.interpol.int/.

George, C., Kaplan, N. & Main, M. (1996) Adult attachment inventory interview protocol cited in Ward, T., Polaschek, D. & Beech, A. R. (2006) *Theories of Sexual Offending*. Chichester: John Wiley & Sons.

Gillespie, A. (2003) Sentences for offences involving child pornography. *Criminal Law Review*, February, 81–92.

Gillespie, A. (2005a) Revisiting Bowden: downloading Internet images. *New Law Journal*, 857–859.

Gillespie, A. (2005b) Child pornography: balancing substantive and evidential law to safeguard children effectively from abuse. *The International Journal of Evidence and Proof*, 1–21.

Gillespie, A. (2005c) Indecent images of children; the ever-changing law. *Child Abuse Review*, **14**, 430–443.

Gillespie, A. (2005d) Tackling child pornography: the approach in England and Wales. In E. Quayle and M. Taylor (eds) *Viewing Child Pornography on the Internet: Understanding the Offence, Managing the Offender, Helping the Victims* (pp. 1–16). Lyme Regis: Russell House Publishing.

Glasser, M., Kolvin, I., Campbell, D. et al. (2001) Cycle of child sexual abuse: Links between being a victim and becoming a perpetrator. *British Journal of Psychiatry*, **179**, 482–494.

Gluckman, M. & Hanson, P. (2006) *Mismatch: Why Our World no Longer Fits our Bodies*. Oxford: Oxford University Press.

Goldstein, S. L. (1999) *The Sexual Exploitation of Children: A Practical Guide to Assessment, Investigation and Intervention*, Boca Raton, FA: CRC Press.

Gotlib, J. I., Gotlib, I. H., Mount, J. H. et al. (1988) Depression and perceptions of early parenting: a longitudinal investigation. *British Journal of Psychiatry*, **152**, 24–27.

Granic, I. & Lamey, A. V. (2000) The self-organisation of the Internet and changing modes of thought, *New Ideas in Psychology*, **18**, 93–107.

Grayson, A. D. & De Luca, R. V. (1999) Female perpetrators of sexual abuse: a review of the clinical and empirical literature. *Aggression and Violent Behavior*, **4** (1), 93–106.

Green, A. H. & Kaplan, M. S. (1994) Psychiatric impairment and childhood victimization experiences in female child molesters. *Journal of the American Academy of Child and Adolescent Psychiatry*, **33**, 954–961.

Greenberg, D., Bradford, J.M., Firestone, P. & Curry, S. (2000) Recidivism of child molesters: A study of victim relationship with the perpetrator. *Child Abuse and Neglect*, **24** (11), 1485–1494.

Greendlinger, V. & Byrne, D. (1987) Coercive sexual fantasies of college men as predictors of self-reported likelihood to rape and overt sexual aggression. *Journal of Sex Research*, **23**, 1–11.

Gresswell, D. M. & Hollin, C. R. (1997) Addictions and multiple murder: A behavioural perspective. In Hodge, J. E., McMurran, M., & Hollin, C. R. (eds) 1997) *Addicted to Crime*. Chichester: John Wiley & Sons.

Griffiths, M. (1999) Internet addiction: Internet fuels other addictions. *Student British Medical Journal*, **7**, 428–429.

Griffiths, M. (2000) Excessive Internet use: implications for sexual behavior. *Cyber Psychology and Behavior*, **3** (4), 537–552.

Groth, A. N. (1979) *Men Who Rape*. New York: Plenum.

Groth, A. N. (1982) The incest offender. In S. Sgroi (ed.) *Handbook of Clinical Intervention in Child Sexual Abuse* (pp. 215–239). Lexington, MA: Lexington Books.

Groth, A. N. & Birnbaum, H. J. (1978) Adult sexual orientation and attraction to underage persons. *Archives of Sexual Behavior*, **7** (3), 175–181.

Grubin, D. (1998) *Sex Offending Against Children: Understanding the Risk*. Police Research Series, Paper 99, Policing and Reducing Crime Unit. London: Home Office.

Grubin, D. & Madsen, L. (2005) Lie detection and the polygraph: a historical review. *British Journal of Forensic Psychiatry and Psychology*, **16,** 357–369.

Grubin, D., Madsen, L., Parsons, S. *et al.* (2004) A prospective study of the impact of polygraphy on high risk behaviors in adult sex offenders. *Sexual Abuse: A Journal of Research and Treatment*, **16**, 209–222.

Haaspasalo, J., Puupponen, M. & Crittenden, P. (1999) Victim to victimizer; the psychology of isomorphism in a case of a recidivist pedophile in Finland. *Journal of Child Sexual Abuse*, 97–115.

Hall, G. C. (1996) *Theory-Based Assessment, Treatment and Prevention of Sexual Aggression*. Oxford: Oxford University Press.

Hall, G. C.. & Hirschman, R. (1991) Towards a theory of sexual aggression: a quad-ripartite model. *Journal of Consulting and Clinical Psychology*, **59**, 662–669.

Hall, G. C. & Hirschman, R. (1992) Sexual aggression against children: a conceptual perspective of etiology. *Criminal Justice and Behavior*, **19**, 8–23.

Hall, G. C. N., Hirschman, R. & Oliver, L. L. (1995) Sexual arousal and arousability to paedophilic stimuli in a community sample of normal men. *Behaviour Therapy*, **26**, 681–694.

Hamilton, G. V. (1929) *A Research in Marriage*. New York: Albert & Charles Boni.

Hammond, S. (2004) The challenge of sex offender assessment: the case of Internet offenders. In M. C. Calder (ed.) *Child Sexual Abuse and the Internet: Tackling the New Frontier* (pp. 85–97). Lyme Regis: Russell House Publishing.

Hanson, R. K. (1997) *The Development of a Brief Actuarial Risk Scale for Sexual Offence Recidivism. User Report 1997-04*. Ottawa: Department of the Solicitor General of Canada.

Hanson, R. K. & Harris, A. J. R. (1998) *Dynamic Predictors of Sexual Recidivism. User Report 1998-01*. Ottawa, Canada: Department of the Solicitor General of Canada.

Hanson, R. K. & Harris, A. J. R (2000) Where should we intervene? Dynamic predictors of sexual offense recidivism, *Criminal Justice and Behavior*, **27** (1), 6–35.

Hanson, R. K. & Morton-Bourgon, K. (2004) *Predictors of Sexual Recidivism: An Updated Meta-analysis*. (User Report No. 2004-02). Ottawa: Public Safety and Emergency Preparedness.

Hanson, R. K. & Morton-Bourgon, K. (2005) The characteristics of persistent sexual offenders: a meta-analysis of recidivism studies. *Journal of Consulting and Clinical Psychology*, **73**, 1154–1163.

Hanson, R. K. & Slater, S. (1988) Sexual victimization in the history of sexual abusers: A review. *Annals of Sex Research*, **1**, 485–499.

Hanson, R. K., Gizzarelli, R. & Scott, H. (1994) The attitudes of incest offenders: sexual entitlement and acceptance of sex with children. *Criminal Justice and Behaviour*, **21** (2), 187–202.

Hanson, R. K. & Bussiere, M. T. (1998) Predicting relapse: a meta-analysis of sexual offender recidivism studies. *Journal of Consulting and Clinical Psychology*, **66** (2), 348–362.

Hanson, R. K. & Thornton, D. (1999) *Static-99: Improving Actuarial Risk Assessments for Sex Offenders* (User Report 99–02). Ottawa: Department of the Solicitor General of Canada.

Hanson, R. K. & Thornton, D. (2000) Improving risk assessments for sex offenders: a comparison of three actuarial scales. *Law and Human Behavior*, **24** (1), 119–136.

Hariton, E. B. & Singer, J. L. (1974) Women's fantasies during sexual intercourse. *Archives of General Psychiatry*, **8**, 86–90.

Hartley, C. C. (1998) How incest offenders overcome internal inhibitions through the use of cognitions and cognitive distortions. *Journal of Interpersonal Violence*, **13**, 25–39.

Hartman, C. R., Burgess, A. W. & Lanning, K. V. (1984) Typology of Collections. In Burgess, A. W. (ed.) *Child Pornography and Sex Rings*. Lexington, MA: D. C. Health.

Haywood, T. W. & Grossman, L. S. (1994) Denial of deviant sexual arousal and psychopathology in child molesters. *Behavior Therapy*, **25**, 327–340.

Hazan, C. & Shaver, P. R. (1994) Attachment as an organizational framework for research on close relationships. *Psychological Inquiry*, **5** (1), 1–22.

Hazelwood, R. R. & Warren, J. L. (1995) The relevance of fantasy in serial sexual crime investigation. In R. R. Hazelwood & A. W. Burgess (eds), *Practical Aspects of Rape Investigation: A Multidisciplinary Approach*, 2 edn (pp. 337–360). New York: CRC Press.

Healy, M. (1997) *Child pornography: an international perspective. Prepared as a working document for the World Congress Against Commercial Sexual Exploitation of Children.* Retrieved 20 February 2003 from http://www.usis.usemb.se/children/csec/215e.htm.

Hebenton, B. & Thomas, T. (1996) Tracking Sex Offenders. *Howard Journal*, **35**, 97–112.

Herdt, G. & McClintock, M. (2000) The magical age of 10. *Archives of Sexual Behavior*, **29**, 587–606.

Herman, J. (1990) Sex offenders: A feminist perspective. In W.L. Marshall, D.R. Laws and H.E. Barbaree (Eds.). *The Handbook of Sexual Assault; Issues, Theories and Treatment of Offenders* (pp. 177–193). London: Plenum Press.

Hetherton, J. (1999) The idealization of women: its role in the minimization of child sexual abuse by females, *Child Abuse and Neglect*, **23** (2), 161–174.

Hetherton, J. & Breadsall, L. (1988) Decisions and attitudes concerning child sexual abuse: does the gender of the perpetrator make a difference to child protection professionals? *Child Abuse and Neglect*, **22** (12), 1265–1283.

Hickman, M (2006) Google reveals UK's most popular internet searches, *Independent*, 18 December 2006. Retrieved 30 December 2006 from http://news.independent.co.uk/world/science_technology/article2083887.ece.

Hilton, M. R. & Mezey, G. C. (1996) Victims and perpetrators of child sexual abuse. *British Journal of Psychiatry*, **169**, 408–415.

Hindman, J. (1988) Research disputes assumptions about child molesters. *National District Attorneys Association Bulletin*, **7**, 1–3.

HMIP (Her Majesty's Inspectorate of Probation) (1998) *Exercising Constant Vigilance: The Role of the Probation Service in Protecting the Public from Sex Offenders* (Report of a Thematic Inspection). London: Home Office.

Hobbs, G. F., Hobbs, C. J. & Wynne, J. M. (1999) Abuse of children in foster and residential care. *Child Abuse and Neglect*, **23** (12), 1239–1252.

Hodge, J. E., McMurran, M. & Hollin, C. R. (eds) (1997) *Addicted to Crime*. Chichester: John Wiley & Sons.

Hoffman, D. L. & Novak, T. P. (1995) *Detailed critique of the TIME article 'On a Screen near You: Cyberporn.'* Retrieved 11 April 2005 from http://trfn.pgh.pa.us/guest/mrcc.html.

Holland, G. (2005) Identifying victims of child abuse images: an analysis of successful identifications. In E. Quayle & M. Taylor (2005) *Viewing Child Pornography on the Internet: Understanding the Offence, Managing the Offender, Helping the Victims.* Lyme Regis: Russell House Publishing.

Holmes, G., Offen, L. & Waller, G. (1997) See no evil, hear no evil, speak no evil: why relatively few males who have been sexually abused receive help for abuse-related issues in childhood, *Clinical Psychology Review,* **17,** 69–88.

Home Office (1993) *Disclosure of Criminal Records for Employment Vetting Purposes* (Cm 2319). London: HMSO.

Home Office (1996a) *Sentencing and Supervision of Sex Offenders–A Consultation Document* (Cm 3304) London: HMSO.

Home Office (1996b) *On the Record: The Government's Proposals for Access to Criminal Records for Employment and Related Purposes in England and Wales* (Cm 3308). London: HMSO.

Home Office (1997) *Aspects of Crime: Children as Victims.* Crime and Criminal Justice Unit, Research and Statistics Directorate. London: Home Office.

Home Office (2001) *Prison Statistics England and Wales, 2001.* London: HMSO.

Home Office (2002) *Protecting the Public: Strengthening Protection against Sex Offenders and Reforming the Law on Sexual Offences* (Cm 5668). London: HMSO.

Home Office (2004a) *Protecting the Public from Sexual Crime: An Explanation of the Sexual Offences Act 2003.* Home Office Communications Directorate (April), SOA/1. London: Home Office.

Home Office (2004b) *Public to play vital role in managing sex and violent offenders in community.* Press release, London, 15 April.

Home Office (27 November 2006) *Memorandum of Understanding between the Government of United Kingdom of Great Britain and Northern Ireland and the Government of Ireland on Information Sharing Arrangements Relating to Sex Offenders.* Home Office Circular 043/2006. Retrieved 4 December 2006 from http://www.knowledgenetwork.gov.uk/HO/circular.nsf/79755433dd36a66980256d4f004d1514/7eea094f4d6975a78025724b00594bd0?OpenDocument.

Home Office (2006) *Government Looking to Ban Computer Generated Images of Child Abuse. Press Release,* 14 December. Retrieved 4 January 2007 from http://press.homeoffice.gov.uk/press-releases/banning-child-abuse-images?version=1.

Home Office Task Force on Child Protection on the Internet (2003) *Good Practice Models and Guidance for the Internet Industry On: Chat Services, Instant Messages; Web based Services.* Retrieved 4 December 2006 from http://police.homeoffice.gov.uk/news-and-publications/publication/operational-policing/ho_model.pdf.

Howells, K., Day, A., Wright, S. (2004) Affect, emotions and sex offending. *Psychology, Crime and Law,* **10** (2), 179–195.

Howitt, D. (1992) *Child Abuse Errors: When Good Intentions Go Wrong.* London: Harvester Wheatsheaf.

Howitt, D. (1995a) *Paedophiles and Sexual Offences Against Children.* Chichester: John Wiley & Sons.

Howitt, D. (1995b) Pornography and the Paedophile: Is it Criminogenic? *British Journal of Medical Psychiatry,* **68,** 15–27.

Howitt, D. (1998a) *Crime, Media and the Law.* Chichester: John Wiley & Sons.

Howitt, D. (1998b) Are causal theories of paedophilia possible? A reconsideration of sexual abuse cycles. In J. Boros, I. Munnich and M. Szegedi (eds) *Psychology and Criminal Justice: International Review of Theory and Practice* (pp. 248–253). Berlin: De Gruyter.

Howitt, D. (2002) *Forensic and Criminal Psychology,* Harlow: Pearson Education Limited.

Howitt, D. (2004) Just what is the role of fantasy in sex offending? *Criminal Behaviour and Mental Health,* **14,** 182–188.

Howitt, D. (2006a) *Introduction to Forensic and Criminal Psychology.* Harlow: Pearson Education Limited.

Howitt, D. (2006b) Paedophilia prevention and the Law. In K. Moss and M. Stephens (eds) *Crime Reduction and the Law.* Abingdon: Routledge.

Howitt, D. (ed.) (1992b) *Concerning Psychology: Psychology Applied to Social Issues*. Milton Keynes: Open University Press.

Howitt, D. & Cumberbatch, G. (1990) *Pornography: Impacts and Influences. A Review of Available Research Evidence on the Effects of Pornography*. London: Home Office Research and Planning Unit.

Howitt, D. & Cramer, D. (2005) *Introduction to Statistics in Psychology*. Harlow: Pearson Education.

Howitt, D. & Sheldon, K. (in press) The role of cognitive distortions in paedophile offending: Internet and contact offenders compared. *Psychology, Crime and the Law*.

Howlett, C (2003) The way forward: A law enforcement perspective. In A. MacVean & P. Spindler (eds) *Policing Paedophiles on the Internet*. John Grieve Centre for Policing and Community Safety. Bristol: The New Police Bookshop.

Hsu, L. M., Santelli, J. & Hsu, R. (1989) Faking detection validity and incremental validity of response latencies to MMPI subtle and obvious items. *Journal of Personality Assessment*, **53**, 278–295.

Hudson, B. (2002) Punishment and control. In M. Maguire, R. Morgan & R. Reiner (eds) *The Oxford Handbook of Criminology*, 3rd edn (pp. 233–263). Oxford: Oxford University Press.

Hudson, K. (2005) *Offending Identities: Sex Offenders' Perspectives on their Treatment and Management*. Cullompton: Willan Publishing.

Hudson, S. M., Ward, T. & McCormack, J. C. (1999) Offence pathways in sexual offenders. *Journal of Interpersonal Violence*, **14**, 779–798.

Huesmann, L. R. (1988) An information processing model for the development of aggression. *Aggressive Behaviour*, **14**, 13–24.

Hunt, M. (1974) *Sexual behaviour in the 70s*. Chicago: Playboy Press.

International Criminal Police Organization (Interpol) (2005) *Legislation of Interpol Member States on Sexual Offences against Children*. Retrieved 7 February 2005 from http://www.interpol.int/public/chidlren/sexualabuse/national laws.asp.

Internet Watch Foundation (1998) *Annual report*. Available from http://www.iwf.org.uk/corporate/page.125.htm on request.

Internet Watch Foundation (2000) *Annual report*. Available from http://www.iwf.org.uk/corporate/page.125.htm on request.

Internet Watch Foundation (2003) *Annual report*. Available from http://www.iwf.org.uk/corporate/page.125.htm on request.

Internet Watch Foundation (2004) *Annual report*. Retrieved 11 April from http://www.iwf.org.uk/corporate/page.125.htm.

Internet Watch Foundation (2005) *2005 Annual and Charity Report*. Retrieved 28 December 2006 from http://www.iwf.org.uk/corporate/page.152.htm.

Irish Examiner (2004) *Child porn hysteria targets the innocent and ignores the victims*. Retrieved 17 August 2004 from http://www.irishexaminer.com/text/story.asp?j=326717884812&p=3z67y7885z3x&n=326717885267.

James, A. C. & Neil, P. (1996) Juvenile sex offenders: one year period prevalence study within Oxfordshire. *Child Abuse and Neglect*, **20** (6), 477–85.

Jenkins, P. (2001) *Beyond Tolerance: Child Pornography on the Internet*. New York: New York University Press.

Jewkes, Y. & Andrews, C. (2005) Policing the filth: the problems of investigating online child pornography in England and Wales, *Policing and Society*, **15** (1), 42–62.

Jones, J. C. & Barlow, D. H. (1990) Self-reported frequency of sexual urges, fantasies, and masturbatory fantasies in heterosexual males and females. *Archives of Sexual Behavior*, **19**, 269–79.

Jones, T. (2003) Child abuse or computer crime? The proactive approach. In A. MacVean. and P. Spindler (eds) *Policing Paedophiles on the Internet*. John Grieve Centre for policing and Community Safety. Bristol: The New Police Bookshop.

Julian, V., Mohr, C. & Lapp, L. (1980) Father-daughter incest. In W. Holder (ed.) *Sexual Abuse of Children: Implications for Treatment* (pp. 17–35). Englewood, CO: American Humane Association.

Kandell, J. J. (1998) Internet addiction on campus: The vulnerability of college students. *CyberPsychology and Behavior*, **1** (1), 46–59.

Kelly, L. (1988) *Surviving Sexual Abuse*. Cambridge: Polity.

Kelly, L., Regan, L. & Burton, S. (1991) *An Exploratory Study of the Prevalence of Sexual Abuse in a Sample of 16–21 Year Olds*. London: Child Abuse Studies Unit, Polytechnic of North London.

Kelly, L. & Scott, S. (1993) The current literature about the organised abuse of children. *Child Abuse Review*, **23**, 281–287.

Kelly, R. J., Wood, J. J., Gonzalez, L. S. *et al.* (2002) Effects of mother-son incest and positive perceptions of sexual abuse experiences on the psychosocial adjustment of clinic-referred men. *Child Abuse and Neglect*, **26**, 425–441.

Kemshall, H. & Maguire, M. (2003) Sex offenders, risk penality and the problem of disclosure to the community. In A. Matravers (ed.) *Managing Sex Offenders in the Community: Context, Challenges and Responses*. Cullompton: Willan Publishing.

Kendall-Tackett, K. A. & Simon, A. F. (1987) Perpetrators and their acts: data from 365 adults molested as children. *Child Abuse and Neglect*, **11**, 237–248.

Killias, M. (1991) The historic origins of penal statutes concerning sexual activities involving children and adolescents, *Journal of Homosexuality*, **20** (1/2), 41–46.

Kim, P. Y. & Bailey, M. J. (1997) Sidestreets on the information superhighway: Paraphilias and sexual variation on the Internet. *Journal of Sex Education and Therapy*, **22** (1), 35–43.

King, S. A. (1999) Internet gambling and pornography: illustrative examples of the psychological consequences of communication anarchy. *CyberPsychology and Behaviour*, **2** (3): 175–193.

King, S. A. & Barak, A. (1999) Compulsive Internet gambling: a new form of an old clinical pathology. *CyberPsychology and Behaviour*, **2** (5), 441–456.

Kinsey, A. C., Pomeroy, W. B., Martin, C. E. and Gebhard, P. H. (1953) *Sexual Behavior in the Human Female*. Philadelphia, PA: Saunders.

Kirkendall, L. A. & McBride, L. G. (1990) Preadolescent and adolescent imagery and sexual fantasies: beliefs and experiences. In M. E. Perry (ed.) *Handbook of Sexology*, Vol. 7, Childhood and Adolescent Sexology (pp. 263–286). Amsterdam: Elsevier.

Knafo, D. & Jaffe, Y. (1984) Sexual fantasizing in males and females. *Journal of Research in Personality*, **18**, 451–467.

Knight, R. A. & Prentky, R. A. (1990) Classifying sexual offenders. The development and corroboration of taxonomic models. In W. L. Marshall, D. R. Laws & H. E. Barbaree (eds) *The Handbook of Sexual Assault; Issues, Theories and Treatment of Offenders*. London: Plenum Press.

Kraft-Ebbing, Richard von (1886/1965) *Psychopathia Sexualis: With Especial Reference to the Antipathic Sexual Interest, A Medico-Forensic Study*. Translation and introduction by Franklin S.Klaf. New York: Stein & Day.

Krauss, D. A., Sales, B. D., Becker, J. V. & Figueredo, A. J. (2000) Beyond prediction to explanation in risk assessment research: A comparison of two explanatory theories of criminality and recidivism. *International Journal of Law and Psychiatry*, **23**, 91–112.

Kutchinsky, B. (1970) The effect of pornography: a pilot experiment on perception, behavior and attitudes. In *Technical Report of the Commission on Obscenity and Pornography, Vol III, Erotica and Social Behavior* (pp. 133–170). Washington, DC: US Government Printing Office.

Kutchinsky, B. (1973) The effect of easy availability of pornography on the incidence of sex crimes: the Danish experiment. *Journal of Social Issues*, **29** (3), 163–191.

La Fontaine, J. S. (1998) *Speak of the Devil*. Cambridge: Cambridge University Press.

Landis, C. (1940) *Sex in Development*. New York: Hoeber.

Landis, J. T. (1956) Experiences of 500 children with adult sexual deviation. *Psychiatric Quarterly Supplement*, **30** (1), 91–109.

Langdridge, D. (2004) *Research Methods and Data Analysis in Psychology*. Harlow: Pearson Education.

Langevin, R. (1991) A note on the problem of response set in measuring cognitive distortions. *Annals of Sex Research*, **4**, 287–292.

Langevin, R., Lang, R. A. & Curnoe, S. (1998) The prevalence of sex offenders with deviant fantasies. *Journal of Interpersonal Violence*, **13** (3), 315–327.

Langevin, R., Lang, R. A., Wright, P. & Hardy, L. (1988) Pornography and sexual offenses. *Annals of Sex Research*, **1** (3), 355–362.

Lanning, K. (1992) *Investigator's Guide to Allegations of 'Ritual Child Abuse'*. Quantico, VA, Behavioral Science Unit, National Center for the Analysis of Violent Crime, FBI Academy.

Lanning, K. (2001 4 Edition) *Child Molesters: A Behavioural Analysis*. Washington, DC: National Center for Missing and Exploited Children.

Laws, D. R. (1996) Relapse prevention or harm reduction? *Sexual Abuse: A Journal of Research and Treatment*, **8** (3), 243–247.

Laws, D. R., Hudson, S. M. & Ward, T. (eds) (2000) *Remaking Relapse Prevention with Sex Offenders: A Sourcebook*. Newbury Park, CA: Sage.

Laws, D. R. & Marshall, W. L. (1990) A conditioning theory of the etiology and maintenance of deviant sexual preference and behaviour. In W. L. Marshall, D. R. Laws & H. E. Barbaree (eds) (1990) *Handbook of Sexual Assault: Issues, Theories and Treatment of the Offender* (pp. 209–229). London: Plenum Press.

Lee, J. K. P., Jackson, H. J., Pattison, P. & Ward, T. (2002) Developmental risk factors for sexual offending. *Child Abuse and Neglect*, **26**, 73–92.

Leitenberg, H. & Henning, K. (1995) Sexual Fantasy. *Psychological Bulletin*, **117** (3), 469–496.

Liberty (2002) *Briefing on the Criminal Justice Bill – 2 Commons Reading* (November) London: Liberty.

Lisak, D. (1994) The psychological impact of sexual abuse: content analysis of interviews with male survivors. *Journal of Traumatic Stress*, **7**, 525–548.

Lloyd, R. (1976) *For Money or Love: Boy Prostitution in America*. New York: Vanguard Press.

Looman, J. (1995) Sexual fantasies of child molesters. *Canadian Journal of Behavioral Sciences*, **27**, 321–332.

Looman, J., Abracen, J., DiFazio, R. & Maillet, G. (2004) Alcohol and drug abuse among sexual and nonsexual offenders: Relationship to intimacy deficits and coping strategy. *Sexual Abuse: A Journal of Research and Treatment*, **16**, 177–189.

Lovell, E. (2001) *Megan's Law: Does it Protect Children*. London: NSPCC.

Lunde, I., Larson, G. K., Fog, E. & Garde, K. (1991) Sexual desire orgasm and sexual fantasies: a study of 625 Danish women born in 1910, 1936 and 1958. *Journal of Sex Education Therapy*, **17**, 111–116.

Luxenburg, J. & Klein, L. (1984) CB radio prostitution technology and the displacement of deviance. *Journal of Offender Counseling (Special Issues: Gender Issues, Sex Offenses and Criminal Justice: Current Trends)*, **9** (1–2), 71–87.

Lyn, T. S. & Burton, D. L. (2004) Adult attachment and sexual offender status. *American Journal of Orthopsychiatry*, **74**, 150–159.

MacCullough, M. J., Snowden, P. R., Wood, P. J. & Mills, H. E., (1983) Sadistic fantasy, sadistic behaviour and offending. *British Journal of Psychiatry*, **143**, 20–29.

Madsen, L., Parsons, S. & Grubin, D. (2004) A preliminary study of the contribution of periodic polygraph testing to the treatment and supervision of sex offenders. *British Journal of Forensic Psychiatry and Psychology*, **15**, 682–695.

Maguire, M. (2002) Crime Statistics: the 'data explosion' and its implications. In M. Maguire, R. Morgan & R. Riener (eds) *The Oxford Handbook of Criminology*, 3rd edn. Oxford: Oxford University Press.

Maguire, M., Kemshall, K., Noaks, L. & Wincup, E. (2001) Risk management of sexual and violent offenders: the work of Public Protection panels. *Police Research Series Paper* No. 139. London: Home Office.

Mah, W. A. & Barak, A. (2000) Online sex shops: phenomenological, psychological and ideological perspectives on Internet sexuality. *CyberPsychology and Behavior*, **3** (4), 575–589.

Mahoney, D., & Faulkner, N. (1997). *Brief overview of pedophiles on the Web.* Retrieved 20 April 2007 from http://www.prevent-abuse-now.com/pedoweb.htm.

Mair, K. J. (1995) Cognitive distortion in the prediction of sexual offending. In N. K. Clark & G. M. Stephenson (eds) *Investigative and Forensic Decision Making, Issues in Criminological and Legal Psychology, No. 26* (pp. 12–17). Leicester: Division of Criminological and Legal Psychology, British Psychological Society.

Malamuth, N. M. (1981a) Rape proclivity among males. *Journal of Social Issues*, **37**, 138–157.

Malamuth, N. M. (1981b) Rape fantasies as a function of exposure to violent sexual stimuli. *Archives of Sexual Behaviour*, **10** (1), 33–47.

Malesky, A. & Keim, J. (2001) Mental health professionals' perspectives on sex offender registry web sites. *Sexual Abuse: A Journal of Research and Treatment*, **13** (1), 53–63.

Maletzky, B. M. & Field, G. (2003) The biological treatment of sexual offenders: a review and preliminary report of the Oregon Pilot *depo-Provera* program. *Aggression and Violent Behavior*, **8**, 391–412.

Marshall, W. (1988) The use of sexually explicit stimuli by rapists, child molesters and non-offenders. *Journal of Sex Research*, **25** (2), 267–288.

Marshall, W. L. (1989) Intimacy, loneliness and sex offenders. *Behavior Research and Therapy*, **27** (5), 491–503.

Marshall, W. L. (1997) Pedophilia: Psychopathology and theory. In D. Laws & W. O'Donohue (eds) *Sexual Deviance: Theory Assessment and Treatment* (pp. 152–174). New York: Guildford Press.

Marshall, W. L., Anderson, D. & Fernandez, Y. (1999) *Cognitive Behavioural Treatment of Sexual Offenders.* Chichester: John Wiley & Sons.

Marshall, W. L. & Barbaree, H. E. (1990) An integrated theory of the etiology of sexual offending. In W. L. Marshall, D. R. Laws & H. E. Barbaree (eds) *Handbook of Sexual Assault: Issues, Theories and Treatment of the Offender* (pp. 257–275). London: Plenum Press.

Marshall, W. L., Cripps, E., Anderson, D. & Cortoni, F. (1999) Self-esteem and coping strategies in child molesters. *Journal of Interpersonal Violence*, **14**, 955–962.

Marshall, W. L. and Marshall, L.E. (2000) The origins of sexual offending. *Trauma, Violence and Abuse: A Review Journal*, **1**, 250–263.

Marshall, W. L., Marshall, L. E., Sachdev, S. & Kruger, R. L. (2003) Distorted attitudes and perceptions and their relationship with self-esteem and coping in child molesters. *Sexual Abuse: A Journal of Research and Treatment*, **15** (3) 171–181.

Marshall, W. L., Serran, G. A. & Cortoni, F. A. (2000) Childhood attachments, sexual abuse and their relationships to adult coping in child molesters. *Sexual Abuse: A Journal of Research and Treatment*, **12**, 17–26.

Maruna, S. & Copes, H. (2005) What have we learned in five decades of neutralization research? *Crime and Justice: A Review of Research*, **32**, 221–320.

Maruna, S. & Mann, R. E. (2006) Invited article. A fundamental attribution error? Rethinking cognitive distortions. *Legal and Criminological Psychology*, **11** (2), 155–177.

Masson, H. & Erooga, M. (1999) *Children and Young People who Sexually Abuse Others: Challenges and Responses.* New York: Routledge.

Masters, W. H. & Johnston, V. E. (1966) *Human Sexual Response.* Boston: Little Brown.

Masters, W. H., Johnson, V. E. & Kolodny, R. C. (1992) *Human Sexuality.* New York: HarperCollins.

May-Chahal, C. & Cawson, P. (2005) Measuring child maltreatment in the United Kingdom: a study of the prevalence of child abuse and neglect. *Child Abuse and Neglect*, **29**, 969–984.

McCabe, K. (2000) Child pornography on the Internet. *Social Science Computer Review*, **18** (1), 73–76.

McCabe, K. & Gregory, S. (1998) Recognizing the illegal activities of computer users. *Social Science Computer Review*, **16**, 419–422.

McFall, R. M. (1990) The enhancement of social skills: an information processing analysis. In W. L. Marshall, D. R. Laws & H. E. Barbaree (eds) *Handbook of Sexual Assault: Issues, Theories and Treatment of the Offender* (pp. 311–330). New York: Plenum Press.

McGrath, G. & Casey, E. (2002) Forensic psychiatry and the Internet: practical perspectives on sexual predators and obsessional harassers in cyberspace. *Journal of American Academic Psychiatry Law*, **30**, 81–94.

McGrath, M., Cann, S. & Konopasky, R. (1998) New measures of defensiveness, empathy and cognitive distortions for sexual offenders against children. *Sexual Abuse: Journal of Research and Treatment*, **10**, 25–36.

McGregor, G. & Howells, K. (1997) Addiction models of sexual offending. In Hodge, J. E., McMurran, M. & Hollin, C. R. (eds) *Addicted to Crime* (pp. 107–137). Chichester: John Wiley & Sons.

McGuire, R. J., Carlisle, J. M. & Young, B. G. (1965) Sexual deviations as conditioned behaviour: a hypothesis. *Behaviour Research and Therapy*, **2**, 185–190.

McKenna, K. Y. A. & Bargh, J. A. (1998) Coming out in the age of the Internet; identity 'demarginalization' through virtual group participant. *Journal of Personality and Social Psychology*, **75**, 681–694.

McKenna, K. Y. A. & Bargh, J. A. (2000) Plan 9 from cyberspace: the implications of the Internet for personality and social psychology. *Personality and Social Psychology Review*, **4**, 57–75.

McLachlan, B. (2002) Child Pornography in B. Long & B. McLachlan (eds) *The Hunt for Britain's Paedophiles*. London: Hodder & Stoughton.

Meerkerk, G.-J., Van Den Eijnden, R. J. J. M & Garetsen, H. F. L. (2006) Predicting compulsive Internet use: it's about sex. *Cyberpsychology and Behavior*, **9** (1), 95–103.

Mehta, M. D. (2001) Pornography in Usenet: a study of 9,800 randomly selected images. *Cyberpsychology and Behavior*, **4** (6), 695–703.

Mehta, M. D. (2002) Censoring Cyberspace. *Asian Journal of Social Science*, **30** (2), 319–338.

Mehta, M. D. & Plaza, D. E. (1994) Pornography on cyberspace: an exploration of what's in Usenet. In S. Kiesler (ed.) *Culture of the Internet* (pp. 53–67). Mahwah, NJ: Lawrence Erlbaum Associates.

Meloy, J. R. (2000) The Nature and dynamics of sexual homicide: an integrative review. *Aggression and Violent Behaviour*, **5** (1), 1–22.

Meloy, J. R., Hempel, A., Mohandie, K. *et al.* (2001) Offender and offense characteristics of a non-random sample of adolescent mass murderers. *Journal of the American Academy of Child Adolescent Psychiatry*, **40**, 719–728.

Middleton, D. (2004) Current Treatment Approaches. In M. C. Calder (Ed.) *Child Sexual Abuse and the Internet: Tackling the New Frontier* (p. 99–112). Lyme Regis, Dorset: Russell House Publishing.

Middleton, D., Beech, A. & Mandeville-Norden, R. (2005) What sort of person could do that? Psychological profiles of Internet Pornography users. In E. Quayle & M. Taylor (ed.) *Viewing Child Pornography on the Internet: Understanding the Offence, Managing the Offender, Helping the Victims*. Lyme Regis: Russell House Publishing.

Middleton, D., Elliott, I. A., Mandeville-Norden & Beech, A. R. (2006) An investigation into the applicability of the Ward and Siegert pathways model of child sexual abuse with Internet offenders, *Psychology, Crime and Law*, **12** (6), 589–603.

Miller, P. Y. & Simon, W. (1980) The development of sexuality in adolescence. In J.Abelson (ed.) *Adolescent Psychology* (pp. 383–407). New York: Wiley.

Morahan-Martin, J. & Schumacher, P. (2000) Incidence and correlates of pathological Internet use among college students. *Computers in Human Behavior*, **16** (1), 13–29.

MORI/News of the World (2000) Naming and shaming poll. Retrieved 3 April 2002 from http://www.mori.com/polls/2000/nowname.shtml.

Morris, I., Scott, I., Mortimer, M. J. & Barker, D. (1997) Physical and sexual abuse of children in the West Midlands. *Child Abuse and Neglect*, **21** (3), 285–293.

Moss, K. & Stephens, M. (2006) (eds) *Crime Reduction and the Law*. Abingdon: Routledge.

Mrazek, P. J., Lynch, M. A. & Bentovim, A. (1983) Sexual abuse of children in the United Kingdom, *Child Abuse and Neglect*, **7** (2), 147–153.

Muensterberg, W. (1994) *Collecting: An Unruly Passion*. Princeton, NJ: Princeton University Press.

Murphy, W. D. (1990) Assessment and modification of cognitive distortions in sex offenders. In W. L. Marshall, D. R. Laws & H. E. Barbaree (eds) *Handbook of Sexual Assault: Issues, Theories and Treatment of the Offender* (pp. 331–342). London: Plenum Press.

Murphy, W. D. & Smith, T. A., (1996) Sex offenders against children. Empirical and clinical issues. In J. Briere, L. Berliner & A. Bulkley (eds) *The APSAC Handbook on Child Maltreatment* (pp. 175–192). London: Sage.

MyHill, A. & Allen, J. (2002) *Rape and Sexual Assault of Women: Findings from the British Crime Survey*. Research Findings No. 159. London: Home Office Research, Development and Statistics Directorate.

National Center for Missing and Exploited Children, *New Study Reveals Child Pornography Not a Crime in Most Countries*, press release, 6 April 2006. Retrieved 28 December 2006 from http://www.missingkids.com/missingkids/servlet/News EventServlet?languageCountry.

National Criminal Intelligence Service (2003) United Kingdom threat assessment of serious and organized crimes: 9. sex offences against children, including online abuse. Retrieved 30 December 2006 from http://www.ncis.co.uk/ukta/2003/ threat09.asp.

National Society for the Prevention of Cruelty to children (2003) *90% of Adults Worried about the Threat Posed to Children by Paedophiles in Internet Chat Rooms*, press release, 21 January. Retrieved 8 April 2003 from http://www.nspcc.org.uk/html/home/ informationresources/paedchatrooms.htm.

Neidigh, L. & Krop, H. (1992) Cognitive distortions among child sexual offenders. *Journal of Sex Education & Therapy*, **18**, 208–215.

Neidigh, L. W. & Tomiko, R. (1991) The coping strategies of child sexual abusers. *Journal of Sex Education and Therapy*, **17**, 103–110.

Nichols, H. R. & Molinder, I. (1984) *Multiphasic Sex Inventory Manual*. Tacoma, WA: Authors.

Nunes, K. L., Firestone, P., Bradford, J. M. *et al.* (2002) A comparison of modified versions of the Static-99 and the Sex Offender Risk Appraisal Guide. *Sexual Abuse: A Journal of Research and Treatment*, **14** (3), 253–269.

Nutter, D. E. & Kearns, M. E. (1993) Patterns of exposure to sexually explicit material among sex offenders, child molesters and controls. *Journal of Sex and Marital Therapy*, **19** (1), 77–85.

O'Carroll, L. & Morris, S. (2003) Newspaper man one of 43 arrested in child porn operation. *Guardian*. Retrieved 19 April 2007 from http://browse.guardian.co.uk/ search?search=o%27carroll+morris&year=2003&search_target=%2Fsearch&fr= cb-guardian.

O'Connell, R. (2000) Child sex iconography. Iconic narratives of child sex myths. In C. von Feilitzen & U. Carlsson (eds) *Children in the New Media Landscape. Games, Pornography, Perceptions* (pp. 211–232). Goteborg: UNESCO.

O'Donohue, W., Letourneau, E. J. & Dowling, H. (1997) Development and preliminary validation of a paraphilic sexual fantasy questionnaire. *Sexual Abuse: A Journal of Research and Treatment*, **9** (3), 167–178.

O'Donohue, W., Regev, L. G. & Hagstrom, A. (2000) Problems with the DSM-IV diagnosis of pedophilia. *Sexual Abuse: A Journal of Research and Treatment*, **12** (2), 95–105.

Okami, P. & Goldberg, S. (1992) Personality Correlates of Pedophilia. *Journal of Sex Research*, **29** (3), 297–328.

Ortmann, J. (1980) The treatment of sexual offenders: Castration and antihormone therapy. *International Journal of Law and Psychiatry*, **3**, 443–451.

O'Shaughnessy, R. J. (2006) Violent adolescent sex offenders. *Child and Adolescent Psychiatric Clinics*, **11**, 749–765.

Ost, S. (2002) Children at risk: legal and societal perceptions of the potential threat that the possession of child pornography poses to society, *Journal of Law and Society*, **29**, 436–460.

OYEZ Project (2002) *Ashcroft v. Free Speech Coalition, 535 U.S. 234.* Retrieved 28 December 2006 from http://www.oyez.org/cases/case?case=2000–2009/2001/2001_00_795.

Parker, G. (1983) *Parental Overprotection: A Risk Factor in Psychosocial Development.* New York: Grune & Stratton.

Parker, G., Tupling, H. & Brown, L. B. (1979) A parental bonding instrument. *British Journal of Medical Psychology,* **52,** 1–10.

Parton, N. (1991) *Governing the Family.* London: Macmillan

Pedhazur, E. J. & Schmelkin, L. P. (1991) *Measurement, Design, and Analysis: An Integrated Approach.* Hillsdale, NJ: Erlbaum.

Petit, J. M. (2004) *Rights of the Child.* Geneva: United Nations.

Pithers, W. D. (1990) Relapse prevention with sexual aggressors: a method of maintaining therapeutic gain and enhancing external supervision. In W. L. Marshall, D. R. Laws & H. E. Barbaree (eds) *Handbook of Sexual Assault: Issues, Theories and Treatment of the Offender* (pp. 257–275). London: Plenum Press.

Pithers, W. D., Kashima, K. M., Cumming, G. F. & Beal, L. S. (1988) Relapse prevention: a method of enhancing maintenance of change in sex offenders. In A. C. Salter (ed.) *Treating Child Sex Offenders and Victims: A Practical Guide* (pp. 131–170). Newbury Park, CA: Sage.

Plotnikoff, J. & Woolfson, R. (2000) *Where Are They Now? An Evaluation of Sex Offender Registration in England and Wales.* London: HMSO.

Pollack, N. L & Hashmall, J. M (1991) The excuses of child molesters. *Behavioral. Sciences and the Law,* **19,** 53–59.

Polaschek, D. L. L. (2003) Classification. In T. Ward, D. R., Laws & S. M. Hudson (eds) *Sexual Deviance: Issues and Controversies* (pp. 154–71). Thousand Oaks, CA: Sage.

Polaschek, D. L. L., Hudson, S. M., Ward, T. & Siegert, R. J. (2001) Rapists' offence process: a preliminary descriptive model. *Journal of Interpersonal Violence,* **16** (6), 523–544.

Polaschek, D. L. L. & Gannon, T. A. (2004) The implicit theories of rapists: what convicted offenders tell us. *Sexual Abuse: Journal of Research and Treatment,* **16,** 299–314.

Polaschek, D. L. L., Ward, T. & Hudson, S. M. (1997) Rape and rapists: theory and treatment. *Clinical Psychology Review,* **17,** 117–144.

Postmes, T. & Spears, R. (1998) Deindividuation and antinormative behavior: a metaanalysis. *Psychological Bulletin,* **123,** 238–259.

Prendergast, W. E. (1993) Sexually abused males who do not enter the victim-to-abuser cycle. In W. Prendergast (ed.) *The Merry-Go-Round of Sexual Abuse: Identifying and Treating Survivors.* New York: Haworth Press.

Prentky, R. A., Knight, R. A. & Lee, A. F. S. (1997) Risk factors associated with recidivism among extra-familial child molesters. *Journal of Consulting and Clinical Psychology,* **65,** 141–149.

Prentky, R. A., Knight, R. A., Sims-Knight, J. E. *et al.* (1989) Developmental antecedents of sexual aggression. *Developmental and Psychopathology,* **1,** 153–169.

Proulx, J., McKibben, A. & Lusignan, R. (1996) Relationships between affective components and sexual behaviours in sexual aggressors. *Sexual Abuse: A Journal of Research and Treatment,* **8,** 279–298.

Putnam, D. E. (1997) *Online Sexual Addiction Questionnaire.* Retrieved 1 November 2002 from http://onlinesexaddict.org/osaq.html.

Putnam, D. E. (2000) Initiation and maintenance of online sexual compulsivity: Implications for assessment and treatment, *CyberPsychology and Behavior,* **3** (4), 553–563.

Quaker Peace and Social Witness (2003) *Circles of Support and Accountability in the Thames Valley: Interim Report* November 2003. London: Quaker Peace and Social Witness.

Quayle, E. (2004) The impact of viewing on offending behaviour. In M. Calder (ed.) *Child Sexual Abuse and the Internet: Tackling the New Frontier* (pp. 25–36). Lyme Regis: Russell House Publishing.

Quayle, E., Erooga, M., Wright, L. *et al.* (2006) *Only Pictures? Therapeutic work with Internet Sex Offenders.* Lyme Regis: Russell House Publishing.

Quayle, E., Holland, G., Linehan, C. & Taylor, M. (2000) The Internet and offending behaviour: a case study. *Journal of Sexual Aggression,* **6,** 78–96.

Quayle, E. & Taylor, M. (2001) Child seduction and self-representation on the Internet. *Cyber Psychology and Behavior*, **4** (5), 597–608.

Quayle, E. & Taylor, M. (2002a) Paedophiles, pornography and the Internet: assessment issues. *British Journal of Social Work*, **32**, 863–875.

Quayle, E. & Taylor, M. (2002b) Child pornography and the Internet: perpetuating a cycle of abuse. *Deviant Behavior: An Interdisciplinary Journal*, **23** (4), 365–395.

Quayle, E. & Taylor, M. (2005) *Viewing Child Pornography on the Internet: Understanding the Offence, Managing the Offender, Helping the Victims*. Lyme Regis: Russell House Publishing.

Quayle, E., Vaughan, M. & Taylor, M. (2006) Sex offenders, Internet child abuse images and emotional avoidance: the importance of values. *Aggression and Violent Behavior*, **11**, 1–11.

Quinsey, V. L. (1986) Men who have sex with children. In D. N. Weisstub (ed.) *Law and Mental Health: International Perspectives*, Vol. 2 (pp. 140–172). New York: Pergamon.

Quinsey, V. L., Harris, G. T., Rice, M. E. & Cormier, C. A. (1998) *Violent Offenders: Appraising and Managing Risk*. Washington, DC: American Psychological Association.

Quinsey, V. L., Rice, M. E. & Harris, G. T. (1995) Actuarial prediction of sexual recidivism. *Journal of Interpersonal Violence*, **10**, 85–105.

Rabb, J. & Rindfleisch, N. (1985) A study to define and assess severity of institutional abuse/neglect. *Child Abuse and Neglect*, **9**, 285–294.

Reifler, C. B., Howard, J., Lipton, M. A. *et al.* (1971) Pornography: An Experimental Study of Effects. *American Journal of Psychiatry*, **128**, 572–582.

Renold, E., Creighton, S. J., Atkinson, C. & Carr, J. (2003) *Images of Abuse: A Review of the Evidence on Child Pornography*. London: The National Society for the Prevention of Cruelty to Children.

Rich, P. (2006) *Attachment and Sexual Offending: Understanding and Applying Attachment Theory to the Treatment of Juvenile Sexual Offenders*. Chichester: John Wiley & Sons.

Righton, P. (1981) The adult. In B. Taylor (ed.) *Perspectives on Paedophilia*. London: Batsford.

Rimm, M. (1995) Marketing pornography on the information superhighway: a survey of 917, 410 images, descriptions, short stories and animations downloaded 8.5 million times by consuming in over 2000 cities in forty countries, provinces and territories. *Georgetown Law Review*, **83**, 1849–934. Retrieved 11 March 2003 from http://xenia. media.mit.edu/~rhodes/Cyberporn/mrtext.html..

Rindfleisch, N. & Rabb, J. (1984) How much of a problem is resident mistreatment in child welfare institutions? *Child Abuse and Neglect*, **8**, 33–40.

Robbins, P. & Darlington, R. (2003) The role of industry and the Internet Watch Foundation. In A. MacVean & P. Spindler (eds) *Policing Paedophiles on the Internet*. John Grieve Centre for Policing and Community Safety (pp. 79–86). Bristol: The New Police Bookshop.

Rosenthal, J. A., Motz, J. K., Edmonson, D. A. & Groze, V. (1991) A descriptive study of abuse and neglect in out-of-home-placement, *Child Abuse and Neglect*, **15**, 249–260.

Rosenthal, S., Feiring, C. & Taska, L. (2003) Emotional support and adjustment over a year's time following sexual abuse discovery, *Child Abuse and Neglect*, **27**, 641–661.

Rosler, A. & Witzum, E. (2000) Pharmacotherapy of paraphilias in the next millennium. *Behavioral Sciences and the Law*, **18**, 43–56.

Russell, D. (1984) *The Secret Trauma; Incest in the Lives of Girls and Women*. New York: Basic Books.

Ruxton, S. (2001) *Child Sexual Exploitation: An Action Plan for Europe*. Stockholm: Swedish Save the Children.

Ryan, G. & Lane, S. (eds) (1991) *Juvenile Sexual Offending: Causes, Consequences and Correction*. Lexington, MA: Lexington Books.

Ryan, G., Miyoshi, T. J., Metzner, J. L. *et al.* (1996) Trends in a national sample of sexually abusive youths. *Journal of American Academy of Child and Adolescent Psychiatry*, **35** (1), 17–25.

Salter, A. C. (1988) *Treating Child Sex Offenders and Victims: A Practical Guide*. Newbury Park, CA: Sage.

Sandfort, Th. G. M. (1992) The argument for adult-child sexual contact: a critical appraisal and new data. In W. O'Donohue & J. H. Geer (eds) *The Sexual Abuse of Children: Clinical Issues*, Vol. 1 (pp. 38–48). Hillsdale, NJ: Lawrence Erlbaum.

Saradjian, J. (1996) *Women who Sexually Abused Children: From Research to Clinical Practice*. New York: John Wiley & Sons.

SAS Library (1995) Factor analysis using SAS Proc Factor. Retrieved August 2006 from ttp://www.ats.ucla.edu/stat/sas/library/factor_ut.htm.

Scharfe, E. (2003) Stability and change of attachment representations from cradle to grave. In S. M. Johnson & V. E. Whiffen (eds) *Attachment Processes in Couples and Family Therapy* (pp. 64–84). New York: Guilford.

Schuijer, J. & Rossen, B (1992) The Trade in Child Pornography. *IPT Forensics Journal, 4*. Retrieved 13 October 2006 from http://www.ipt-forensics.com/journal/volume4/j4_2.

Scott, K. (29 June 2005) Hamilton hit by indecency claim. *British Journal of Photography*. Retrieved 4 December 2006 from http://www.bjp-online.com/public/showPage.html?page=285424.

Scott, S. (2001) *The Politics and Experience of Ritual Abuse. Beyond Disbelief*. Buckingham: Open University Press.

Seghorn, T. K., Prentky, R. A. & Boucher, R. J. (1987) Childhood sexual abuse in the lives of sexually aggressive offenders. *Journal of American Academy of Child and Adolescent Psychiatry, 9*, 103–116.

Sentencing Advisory Panel (2002) *Advice to the Court of Appeal–10. Offences Involving Child Pornography*. Home Office Communications Directorate. Retrieved 1 March 2003 from http://www.sentencing-advisory-panel.gov.uk/index.htm.

Serran, G. A. & Marshall, L. E. (2006) Coping and mood in sexual offenders. In W. L. Marshall, Y. M. Fernandez, L. E. Marshall & G. E. Serran (eds) *Sexual Offender Treatment: Controversial Issues* (pp. 109–124). Chichester: John Wiley & Sons.

Seto, M. (2004) Pedophilia and sexual offences against children, *Annual Review of Sex Research, 15*, 329–369.

Seto, M., Cantor, J. M. and Blanchard, R. (2006) Child pornography offenses are a valid diagnostic indicator of pedophilia. *Journal of Abnormal Psychology, 115* (3), 610–615.

Seto, M. & Eke, A. W. (2005) The criminal histories and later offending of child pornography offenders. *Sexual Abuse: A Journal of Research and Treatment, 17* (2), 201–210.

Seto, M., Maric, A. and Barbaree, H. (2001) The role of pornography in the etiology of sexual aggression. *Aggression and Violent Behavior, 6* (1), 35–53.

Shaffer, H. J., Hall, M. N., Vander Bilt, J. (2000) 'Computer addiction': a critical consideration. *American Journal of Orthopsychiatry, 70*, 162–168.

Shaw, J. A. (2000) Summary of the practice parameters for the assessment and treatment of children and adolescents who are sexually abusive of others. *Journal of American Academy of Child and Adolescent Psychiatry, 39* (1), 127–130.

Sheldon, K (2004) A new type of sex offender? *Forensic Update, 79*, 24–31.

Sheldon, K. & Howitt, D. (2005) *A New Kind of Paedophile? Contact and Internet Offenders Against Children Ccompared*. Fifteenth European Conference on Psychology and Law, Vilnius, Lithuania 29 June – 2 July 2005.

Sheldon, K. & Howitt, D. (in press) Sexual Fantasy in Paedophile Offenders. Can any model explain satisfactorily new findings from a stuffy of Internet and Contact Sexual Offenders? *Legal and Criminological Psychology*.

Shytov, A. (2005) Indecency on the Internet and international law. *International Journal of Law and Information Technology, 13* (2), 260–280.

Silverman, J. & Wilson, D. (2002) *Innocence Betrayed: Paedophilia, the Media and Society*. Cambridge: Polity Press.

Simpson, J. B. (1988) *Simpson's Contemporary Quotations*. Boston: Houghton Mifflin.

Smallbone, S. W. & Dadds, M. R. (1998) Childhood attachment and adult attachment in incarcerated adult male sex offenders, *Journal of Interpersonal Violence, 13*, 555–573.

Smallbone, S. W. & Dadds, M. R. (2000) Attachment and coercive sexual behavior, *Sexual Abuse: A Journal of Research and Treatment*, **12**, 3–15.

Smallbone, S. W. & Dadds, M. R. (2001) Further evidence for a relationship between attachment insecurity and coercive sexual behavior. *Journal of Interpersonal Violence*, **16**, 22–35.

Smallbone, S. W. & McCabe, B. (2003) Child attachment, childhood sexual abuse, and onset of masturbation among adult sexual offenders. *Sexual Abuse: A Journal of Research and Treatment*, **15**, 1–9.

Smallbone, S. W. & Wortley, R. K. (2000) *Child Sexual Abuse in Queensland: Offender Characteristics and Modus Operandi*. Brisbane: Queensland Crime Commission

Smallbone, S. W. & Wortley, R. K. (2004) Onset, persistence and versatility of offending among adult males convicted of sexual offences against children. *Sexual Abuse: A Journal of Research and Treatment*, **16**, 285–298.

Smith, D. (2005) Home Office figures supplied upon request. *Office for Criminal Justice Reform, Research and Statistics Directorate* London; Home Office, 3 June.

Snyder, H. N. (2000, July) *Sexual Assault of Young Children as Reported to Law Enforcement: Victim, Incident and Offender Characteristics* (NCJ 182990) Washington DC: Bureau of Justice Statistics.

Sommer, P. (2003) Evidence: a case for the defence. In A. MacVean & P. Spindler (eds) *Policing Paedophiles on the Internet*. John Grieve Centre for Policing and Community Safety (pp. 97–118). Bristol: The New Police Bookshop.

Soothill, K., Francis, B. & Ackerley, E. (1998) Paedophilia and paedophiles. *New Law Journal*, **148**, 882–883.

Soothill, K., Peelo, M. & Taylor, C. (2002) *Making Sense of Criminology*. Cambridge: Polity.

Spaccarelli, S. & Kim, S. (1995) Resilience criteria and factors associated with resilience in sexually abused girls, *Child Abuse and Neglect*, **19** (9), 1171–1182.

Sparrow, P. & Griffiths, M. D. (1997) Crime and IT: Hacking and pornography on the Internet. *Probation Journal*, **44**, 144–147.

Spencer, J. W. & Knudsen, D. D. (1992) Out-of-home maltreatment: an analysis of risk in various settings for children, *Children and Youth Services Review*, **14**, 485–492.

Sperry, D. M. & Gilbert, B. O. (2005) Child peer sexual abuse: preliminary data on outcomes and disclosure experiences. *Child Abuse and Neglect*, **29**, 889–904.

Sprenger, P. (1999) Porn pioneers. *Guardian*, 30 September.

Stanley, L. A. (1991) Art and 'perversion': censoring images of nude children, *Art Journal*, **50** (4), Censorship II, pp. 20–27.

Stermac, L. E. & Segal, Z. V., (1990) The role of cognition in sexual assault. In W. L. Marshall, D. R. Laws & H. E. Barbaree (eds) *Handbook of Sexual Assault: Issues, Theories and Treatment of the Offender* (pp. 161–174). London: Plenum Press.

Studer, L. H., Aylwin, A. S., Clelland, S. R. *et al.* (2002) Primary erotic preference in a group of child molesters. *International Journal of Law and Psychiatry*, **25**, 173–180.

Studer, L. H., Clelland, S. R., Aylwin, A. S. *et al.* (2000) Re-thinking risk assessment for incest offenders. *International Journal of Law and Psychiatry*, **23**, 15–22.

Sturup, G. K. (1968) Treatment of sexual offenders in Herstedrester, Denmark: the rapists. *Acta Psychiatrica Scandinavica Supplementum*, **204**, 44.

Sue, D. (1979) Erotic fantasies of college students during coitus. *Journal of Sex Research*, **15**, 299–305.

Sullivan, J. & Beech, A. (2003) Are collectors of child abuse images a risk to children? In A. MacVean & P. Spindler (eds) *Policing Paedophiles on the Internet* (pp. 49–60). John Grieve Centre for Policing and Community Safety. Bristol: The New Police Bookshop.

Svedin, C. G. & Back, K. (1996) *Children Who Don't Speak Out*. Stockholm: Radda Barnen Swedish Save the Children.

Swaffer, T., Hollin, C., Beech, A. *et al.* (2000) An exploration of child sexual abusers' sexual fantasies before and after treatment. *Sexual Abuse: Journal of Research and Treatment*, **12** (1), 61–68.

Sykes, G. & Matza, D. (1957) Techniques of neutralisation: A theory of delinquency. *American Sociological Review*, **22**, 664–670.

Tardif, M., Auclair, N., Jacob, M. & Carpentier, J. (2005) Sexual abuse perpetrated by adult and juvenile females: An ultimate attempt to resolve a conflict associated with maternal identity. *Child Abuse and Neglect*, **29**, 153–167.

Tate, T. (1990) *Child Pornography*. London: Methuen.

Tate, T. (1992) The Child Pornography Industry: International Trade in Child Sexual Abuse. In Itzin, C. (ed.) *Pornography: Women, Violence and Civil Liberties* (pp. 203–216). Oxford: Oxford University Press.

Taylor, M. (1999) The nature and dimensions of child pornography on the Internet. Paper presented at the US/EU international Conference 'Combating child Pornography on the Internet' Vienna, Austria, September 29 to October 1. Retrieved 11 March 2003 from http://www.stop-childporn.at/.

Taylor, M., Holland, G. & Quayle, E., (2001) Typology of paedophile picture collections, *The Police Journal*, **74** (2), 97–107.

Taylor, M. & Quayle, E. (2003) *Child Pornography: An Internet Crime*. Hove: Brunner-Routledge.

Taylor, M., Quayle, E. & Holland, G. (2001) Child pornography, the Internet and offending, ISUMA *The Canadian Journal of Policy Research*, **2** (2), 94–100.

Templeman, T. L. & Stinnett, R. D. (1991) Pattern of sexual arousal and history in a 'normal' sample of young men. *Archives of Sexual Behavior*, **20**, 137–50.

Terman, L. M. (1938) *Psychological Factors in Marital Happiness*. New York: McGraw Hill.

Terman, L. M. (1951) Correlates of orgasm adequacy in a group of 556 wives. *Journal of Psychology*, **32**, 115–172.

Tewksbury, R (2002) Validity and utility of the Kentucky sex offender registry. *Federal Probation*, **66** (1), 21–26.

Thomas, G. & Wyatt, S. (1999) Shaping cyberspace–Interpreting and transforming the Internet, *Research Policy*, Vol. 28, 681–698.

Thomas, T. (2005) *Sex Crime: Sex Offending and Society*. Cullompton: Willan Publishing.

Thompson, B. & Williams, A. (2004) Virtual Offenders: The Other Side of Internet Allegations. In M. C. Calder (ed.) *Child Sexual Abuse and the Internet: Tackling the New Frontier* (pp. 113–132). Lyme Regis, Dorset: Russell House Publishing.

Thompson, R. W., Authier, K. & Ruma, P. (1994) Behavior problems of sexually abused children in foster care: A preliminary study. *Journal of Sexual Abuse*, **3**, 79–91.

Thornton, D. (2002) Constructing and testing a framework for dynamic risk assessment. *Sexual Abuse: A Journal of Assessment and Treatment*, **14**, 139–153.

Thornton, D., Mann, R. E., Webster, S. *et al.* (2003) Distinguishing and combining risks for sexual and violent recidivism. In R. A. Prentky, E. S. Janus & M. C. Seto (eds) *Sexually Coercive Behavior: Understanding and Management, Annals of the New York Academy of Science*, vol. 989 (pp. 225–235). Available from http://www.nyas.org/annals/browse.

Tierney, D. W. & McCabe, M. P. (2001) The assessment of denial, cognitive distortions and victim empathy among paedophilic sex offenders; an evaluation of the utility of self-report measures. *Trauma, Violence and Abuse*, **2** (3), 259–270.

Tikkanen R & Ross MW (2000) Looking for sexual compatibility: experiences among Swedish men visiting internet gay chatrooms. *Cyberpsychology and Behaviour*, **3** (4): 605–616.

Tingle, D., Barnard, G. W., Robbins, L. *et al.* Childhood and adolescent characteristics of pedophiles and rapists. *International Journal of Law and Psychiatry*, **9** (1), 103–116.

Tomlinson, B., Stephens, M., Cunes, J. W. *et al.* (1991) Characteristics of Canadian male and female child sexual abuse victims. *Journal of Child and Youth Care*, (special issue): 65–76.

Travin, S., Cullen, K. & Protter, B. (1990) Female sex offenders: severe victims and victimizers, *Journal of Forensic Sciences*, **35** (1), 140–150.

Travis, A. (2004) Sex offenders may face lie detector tests, *Guardian*, 28 May. Retrieved 28 May 2003 from http://www.guardian.co.uk/child/story/0,,1226459,00.html.

Turkle, S. (1995) *Life on the Screen*. New York: Simon & Schuster.

Turvey, B. E. (1995) *The Impressions of a Man: An Objective Forensic Guideline to Profiling Violent Serial Sex Offenders*. Retrieved 20 July 2006 from http://www.corpus-delicti.com/impress.html.

Tyler, R. P. & Stone, L. E. (1985) Child pornography: perpetuating the sexual victimisation of children. *Child Abuse and Neglect: The International Journal*, **9**, 313–318.

United Nations (1996) *Sexual Exploitation of Children*. Study Series 8. Geneva: Centre for Human Rights.

US Attorney General's Commission on Pornography (1986) *Final Report*. Washington, DC: US Department of Justice.

US Department of Justice (2004) *Criminal Victimization in the United States, 2004 Statistical Tables*. Retrieved 2 September 2006 from http://www.ojp.usdoj.gov/bjs/pub/pdf/cvus0405.pdf.

US Postal Service (2002) *Annual Report of Investigations*. Retrieved 18 April 2007 from http://www.usps.com/postalinspectors/ar02/ar02text.htm.

Utting, W. (1991) *Children in Public Care: A Review of Residential Care*. London: SSI/HMSO.

Valios, N. (1998) Social workers warn register is flawed. *Community Care*, 27 August – 2 September.

Veneziano, C., Veneziano, L. & LeGrand, S. (2000) The relationship between adolescent sex offender behaviors and victim characteristics with prior victimization. *Journal of Interpersonal Violence*, **15** (4), 363–374.

Ward, T. (2000) Sexual offenders' cognitive distortions as implicit theories. *Aggression and Violent Behavior*, **5**, 491–507.

Ward, T. (2001) Hall and Hirschman's quadripartite model of child sexual abuse: a critique. *Psychology, Crime and Law*, **7**, 291–307.

Ward, T. (2002) Marshall and Barbaree's integrated theory of child sexual abuse: a critique. *Psychology, Crime and Law*, **8**, 209–228.

Ward, T., Fon, C., Hudson, S. M. & McCormack, J. (1998) A descriptive model of dysfunctional cognitions in child molesters. *Journal of Interpersonal Violence*, **13** (1), 129–155.

Ward, T. & Hudson, S. M. (2000) Sexual offenders implicit planning: a conceptual model. *Sexual Abuse: A Journal of Research and Treatment*, **12**, 189–202.

Ward, T. & Hudson, S. M. (2001) A critique of Finkelhor's precondition model of child sexual abuse: a critique. *Psychology, Crime and Law*, **7**, 333–350.

Ward, T., Hudson, S. M., Johnston, L. & Marshall, W. L. (1997) Cognitive distortions in sex offenders: an integrative review, *Clinical Psychology*, **17**, 479–507.

Ward, T., Hudson, S. M. & Marshall, W. L. (1996) Attachment style in sex offenders: a preliminary study. *Journal of Sex Research*, **33**, 17–26.

Ward, T. & Keenan, T. (1999) Child molesters' implicit theories. *Journal of Interpersonal Violence*, **14**, 821–838.

Ward, T., Keenan, T. & Hudson, S. M. (2000) Understanding cognitive, affective and intimacy deficits in sexual offenders; a developmental perspective. *Aggression and Violent Behaviour*, **5** (1), 41–62.

Ward, T., Louden, K., Hudson, S. M. & Marshall, W. L. (1995) A descriptive model of the offense chain for child molesters. *Journal of Interpersonal Violence*, **10**, 452–72.

Ward, T., Polaschek, D. & Beech, A. R. (2006) *Theories of Sexual Offending*. Chichester: John Wiley & Sons.

Ward, T. & Siegert, R., (2002) Toward a comprehensive theory of child sexual abuse: a theory of knitting perspective. *Psychology, Crime and Law*, **8**, 319–351.

Warmoll, C. (23 June 2005) Hamilton's naked girl shots ruled 'indecent'. *Guardian*. Retrieved 4 December 2006 from http://arts.guardian.co.uk/news/story/0,11711,1512621,00.html. Webster, S. D., Mann, R. E., Carter, A. J. *et al.* (2006) Inter-rater reliability of dynamic risk assessment with sexual offenders. *Psychology, Crime and Law*, **12** (4), 439–452.

West, D. (1996) Sexual Molesters. In N. Walker (ed.) *Dangerous People*. London: Blackstone.

Whitfield, D. (1997) *Tackling the Tag: The Electronic Monitoring of Offenders*. Winchester: Waterside Press.

Widom, C.S., Morris, S. (1997). Accuracy of adult recollections of childhood victimization: Part 2. Childhood sexual abuse. *Psychological Assessment*, **9** (4): 34–46.

Widom, C.S., Shepared, R.L. (1996). Accuracy of adult recollections of childhood victimization: Part 1. Childhood sexual abuse. *Psychological Assessment*, **8**, 412–421

Wild, N. J. (1987) Child sex rings in context. *Child Abuse Review*, **1** (5), 7–9.

Wild, N. J. & Wynne, J. M. (1986) Child sex rings, *British Medical Journal*, **293**, 183–5.

Williams, B. (1979) *Report of the Committee on Pornography and Censorship*. Cmd. 7772. London: HMSO.

Williams, K. S. (2005) Facilitating safer choices: use of warnings to dissuade viewing of pornography on the Internet. *Child Abuse Review*, **14**, 415–429.

Williams, L. M. & Finkelhor, D. (1990) The characteristics of incestuous fathers: a review of recent Studies. In W. L. Marshall, D. R. Laws & H. E. Barbaree (eds) *Handbook of Sexual Assault: Issues, Theories and Treatment of the Offender* (pp. 231–255). London: Plenum.

Wilson, G. D. (1987) Male-female differences in sexual activity, enjoyment and fantasies. *Personality and Individual Differences*, **8**, 123–127.

Wilson, R. J. (1999) Emotional congruence in sexual offenders against children. *Sexual Abuse: Journal of Research and Treatment*, **11** (1), 33–46.

Winick, B. J. (1998) Sex offender law in the 1990s: a therapeutic jurisprudence analysis. *Psychology, Public Policy and the Law*, **4**, 505–570.

Wolak, J., Finkelhor, D. & Mitchell, K. J. (2005) The varieties of child pornography production. In E. Quayle & M. Taylor (2005) *Viewing Child Pornography on the Internet: Understanding the Offence, Managing the Offender, Helping the Victims*. Lyme Regis: Russell House Publishing.

Wyatt, G. W. (1985) The sexual abuse of Afro-American and white American women in childhood. *Child Abuse and Neglect*, **9**, 507–519.

Wyatt, G. E. & Peters, S. D. (1986) Issues in the definition of child sexual abuse in prevalence research. *Child Abuse and Neglect*, **10**, 231–240.

Wyre, R. (1987) *Working with Sex Offenders*. Oxford: Perry Publications.

Young, K. (1997a) The relationship between depression and pathological Internet use. *Proceedings and abstracts of the Annual Meeting of the Eastern Psychological Association*, Vol. 68, Washington, DC: Eastern Psychological Association.

Young, K. (1997b) *What Makes Online Usage Stimulating: Potential Explanations for Pathological Internet Use*. Paper presented at the 105th Annual Convention of the American Psychological Association, Chicago, IL.

Young, K. S. (1996) *Internet Addiction: The Emergence of a New Clinical Disorder*. Paper presented at the 104th Annual Convention of the American Psychological Association, Toronto, Ontario, Canada, August.

Young, K. S. & Rogers, R. C. (1998) The relationship between depression and Internet addiction. *CyberPsychology and Behavior*, **1** (1), 25–28.

Zevitz, R. G. (2006) Sex offender community notification: its role in recidivism and offender reintegration. *Criminal Justice Studies*, **19** (2), 193–208.

Zimbardo, P. (1969) The human choice: individuation, reason and order, versus deindividuation, impulse and chaos. In W. Arnold & D. Levine (eds). *Nebraska Symposium on Motivation*, **17**, 237–307. Lincoln: University of Nebraska Press.

# Author Index

# Subject Index